HOUSEKEEPING

IN OLD VIRGINIA.

CONTAINING

CONTRIBUTIONS FROM TWO HUNDRED AND FIFTY OF VIRGINIA'S
NOTED HOUSEWIVES, DISTINGUISHED FOR THEIR SKILL
IN THE CULINARY ART AND OTHER BRANCHES
OF DOMESTIC ECONOMY.

EDITED BY

MARION CABELL TYREE.

"Who can find a virtuous woman? for her price is far above rubies. . . . She looketh well to the ways of her household, and eateth not the bread of idleness."—*Prov.* xxxi, 10, 27.

Creative Cookbooks
Monterey, California

Housekeeping in Old Virginia

Edited by
Marion Cabell Tyree

ISBN: 1-4101-0508-3

Copyright © 2004 by Fredonia Books

Reprinted from the 1879 edition

Creative Cookbooks
An Imprint of Fredonia Books
Monterey, California
http://www.creativecookbooks.com

All rights reserved, including the right to reproduce this book, or portions thereof, in any form.

In order to make original editions of historical works available to scholars at an economical price, this facsimile of the original edition of 1879 is reproduced from the best available copy and has been digitally enhanced to improve legibility, but the text remains unaltered to retain historical authenticity.

GENERAL CONTENTS.

	PAGE
Preface	7
List of Contributors	11
Bread	19
Coffee, Tea, and Chocolate	61
Milk and Butter	65
Soup	68
Oysters and other Shell Fish	85
Fish	97
Game	107
Meats	114
Beef and Veal	136
Mutton and Lamb	168
Poultry	176
Salads	190
Sauces	200
Brunswick Stews, Gumbo, and Side Dishes	211
Eggs	232
Vegetables	238
Pickles and Catsups	255
Cake	304

CONTENTS.

	PAGE
Icing	348
Gingerbread	350
Small Cakes	353
Puddings	365
Pudding Sauces	401
Pastry	404
Fritters and Pancakes	416
Jelly, Blanc-mange, Charlotte Russe, Baked Custard, Creams, and Miscellaneous Desserts	417
Ice Cream and Frozen Custard	430
Fruit Desserts	442
Preserves and Fruit Jellies	443
Confectionery	458
Wines	461
Beverages, Cordials, etc	468
The Sick-Room—Diet and Remedies for the Sick	476
House-cleaning, etc	497
Recipes for Restoring Old Clothes, Setting Colors, Removing Stains, etc	505
Miscellaneous Recipes	508

PREFACE.

VIRGINIA, or the Old Dominion, as her children delight to call her, has always been famed for the style of her living. Taught by the example of her royal colonial governors, and the numerous adherents of King Charles, who brought hither in their exile the graces and luxuriousness of his brilliant court, she became noted among the colonies for the princely hospitality of her people and for the beauty and richness of their living. But when at length her great son in the House of Burgesses sounded the cry of war, and her people made haste to gird themselves for the long struggle, her daughters, not to be outdone either in services or patriotism, set about at once the inauguration of a plan of rigid retrenchment and reform in the domestic economy, while at the same time exhibiting to their sisters a noble example of devotion and self-sacrifice.

Tearing the glittering arms of King George from their sideboards, and casting them, with their costly plate and jewels, as offerings into the lap of the Continental Congress, they introduced in their homes that new style of living in which, discarding all the showy extravagance of the old, and retaining only its inexpensive graces, they succeeded in perfecting that system which, surviving to this day, has ever been noted for its beautiful and elegant simplicity.

This system, which combines the thrifty frugality of New England with the less rigid style of Carolina, has been justly pronounced, by the throngs of admirers who have gathered from all quarters of the Union around the generous boards of her illustrious sons, as the very perfection of domestic art.

It is the object of the compiler of this book, for she does not claim the title of author, to bring within the reach of every American housekeeper who may desire it, the domestic principles and practices of these famous Virginia homes. In doing this she has not sought to pursue the plan adopted by so many authors of such books—to depend upon her own *authorship* for her rule. She confesses that in this matter her labors have been largely editorial.

Through a long life it has been her good fortune to be a frequent visitor, and often the intimate guest and kinswoman, at many of these homes; and she has sought, by the opportunities thus afforded, and guided by her own extensive experience as a housekeeper, to gather and select from these numerous sources those things which seemed to her best and most useful to the practical housewife, and which, carefully observed, would bring the art within reach of all who have the ambition to acquire it.

It will be seen that she is indebted to near 250 contributors to her book Among these will be found *many names famous through the land.* Associated with them will be discovered others of less national celebrity, but who have acquired among their neighbors an equally merited distinction for the beautiful order and delightful cuisine of their homes.

The labors of the writer have been greatly lightened by the kindness of these contributors. And she desires in this public way to renew her thanks for the aid which they have given her, but even more for the goodness which prompts them, at cost of their sensitiveness, to allow her to append their names to the recipes which they furnish.

The book, after great care in its preparation, is now offered to the public with much confidence. All that is here presented has been so thoroughly tested, and approved by so many of the best housekeepers in Virginia, that she feels it must meet with a cordial and very general reception at the hands of all accomplished housewives throughout the land, and will supply a long-felt and real need.

If she shall thus succeed in disseminating a knowledge of the practice of the *most admirable system of domestic art known in our country ;* if she shall succeed in lightening the labors of the housewife by placing in her reach a guide which will be found *always trusty and reliable ;* if she shall thus make her tasks lighter and home-life sweeter; if she shall succeed in contributing something to the health of American children by instructing their mothers in the art of preparing light and wholesome and palatable food; *if she, above all, shall succeed in making American homes more attractive to American husbands, and spare*

1*

them a resort to hotels and saloons for those simple luxuries which their wives know not how to provide; if she shall thus add to the comfort, to the health and happy contentment of these, she will have proved in some measure a public benefactor, and will feel amply repaid for all the labor her work has cost.

MARION CABELL TYREE.

LYNCHBURG, VA., January, 1877.

LIST OF CONTRIBUTORS.

Mrs. Robert Alexander. ....Fredericksburg, Va.
Mrs. John J. Ambler............................Lynchburg
Mrs. Judge Anderson ....Lexington.
Mrs. Charlotte Armstrong......................Richmond.
Miss Nannie Averett..........................Amherst Co.
"Mozis Addums.".................................Richmond.
Mrs. R. T. H. Adams........................... Lynchburg.
Mrs. John T. Anderson............................Virginia.
Mrs. John Thompson Brown ....Nelson Co.
Mrs. Benjamin J. Barbour......................Orange Co.
Mrs. Judge Barton.......................... Fredericksburg.
Miss Mary Bella Beale..........................Richmond.
Mrs. Orville Bell..................................Liberty.
Mrs. C. S. Bliss ....Lynchburg.
Mrs. S. Brady............................Wheeling, West Va.
Mrs. Emma Breckinridge..........................Fincastle.
Mrs. Julia Breckinridge............................ "
Mrs. Brinckerhoff..........................Fredericksburg
Mrs. John Brooke..............................Lexington.
Mrs. M. B............................Warrenton, Fauquier Co.
Mrs. Bruce..Virginia.
Mrs. Marcus B. Buck................Front Royal, Warren Co.
Mrs. Armstead Burwell..........................Franklin Co.

LIST OF CONTRIBUTORS.

Mrs. Charles W. Burwell..................Ellicot City, Md
Mrs. Wm. Burwell....................................Georgia.
Mrs. Charles Button............................Lynchburg
Dr. Burney..................................Montgomery, Ala
Mrs. George A. Burks...........................Lynchburg.
Mrs. Broaddus................................Mecklenburg Co.
Mrs. Byrd..Virginia.
Mrs. William Cameron...........................Petersburg.
Mrs. Clara Cabell..................................Nelson Co.
Mrs. Louis W. Cabell.........................Buckingham Co
Mrs. Margaret C. Cabell.....................   "   "
Mrs. H. Coalter Cabell..........................Richmond.
Mrs. Mary C. Campbell.......................Baltimore, Md.
Mrs. Thos. Campbell............................Bedford Co.
Mrs. Wm. Campbell..........................   "   "
Mrs. Eliza H. Carrington.......................Halifax Co.
Mrs. Paul Carrington.......................   "   "
Mrs. Fannie Carrington........................Charlotte Co.
Mrs. Henry Carrington......................   "   "
Mrs. Theo. M. Carson............................Lynchburg
Mr. Edward Camm ....   "
Mrs. Fannie Chalmers ....   "
Mrs. Addison Cobbs.....................Charleston, West Va.
Mrs. Alice Coleman..............................Halifax Co.
Mrs. Dr. Coleman..............................Williamsburg.
Mrs. John L. Coles.........................Northumberland Co
Mrs. Peyton Coles............................Albemarle Co.
Mrs. Tucker Coles..........................   "   "
Mrs. Raleigh Colston.............................Richmond.
Mrs. H. P. Chew..............................Fredericksburg.
Mrs. Camillus Christian........................Lynchburg
Dr. E. A. Craighill................................   "
Mrs. D. Cone.....................................Warren Co

LIST OF CONTRIBUTORS.

Mrs. Davis...Chesterfield Co
Mrs. Robert J. Davis..............................Lynchburg.
Mrs. Mary M. Dame................................Danville.
Mrs. John B. Dangerfield.....................Alexandria.
Mrs. Addison M. Davies........................Lynchburg
Mrs. Horatio Davis...............................Pittsylvania Co.
Mrs. Frank Deane..................................Lynchburg
Mrs. Jos. Deans.....................................Gloucester Co.
Mrs. Judge Asa Dickinson...................Prince Edward Co.
Mrs. Melville Dunn..............................Richmond.
Mrs. Andrew Dunn.................................Petersburg
Mrs. Duke..Suffolk Co.
Miss D. D..Norfolk.
Miss Didlake...Lynchburg.
Mrs. Maria Edmonds..............................Prince Edward Co.
Mrs. John T. Edwards............................Lynchburg.
Mrs. Dr. Early... "
Mrs. Early... "
Mrs. J. D. Ewing....................................Harrisonburg.
Mrs. Elam..Virginia.
Mrs. Fitz Hugh....................................... "
Mrs. F. B. Ficklin...............................Fredericksburg.
Mrs. F. F. Fitzgerald..........................Farmville.
Mrs. J. H. Figgat..................................Fincastle.
Mrs. Col. Forsberg...............................Lynchburg.
Mrs. Graves..Kentucky.
Mrs. Caroline Garland........................Lynchburg.
Mrs. Mary L. Garland........................... "
Mrs. John F. Gardner............................Nelson Co.
Mrs. Judge Geo. H. Gilmer..................Pittsylvania Co.
Mrs. F. D. Goodwin...............................Wytheville.
Mrs. Judge Goolrick............................Fredericksburg
Mrs. Jane V. Goolrick.......................... "

LIST OF CONTRIBUTORS.

Mrs. E. P. Goggin..................................Lynchburg.
Mrs. Susan Goggin.................................Bedford Co.
Mrs. Newton Gordon...............................Lynchburg.
Mrs Isabella Gilmer................................ "
Mrs. Isabella Harrison......................Charles City Co.
Mrs. Elvira Henry................................Charlotte Co.
Mrs E. Winston Henry..........................   "   "
Mrs. Mary G. Harding..............................Staunton.
Mrs. Fred. Hickey.................................Lynchburg.
Mrs. John W. Holt.................................   "
Mrs. Ann Holt......................................Liberty.
Mrs. Ferdinand C. Hutter.........................Lynchburg.
Mrs. J. P. Hubbard................Shepherdstown, West Va.
Mrs. Wm. L. Hyland...............Parkersburg, West Va.
Mrs. Edward Ingle................................Roanoke Co.
Mrs. J. J. Irby................................New Orleans, La.
Mrs. Joseph M. Jones...............................Kentucky.
Mrs. Dr. Jones.....................................Bedford Co.
Mrs. Arthur Johns..............................Northampton Co.
Mrs. Col. Johnson..................................Lexington.
Mrs. J. Johnson.....................................Abingdon.
Mrs. Thomas L. Johnson..........................Lynchburg.
Mrs. David Kent....................................Pulaski Co.
Mrs. D. B. Kinckle.................................Lynchburg.
Mrs. Kinsolving....................................Halifax Co.
Mrs. Knox.......................................Fredericksburg.
Mrs. Dr. Henry Latham...........................Lynchburg.
Mr. K..Norfolk.
Mrs. L. D. Leighton...............................Petersburg.
Mrs. Col. Augustine Leftwich....................Lynchburg.
Mrs. Gen. Robert E. Lee........"Arlington," Westmoreland Co
Miss Mildred C. Lee................................Lexington
Mrs. Gov. John Letcher...........................   "

LIST OF CONTRIBUTORS.

XV

Mrs. Dr. Robert T. Lemmon.................Campbell Co
Mrs. Andrew Lewis..........................Harrisonburg
Mrs. James Langhorne..........................Lynchburg
Mrs. John A. Langhorne....................Montgomery Co
Mrs. Nannie A. Langhorne.....................Lynchburg
Mrs. Richard T. Lacy.................................."
Mrs. M. L.."
Mrs. Geo. D. Lawrence.............................Miss.
Mrs. Wm. H. Little.........................Fredericksburg.
Mrs. J. D. L...................................Lynchburg.
L. D. L......................................Albemarle Co.
Mrs. Gov. Marye............................Fredericksburg.
Mrs. John Mason......................................"
Mrs. O. Massie............................Brooklyn, N. Y.
Mrs. Patrick Massie............................Nelson Co.
Mrs. Sarah Meem..................................Abingdon.
Mrs. John F. Miller............................Lynchburg.
Mrs. Charles L. C. Minor.......................Blacksburg.
Mrs. C. C. McPhail............................Charlotte Co.
Mrs. John R. McDaniel..........................Lynchburg
Mrs. Mary McNutt..........................Prince Edward Co
Mrs. R. K. Meade..............................Petersburg.
Mrs. Wm. H. Mosby.............................Amherst Co.
Mrs. Alice Murrel..............................Lynchburg.
Mrs. Wm. McFarland..............................Missouri
Mrs. C. V. McGee....................................Ala
Mrs. McGavock..................................Pulaski Co.
Gen. M...Virginia.
Mrs. James J. Moore.............................Richmond.
Mrs. Geo. Newton.................................Norfolk.
Miss Fannie Nelson..............................Yorktown
Mrs. Geo. Nichols.............................Bedford Co
Mrs. Gen. F. T. Nichols.....................New Orleans, La

LIST OF CONTRIBUTORS.

Mrs. Charles Norvell	Lynchburg
Miss Norwood	Richmond
Mrs. Robert L. Owen	Lynchburg
Mrs. Geo. W. Palmer	Saltville
Mrs. R. L. Page	Norfolk
Mrs. David Pierce	Wytheville
Mrs. John D. Powell	Portsmouth.
Mrs. Wm. Ballard Preston	Montgomery Co
Mrs. Gen. Robert Preston	" "
Mrs. Jas. Preston	" "
Mrs. Preston	Virginia.
Mrs. Annis E. Preston	Lynchburg.
Mrs. Richard Pollard	"
Mrs. James F. Payne	"
Miss Eliza Payne	"
Mrs. Annie Phillips	Fredericksburg.
Mrs. Edmund H. Pendleton	Cincinnati, Ohio.
Mrs. Price	Charlotte Co.
Mrs. John H. Parker	Chesterfield Co.
Mrs. Reid	Norfolk.
Mrs. Mattie Reid	Winchester.
Mrs. David S. Read	Roanoke Co.
Mrs. Wm. C. Rives	Albemarle Co.
Mrs. J. Henry Rives	Lynchburg.
Mrs. Roane	"
Mrs. J. H. Robinson	"
Mrs. W. Russell Robinson	Richmond.
Mrs. Dr. Edward T. Robinson	"
Mrs. John Roberts	Fredericksburg.
Mrs. E. M. Ruggles	"
Mrs. Dr. Sale	Liberty.
Mrs. Geo. D. Saunders	Buckingham Co
Mrs. Ann Saunders	Lynchburg

LIST OF CONTRIBUTORS.

Mrs. James A. Seddon..........................Goochland Co
Mrs. Dr. Semple.......................................Ala.
Mrs. H. H. Service.............................Alexandria
Mrs. J. W. Shields..............................Richmond.
Mrs. Jas. W. Shields..........................King Geo. Co.
Mrs. H. T. Silverthorn..........................Lynchburg.
Mrs. Wm. A. Strother................................ "
Mr. Wm. A. Strother................................. "
Mrs. John W. Stone .... "
Mrs. John F. Slaughter .... "
Miss Lillie Slaughter............................... "
Mrs. Kate Slaughter................................. "
Mrs. Judge Spence................................... "
Mrs. Henderson Suter............................Liberty.
Mrs. Harriet Stansbury....................New Orleans, La.
Mrs. Shannon ....Miss
Miss Ellen Shute..........................New Orleans, La
Miss Rebecca Smith..............................Norfolk.
Mrs. Charles Sharp.................................. "
Mrs. Sparks.....................................Virginia
Mrs. Col. Smith...........................Pittsylvania Co
Mrs. A. H. M. Taliaferro.......................Orange Co
Mrs. Mary W. Taylor...........................Campbell Co
Mrs. Major Thos. L. Taylor...................Campbell C. H
Miss Julia Thompson.........................Williamsburg.
Mrs. C. L. Thompson............................Richmond.
Mrs. J. Hanson Thomas.......................Baltimore, Md.
Mrs. Eli Tutwiler..............................Lexington.
Mrs. Samuel Tyree..............................Lynchburg
Mrs. John H. Tyree .... "
Mrs. Jas. Taylor..........................Fredericksburg.
Miss Edmonia Taylor............................Orange Co.
Mrs. Tucker....................................Virginia.

LIST OF CONTRIBUTORS.

Mrs. Judge Watson..................................Abingdon
Mrs. Dr. Thos. Walker..........................Lynchburg
Mrs. Col. W..."
Mrs. Col. Robert E. Withers....................Wytheville.
Mrs Philip T. Withers..........................Lynchburg.
Mrs. Dr. R. W. Withers........................Campbell Co.
Mrs. Edmund Withers............................Nelson Co.
Mrs. Dr. Wingfield...............................Maryland
Mrs. R. M. C. Wingfield.........................Portsmouth.
Mrs. J. C. Wheat..................................Winchester.
Mrs. Judge Wharton................................Liberty.
Miss Emily Whitehead..............................Norfolk.
Mrs. Robert Whitehead.............................Nelson Co
Mrs. John M. Warwick..............................Lynchburg.
Mrs. Wm. N. Welford.................................."
Mr. Philip Withers.................................."
Miss Kate Wilson ...."
Dr. Thos. L. Walker................................."
Miss Nannie S. Langhorne........ ...."

HOUSEKEEPING IN OLD VIRGINIA.

BREAD.

BREAD is so vitally important an element in our nourishment that I have assigned to it the first place in my work. Truly, as Frederika Bremer says, "when the bread rises in the oven, the heart of the housewife rises with it," and she might have added that the heart of the housewife sinks in sympathy with the sinking bread.

I would say to housewives, be not daunted by one failure, nor by twenty. Resolve that you *will* have good bread, and never cease striving after this result till you have effected it. If persons without brains can accomplish this, why cannot you? I would recommend that the housekeeper acquire the practice as well as the theory of bread-making. In this way, she will be able to give more exact directions to her cook and to more readily detect and rectify any blemish in the bread. Besides, if circumstances should throw her out of a cook for a short time, she is then prepared for the emergency. In this country fortunes are so rapidly made and lost, the vicissitudes of life are so sudden, that we know not what a day may bring forth. It is not uncommon to see elegant and refined women brought suddenly face to face with emergencies which their practical knowledge of household economy and their brave hearts enable them to firmly meet and overcome.

To return to the bread question, however. Good flour is an indispensable requisite to good bread. Flour, whether old or new, should always be sunned and aired before being used. In the morning, get out the flour to be made up at night for next morning's breakfast. Sift it in a tray and put it out in the sun, or, if the day is damp, set it near the kitchen fire. Only experience will enable you to be a good judge of flour. One test is to rub the dry flour between your fingers, and if the grains feel round, it is a sign that the flour is good. If after trying a barrel of flour twice, you find it becomes wet and sticky, after being made up of the proper consistency, you had better then return it to your grocer.

The best flour is worthless without good yeast. Yeast made up in the morning ought to be fit for use at night. It should be foamy and frothy, with a scent slightly like ammonia. After closely following the directions for yeast-making, given in the subsequent pages, the bread will be apt to succeed, if the flour employed is good.

There is a great art in mixing bread, and it is necessary to observe a certain rotation in the process. To make a small quantity of bread, first sift one quart of flour; into that sift a teaspoonful of salt, next rub in an Irish potato, boiled and mashed fine, then add a piece of lard the size of a walnut, and next a half teacup of yeast in which three teaspoonfuls of white sugar have been stirred. (Under no circumstances use soda or saleratus in your light dough.) Then make into a soft dough with cold water in summer, and lukewarm in winter. Knead without intermission for half an hour, *by the clock* Otherwise five minutes appear to be a half hour when bread is being kneaded or beaten. Then place it in a stone crock, greased with lard at the bottom, and set it to rise. In summer, apply no artificial heat to it, but set it in a cool place. As bread rises much more quickly in summer than in winter, you must make allowance for this difference, during the respective seasons. The whole process, including both the first and second rising, may be accomplished in seven or eight hours in summer, though this will be regulated partly by the flour, as some kinds of flour rise much more quickly than others. In summer you may make it up at nine o'clock P.M., for an eight o'clock breakfast next morning; but in winter, make it up at seven P.M., and then set it on a shelf under which a lighted coal-oil lamp is placed. If you can have a three-cornered shelf of slate or sheet-iron, placed in a corner of the kitchen, just above the bread block, it will be all the better, though a common wooden shelf, made very thin, will answer, where you cannot get the other. The coal-oil lamp underneath without running the risk of burning the shelf (it wooden), will keep the bread gently heated all night, and will answer the double purpose of keeping a light burning, which most persons like to do at night, and which they can do with scarcely any expense, by using a coal-oil lamp.

Never knead bread a second time in the morning, as this ruins it. Handle lightly as possible, make into the desired shapes and put into the moulds in which it is to be baked. Grease your hands before doing this, so as to grease the loaf or each roll as you put it in, or else dip a feather in lard and pass lightly over the bread just before putting it in the oven to bake. Let it be a little warmer during the second rise than during the first. Always shape and put in the moulds two hours before breakfast. If hot bread is desired for dinner, reserve part of the breakfast dough, keeping it in the kitchen in winter, and in the refrigerator in summer till two hours before dinner.

In baking, set the bread on the floor of the stove or range, never on the shelf. Always turn up the damper before baking any kind of bread. As you set the bread in the stove, lay a piece of stiff writing paper over it to keep it from browning before heating through. Leave the door ajar a few minutes, then remove the paper and shut the door. When the top of the loaf is a light amber color, put back the paper that the bread may not brown too much while thoroughly baking. Turn the mould around so that each part may be exposed to equal heat. Have an empty baking-pan on the shelf above the bread, to prevent it from blistering: some persons fill the pan with water, but I think this is a bad plan, as the vapor injures the bread. When thoroughly done, wrap the bread a few moments in a clean, thick, bread towel and send to the table with a napkin over it, to be kept on till each person has taken his seat at table.

I would suggest to housekeepers to have made at a tinner's, a sheet-iron shape for bread, eight inches long, four and one-half inches wide, and five and one-half deep. This is somewhat like a brickbat in shape, only deeper, and is very desirable for bread that is to be cut in slices, and also for bread that is to be pulled off in slices. A quart of flour will make eight large rolls, six inches high, for this mould, and three or four turnovers. It is a nice plan after making out the eight rolls to roll them with greased hands till each one will reach across the pan (four and one-half inches), making eight slices of bread which will pull off beautifully when well done, and thus save the task of slicing with a knife. It requires an hour to bake this bread properly.

Do not constantly make bread in the same shapes: each morning, try to have some variation. Plain light bread dough may be made into loaves, rolls, twist, turnovers, light biscuit, etc., and these changes of shape make a pleasant and appetizing variety in the appearance of the table. The addition of three eggs to plain light bread dough will enable you to make French rolls, muffins, or Sally-Lunn of it. As bread is far more appetizing, baked in pretty shapes, I would suggest the snow-ball shape for muffins and egg bread. Very pretty iron shapes (eight or twelve in a group, joined together) may be procured from almost any tinner.

If you should have indifferent flour of which you cannot get rid, bear in mind that it will sometimes make excellent beaten biscuit when it will not make good light bread. In making beaten buscuit, always put one teaspoonful of salt, a piece of lard the size of an egg, and a teacup of milk to a quart of flour, adding enough cold water to make a stiff dough: no other ingredients are admissible. Make the dough much stiffer than for other breads, beat steadily a half hour, *by the clock*. Cut with a biscuit cutter or shape by hand, being careful to have the shape of each alike and perfect. Make them not quite half an inch thick, as they rise in baking. Do not let them touch each other in the pan, and let the oven be very hot. It is well not to have beaten biscuit and light bread baked at the same time, as they require different degrees of heat. When two kinds of bread are required, try to have two such as require the same amount of heat. Egg bread and corn muffins require the same degree of heat as beaten biscuit, while Sally-Lunn and muffins need the same as light bread.

There is no reason why the poor man should not have as well prepared and palatable food as the wealthy, for, by care and pains, the finest bread may be made of the simplest materials, and surely the loving hands of the poor man's wife and daughter will take as much pains to make his bread nice and light as hirelings will do for the wealthy. The mistake generally made by persons in restricted circumstances is to make too great a use of soda bread, which is not only less wholesome, but is more expensive than light bread or beaten biscuit, as it requires more ingredients. The bread, coffee and meat, which constitute the poor man's breakfast, properly cooked, furnish a meal fit for a prince.

The furnishing of the kitchen is so important that I must here say a few words on the subject. First, the housekeeper must have a good stove or range, and it is well for her to have the dealer at hand when it is put up, to see that it draws well. Besides the utensils furnished with the range or stove, she must provide every kitchen utensil needed in cooking. She must have a kitchen safe,—a bread block in the corner, furnished with a heavy iron beater; trays, sifters (with iron rims) steamers, colanders, a porcelain preserving kettle, perforated skimmers and spoons, ladles, long-handled iron forks and spoons, sharp knives and skewers, graters, egg beaters (the Dover is the best), plenty of extra bread pans, dippers and tins of every kind, iron moulds for egg bread and muffins, wash pans, tea towels, bread towels, and hand towels, plates, knives, forks and spoons for use of the servants, a pepper box, salt box and dredge box (filled), a match safe, and last, but not least, a clock. Try as far as possible to have the utensils of metal, rather than of wood. In cases where you cannot have cold and hot water conveyed into the kitchen, always keep on the stove a kettle of hot water, with a clean rag in it, in which all greasy dishes and kitchen utensils may be washed before being rinsed in the kitchen wash pan. Always keep your cook well supplied with soap, washing mops and coarse linen dish rags. I have noticed that if you hem the latter, servants are not so apt to throw them away. Insist on having each utensil cleaned immediately after being used. Have shelves and proper places to put each article, hooks to hang the spoons on, etc. If you cannot have an oilcloth on your kitchen floor, have it oiled and then it may be easily and quickly wiped over every morning. Once a week, have the kitchen and every article in it thoroughly cleaned. First clean the pipe of the stove, as the dust, soot and ashes fly over the kitchen and soil everything. Then take the stove to pieces, as far as practicable, cleaning each part, especially the bottom, as neglect of this will prevent the bread from baking well at the bottom. After the stove is thoroughly swept out,— oven and all, apply stove polish. I consider "Crumbs of Comfort" the best preparation for this purpose. It comes in small pieces, each one of which is sufficient to clean the stove once, and is thus less apt to be wasted or thrown away by servants than stove polish that comes in a mass. Next remove everything from the kitchen safe and shelves, which must be scoured before replacing the utensils belonging to them, and these too must first be scoured, scalded, and wiped dry. Then wash the windows, and lastly the floor, scouring the latter unless it is oiled, in which case, have it merely wiped over.

Never let a servant take up ashes in a wooden vessel. Keep a sheet-iron pan or scuttle for the purpose. At night, always have the water buckets filled with water and also the kettles.

HOUSEHOLD MEASURES—YEAST.

setting the latter on the stove or range, in case of sickness or any emergency during the night. Have kindling wood at hand also, so that a fire may be quickly made, if needed.

Sometimes a discoloration is observable in iron kettles or other iron vessels. This may be avoided by filling them with hay before using them. Pour water over the hay, set the vessel on the fire and let it remain till the water boils. After this, scour in sand and ashes—then wash in hot soap-suds, after which process, there will be no danger of discoloration.

HOUSEHOLD MEASURES.

Wheat Flour. 1 lb. is 1 quart.
Indian Meal. 1 lb. 2 oz. are 1 quart.
Butter, when soft, 1 lb. is 1 pint.
Loaf sugar, broken, 1 lb. is 1 quart.
White sugar, powdered, 1 lb. 1 oz. are 1 quart.
Best brown sugar, 1 lb. 2 oz. are 1 quart.
Ten eggs are 1 lb.
Flour. 8 quarts are 1 peck.
" 4 pecks are 1 bushel.
16 large tablespoonfuls are ½ pint.
8 large tablespoonfuls are 1 gill.
2 gills are ½ pint.
A common sized tumbler holds ½ pint.
A tablespoonful is ½ oz.
60 drops are equal to a teaspoonful.
4 teaspoonfuls are equal to 1 tablespoonful.

YEAST.

Boil one quart of Irish potatoes in three quarts of water. When done, take out the potatoes, one by one, on a fork, peel and mash them fine, in a tray, with a large iron spoon, leaving the boiling water on the stove during the process. Throw in this water a handful of hops, which must scald, not boil, as in turns the tea very dark to let the hops boil.

Add to the mashed potatoes a heaping teacupful of powdered white sugar and half a teacupful of salt; then slowly stir in the strained hop tea, so that there will be no lumps. When milk-warm add a teacupful of yeast and pour into glass fruit jars, or large, clear glass bottles, to ferment, being careful not to close them tightly. Set in a warm place in winter, a cool one in summer. In six hours it will be ready for use, and at the end of that time the jar or bottle must be securely closed. Keep in a cold room in winter, and in the refrigerator in summer. This yeast will keep two weeks in winter and one week in summer. Bread made from it is always sweet.—*Mrs. S. T.*

Irish Potato Yeast.

1 quart of potatoes, boiled and mashed fine.
1 teaspoonful of salt.
½ teacup of sugar.

Put two cups of flour in a bowl, and pour over it three cups of strong hop-water, sealding hot, and stir it briskly.

Then put all the ingredients in a jar together, and when cool enough, add a cup of yeast, or leaven.

Set it by the fire to rise.

It will be ready for use in five or six hours.—*Mrs. E.*

Another Recipe for Yeast.

12 large potatoes, boiled and mashed fine.
1 teacup of brown sugar.
1 teacup of salt.
1 gallon of hop tea.

Mix the ingredients well, and when milk-warm, add a pint of yeast. Set it in a warm place to rise. Put one teacupful of this yeast, when risen, to two quarts of flour.—*Mrs. Dr. S.*

Yeast that Never Fails.

Boil twelve potatoes in four quarts of water till reduced to three quarts.

Then take out and mash the potatoes, and throw into the water three handfuls of hops.

When the hops have boiled to a good tea, strain the water over the potatoes, a small quantity at a time, mixing them well together.

Add one teacup of brown sugar.

1 teacup of salt.

1 tablespoonful of ground ginger.

When milk-warm, add yeast of the same sort to make it rise.

Put it in bottles, or a jug, leaving it uncorked for a day.

Set it in a cool place.

Put two large tablespoonfuls of it to a quart of flour, and when making up, boil a potato and mix with it.

This yeast never sours, and is good as long as it lasts.—*Mrs. A. F.*

Alum Yeast.

On one pint of flour pour enough boiling water to make a thick batter, stirring it until perfectly smooth, and then let it stand till milk-warm.

  Then add a teaspoonful of powdered alum.

  1 teaspoonful of salt.

  1 tablespoonful of sugar.

  Half a teacup of yeast.

After it ferments, add enough meal to make it a stiff dough.

Let it stand till it works, and then spread it in the shade to dry.

To a quart of flour put a tablespoonful of crumbs.—*Mrs. P.*

Leaven.

  2 tablespoonfuls of flour.

  1 tablespoonful of lard or butter.

  2 tablespoonfuls of yeast.

  2 eggs.

  1 potato.

  2 teaspoonfuls of sugar.

Make the leaven soon after breakfast in winter, and at one o'clock P. M. in summer. Let it be of the consistency of batter. Put it in a small bucket, in a warm place, to rise till four o'clock P. M. This amount of leaven is sufficient for two quarts of flour. If for loaf bread, leave out the eggs and butter.—*Mrs. M.*

EXCELLENT BREAD FOR BREAKFAST.

1 quart of flour.
Lard the size of a walnut.
1 small Irish potato, boiled and mashed fine.
1 heaping teaspoonful of salt.
Half a teacup of good yeast, into which put a tablespoonful of white sugar.

Make up a soft dough with cold water in summer and milk-warm water in winter. This must be kneaded for thirty minutes, and then set to rise, in a cool place in summer, and a warm one in winter; must never be kept more than milk warm.

Two hours before breakfast, make the dough into the desired shapes, handling it lightly, *without kneading it*, first rubbing lard over the hands, and taking especial care to grease the bread on top. Then set it to rise again.

Thirty minutes are sufficient for baking it, unless it be in the form of a loaf or rolls, in which case, it must be baked fifteen minutes longer. Excellent muffins may be made by the above receipt, adding two eggs well beaten, so that from the same batch of dough both plain bread and muffins may be made.

Iron moulds are best for baking.

For those who prefer warm bread for dinner, it is a good plan to reserve a portion of the breakfast dough, setting it away in a cool place till two hours before dinner, then make into turnovers or twist, set it to rise and bake it for dinner, as for breakfast. Very nice on a cold day, and greatly preferable to warmed-over bread.—*Mrs. S. T.*

FAMILY BREAD—OLD VIRGINIA LOAF BREAD.

Recipe for Family Bread.

2 quarts of flour.
2 tablespoonfuls of lard or butter.
2 teaspoonfuls of salt.
Enough sponge for a two quart loaf of bread.
Mix with one pint of sweet milk.

Make into rolls and bake with very little fire under the oven.
—*Mrs. A. C.*

Loaf Bread.

First make a batter of the following ingredients.

1 pint of flour.
1 teaspoonful of salt.
1 teaspoonful of sugar.
A cup of water.
A cup of good yeast.

Set this to rise and when risen work in two pints of flour, or, if the batter is not sufficient to work up this flour, add a little water.

Work it smoothly and set it to rise.

When risen, add a small piece of lard, work it well again, let it stand an hour and then bake it slowly.—*Mrs. P. W.*

Old Virginia Loaf Bread.

Sponge for the same.

Boil one large Irish potato, until well done, then peel and mash it fine, adding a little cold water to soften it. Stir into it

1 teaspoonful of brown sugar.
1 tablespoonful of sweet lard.

Then add three tablespoonfuls of good hop yeast.

Mix the ingredients thoroughly, then put the sponge in a mug with a close-fitting top, and let it stand several hours to rise.

Sift into the tray three pints of the best family flour, to which add a teaspoonful of salt. Then pour in the sponge and add enough cold water to the flour to work it up into a rather stiff dough. Knead it till the dough is smooth, then let it stand all night to rise. Work it over in the morning, using just enough flour to keep it from sticking to the hands. Allow it one hour to rise before baking and one hour to bake in a moderate oven. Then it will be thoroughly done and well dried.

Use a little lard on the hands when making out the loaf, as it keeps the crust from being too hard.—*Mrs. S.*

Another Recipe for Loaf Bread.

Good flour is the first requisite, and next, good yeast and sufficient kneading.

For a loaf of ordinary size, use

    2 lbs. of flour.
    Lard the size of a hen's egg.
    A saltspoonful of salt.
    2 gills of yeast.

Mix up these ingredients into a moderately stiff dough, using for the purpose, from three gills to a pint of water. Some flour being more adhesive than others, you have to learn by experience the exact amount of water required.

Knead the dough till perfectly smooth, then set it to rise, in a cool place, in summer, but in a warm place, free from draughts, in winter. In the latter season it is better to keep a blanket wrapped around it.

This amount of flour will rise to the top of a gallon and a half jar or bucket. If it is ready before time, stir it down and set it in a cooler place.

When you put it in the baking-pan (in which it will be in an inch of the top, if the pan be of a suitable size for the amount of flour) cover it well, or a hard crust will form from the effects of the atmosphere. Keep it a little warmer during the second rise than during the first. When ready for baking, set it in the oven and bake it for three-quarters of an hour with a moderate fire, evenly kept up. It will then come out without sticking, if the pans are well cared for.—*Mrs. J. J. A.*

Light Bread.

2 quarts of flour.
1 teaspoonful of sugar.
1 teaspoonful of salt.
Half a teacup of yeast.
One egg, well beaten.
1 pint of water.

Sift the flour and divide it into three parts. Mix one third in the batter, one third in the jar to rise in, and pour the other third over the batter. Let it stand two hours and then work it well, adding a small piece of lard before baking.—*Mrs. Dr. S.*

Recipe for Hot Rolls or Cold Loaf Bread.

Mix the following ingredients.

Four pints of flour.
1 pint of fresh milk.
2 eggs, well beaten.
1 large tablespoonful of melted lard.
1 large tablespoonful of hop yeast.

Set it to rise at eleven o'clock in the morning, for early tea. Make into rolls at five o'clock P. M., and bake as soon as risen. In cool weather, set before the fire, both before and after making it into rolls.—*Mrs. S.*

French Rolls.

1 quart of flour.
1 teaspoonful of salt.
2 eggs.
1 large tablespoonful of lard.
2 tablespoonfuls of yeast.

Work and knead it well at night, and in the morning work it well again, make it into rolls, put them in the oven to take a second rise, and when risen, bake them.—*Mrs. Col. W.*

Another Recipe for French Rolls.

>3 pints of flour.
>1 gill of yeast.
>1 egg (beaten up).
>1 tablespoonful of butter.

Mix up with milk and warm water and set to rise.—*Mrs. Dr. E.*

Another Recipe for French Rolls or Twist.

>1 quart of lukewarm milk.
>1 teaspoonful of salt.
>1 teacup of yeast.
>Enough flour to make a stiff batter.

When very light, add one beaten egg and two teaspoonfuls of butter, and knead in the flour till stiff enough to roll. Let it rise a second time, and, when very light, roll out, cut in strips and braid it. Bake thirty minutes, on buttered tins.—*Mrs. S.*

VELVET ROLLS.

Three pints of flour.
Two eggs.
One teacup of sweet milk.
One teacup of yeast.
1 tablespoonful of lard, and the same of butter.

Mix well and beat the dough till it blisters.

Let it rise, work in a small quantity of flour, beat as before and make into rolls. After the second rising, bake quickly.—*Mrs. Dr. S.*

Pocketbook Rolls.

1 quart of flour.
1 teaspoonful of salt.
2 teapoonfuls of sugar.
2 tablespoonfuls of lard.
3 tablespoonfuls of yeast.
2 eggs.

Mix up these ingredients with warm water, making up the dough at ten A. M. in summer and eight A. M. in winter. Put in half the lard when it is first worked up, and at the second working put in the rest of the lard and a little more flour.

Roll out the dough in strips as long and wide as your hand, spread with butter and roll up like a pocketbook. Put them in buttered tins, and, when they are light, bake them a light brown—*Mrs. L. C. C.*

Turnovers.

1 quart of flour.
1 large Irish potato, boiled and mashed.
3 eggs.
1 tablespoonful of butter or lard.
2 tablespoonfuls of yeast.
1 teacup of milk.

Rub the potato in the flour, then the lard and other ingredients, making it into a soft dough. Then set it to rise, at night if you wish it for breakfast next morning. Early in the morning, take off a piece of dough, the size of a biscuit, roll it out, about five inches long, then turn it about half over. When you have made up all the dough, in shapes like this, place them on a dish or board, cover with a napkin and set aside for a second rising. When ready to bake, dip a feather in water and pass over them to prevent the crust being too hard. If the dough should be sour, knead in a little soda, which will correct it—*Mrs. A. C.*

Another Recipe for Turnovers.

1 quart of flour.
4 eggs.
1 tablespoonful of lard or butter.
1 tablespoonful of yeast.

Set it to rise, then make them up round and flat, greasing the upper side with lard and turning over one side. When well risen the second time, bake.—*Mrs. I.*

TWIST.

From the dough of loaf bread or French rolls, reserve enough to make two long strips or rolls, say, fifteen inches long and one inch in diameter. Rub lard well between the hands before handling and shaping these strips. Pinch the two ends so as to make them stick together. Twist them, pressing the other ends together to prevent unrolling.—*Mrs. S. T.*

POCKETS.

1 quart of flour.
4 eggs.
1 cup of butter.
1 cup of yeast.
1 large Irish potato, boiled and mashed into the flour.

Add the yeast, butter and eggs, after mashing the potato in the flour. Knead all together and set to rise.

SALLY-LUNN.

1 quart of flour.
1 teaspoonful of salt.
1 tablespoonful of white sugar.
Rub in a heaping tablespoonful of butter and lard in equal parts, then rub in an Irish potato, mashed fine.
Half a teacup of yeast.
3 eggs well beaten.
Make up the dough to the consistency of light bread dough.

with warm water in winter, and cold in summer. Knead half an hour. When it has risen light, handle lightly, put into a cake-mould and bake without a second kneading.—*Mrs. S. T.*

Another Recipe for Sally-Lunn.

1 quart of flour.
1 tablespoonful of yeast.
4 eggs well beaten.
2 oz. of butter or lard.
1 pint of milk.

Set it to rise in the pan in which it is to be baked.—*Mrs. A. C.*

Another Recipe for Sally-Lunn.

3 pints of flour.
1 tablespoonful of butter and the same of lard.
3 eggs.
1 light teacup of yeast.
2 large tablespoonfuls of sugar.

Use as much milk in mixing as will make a soft dough. Work this well, as it gets only one working. Then grease it, put it in a greased pan, and set it in a warm place to rise. Bake about an hour.—*Mrs. Dr. T.*

Recipe for the Same.

1 quart of flour.
3 tablespoonfuls of yeast.
3 eggs.
1 saltspoonful of salt.
Butter the size of an egg.

Make up with new milk into a tolerably stiff batter. Set it to rise and when risen pour into a mould and set to rise again, as light bread. Bake quickly.—*Mrs. L.*

Quick Sally-Lunn.

1 quart of flour.
Half cup of butter.
2 eggs.
2 cups of milk.
Two teaspoonfuls of cream of tartar.
1 teaspoonful of soda.
2 tablespoonfuls of sugar.
1 saltspoonful of salt.

Bake fifteen minutes.—*Mrs. Dr. S.*

Muffins.

1 quart of flour.
6 eggs, beaten very light.
2 tablespoonfuls of butter.
2 tablespoonfuls of yeast.—*Mrs. Dr. E.*

Sweet Spring Muffins.

Sift three good pints of flour. Beat well six eggs, leaving out one and a half of the whites. Then beat into them as much flour as they will take in; then add milk and flour alternately (beating all the while) till all the flour is used. Add five tablespoonfuls of yeast, and when this batter is well beaten, stir into it two ounces of melted butter, cooled but liquid. The batter must be as stiff as can be beaten with an iron spoon. Bake in a hot oven.—*Mrs. L.*

Salt Sulphur Muffins.

Work together, about twelve o'clock in the day, one pint of yeast, half a pint of water, six eggs, one pound of butter and enough flour to make a dough just stiff enough not to stick to the fingers. After the dough is risen, make it out in biscuit and allow half an hour or more for them to rise before baking.—*Mrs. L.*

Superior Muffins.

1 quart of flour.
1 teaspoonful of salt.
1 tablespoonful of white sugar.

Rub in one heaping tablespoonful of butter and lard mixed, and one tablespoonful of Irish potato, mashed free from lumps.

Pour in three well beaten eggs and a half teacup of yeast. Make into a soft dough with warm water in winter and cold in summer. Knead well for half an hour. Set to rise where it will be milk-warm, in winter, and cool in summer. If wanted for an eight o'clock winter breakfast, make up at eight o'clock the night before. At six o'clock in the morning, make out into round balls (without kneading again), and drop into snow-ball moulds that have been well greased. Take care also to grease the hands and pass them over the tops of the muffins. Set them in a warm place for two hours and then bake.

These are the best muffins I ever ate.—*Mrs. S. T.*

Parker House Muffins.

Boil one quart of milk. When nearly cool stir in one quart sifted flour, one teaspoonful salt, one half cup of yeast. Then stir in three well beaten eggs. Let it rise in a warm place in winter and a cool one in summer, eight or ten hours. When risen light, stir in one tablespoonful melted butter and bake in iron muffin moulds.—*Mrs. W. H. M.*

Muffins.

1 quart of flour.
1 pint milk.
3 eggs.
1 heaping tablespoonful lard.
1   "   "   butter.
½ cup yeast.
1 teaspoonful sugar.

Mix and beat till perfectly light.—*Mrs. W. S.*

Another Recipe for Muffins.

One quart of milk, one dozen eggs, one pound of butter. Beat the butter and yolks together. Beat the whites to a stiff froth. Make the batter the consistency of pound cake, and bake in snow-ball cups as soon as made.—*Mrs. C. W. B.*

Muffin Bread.

3 pints of flour.
4 eggs.
1 pint of milk.
1 large tablespoonful of butter.
1 gill of yeast.
A little salt.

Make up at night. This makes two loaves.—*Mrs. A F.*

Soda Muffins.

1 quart of flour.
2 eggs.
3 teaspoonfuls of cream of tartar.
1 teaspoonful of soda.

Add enough buttermilk to make a stiff batter, and bake immediately.

White Egg Muffins.

1 pint of flour.
Whites of 8 eggs, beaten to a stiff froth.

Add enough milk to make it into a thin batter. Put in a little salt. Very nice.—*Mrs. C. C. McP.*

Cream Muffins.

Beat the whites and yolks of four eggs separately. When well beaten, mix them and add to them a half pint of cream, a lump of melted butter half the size of an egg. Then mix in slowly one pint of flour and bake it quickly, in small tins, without any further beating. A delicious breakfast bread.—*Mrs. McG., Ala.*

Miscellaneous Yeast Breads.

BUNNS.

1 pint of potato yeast.
4 ounces of sugar.
4 ounces of butter.
1 egg and as much flour as will make a soft dough.

Make as Sally-Lunn and bake in rolls.—*Mrs. Dr. S.*

COTTAGE LOAF.

1 quart of flour.
1 tablespoonful of sugar.
1 tablespoonful of butter.
1 tablespoonful of yeast.
2 eggs, and a little salt.

Make up at night for breakfast, mixing it with water. Bake in a quart tin pan.—*Mrs. A. B.*

POTATO BREAD.

1 quart of flour.
4 eggs.
4 good sized Irish potatoes, boiled, mashed and strained through a colander.
2 ounces of butter.
As much yeast as is needed to make it rise.

To be made up with water, not so stiff as light bread dough. Bake in a loaf or rolls.—*Mrs. J. H. F.*

OLD MAIDS.

Made at night like common light bread. Roll out the size of saucers in the morning, for the second rising. Bake on a hoe, turning over as a hoe cake. Then toast the sides, in front of a fire. A very nice, old-fashioned bread.—*Mrs. Dr. E.*

GRAHAM BREAD.

The night before baking, make a sponge of white flour, using half new milk and half cold water, with a teacup two thirds full of home-made yeast. In the morning, put four tablespoonfuls of this sponge in a separate dish, adding three tablespoonfuls of molasses, a little milk or water, and stirring in as much Graham flour as you can with a spoon. Then let it rise and mould the same as white bread.

BROWN BREAD.

One quart of light bread sponge, one-half teacup of molasses. Stir into the above, with a large spoon, unbolted wheat meal, until it is a stiff dough. Grease a deep pan, put the mixture in; when light, put the pan over a kettle of hot water (the bread well covered), and steam for half an hour. Then put in the oven and bake until done. Especially good for dyspeptics.
—*Mrs. D. Cone.*

BOX BREAD.

One quart of flour, one teacup of yeast, one teacup of melted lard or butter, four eggs, one teaspoonful of salt. Let it rise as light bread, and, when risen, make it into square rolls, without working it a second time. Let it rise again and then bake it.
—*Mrs. R. E. W.*

RUSKS.

1 cup of yeast.
1 cup of sugar.
1 cup of cream.
4 eggs.

Enough flour to make a batter, mixed with the other ingredients. Let it rise; then add enough flour to make rolls, and also add a teacup of lard and butter mixed. Bake as rolls after they have risen.—*Mrs. H.*

EGG RUSKS.

Melt three ounces of butter in a pint of milk. Beat six eggs into one-fourth of a pound of sugar. Mix these ingredients with enough flour to make a batter, adding a gill of yeast and half a teaspoonful of salt. When light, add flour to make a dough stiff enough to mould. Make into small cakes and let them rise in a warm place while the oven is heating.—*Mrs. Dr. S.*

GERMAN RUSKS.

1 quart of flour.
2 eggs.
2 cups of sugar.
2 cups of lard and butter mixed.
2 cups of potato yeast.
2 cups of milk.
1 nutmeg.

Put all the ingredients in the middle of the flour, work well together and set to rise as loaf bread. Wash the rolls over with butter and sugar.—*Mrs. C. L. T.*

FRENCH BISCUIT.

1 quart of flour.
1 teaspoonful of salt.

Rub in one tablespoonful of butter and lard mixed.

Pour in half a teacup of yeast, two well beaten eggs, and enough water to make a soft dough. Knead half an hour. Then set to rise; when well risen, roll out, without kneading again. Handle lightly, first greasing the hands with butter. Cut with a biscuit cutter, greasing one biscuit and placing another on it. Set to rise a second time before baking.—*Mrs S. T.*

Vanity Biscuit.

One pint of flour, one of milk, three eggs beaten well together Bake in cups.—*Miss D*.

Beaten Biscuit.

One quart of flour, lard the size of a hen's egg, one teaspoonful of salt. Make into a moderately stiff dough with sweet milk. Beat for half an hour. Make out with the hand or cut with the biscuit cutter. Stick with a fork and bake in a hot oven, yet not sufficiently hot to blister the biscuit.—*Mrs. S. T*.

Another Recipe for Beaten Biscuit.

1 quart of flour.
1 teaspoonful of salt.
1 egg.
1 tablespoonful of butter and the same of lard.

Mix up these ingredients with skimmed milk, work them well together and beat fifteen minutes. Stick with a fork and bake quickly.—*Mrs. E. B*.

Soda Biscuit.

1 quart of flour.
1 heaping teaspoonful of cream of tartar, the same of soda, and the same of salt. Sift these together, then rub in a tablespoonful of lard and make up the dough with milk and water.—*Mrs. E. B*.

Cream Biscuit.

1 quart of sifted flour.

Four teaspoonfuls of cream of tartar and two teaspoonfuls of fine table salt, which must be well diffused through the flour. Then add two ounces of fresh, good butter. Take one pint of pure, sweet cream, put in it two even teaspoonfuls of soda and then add it to the flour. The dough ought to be very soft; but should it be too soft, add a little more flour. Work it well, roll it out half an inch thick, cut with a biscuit cutter and bake in a quick oven five minutes.—*Mrs. J. H. F.*

Excellent Light Biscuit.

Boil four large Irish potatoes. While hot, mash them with a piece of lard the size of an egg. Add one teacup of milk and one of yeast. Stir in enough flour to make a good batter and set it to rise. It will take about two quarts of flour. When light, make up the dough. You generally have to add more water or milk. Roll thick, let them rise slowly, but bake them quickly.—*Mrs. M. G. H.*

Light Biscuit.

Two quarts flour, one large tablespoonful lard, and the same of butter. Salt to the taste. One teaspoonful soda and enough buttermilk to make a soft dough. Bake quickly.—*Mrs. Dr. S.*

Thick Biscuit.

One quart flour, one large tablespoonful lard and butter mixed, one teaspoonful salt, enough morning's milk to make a stiff dough. Work well and beat with a rolling-pin or iron pestle, at least half an hour. Make into small biscuit and bake in a quick oven. This will make sixteen biscuit.—*Mrs. M. A. P.*

Thin Biscuit or Crackers.

One quart of flour, one tablespoonful lard and butter mixed, a little salt. Make a stiff paste with water. Beat the dough till it blisters. Roll thin, stick, and bake quickly.--*Mrs A. C.*

Soda Crackers.

1 quart of flour.
1 tablespoonful of lard and butter mixed.
1 egg; a little salt.
1 teaspoonful of soda, sifted into the flour.

Make a stiff paste with buttermilk, beat until light, roll tolerably thin, cut in squares, prick, and bake quickly.—*Mrs. A. C.*

HUNTSVILLE CRACKERS.

Take a lump of risen dough, as large as your double fist, a heaping teaspoonful of loaf sugar, beaten with the yolk of an egg. Mix with the dough a lump of butter the size of a hen's egg and an equal quantity of lard, a tablespoonful of soda, dissolved in a cup of cream. Beat a long time, stirring in flour all the while, till quite stiff. Roll out, cut in square cakes and bake in a brisk oven.—*Miss E. P.*

WATER CRACKERS.

1 lb. of flour.
1 teaspoonful of salt and the same of soda.
1 tablespoonful of lard.

Make up with sweet milk, beat well, roll thin, and bake quickly.

WAFERS.

1 quart flour.
Yolk of one egg.
1 heaping tablespoonful lard.
A little salt.

Mix with milk, as stiff as you would for biscuit. Beat well with the biscuit beater, roll out thin and put in the wafer irons. Put in the fire and bake.—*Mrs. W. S.*

NUN'S PUFFS.

Boil one pint of milk with half a pound of butter. Stir them into three-quarters of a pound of flour and let them cool. Then add nine eggs, yolks and whites to be beaten separately, and whites to be added last. Fill cups or tins half full and bake. When done, sprinkle with white sugar while hot. Very nice for tea.—*Mrs. A. D.*

Miscellaneous Flour Breads.

LAPLAND BREAD.

1 quart of flour.
1 quart of cream.
1 teaspoonful of salt.

Twelve eggs (whites and yolks beaten separately and very light). Put the whites in the batter the last thing, beat very light, bake in a quick oven, in small tins, which must be perfectly dry and sprinkled with a little flour before being greased. A delicious bread.—*Mrs. Dr. J.*

A Plainer Recipe for the Same.

1 pint of flour.
1 pint of milk.
2 eggs.

Beat the eggs well and stir in the flour and milk. Bake in little pans.

NEW BREAD.

1 quart of flour.
1 dessertspoonful of lard and the same of butter.
1 teaspoonful of soda.

Work the lard and butter in the flour, and sprinkle in the soda, with salt to taste. Mix with buttermilk or clabber to the consistency of biscuit. Roll it round to the size of a teaplate. Made just before eating.—*Mrs. F.*

HENRIETTA BREAD.

1 pint of flour.
1 pint of sweet milk.
2 eggs, beaten separately.
1 tablespoonful of lard or butter.

Make the consistency of poor man's pudding. Bake in cups —*Mrs. K.*

Jenny Lind Bread.

1 quart of sifted flour.
A lump of butter the size of an egg
2 teacups of milk.
4 eggs.
1½ teaspoonfuls of soda.
2 teaspoonfuls of cream of tartar.

Bake twenty minutes.—*Mrs. L.*

Lunch Bread.

1 pint of flour.
1 tablespoonful of butter.
3 tablespoonfuls of sugar.
1 teaspoonful of soda.
2 teaspoonfuls cream of tartar.
2 eggs.
1 cup of milk and a little salt.

Bake in a flat pan in a quick oven. To be eaten hot with butter.—*Mrs. I. H.*

Breakfast Puffs.

One tumbler of flour, one tumbler of milk, and one egg. Beat the yolk and milk together, then add the flour, and lastly the white of the egg. Bake a few minutes in a hot oven.—*Mrs. I. H.*

Another Recipe for the Same.

Take two eggs well beaten and stir into a pint of milk; add a little salt, two spoonfuls of melted butter, one and one-half pints of flour. Stir thoroughly, so as to avoid lumps. Grease the cups in which you pour the batter, and fill them two-thirds full.

Salt-Risen Bread.

Make into a thin batter:

>1 pint of flour.
>1 tablespoonful of corn meal.
>Half-teaspoonful salt.

Set in a warm place to rise. After it has risen, pour into it two quarts of flour, with sufficient warm water to make up a loaf of bread. Work it well, set it to rise again, and when risen sufficiently, bake it.—*Mrs. T. L. J.*

Another Recipe for the Same.

Into a pitcher, put one teacup of milk fresh from the cow, two teacups of boiling water, one tablespoonful of sugar, one teaspoonful of salt. Into this stir thoroughly a little less than a quart of flour. Set the pitcher in a kettle of moderately warm water and keep it at a uniform temperature. Keep a towel fastened over the mouth of the pitcher. Set the kettle in front of the fire to keep the water warm. Let it stand three hours, then beat it up well, after which do not interrupt it. If in two hours it does not begin to rise, put in a large slice of apple. As soon as it rises sufficiently, have ready two quarts of flour, half a tablespoonful of lard and more salt, and make up immediately. Should there not be yeast enough, use warm water. Put into an oven and set before a slow fire to rise, after which bake slowly. The yeast must be made up at seven o'clock in the morning.—*Miss N. C. A.*

Waffles.

>1 pint milk.
>3 tablespoonfuls flour.
>1 tablespoonful corn meal.
>1 tablespoonful melted butter.
>1 light teaspoonful salt.

Three eggs, beaten separately, the whites added last. To have good waffles, the batter must be made thin. Add another egg and a teacup of boiled rice to the above ingredients, if you wish to make rice waffles.—*Mrs. S. T.*

Waffles.

1 quart of flour.
1 quart of sour cream (or buttermilk, if you have no cream).
6 eggs.
1½ teaspoonful of soda.
Half a tablespoonful of melted lard, poured in after the batter is mixed.

This may be baked as flannel cakes or muffins.—*Mrs. H. D.*

Another Recipe for Waffles.

1 quart of flour.
6 eggs beaten very light.
1½ pint of new milk.
2 teaspoonfuls of salt.
3 tablespoonfuls of yeast.

Set it to rise at night, and stir with a spoon, in the morning, just before baking. When you want them for tea, make them up in the morning, in winter, or directly after dinner, in summer.—*Mrs. Dr. J.*

Soda Waffles.

1 pint of flour.
1 pint of milk.
1 teaspoonful of soda, dissolved in the milk.
2 teaspoonfuls of cream of tartar, mixed in the flour.
2 eggs.
1 tablespoonful of butter.
Beat up and bake quickly.

Another Recipe for Waffles.

1 quart of flour, with a kitchen-spoonful of corn meal added

3 eggs beaten separately.
1 quart of milk.
1 teacup of water.
1 teaspoonful of salt.
Lump of butter large as a walnut, melted and poured in.
Bake in hot irons.
One secret of having good waffles is to have the batter thin.
—*Miss R. S.*

Superior Rice Waffles.

1 quart flour.
3 eggs.
1 cup boiled rice, beaten into the flour.
1 light teaspoonful soda.

Make into a batter with buttermilk. Bake quickly in waffle irons. Batter made as above and baked on a griddle makes excellent breakfast cakes.—*Mrs. D. B. K.*

Rice Waffles.

1 pint of flour.
1 pint of new milk.
The yolks of three eggs.
Lump of butter the size of an egg.
Half teacup of boiled rice.
A pinch of salt and a pinch of soda, sprinkled in the flour and sifted with it.
Beat well.—*Mrs. F.*

Another Recipe for the Same.

Two gills of rice, mixed with three ounces of butter, three eggs, three gills of flour, a little salt, and cream enough to make the batter. Beat till very light.—*Mrs. Dr. S.*

Mush Waffles.

With one pint of milk, make corn mush. When cool, add a

tablespoonful of butter, a little salt, and thicken with flour to a stiff batter. Bake quickly in irons.—*Mrs. C. L. T.*

BREAKFAST CAKES.

In the morning take the dough of a pint of flour. Beat two eggs light and mix them with a half pint of milk, then add these ingredients to the dough, let it stand an hour to rise, and then bake as buckwheat cakes.—*Mrs. Dr. J.*

MADISON CAKES.

Two pounds of flour, two eggs, two ounces of lard, three tablespoonfuls of yeast. Make up with new milk, the consistency of roll dough, at night. Flour the biscuit board and roll out the dough in the morning about three quarters of an inch thick, cutting the cakes with a dredging-box top. Let them rise, covered with a cloth, till fifteen minutes before breakfast. —*Mrs. L.*

ORANGE CAKES.

1 quart of flour.
1 teacup of butter.
4 eggs.
1 tablespoonful of yeast.

Make into a stiff batter with milk, the over-night. Next morning, add a teacup of Indian meal. Beat well and put in cups to rise before baking.—*Mrs. A. C.*

VELVET CAKES.

1 quart of flour.
1 quart of milk.
1 tablespoonful of yeast.
1 tablespoonful of melted butter.
3 eggs.

Bake in muffin rings.—*Mrs. A. C.*

Flannel Cakes.

1 quart of flour.
1 pint of meal.
1 teacup of milk.
1 teacup of yeast.
3 eggs.
2 teaspoonfuls of salt.

Beat well together and let it rise till usual time in a warm place. Excellent.—*Mrs. W. B.*

Another Recipe for Flannel Cakes.

1 quart of flour.
2 eggs.
1½ pint boiled milk (used cold).
2 teaspoonfuls of salt.
3 tablespoonfuls of yeast (added after the other ingredients have been mixed).

Beat light, and set to rise till morning.
Bake on a griddle.—*Mrs. Dr. J.*

Another Recipe for the Same.

4 eggs.
1 quart of milk.
Half teacup of butter or lard.
2 tablespoonfuls of yeast.
1 teaspoonful of salt.

Flour to make the batter like pound cake.—*Mrs. S.*

Buckwheat Cakes.

1 quart buckwheat flour.
1 pint sifted corn meal.
Half teacup of yeast.
1 teaspoonful of salt.
Enough water to make a stiff batter.

After rising, stir in a half teacup of butter or lard. Let it rise a second time, grease the griddle, dip the spoon in lightly, and cook quickly.—*Mrs. P. W.*

Another Recipe for Buckwheat Cakes.

1 pint of buckwheat flour.
1 tablespoonful of meal.
1 tablespoonful of yeast.
1 teaspoonful of salt.

Make up with water the over-night, and beat till it bubbles. In the morning beat again, and just before baking stir in a pinch of soda dissolved in milk or water.—*Mrs. Col. W.*

BUCKWHEAT CAKES.

1 quart buckwheat flour.
1 pint wheat flour.
½ teacup yeast.
A pinch of salt.

Make into a batter with warm water. Set to rise. Thin the batter with a cup of milk (to make them brown well). Add a pinch of soda and bake quickly on a griddle. Butter and send to the table hot.—*Mrs. D. B. K.*

Another Recipe for the Same.

1 pint buckwheat.
½ pint sifted meal.
2 teaspoonfuls of salt.
4 tablespoonfuls of yeast.
1½ pint lukewarm water.

Beat well and set to rise till morning.—*Mrs. Dr. J.*

CREAM CAKES.

1 pint of flour.
1 pint of cream (or milk).
2 eggs, well beaten.
Lump of butter size of an egg.

Put the milk and butter on the fire till it boils. Mix and bake quickly in pans. Salt to taste.

Another Recipe for Cream Cakes.

1 quart of cream (sour is preferable).
4 eggs.
1 teaspoonful of soda.
1 teaspoonful of salt.

Flour for a thick batter.—*Mrs. G.*

Another Recipe for the Same.

   1 quart of flour.
   3 eggs.
   1 tablespoonful of lard.
   1 pint of cream.
   1 teaspoonful of salt.

Bake in tins.—*Mrs. A. C.*

BOSTON CREAM CAKES.

   2 cups of flour.
   2½ cups of water.
   1 cup of butter.
   5 eggs.

Boil the butter and water together, stir in the flour while boiling; after it is cool, add the eggs, well beaten. Put a large spoonful in muffin rings, and bake twenty minutes in a hot oven.

The cream for them is made as follows:

Put over the fire one cup of milk and not quite a cup of sugar, one egg, mixed with three teaspoonfuls of corn starch and one tablespoonful of butter. Boil a few moments only. When cool, add vanilla to the taste.

Open the cakes and fill them with this cream.—*M. H. K.*

Buttermilk Cakes.

1 quart of flour.
2 eggs, well beaten.
1½ pint of buttermilk.
1 teaspoonful of salt.

Beat very light, after mixing the ingredients. Just before baking, stir in a little soda, mixed in a little of the buttermilk. Bake on a griddle, free from grease.—*Mrs. L.*

Sour Milk Cakes.

1 pint sour milk.
1 pint flour.
Butter size of a small egg.
1 tablespoonful of sugar.
1 saltspoonful of salt.
Half teaspoonful of soda.

Bake in hot and well greased iron clads.

Farina Cakes.

Melt together one pint of milk and one tablespoonful of butter. Then add four tablespoonfuls of farina and boil till quite thick. Set aside to cool. When ready to bake, add three well beaten eggs, a few spoonfuls of flour, and salt to your taste.—*Mrs. S.*

Rice Cakes.

Put one pound of rice in soak the over-night. Boil very soft in the morning, drain the water from it and mix with it, while hot, a quarter of a pound of butter. After it has cooled, add to it one quart of milk, a little salt, and six eggs. Sift over it and stir into it gradually a half pound of flour. Beat the whole well and bake on a griddle like other batter cakes.—*Mrs. W.*

Another Recipe for Rice Cakes.

One cup of cold boiled rice, rubbed in a quart of milk, one pint of flour, a teaspoonful of salt, two eggs beaten light. Beat all till free from lumps. Bake as soon as made, on a well greased griddle.

BATTER CAKES.

Two eggs beaten separately. Pour into the yolks a pint of buttermilk, then put in two handfuls of meal and one of flour, then the whites of the eggs, half a teaspoonful of soda and a little salt. Fry with very little grease, or with egg shells. Put two spoonfuls of batter to a cake.—*Mrs. C. L. T.*

Another Recipe for Batter Cakes.

1 quart of flour.
1 pint of meal.
1 teaspoonful of soda.
1 teaspoonful of salt.
3 eggs.

Make up with buttermilk.—*Mrs. Dr. J.*

Batter Cakes made of Stale Bread.

Put a loaf of stale bread to stand all day in a pint of milk. Just before tea add three eggs and one large spoonful of butter. If too thin, add a little flour.—*Mrs. R.*

Old Virginia Batter Cakes.

Beat two eggs very light in a bowl. Add one teacup of clabber, one of water, one of corn meal, a teacup of flour, one-half teaspoonful of salt. Just before baking, sift in half a teaspoonful of soda and stir well. It is better to grease the griddle with fat bacon than with lard.

The above proportions will make enough batter cakes for two or three persons.—*Mrs. S. T.*

Another Recipe for the Same.

1 quart sweet milk.
1 heaping pint corn meal.
4 eggs.
1 teaspoonful of salt.
Half teaspoonful of soda.
1 tablespoonful of warmed butter or fresh lard.

Break the eggs, whites and yolks together, beat slightly, then add the milk, stir in the meal and beat until it looks light. Bake on a griddle.—*Mrs. J. P.*

Cheap Recipe for Batter Cakes.

1 pint of sour milk.
1 teaspoonful of soda.
1 tablespoonful of flour.
Enough meal to make a good batter.

Bake on a hoe.—*Miss E. P.*

INDIAN GRIDDLE CAKES.

1 quart of sour milk.
1 large tablespoonful of butter, melted after measuring.
2 eggs.
1 teaspoonful of soda.
Half a teaspoonful of salt.

Make a thin batter, with two-thirds Indian meal, and one-third flour.

A small bag made of coarse but thin linen or cotton, and filled with common salt, is much better to rub over the griddle than lard, when cakes are to be fried or baked.

BATTER BREAD.

Break two eggs into a bowl. Beat to a stiff froth. Pour in one teacup of clabber or butter-milk, one of water, one of corn meal, one of flour, half teaspoonful of salt, a heaping teaspoonful of butter melted. Beat all well together. Have already heated on the stove or range, iron-clad muffin moulds (eight or ten in a group). Grease them well with a clean rag, dipped in lard. Fill each one nearly full with the batter, first sifting in half a teaspoonful soda. Set in a hot oven and bake a nice brown. Oblong shapes are the nicest. If preferred, sweet milk may be used instead of sour milk and water. In this case add another egg and dispense with the soda.—*Mrs. S. T.*

Batter Bread.

Four cups of meal, two cups sweet milk, four eggs, two tablespoonfuls flour, one tablespoonful lard, one teaspoonful salt, half teaspoonful soda.—*Mrs. F.*

Batter Bread.

One cup meal, one cup sweet milk, one cup butter-milk, two eggs, one tablespoonful butter, one tablespoonful flour, half teaspoonful of salt, and same of soda.

Bake in cups.—*Mrs. G.*

Corn Muffins.

3 eggs, beaten light.
1 pint of buttermilk (if very sour, use less).
1 teacup of cream or milk.
1 small teaspoonful of soda.
Lard or butter size of an egg.

Meal enough to make the batter of the consistency of poundcake batter.—*Mrs. I.*

Corn Meal Waffles.

One pint of corn meal scalded. While hot add to it, two tablespoonfuls of lard or butter, three well beaten eggs, a cup of boiled rice, a pint of flour, a teaspoonful of salt.

Thin to the proper consistency with milk.—*Mrs. Dr. S.*

ST. NICHOLAS' PONE.

1 quart of meal.
1 quart of milk.
4 eggs.
1 tablespoonful of melted butter.
1 teaspoonful of salt.
2 teaspoonfuls cream of tartar.
1 teaspoonful of soda.—*Mrs. C. C.*

GRIT OR HOMINY BREAD.

2 eggs, beaten separately.
1 pint of milk.
Small piece of butter.

Add enough meal and hominy to make a batter, and bake quickly.—*Mrs. C. L. T.*

HOMINY BREAD.

Mix with two teacups of hot hominy a very large spoonful of butter. Beat two eggs very light and stir into the hominy. Next add a pint of milk, gradually stirring it in. Lastly, add half a pint of corn meal. The batter should be of the consistency of rich boiled custard. If thicker, add a little more milk. Bake with a good deal of heat at the bottom, but not so much at the top. Bake in a deep pan, allowing space for rising. When done, it looks like a baked batter pudding.—*Mrs. F. D.*

CORN CAKE.

1 pint of corn meal.
1 pint of sweet milk.
2 eggs.
1 tablespoonful of butter.
2 tablespoonfuls of flour.
1 teaspoonful of salt.

Boil the milk and pour it over the meal, flour, and butter.

Beat light. When cool, add eggs well beaten. Bake in a buttered pan.—*Mrs. G. W. P.*

Mush Bread.

Make a thin mush of corn meal and milk (or hot water, if milk is scarce). Cook till perfectly done, stirring all the time to keep it smooth. Then add a good lump of butter; and, after it cools a little, two eggs, one at a time. Beat in a very small pinch of soda and a little salt.

Butter a yellow dish and bake slowly till brown.—*Mrs. C. L. T.*

Light Corn Bread.

Pour one quart of boiled milk over one pint of corn meal. Add a teaspoonful of salt, a teaspoonful of cream of tartar, half teaspoonful of soda, three well beaten eggs, four tablespoonfuls of flour, a little butter.—*Miss E. P.*

Soft Egg Bread.

1 quart of milk.
Half pint of meal.
3 eggs.
Large spoonful of butter.

Make in a pudding dish. Rice is an improvement to the above.—*Mrs. P.*

Old-fashioned Egg Bread.

1 pint of meal.
3 eggs well beaten.
1 teaspoonful of salt.
1 tablespoonful melted butter.

Add enough sweet milk to make a rather thin batter. Bake quickly.—*Mrs. S. T.*

Another Recipe for Egg Bread.

1 quart of milk.
3 eggs.
1 tablespoonful of butter.
1 pint of corn meal.
1 teaspoonful of salt.

Beat the eggs very light and add to the other ingredients. Bake in a pan or dish. Add a little soda dissolved in milk, if you desire it.—*Mrs. I. H.*

INDIAN BREAD.

Beat two eggs very light, mix alternately with them one pint of sour milk or buttermilk, and one pint of fine corn meal. Melt one tablespoonful of butter, and add to the mixture. Dissolve one teaspoonful of soda in a small portion of the milk, and add to the other ingredients, last of all. Beat hard and bake in a pan, in a hot oven.

RICE BREAD.

1 pint sweet milk.
1 teacup boiled rice.
2 teacups sifted corn meal.
½ teacup melted butter.
3 eggs, beaten separately.
½ teaspoonful salt.

Bake in a very hot oven, using buttered iron muffin moulds. —*Mrs. S. T.*

CRACKLIN BREAD.

Take one quart sifted corn meal and a teacup of cracklins. Rub the latter in the meal as fine as you can. Add a teaspoonful of salt and make up with warm water into a stiff dough. Make into pones, and eat hot.—*Mrs. P. W.*

Virginia Ash Cake.

Add a teaspoonful of salt to a quart of sifted corn meal. Make up with water and knead well. Make into round, flat cakes. Sweep a clean place on the hottest part of the hearth. Put the cake on it and cover it with hot wood ashes.

Wash and wipe it dry, before eating it. Sometimes a cabbage leaf is placed under it, and one over it, before baking, in which case it need not be washed.—*Mrs. S. T.*

Plain Corn Bread.

1 pint sifted meal.
1 teaspoonful salt.
Cold water sufficient to make a stiff dough.

Work well with the hands, pat out in long, narrow pones, six or seven inches long and as wide as the wrist. Bake quickly in a hot pan.—*Mrs. P. W.*

COFFEE, TEA, AND CHOCOLATE.

To toast Coffee.

Wash and pick the coffee, put it in a very large stove-pan in a hot oven. Stir often, giving constant attention. It must be toasted the darkest brown, yet not one grain must be burned. It should never be glazed, as this destroys the aroma.

Two pints of coffee become three pints after toasting.—*Mrs. S. T.*

Boiled Coffee.

To one quart of boiling water (poured in after scalding the pot) stir in three gills of coffee, not ground too fine. Boil twenty minutes, scraping from the sides and stirring occasionally. Five minutes before breakfast, scrape from the spout, pour out half a teacupful, and return to the pot. Do this a second time. Set it with the side of the pot to the fire, so that it will be just at the boiling point. Do not let it boil, however. Serve in the same coffee-pot.

Coffee should never be glazed.

Have a liberal supply of thick, sweet cream, also of boiled milk, to serve with the coffee.

If the members of the family drop in at intervals, it is well to keep the coffee over a round iron weight, heated just enough to keep the coffee hot, without boiling it. This answers better than a spirit lamp for keeping coffee hot.—*Mrs. S. T.*

Coffee.

Take equal quantities of Mocha, Java, Laguayra and Rio coffee. Have the coffee roasted a chestnut brown. To every twelve cups of coffee to be drawn, use eighteen heaping tablespoons of the ground coffee. Have the water boiling hot, scald the biggin or percolator, put the ground coffee in the upper part, then pour on some boiling water for it to draw—about two teacups if you are to make twelve cups of coffee. Let it stand a few moments and pour again into the upper part of the percolator the first drawn coffee. Then add, one by one, the cups of boiling water required. It will take ten minutes for the coffee to be ready for the table.

Use the best white sugar, and in winter let the milk stand twenty-four hours for the cream to rise. Use together with rich cream, a cream jug of boiling sweet milk.—*Mrs. M. C. C.*

Coffee

Buy Java and Laguayra mixed, two-thirds Java and one-third Laguayra, which will give a delightful aroma to the Java.

Scald the pot. Then put in a teacup of coarsely ground

coffee, parched a light brown and mixed with cold water till it forms a paste, to six cups of boiling water. Before you put in the boiling water, add to the grounds one or more egg-shells or whites of eggs, to keep it clear. Let it boil ten or fifteen minutes. Before taking it off the fire, drop in about a teaspoonful of cold water, which will settle all the floating grounds.—*Mrs. J. P.*

Dripped or Filtered Coffee.

If one quart of coffee is desired, grind three gills of coffee, put it in the filterer and pour boiling water over it. If not sufficiently strong, pour out and return to the filterer. Then set on the fire and boil up, taking from the fire immediately.—*Mrs. S. T.*

Dripped Coffee.

One-half pint Java coffee ground and put in the dripper. Pour over it two and one-half pints boiling water. If not strong enough, pass through the dripper a second time.—*Mrs. J. R. McD.*

Café au Lait.

1 cup German chiccory.
2 cups ground coffee.

Put in three pints boiling water with a pinch of isinglass, boil five minutes and allow it to settle, or, if made in a percolator it will be better. Use three-quarters of a cup boiling milk and one-quarter of strong coffee, with sugar to suit the taste.—*Mrs. J. W. S.*

Green Tea.

Scald the teapot, and add one-half pint boiling water to two teaspoonfuls of the best green tea. Set it where it will keep hot, but not boil. When it has drawn fifteen or twenty minutes, add boiling water till it has the strength desired.—*Mrs. J R. McD.*

Green Tea.

Scald the teapot. If you wish a pint of tea, put in one heaping teaspoonful tea after putting in a pint boiling water. Set this where it will keep hot, but not quite boil.—*Mrs. S. T.*

A good Cup of Green Tea.

Before putting in any water, set the teapot with the tea in it before the fire and let it get thoroughly hot. Then fill the pot with boiling water and let it stand five minutes.—*Mrs: M. E L. W.*

Black Tea.

If you wish a quart of tea, put that quantity of boiling water into the teapot, after scalding it. Add four teaspoonfuls of tea. Boil twenty minutes. It is a great improvement to put in a little green tea.—*Mrs. S. T.*

Black Tea.

Add one and one-half pint boiling water to a half-teacupful of the best black tea. Boil gently for ten or fifteen minutes. If too strong, weaken with boiling water.—*Mrs. J. R. McD.*

Iced Tea.

After scalding the teapot, put into it one quart of boiling water and two teaspoonfuls green tea. If wanted for supper, do this at breakfast. At dinner time, strain, without stirring, through a tea-strainer into a pitcher. Let it stand till tea time and then pour into decanters, leaving the sediment in the bottom of the pitcher. Fill the goblets with ice, put two teaspoonfuls granulated sugar in each, and pour the tea over the ice and sugar. A squeeze of lemon will make this delicious and healthful, as it will correct the astringent tendency.—*Mrs. S. T.*

CHOCOLATE.

Scrape fine one square of Baker's chocolate (which will be an ounce). Put it in a pint of boiling water and milk, mixed in equal parts. Boil it ten minutes, and during this time mill it or whip it with a Dover egg-whip (one with a wheel), which will make it foam beautifully. Sweeten to the taste, at table.—*Mrs. S. T.*

COCOA.

To one pint milk and one pint cold water add three tablespoonfuls grated cocoa. Boil fifteen or twenty minutes, milling or whipping as directed in foregoing recipe. Sweeten to taste, at the table. Some persons like a piece of orange-peel boiled with it.—*Mrs. S. T.*

BROMA.

Dissolve one large tablespoonful broma in one tablespoonful warm water. Pour on it one pint boiling milk and water (equal parts). Boil ten minutes, milling or whipping as above directed. Sweeten to the taste.—*Mrs. S. T.*

A cream-pitcher of whipped cream should always accompany chocolate or any preparation of it, such as cocoa or broma.—*Mrs. S. T.*

MILK AND BUTTER.

THE most exquisite nicety and care must be observed in the management of milk and butter. A housekeeper should have two sets of milk vessels (tin or earthenware, never stoneware, as this is an absorbent). She should never use twice in succes sion the same milk vessels without having them scalded and aired.

In warm weather, sweet milk should be set on ice, if practicable, or if not, in a spring-house. Never put ice in sweet milk, as this dilutes it. One pan of milk should always be set aside to raise cream for coffee. A bucket with a close-fitting lid should be filled with milk and set aside for dinner, one for supper, one for breakfast, and a fourth for cooking purposes.

For making butter, strain unskimmed milk into a scalded churn, where the churning is done daily. This will give sweeter butter and nicer buttermilk than when cream is skimmed and kept for churning, as this sometimes gives a cheesy taste to the butter. Do not let the milk in the churn exceed blood heat. If overheated, the butter will be white and frothy, and the milk thin and sour. Churn as soon as the milk is turned. In summer try to churn early in the morning, as fewer flies are swarming then, and the butter can be made much firmer.

A stone churn is in some respects more convenient than a wooden churn; but no matter which you use, the most fastidious neatness must be observed. Have the churn scalded and set out to sun as soon as possible after churning. Use your last made butter for buttering bread, reserving the staler for cookery.

Butter should be printed early in the morning, while it is cool. A plateful for each of the three meals should be placed in the refrigerator ready for use. Do not set butter in a refrigerator with anything else in it but milk, or in a safe with anything but milk. It readily imbibes the flavor of everything near it. After churning, butter should be taken up in what is called "a piggin," first scalded and then filled with cold water. With an old-fashioned butter-stick (scalded) wash and press the butter till no water is left. Then add a little salt, finely beaten. Beat again in a few hours, and make up in half-pound prints. I would advise all housekeepers (even those who do not make their own butter) to keep a piggin, a butter-stick, and a pretty butter-print.

To secure nice Butter for the Table in Winter.

In October and November, engage butter to be brought weekly, fresh from the churn in rolls. Wrap each roll in a piece of old table cloth, and put in a sweet firkin or stone jar which has been washed with soda water, scalded and sunned for a month before using. Pour over it a clear strong brine, which also must have been prepared at least a week beforehand, by pouring off the settlings and repeated strainings. Have a nice flat rock washed and weight the butter down with it, being careful to keep it always under the brine.—*Mrs. S. T.*

Recipe for Putting up Butter

2 quarts best common salt.
1 ounce pulverized saltpetre.
1 ounce white sugar.

Work the butter over three times, the last time adding an ounce of the above mixture to every pound butter. Of course, the butter is salted, when first made. Make the butter into rolls and wrap in cloths or pack in jars, within four inches of the top of each jar. If the latter is done, fill the jars with brine and tie up closely. If the former is preferred, drop the rolls into brine, prepared as follows:

To every gallon brine that will bear an egg, add one pound white sugar and one-half ounce saltpetre. Boil well and skim. Keep the brine closely covered. I have used butter on my table in May, put up in this way, and it tasted as well as when put up in October.—*Mrs. R. C.*

CLABBER.

To have clabber in perfection, place in small glass dishes or bowls enough milk to make clabber for each person. After it has turned, set it in the refrigerator, if in summer, till called for. By the way, refrigerators (as well as water-coolers) should be washed every morning with water in which a tablespoonful of common soda has been dissolved. They should then be aired before filling with ice for the day.—*Mrs. S. T.*

COTTAGE CHEESE.

When the tea-kettle boils, pour the water into a pan of "loppered" milk. It will curd at once. Stir it and turn it into a colander, pour a little cold water over it, salt it and break it up. A better way is to put equal parts of buttermilk and thick milk in a kettle, over the fire, heat it almost boiling hot, pour into a linen bag and let it drain till next day. Then take it out, salt it, put in a little cream or butter, as it may be thick or not, and make it up into balls the size of an orange.

SOUP.

As making soup is a tedious process, it is best to make enough at once to last several days. Beef shank is most generally used in making nutritious soup. It is best to get this the day before using it, and soak it all night in cold, clear water. If you cannot do this, however, get it as early in the morning as you can. Break the bones, wash it, soak it a few minutes in weak salt and water, and put it in a large boiler of cold water. As soon as it begins to simmer, remove the dark scum that rises on top. Keep the boiler closely covered, and boil very slowly till an hour or two before dinner. Then, with a ladle, remove all the fat from the top, as it is this element that makes soup unwholesome. Strain and season, or, if you prefer, season just enough for one meal, reserving the rest as foundation for another sort of soup. It is well always to keep some of this stock on hand in cold weather, as by the addition of a can of tomatoes, or other ingredients, a delicious soup may be quickly made of it. Never throw away water in which any sort of meat has been boiled, as it is much better to simmer hash or a stew in this liquor than in water, and it is also invaluable for basting fowls or meats that have not been parboiled.

Directions for soup making are so fully given in the following pages that it is needless for me to say anything further on the subject here.

Oyster Soup.

100 oysters.
1 teaspoonful salt.
1 tablespoonful black pepper.
¼ pound butter.
Yolks of 3 eggs.
1 pint rich milk, perfectly fresh.
3 tablespoonfuls flour.

Separate the oysters from the liquor: put the liquor to boil, when boiled add salt, pepper and butter, then the flour, having previously made it into a batter. Stir all the time. When it comes to a boil, add the eggs well beaten, then the milk, and when the mixture reaches a boil, put in the oysters; let them also just boil, and the soup is done. Stir all the time to prevent curdling.—*Mrs. Judge M.*

Economical Oyster Soup.

1 quart oysters.
2 quarts water.
Boil with salt and pepper.

Cut up one tablespoonful butter with flour and put in while boiling; beat the yolks of four eggs light, mix them with one-half pint milk.

When the oysters are well cooked, pour on the milk and eggs, stirring all the time. Let it boil up, and take off quickly, and pour into the tureen, over toasted bread cut into dice—if preferred rich, leave out some of the water.—*Mrs. Lt. Gov. M.*

Oyster Soup.

Empty the oysters into a colander and drain off all the liquor; then strain the liquor through a very coarse cloth to rid it of all scum, etc. To a whole can of oysters take a quart of milk

Put the milk, oyster liquor, one level tablespoonful flour rubbed very smooth with one heaping tablespoonful of butter, one tablespoonful salt, one-half teaspoonful pepper, all on the fire together in a farina-boiler (or put a skillet one-third filled with boiling water under the saucepan, to prevent the milk burning). When it comes to a boil, put in the oysters and let them stew for twenty minutes or till the gill of the oyster turns and begins to ruffle and crimp at the edge. Serve immediately, for if they are cooked too long, they become hard, dark and tasteless. If you put the salt in last, it will not curdle the soup. Some add one level teaspoonful whole cloves and same of mace, tied up in a net bag, but they are little improvement.—*Mrs. R.*

Purée of Oysters.

For fifty oysters.

Put the oysters on in their own liquor—let them come to a boil—take them out and mince them; skim the liquor when nearly done. Beat well together:

    1 egg.
    1 dessertspoonful butter.
    ½ pint milk.
    1 cracker sifted.
    Salt, pepper (mace, also, if liked).

Pour this into boiling liquor and then add the minced oysters. When done, the soup is smooth. The milk must be fresh or it will curdle.—*Mrs. John Walker, Alabama.*

Oyster Soup.

Take two quarts of oysters, wash them, and add,
    2 quarts water.

A bundle of herbs.
1 small onion sliced.

Let it boil until all the substance is out of the oysters Strain the liquor from the ingredients and put it back in the pot. Add a large spoonful butter mixed with flour. Have ready two dozen oysters to throw in just as it is ready to be dished—at the same time stir up two yolks of eggs with a cup of cream. Cayenne pepper is an improvement.—*Mrs. E. W.*

TURTLE SOUP.

Kill the turtle at daylight in summer, the night before in winter, and hang it up to bleed. After breakfast, scald it well and scrape the outer skin off the shell; open it carefully, so as not to break the gall. Break both shells to pieces and put them into the pot. Lay the fins, the eggs and some of the more delicate parts by—put the rest into the pot with a quantity of water to suit the size of your family.

Add two onions, parsley, thyme, salt, pepper, cloves and allspice to suit your taste.

About half an hour before dinner thicken the soup with brown flour and butter rubbed together. An hour before dinner, take the parts laid by, roll them in brown flour, fry them in butter, put them and the eggs in the soup; just before dinner add a glass of claret or Madeira wine.—*Mrs. N.*

Turtle Soup.

To one turtle that will weigh from four to five pounds, after being dressed, add one-half gallon water, and boil until the turtle will drop to pieces, then add:

  2 tablespoonfuls allspice.
  1 tablespoonful black pepper.
  2 tablespoonfuls butter, and salt to the taste.

When nearly done, put in a small handful pot marjoram, thyme and parsley tied together, and two large onions; when ready to come off, add two sliced lemons, one pint good wine, and a small quantity of curry powder; thicken with flour.—*Mrs. D.*

Turtle Soup.

To 2½ quarts soup add:

1 ounce mace.
1 dessertspoonful allspice.
1 teaspoonful cloves.
Pepper, black and cayenne, and salt to your taste.

Tie up a bunch of parsley, thyme, and onion in a cloth, and throw into soup when boiling. When nearly done, thicken with two tablespoonfuls flour. To give it a good color, take one tablespoonful brown sugar and burn it; when burnt, add a wine-glass of water. Of this coloring, put two tablespoonfuls in soup, and just before serving, add half a pint Madeira wine.—*Miss E. W.*

Mock Turtle Soup.

Put on beef and boil very tender; take out, chop fine, and put back to boil. Put potatoes, mace, cloves, cinnamon, parsley, thyme, spice, celery seed, and ten hard-boiled eggs; pepper and salt to your taste.

Thicken with flour and add brandy and wine.—*Miss E. P.*

Mock Terrapin Soup.

Cut up two pounds roast or boiled beef in small pieces. Put one large teacup new milk, one large teacup of wine, a piece of butter size of an egg (rolled in flour), a little nutmeg, two or three spoonfuls mixed mustard—all in a stewpan, and cook ten or fifteen minutes. Good way to use up cold meats.—*Mrs. S. M.*

Clam Soup.

Boil half a peck of clams fifteen minutes; then take them from the shells, clean and wash them. Have ready the stew-kettle; strain the water, in which clams have been boiled; chop up clams, and put in with three or four slices of salt pork, some mashed potatoes, salt and pepper to taste. Thicken with grated cracker, and add two spoonfuls butter rolled in flour. Let it boil twenty minutes and serve.—*Mrs. C.*

Clam Soup.

Open the clams and chop them up fine. To twenty clams, add:

½ gallon water.
3 good onions.
2 tablespoonfuls butter.
A small bunch of parsley and thyme.

Just before taking off, add one quart rich milk and thicken with flour.—*Mrs. D.*

Crab Soup.

Open, and cleanse of the deadman's fingers and sandbag, twelve small fat crabs raw. Cut the crabs into two parts. Parboil and extract the meat from the claws, and simply extract the fat from the back shells of the crabs. Scald eighteen ripe tomatoes, skin them and squeeze the pulp from the seeds through a colander. Chop them fine and pour boiling water over the seeds and juice, and strain them. Stew a short time in the soup-pot one large onion, one clove of garlic, in one spoonful butter and two spoonfuls lard, and put them in the tomatoes.

After stewing a few minutes, add the meat from the claws, then the crabs, and lastly the fat from the back shells. Season with salt, cayenne and black pepper, parsley, sweet marjoram and thyme, one-half teaspoonful lemon juice, and peel of one lemon. Pour in the water with which the seeds were scalded, adding more should there not be the quantity of soup required. Boil moderately one hour. About a quarter of an hour before serving, sift in grated bread crumbs or pounded crackers as a thickening. Any firm fish prepared by this recipe is excellent. —*Mrs. J. I.*

Crab Soup.

One dozen crabs to one gallon water. Take off top shell; clear body of crabs. Cut through the middle, put them into a kettle, mix with some butter, and brown them. Then add one gallon water, and simmer for half an hour. Skim slightly, and add the hock of an old ham, and strained tomato juice one pint. Boil two hours. Season with pepper, spice if liked, and half-pint wine.

The claws are to be cracked and divested of the jaws. A Hampton recipe.—*Miss E. W.*

Beef Soup.

Crack the bone of a shin of beef, and put it on to boil in one quart water. To every pound meat add one large teaspoonful salt to each quart water. Let it boil two hours and skim it well. Then add:

    4 turnips, pared and cut into quarters.
    4 onions, pared and sliced.
    2 carrots, scraped and sliced.
    1 root of celery, cut into small pieces.

When the vegetables are tender, add a little parsley chopped fine, with salt and pepper to the taste. Serve hot.—*Mrs. P. McG.*

Another Recipe for Beef Soup.

One shin beef in one-half gallon water, put on before breakfast and boiled until dinner. Thicken with brown flour two or three hours before dinner. Put in one carrot, two turnips, one onion, thyme, cabbage, and celery-seed.—*Mrs. H. P. C.*

To prepare a Beef's Head as Stock for Soup.

Cut up the head into small pieces, and boil in a large quantity of water until it is all boiled to pieces. Take out all the bones as for souse cheese, and boil again until thick. Then while hot, season very highly with pepper, salt, catsup, allspice, and onions chopped fine.

Put into a mould to get cold. For a small family cut a thick slice, say five inches square, whenever you want soup in a hurry, adding about a quart of water. It need cook for a few minutes only, and is valuable as keeping well and being ready in times of emergency. By adding a few slices of hard-boiled egg and a gill of good cooking wine, this soup may have very nearly the flavor of mock turtle.—*Mrs. A. M. D.*

CALF'S HEAD SOUP.

Take one-half liver and the head of a mutton, veal or beef, and boil until the meat drops from the bone. Cut up fine and add one-half the brains; then:

1 onion.
1 spoonful spice.
½ spoonful cloves.
1 spoonful black pepper and a piece of mace.
3 tablespoonfuls flour.
3 tablespoonfuls flour, and salt to the taste.

Put in enough water at first, as adding it makes the soup thin.

Cut up three hard boiled eggs, and add, when done, one glass of wine.

A little brandy and walnut catsup, with more eggs, will improve it, though it is a delightful soup as it is.—*Mrs. W. A. C.*

Calf's Head Soup.

Clean the head, laying aside the brains. Put the head in a gallon of water, with pepper and salt. Boil to pieces and take out bones; return to the pot with—

1 teacup of mushroom or tomato catsup.
1 teaspoonful allspice.
1 lemon rind, grated.

CALF'S HEAD SOUP.

    1 grated nutmeg.
    1 tablespoonful butter.
    1 teacup of browned flour.

Fry, and add the brains when nearly ready for the table.
About five minutes before serving, add:

          1 teacup of wine.
          1 teaspoonful cloves.
          1 teaspoonful mace.

When sent to the table have two hard-boiled eggs sliced and floating on top.—*Mrs. J. D.*

Calf's Head Soup.

Take a large calf's head and boil it with four gallons water and a little salt; when tender, bone and chop it fine, keeping out the brains, and put the meat back in the pot and boil down to a tureenful. Half an hour before serving the soup, add:

    1 tablespoonful mustard.
    1 teaspoonful black pepper.
    1 teaspoonful powdered cloves.
    1 teaspoonful mace.
    1 teaspoonful nutmeg.

Brown a cup of flour to thicken and just as the soup is dished, add one cup walnut catsup, and one cup port or claret wine.

The brains must be beaten up with an egg, fried in little cakes, and dropped in the tureen.—*Miss N.*

CALF'S HEAD SOUP.

Take the head, split it open and take out the brains; then put the head, brains, and haslet in salt water—let them soak one hour. Put on to boil at eight o'clock; after boiling four hours, take it up and chop up the head and haslet, removing all the bones; return to the soup, with a small pod of pepper. Thicken it with one pint browned flour with one tablespoonful butter rubbed in it. Have—

1 tablespoonful mace.
1 tablespoonful allspice.
⅓ doz. cloves.

Beat all together and put in the tureen with,

1 teacup of tomato catsup.
1 teacup of cooking wine.

Pour the soup on them. Have the brains fried, and two hard boiled eggs sliced and dropped in the soup.—*Mrs. T. C.*

Brown Calf's Head Soup.

Scald and clean the head, and put it to boil in two gallons water, with

A shank of veal.
2 carrots.
3 onions.
A small piece of bacon.
A bunch of sweet herbs.

When they have boiled half an hour, take out the head and shank, and cut all the meat off the bone in pieces two inches square. Let the soup boil half an hour longer, then strain it and put in the meat, and season with salt, black and cayenne pepper (and a few cloves, if you like them). Thicken with butter and brown flour.

Let it now boil nearly an hour longer, and just before serving it, stir in one tablespoonful sugar browned in a frying-pan, and half a pint wine. A good substitute for turtle soup.—*Mrs. Col. A. F.*

Calf's Head Soup.

Have a head nicely cleaned, the brains taken out and the head put to soak. Put it on with.

1 gallon water.
1 piece of fat ham.
Thyme, parsley, pepper and salt.

Boil together until the flesh is tender; take out and chop—strain the water—two tablespoonfuls brown flour, four ounces butter—returning the "dismembered" fragments; let it boil till reduced to two quarts. Season with one-half pint wine, one gill catsup, nutmeg, mace, allspice.

Cut up the liver, and fry; beat the brains up with an egg, pepper and salt; fry in cakes and lay in the soup when served up, and hard boiled eggs sliced up and put in.—*Miss B. L.*

Ox-tail Soup.

Wash and soak three tails; pour on them one gallon cold water; let them be brought gradually to boil, throw in one and a half ounce salt, and clear off the scum carefully as soon as it forms on the surface. When it ceases to rise, add:

- 4 moderate sized carrots.
- 2 or 3 onions.
- 1 large bunch savory herbs.
- 1 head celery.
- 2 turnips.
- 6 or 8 cloves, and ½ teaspoonful peppercorns.

Stew these gently from three hours to three and a half hours. If the tails be very large, lift them out, strain the liquor and strain off all the fat. Cut the meat from the tails and put it in two quarts or more of the stock. Stir in, when this begins to boil, a thickening of arrow-root or of rice flour, mixed with as much cayenne and salt as may be required to flavor the soup, and serve very hot.—*Mrs. P.*

Chicken Soup.

Put on the chickens with about three quarts water and some thin slices bacon. Let it boil well, then put in:

- A spoonful butter.
- 1 pint milk.
- 1 egg, well beaten.
- Pepper, salt, and celery or celery-seed or parsley.

Let all boil up. Some dumplings made like biscuits are very nice in it.—*Mrs. W.*

Roast Veal and Chicken-bone Soup.

Boil the veal and chicken bones with vegetables, and add one handful maccaroni, broken up fine. Boil the soup half an hour. Color with a little soy or catsup.—*Mrs. S.*

Chicken Soup.

Put on the fire a pot with two gallons water and a ham bone, if you have it; if not, some slices of good bacon. Boil this two hours, then put in the chickens and boil until done: add one-half pint milk and a little thickening; pepper and salt to the taste. After taking off the soup, put in a piece of butter size of an egg. Squirrel soup is good made the same way, but takes much longer for a squirrel to boil done.—*Mrs. P. W.*

Giblet Soup.

1 pint dried green English peas.
1 pound giblets.
1 dozen cloves.
1 small piece red pepper.
Nearly 1 gallon water.

Boil peas slowly seven hours. Add giblets, spices, and salt to taste, two hours before dinner. When peas are dissolved, strain through sieve; cut giblets into dice and return to soup; boil up and serve. Will be enough for six or eight persons.—*Mrs. R. R.*

Okra Soup.

1½ gallons water.
2 quarts young okra, cut very fine.
2 quarts tomatoes.
Onions, prepared as for pea soup.
Pepper; salt.
1 large spoonful butter.

Add the tomatoes about twelve o'clock. Put the soup on early in the morning.—*Mrs. I.*

Gumbo Soup.

1 fried chicken.
1 quart okra, cut up.
1 onion.
1 bunch parsley.
Few celery tops—fry all together. Put in one quart skinned tomatoes.
1½ gallons water, boil to ½ gallon.
Teacup of wine after taking from the fire.—*Mrs. R. A.*

Gumbo Soup.

Fry two fowls, old or young, with parsley, pepper, salt, onion, lard or bacon.

Put it in the pot with water sufficient for the soup. One quart sliced okra, scrap of ham or fried sausage to boil with it.

Sassafras Gumbo is made in the same way, except after the fowl has boiled until the flesh has left the bone, just before taking off the fire, stir in one tablespoonful sassafras flour. Oysters are a great improvement to sassafras gumbo. Gather the sassafras leaves green, and dry in the shade, as sage; when thoroughly dry, rub through a sieve and bottle and cork tightly. It is nice in beef soup instead of okra.—*Mrs. T.*

Fine Vegetable Soup.

Put on two pounds of fresh beef, or a good-sized chicken, or ham bone if you have it, early in the morning. Put your boiler on filled with water. Keep boiling, and when boiled down, about one hour or more before dinner, add:

Grated lemon peel.
6 ears corn.
1 dozen good tomatoes.

Beans.

1 small head of cabbage.

A few Irish potatoes.

Sweet herbs, pepper and salt to the taste.

A few leaves of dried sassafras rubbed up will improve the taste. Serve hot with toast, a small quantity of sugar and vinegar. Boil till thick.—*Mrs. Dr. L.*

VEGETABLE SOUP.

Before breakfast, wash a beef shank in several waters, break the bone, and put it in a large pot of cold water. Keep it steadily boiling until one hour before dinner, when the following vegetables, previously prepared, must be added to the soup after it has been carefully skimmed of all grease, and strained.

1 quart peeled and chopped tomatoes.

1 pint lima or butter beans.

1 pint grated corn.

1 pint chopped cabbage.

1 pint sliced Irish potatoes.

1 sliced turnip.

1 carrot.

A little minced onion.

Parsley.

1 tablespoonful pepper sauce.

1 heaping tablespoonful flour rubbed into—

1 teacup milk.

1 teacup brown sugar.

1 teaspoonful black pepper.

Boil an hour: thicken with mixed milk and flour, and serve.

A piece of middling, bacon, or any other kind of meat, may be used instead of the beef shank. The best meat of the shank may be freed from gristle, chopped fine and made into a nice stew by adding

1 grated turnip.

1 mashed potato.

TOMATO SOUP.

    1 tablespoonful pepper sauce.
    1 tablespoonful made mustard.
    1 tablespoonful butter.
    1 teaspoonful celery seed.
    1 teaspoonful fruit jelly.
    1 teacup milk.
    Minced onion and parsley.

Boil up and serve.—*Mrs. S. T.*

TOMATO SOUP.

Take one quart ripe tomatoes, peeled and chopped up, or a three-pound can of same, put in an earthenware baking dish with

    1 pint grated corn (or, if in winter, dried corn prepared as if for the table), and add—
    1 teacup sugar.
    1 teacup grated cracker.
    1 teacup butter.
    1 teaspoonful black pepper.
    2 teaspoonfuls salt.

Set this in a hot oven with a tin plate over it to prevent browning. Have ready, in a porcelain kettle or pan, two quarts new milk boiling hot. When the tomatoes and corn are thoroughly done, stir in one large Irish potato mashed smooth, a little minced onion and parsley, and pour into the boiling milk and serve.—*Mrs. S. T.*

Tomato Soup.

A shin of beef, season to your taste with all kinds of vegetables:

Tomatoes, turnips, carrots, potatoes, cabbage cut fine, corn, butter beans and celery.

When nearly done, take vegetables out and mash them well, and also cut the beef up fine. It is best to season with salt and pepper when you first put it on. The beef should be put on very early.—*Mrs. J. L.*

Clear Tomato Soup.

1 large can tomatoes.
1 beef shin.
1 bunch soup herbs.
1 gallon water.

Boil eight hours, stir and skim several times. Strain through wire sieve, add one tablespoonful Worcester sauce and same of brown sugar. Serve with dice of toasted bread; pepper and salt to taste.—*Mrs. R. R.*

Asparagus Soup.

Cut the asparagus into small pieces and put on to boil in salt water, with slices of middling; just before dinner, taking it off, beat four eggs and stir in one pint milk or cream, a piece of butter. A piece of veal may be boiled with it, if you wish meat.—*Mrs. H.*

Asparagus Soup.

Parboil the asparagus with as much water as will cover them; then pour the water and asparagus into milk, then add butter, pepper and salt, also bread crumbs, and boil until the asparagus is done.—*Mrs. S.*

Pea Soup.

Soak one pint of split peas in water for twelve hours; drain off the water, put the peas into a saucepan with three pints cold water, one-half pound bacon, two sprigs of dried mint, a bay leaf, some parsley, an onion stuck with one or two cloves, some whole pepper, and salt to taste.

Let the whole boil three hours, then pass the purée through a hair sieve; make it hot again and serve with dice of bread fried in butter.—*Mrs. A.*

Green Pea Soup.

Boil one quart peas in two quarts water, and two thin slices bacon. When done mash through a colander; then put back in the same water, throwing away the slices of bacon. Season with pepper, salt, spoonful butter rolled in flour.

Boil well again. Toast some bread and cut in slices, and put in the tureen when the soup is served. The hulls of green peas will answer; boil them well with a few peas, then season as above and boil. Two hours will be enough to boil green pea soup.—*Mrs. W.*

Green Pea Soup.

Boil half a peck of peas in one and a half gallons water, till perfectly done. Take out, mash and strain through a colander, then pour a little of the water well boiled over them, to separate the pulp from the hull. Return it to the water they were boiled in; chop up one large or two small onions; fry them in smallest quantity of lard, not to brown them. Add this with chopped thyme, parsley, pepper and salt.

Just before taking off the fire stir in one tablespoonful butter. If the soup is too thin, cream a little butter with flour to thicken.—*Mrs. I.*

Potato Soup.

Mash potatoes, pour on them one teacup cream, one large spoonful butter.

Pour boiling water on them till you have the desired quantity. Boil until it thickens; season with salt, parsley, and pepper to your taste.—*Mrs. R. E.*

Potato Soup.

Pour two quarts water on six or seven large peeled potatoes, adding two or three slices of middling; boil thoroughly done. Take them out, mash the potatoes well and return all to the same water, together with pepper, salt, one spoonful butter, and one quart milk, as for chicken soup.—*Mrs. W.*

OYSTERS AND OTHER SHELL FISH.

STEWED OYSTERS.

Put butter, salt and pepper in a stew-pan, and put the oysters to the butter and stew until perfectly done.—*Mrs. D.*

Stewed Oysters.

Take one-quarter pound nice butter, put it in a pan and melt, then pepper and salt, add a small piece of cheese. When it is all melted add one pint of oyster liquor, and boil; when hot, strain and put back in pan, then add oysters and boil five minutes.—*Mr. K. N.*

Stewed Oysters.

Pour into a stew-pan ½ gallon oysters.

2 tablespoonfuls pepper vinegar.

1 teaspoonful black pepper.

1 teaspoonful salt.

Let them simmer until the oysters are plump; take them out with a fork and drop them into a tureen, on a handful of crackers and three heaping tablespoonfuls fresh butter.

Pour one pint milk to the liquor, let it boil up and strain it on the oysters. Rinse out the stew-pan and pour the oysters, liquor, etc., back into it, and set it on the fire. When it comes to a boil, serve.

This method deprives the oysters of the bits of shell.—*Mrs. S. T.*

To Stew Oysters.

Put into the kettle one pint liquor, one-half pound butter, and pepper.

Let it boil, then put in the oysters, after draining them in a colander. They will be done as soon as they boil up, or when they curl right well. When ready to take up, add half tea-cup cracker crumbs and a little salt in the stew.—*Mrs. P. W.*

To Stew Oysters.

Put into a shallow stew-pan the oysters. As soon as the gills begin to open pour off all the liquor. Continue to cook them, stirring all the time until done. The liquor that was poured off must be thickened with a good lump of butter rubbed up with flour, and seasoned with pepper and salt, and poured boiling-hot onto the oysters.

The advantage of this way of cooking is that the oysters become large and plump.—*Mrs. Dr. E. R.*

To Cook Oysters.

½ gallon oysters.
1 quart fresh milk.
½ pound butter.
1 tablespoonful flour.
1 teaspoonful salt.
1 teaspoonful pepper.
1 egg.

Rub the egg and flour together and thin with a little of the milk. Mix the oysters, pepper and salt, and let them come to a boil; then add the milk, and when this boils add the egg and flour with the butter. Let the whole boil three minutes.—*Miss N. S. L.*

SCALLOPED OYSTERS.

Do not drain the liquor from the oysters, but fork them out of it as you use them; in that way as much liquor as you require adheres to them. Use stale bread, and do not crumb it too fine, or it will be clammy.

½ teacupful cream.
2 great spoonfuls butter.
Salt and pepper.

Oysters part with a great deal of moisture in cooking, and if the mixture is too wet it is not as good; it should be rather dry when done. Cover the bottom of a well-buttered dish with a layer of very dry bread crumbs, dust over a little salt and pepper, and stick little bits of butter all over the crumbs; then, with a spoon, moisten it with cream. Next, place a layer of oysters, alternating with bread crumbs, until the dish is filled, finishing with butter and cream; invert a plate over it to keep in the flavor. Bake three-quarters of an hour, or until the juice bubbles to the top. Remove the plate, and brown on the upper shelf of the oven for two or three minutes only.—*Mrs. R.*

Scalloped Oysters.

Those who are fond of oysters prepared in this way will find them much more delicate when cooked entirely by reflected heat. Have your tinner make you an old-fashioned "tin-kitchen" with *sloping* sides. Take small oblong dishes, such as are in general use at hotels, fill them with alternate layers of oysters and rolled crackers, and lay lumps of fresh butter liberally on top of each dish. Arrange them in the "kitchen," set the open dish in front of a bright fire or very warm grate, and in fifteen or twenty minutes you will find the oysters delicious. —*Mrs. D. P.*

Scalloped Oysters.

Put on the oysters with just enough liquor to keep from burning, and parboil slightly. Season the rest of the liquor as for stewed oysters with butter, pepper, salt, and a little flour, and boil until done. Put the parboiled oysters in a baking-dish, with a piece of butter and a grated cracker or stale bread and pepper, and pour as much of the gravy as the dish will hold. Put a little of the grated cracker on top, and set it in the oven to brown.—*Mrs. W.*

Oysters Scalloped in the Shell.

Open the shells, setting aside for use the deepest ones. Have ready some melted butter, not hot, seasoned with minced parsley and pepper.

Roll each oyster in this, letting it drip as little as may be, and lay in the shell, which should be arranged in a baking-pan.

Add to each a little lemon juice, sift bread crumbs over it, and bake in a quick oven till done. Serve in the shells.—*Mrs. S.*

Scalloped Oysters.

Put in the scallop shells as many oysters as each will hold. Season with butter, salt and pepper; a few bread crumbs.

Cook until well done; add a piece of butter just before they are served.—*Mrs. R. L. O.*

DEVILLED OYSTERS.

Put a layer of raw oysters in a pan, and then a layer of bread crumbs, black and red pepper, salt, butter, mustard, and a little vinegar mixed together.

Put alternate layers of each until full, and then bake.—*Mrs. Duke.*

Devilled Oysters.

Drain one quart oysters; chop thoroughly and season with cayenne pepper, lemon-juice, salt, and yolks of two hard-boiled eggs, and yolks of two raw eggs beaten and stirred in; one-half as much bread crumbs as you have oysters, and one large tablespoonful butter.

Have ready one dozen deep shells, nicely cleaned, and fill them with the oysters; sprinkle with bread crumbs, and bake in a few minutes.—*Mrs. H. S.*

To Cook Oysters.

Put into a baking-bowl a layer of cracker-crumbs, pepper, and butter. If the butter is salty do not use any salt. Then a layer of oysters, after they have been drained from their liquor; do this alternately till the dish is full. Be sure and put the cracker crumbs at the top of the dish, and bits of butter, also pepper: this makes it brown nicely. Set it in a hot oven; as soon as browned it will be ready for the table.—*Mrs. P. W.*

Fried Oysters.

Take each oyster separately and put salt and pepper on them; then roll them in equal portions of meal and flour. Fry them in hot lard until a light brown.—*Mrs. D.*

Oyster Fritters.

Beat two eggs very light; then stir in two tablespoonfuls cream or milk, three tablespoonfuls sifted flour, a pinch of salt; dip the oysters in this and fry them in hot lard.—*Mrs. B.*

Oyster Fritters.

Wipe the oysters dry. Beat 6 eggs light, and stir into them:
6 tablespoonfuls flour.
1½ pint rich milk.

Beat to smooth batter. Have in a pan some butter and lard; when it begins to froth, put a small ladleful of the batter, with an oyster in the middle, into it to fry. If too thin, add flour; if too thick, milk.—*Mrs. R.*

To Fry Oysters.

Drain the oysters through a sieve; sprinkle a little salt and pepper over them. Dip each oyster into meal. Have the pan hot, and drop in an equal portion of lard and butter; when boiling, put in the oysters and fry. Do not let them stand, but serve hot.—*Mrs. E.*

Fried Oysters.

Drain the oysters through a sieve. Beat up two or three eggs. Have ready some grated bread crumbs. Sprinkle some salt and a little pepper over the oysters; then dip each oyster into the egg and bread crumbs. Have the pan hot and clean; put equal portions of butter and lard into the pan. Be careful to keep the fat of oysters from burning.—*Mrs. R.*

To Fry Oysters.

Wash them and dry them on a clean napkin; dip in beaten egg and pounded crackers sifted, and let them lie several hours before frying, and they will not shrink.—*Mrs. P.*

To Fry Oysters.

Drain the oysters dry. Three eggs beaten, and grated crackers. Dip the oyster first in the egg and then in the crackers; do this twice. Grease the pan with butter or lard. Add pepper and salt to taste, and fry.—*Mrs. P. W.*

Clam or Oyster Fritters.

Chop up the clam very fine (when of oysters, leave them whole); put them in a batter and fry them.—*Mrs. D.*

Broiled Oysters.

Select the largest oysters, examining each one, to see that no particle of shell adheres to it. Dry with a nice linen cloth; then pepper and salt them, and sift over a little finely-powdered cracker. Place them on an oyster gridiron over a quick fire. As soon as plump, dip each one in a cup of melted fresh butter; lay on a hot dish garnished with scraped horseradish and parsley, and serve.—*Mrs. S. T.*

Steamed Oysters.

Wash shell oysters perfectly clean; lay them on a steamer, so the juice will not escape from the shells when opened. It is best to lay the upper shells down. Cover the lid of the steamer with a coarse towel and press closely on. Set this over a pot of water boiling hard. In from twenty minutes to half an hour, the shells will have opened. Have ready a hot dish, on which lay the oysters; sprinkle over them a little salt and pepper with a bit of fresh butter on each oyster. Serve immediately.—*Mrs. S. T.*

To Roast Oysters.

Wash and wipe one peck large shell oysters. Put in a hot oven, taking care to put the upper shell downward, so the juice will not escape. As soon as the shells open, lay on a hot dish and serve with horseradish or pepper-sauce, after sprinkling on them a little salt, and putting a bit of fresh butter on each oyster.—*Mrs. S. T.*

Pickled Oysters.

1 gallon oysters.
1 tablespoonful salt.
1 " unground black pepper.
1 " allspice.
6 blades mace.
1 small piece cayenne pepper.

Pick oysters out from the juice with a fork; stew until gills are opened well, then lay on flat dishes until cold; put in a jar, and cover with equal parts of stewed juice and vinegar. Let stand two days.—*Mrs. R. R.*

Pickled Oysters.

Take two hundred oysters of largest size, rinse them in their own liquor and put them in a stew-pan. Strain the liquor to them, let them come to a boil, and *no more*. Take them out of the liquor; have ready one quart or more of pure cider vinegar, with which boil whole pepper, a little salt, mace, cloves, and nutmeg.

When it is cool, pour over the oysters. Before serving add a few raw cranberries and thin slices of lemon.—*Mrs. S. T.*

Pickled Oysters.

Take one gallon oysters and cook them in their own liquor till nearly done. Then skim out the oysters and add to the liquor one teaspoonful whole black pepper, one teaspoonful allspice, one teaspoonful mace, a little red pepper and half a pint of strong vinegar.

Let it boil a few minutes and then pour over the oysters. When nearly cool, slice in them a large fresh lemon.—*Mrs. Col. A. F.*

Oyster Pie.

Stew the oysters, not entirely done, with butter, pepper and one tablespoonful pepper-sauce, and salt. Make a paste of one pound flour and one-half pound butter. Line the dish and put in the oysters, grate bread crumbs over top, and bake.—*Mrs. T.*

Oyster Pie.

Put a paste in a deep dish. Wash the oysters, drain and put them in the dish, seasoning with butter, pepper, salt, and a little mace, if liked; then put in a layer of grated cracker. When the dish is full, cover with paste and slips of paste laid across; then bake.—*Mrs. W——.*

Oyster Pâtés.

Stew some large oysters with a little nutmeg, a few cloves, some yolk of egg boiled hard and grated, a little butter and as much liquor from the oysters as will cover them. When stewed a few minutes, take them out of the pan to cool. Have shells of puff paste, previously baked in patty pans, and lay two or three oysters in each.—*Mrs. D.*

Oyster Short Cake.

1 quart flour.
3 teaspoonfuls baking powder.
1 tablespoonful butter.
A pinch of salt.
Enough sweet milk to moisten well.

Roll about one inch thick and bake on tin pie plates quickly While it is baking, take one quart oysters and one-half cup water and put on the stove; then take one-half cup milk, and one-half cup butter mixed with one tablespoonful flour, and a little salt or pepper; add all together and boil up once.

When the cakes are done, split them open and spread the oysters between them, and some on the top. Put the oysters that are left in a gravy-dish and replenish when needed.—*Mrs. K.*

Oyster Sausage.

Chop one pint oysters, with one-quarter pound veal, and one-quarter pound suet.

Mix with bread crumbs, and pound all in a mortar. Season with salt and pepper, adding an egg, well beaten.

Make into cakes like pork sausage.—*Mrs. E.*

Raw Oysters.

Take each oyster separately on a fork and drain from the liquor. Place on the table in an oyster tureen or salad bowl; have near a pile of small oblong dishes; scraped horseradish, pepper sauce, and Worcestershire sauce, etc., so that after being helped, each guest may season to taste.

When oysters are transported some distance, it is well to boil the liquor from which they have been taken and pour over them: this makes them plump and prevents them from being slimy.—*Mrs. S. T.*

To keep Oysters alive and Fatten.

Mix one pint of salt with thirty pints of water. Put the oysters in a tub that will not leak, with their mouths upwards and feed them with the above, by dipping in a broom and frequently passing over their mouths. It is said that they will fatten still more by mixing fine meal with the water.—*Mrs. R——.*

To Cook Crabs.

Take live crabs and put them in cool water, let them remain for half an hour. Then put them in a vessel, pour boiling water on them sufficient to cover them; boil ten minutes. Take them off and wipe them clean, first removing the dead men, and proceed to remove the meat. Take the upper shell, clean it. Season the meat with pepper, salt, mustard, and plenty of butter; put all in the shell again and bake half an hour.—*Mr. K. Norfolk.*

Crab Stew.

One peck live crabs, steam twenty minutes, bone and pick the claws and bodies. Stew with one pint milk or cream, the flesh and eggs of the crabs, fifteen minutes. Flavor with salt and cayenne pepper.—*Mrs. R. L. O.*

Devilled Crab.

After crabs are picked, season with mustard, pepper, salt, and catsup to taste. Add olive oil or butter.

Cover with bread crumbs moistened with milk and lumps of butter (put a little milk in the crab also). Bake in the shells or in a pan.—*Miss E. W.*

Devilled Crabs.

To the flesh of one dozen crabs boiled fifteen minutes and picked free from shell, add:

3 tablespoonfuls of stale bread crumbs.
½ wine glass of cream.
Yolks of 3 eggs.
A little chopped parsley.
1 tablespoonful butter.
Salt and pepper to the taste.

Put them in the shell and bake in a quick oven.—*Mrs. M. E. L. W.*

SOFT CRABS.

Turn up the ends of the shells and take out the dead man's fingers and take off the flap, and cut out the sand-bag; lay them in cold water until ready to fry. Then dust flour over them, a little salt, and fry them in hot lard.—*Mrs. D.*

DEVILLED CRABS.

After the crabs are boiled, pick them up fine and add one third the quantity of crab, in cracker dust or bread crumbs, mustard, red and black pepper, salt, and butter. Return them to the top shells, and bake.—*Mrs. D.*

TO DEVIL HARD CRABS.

Take them while alive, put them in very little water and steam them till perfectly done and brown, set them away till cold, take all out of the shell. Mix with eggs, bread crumbs, butter, and pepper. Either put back in the *top* shell and bake, or bake in pans.—*Mrs. J. C.*

LOBSTER CURRY.

Put the meat of a large lobster into a stewpan with one blade of mace.

1 large cup of meat stock, or gravy.

1 tablespoonful corn starch, mixed smooth, with a little milk or cream.

Add salt.

1 small piece of butter.

1 dessertspoonful curry powder.
Juice of one lemon.
Simmer for an hour and serve hot.—*Mrs. C.*

Turtle or Terrapin Stew.

After they are well cleaned, parboil the meat, then pick it to pieces. Season highly with pepper, salt, cayenne pepper, hard-boiled egg, spices, lemon, and champagne or other wine.

Stew until well done.

Stewed Turtle.

Make a stew of the turtle and add all the ingredients used in the turtle-soup, except wine and lemons.—*Mrs. D.*

Terrapin.

First cut up the head and put it in the pot to boil with the shell on; when done enough to remove the under shell, take it up and pick to pieces. Clean the top shell well; add a few crackers, onions, parsley, allspice, black pepper, butter, and wine.

Return it to the shell, put sliced lemon on and bake it.—*Mrs. D.*

Turtle or Terrapin Steaks.

Cut the turtle or terrapin in thin slices; broil or fry them with pepper, salt, and butter.

Turtle or Terrapin in Batter.

Smother the steaks in an egg-batter. Season with pepper, salt, butter, and with a little bread crumbs; fry or broil.

To Cook Turtles.

Drop four turtles into boiling water, and boil one hour; then take them out and remove the skin from the legs and feet, and replace them in fresh boiling water, where they should continue to boil one and one-half hour and then be taken out to cool. When cold, clean them thoroughly, removing the round liver which contains the gall. Cut them into small bits and place them in a stewpan, adding pepper, salt, the eggs that are found within, one quart water, one-half pound butter, and two tablespoonfuls flour mixed with a little cold water. Stir the flour and water well into the other ingredients, and stew about twenty minutes. As you remove them from the fire, pour in one-half pint Madeira wine.—*Mrs. A. D.*

FISH.

In selecting fish, notice if the flesh is firm and hard, the eyes full and prominent, the scales bright, the fins stiff, and the gills red, as all these indications denote their being fresh. Wash the fish, rub it with salt and pepper, and lay it on a dish, or hang it up till ready to cook. Never keep it lying in water, either in preparing it for cooking, or in trying to keep it till the next day.

In boiling fish, put it in boiling water, and simmer very slowly. It will require an hour to boil a large fish, and about twenty minutes for a small one. Every housekeeper should have a fish-kettle for fish.

Be careful to have boiling-hot lard in the frying-pan when you go to fry fish. First rub salt and pepper and flour or meal on the fish, then keep it well covered while frying, as you should do to every thing that is being fried. Doing this will enable you to fry the fish (or other article of food) a pretty amber color, while at the same time it will be perfectly done.

Always have a tin sheet for lifting boiled fish and for turning broiled fish. Before broiling, rub with pepper and salt, and then grease with fresh butter. Lay the fish on a gridiron well greased with sweet lard and lay the tin sheet over it. When you wish to turn, take the gridiron from the fire, holding the tin sheet on top the fish. Hold them together, then lay them on a table with the tin sheet down and the gridiron uppermost. Carefully raise the gridiron, leaving the fish lying unbroken on the tin sheet. The cook may now easily slide the fish on the gridiron, put it again on the fire and brown the other side, putting the tin sheet back on top of it. Every thing should be covered while being broiled. When done, lay it on a dish and pour over it melted butter in which has been stirred pepper, salt, and minced parsley. If devilled fish is desired, add to this dressing, one tablespoonful pepper vinegar, one of celery vinegar, one of walnut catsup, one of made mustard, one wine-glassful of acid fruit jelly. In making sauces for fish, never use the water in which the fish has been boiled.

Full directions for stewing fish are to be found in the subsequent pages.

Fish à la Crème.

Boil a firm fish, remove the bones, pick it to pieces. Mix one pint cream or milk with two tablespoonfuls flour, one onion, one-half pound butter (or less), and salt.

Set it on the fire and stir until it is as thick as custard. Fill a baking-dish alternately with fish, cracker, and cream. Bake for thirty minutes, use four crackers.—*Mrs. W. C. R.*

Halibut.

Boil one pound halibut, then chop it very fine and add eight eggs well beaten; pepper and salt to taste, then one cup butter.

Put it in a stewpan and cook until the eggs are done sufficiently. Serve very hot on toast.—*Miss F. N.*

Halibut.

Halibut should be cut in slices of four pounds each. If to

be boiled, cover with salt water, and skim often; drain off and serve with butter sauce.

If baked or fried, garnish with horseradish and serve with melted butter.

Fish Chowder.

Fry a few slices of salt pork, cut the fish in small pieces, pare and slice the potatoes, add a little onion chopped fine.

Place all in layers in the kettle; season with salt and pepper. Stew over a slow fire thirty minutes.

Cat-fish Chowder.

To be made of New River cat-fish.

Wash the fish in warm water, put it on in just water enough to cover it, boil until tender or until the bones will slip out; take out the largest bones, chop up the fish, put it in a stewpan with a pint of water, a large lump of butter.

1 cup of cream, pepper and not much salt.

1 onion, one teaspoonful mustard, one-half teacupful walnut catsup.

Stew until quite thick, garnish with sliced lemon and serve hot.—*Mrs. P. W.*

Cat-fish Chowder or Hog-fish.

Take two cat-fish, skin, and boil till thoroughly done; pick very fine and add:

    2 good sized onions.
    ¼ pound butter.
    1 tablespoonful salt.
    1 tablespoonful pepper.
    2 tablespoonfuls Worcestershire sauce.

Add a little celery or celery-seed, a little thyme, a little parsley.

Pour over all about one quart of boiling water and cook fast bout half an hour.—*Miss F. N.*

Fish Chowder.

Take any large fish, and cut in thin slices, lay some slices of fat bacon at the bottom of the pot and then a layer of fish, onions, cracker dust, red and black pepper, salt, and butter.

Then more layers, until you have used all the fish. Cover the whole with water and cook until well done.—*Mrs. D.*

Boiled Sheep's-head.

Clean the fish and boil well done. Serve hot with butter and egg sauce.

To Bake a Sheep's-head.

Put two tablespoonfuls butter and two tablespoonfuls lard in a skillet; also, with that, two tablespoonfuls flour, a little parsley, one pint boiling water, a little wine, catsup, salt, and cayenne pepper. Boil a few minutes; then take four eggs, half a pint cream or butter; beat well together. Lay the fish in a large deep dish, pour gravy from skillet over it; spread butter over top of fish. The bottom of the oven to be quite hot, top slow.—*Miss E. W.*

Boiled Sheep's-head or Rock.

Lay the fish in a fish boiler, in a cloth, to prevent breaking. Throw into the water a handful parsley, and when the fish is done, lay some sprigs on it in the dish.—*Mrs. D.*

Baked Sheep's-head.

Put the fish in a pan and cover with water; put a little parsley, onions, and fat bacon, chopped up together, black pepper and salt, in the fish and over it, and when nearly done, beat up one egg and a little flour, and pour over it to thicken the gravy. Rock or shad may be cooked the same way.—*Mrs. D.*

Baked Sheep's-head.

When ready for cooking, salt and pepper well, gash the sides in three or four places. Cut four onions very fine, to which add one pint bread crumbs, fat meat minced very fine, as it suits better than lard, cayenne pepper, thyme, a little salt, and the yolks of two eggs, all mashed together, with which stuff the fish inside and gashes on the outside. Then sprinkle over with flour and black pepper; put into a large pan with one quart cold water. Bake two hours, slowly. Serve with or without sauce, according to taste.—*Miss F. N.*

BOILED ROCK-FISH.

Clean the fish nicely, rub well with salt and pepper. Put into a large deep pan, that it may lie at full length; cover with cold water, adding salt and pepper. Boil steadily for three-quarters of an hour; dish and serve with melted butter and sauce or catsup.—*Miss F. N.*

Boiled Rock-fish.

Clean nicely and hang it up; do not lay it in water, but wash it when ready for cooking. Put on in boiling water, seasoning with salt to taste. It takes two hours to boil, if large. Serve with egg sauce, and send to the table in a napkin to keep hot.—*Mrs. W.*

To Stew Rock-fish.

Take a rock, clean and season with parsley, sweet marjoram, onions, one-half pint water, salt to taste, one pint Port wine, one-half pound butter, and a little flour. Put them in a dish, and set in a stewpan. One hour is sufficient for cooking.—*Mrs. J. T.*

Baked Rock.

Boil the fish and take out the bones. Season with cream,

butter, pepper, and salt, and grated bread crumbs over the top. Bake slightly in a flat dish or scollop shells.—*Mrs. R.*

To Pickle Rock.

Cut a rock-fish into pieces and put in a kettle with sufficient water to cover it. Put in a handful of salt, some white pepper, one tablespoonful allspice, a few cloves and mace.

When the fish is nearly done, add a quart of vinegar. In putting away, use as much liquor as will cover it.—*Mrs. J. W. S.*

Baked Shad.

Open the shad down the back, wash well and salt it; wipe dry and rub inside and out with a little cayenne pepper. Prepare a stuffing of bread, seasoned with pepper, salt, thyme, or parsley, celery-seed, a little chopped onion, piece of butter, size of a walnut.

Tie up the fish and put in a baking pan with one pint water (to a good sized fish) and butter, size of a hen's egg. Sprinkle with flour, baste well and bake slowly an hour and a half.—*Mrs. J. H. F.*

To Fry Shad.

Clean and hang in a cool place. When ready to use wash thoroughly, cut up and sprinkle lightly with flour, pepper, salt, and fry with lard.—*Mrs. R——.*

To Roast Shad.

Fill the inside with forcemeat, sew it up and tie it on a board, not pine, cover with bread crumbs, a little salt, and pepper, and place before the fire. When done one side, turn it; when sufficiently done, pull out the thread; dish and serve with drawn butter and parsley.—*Mrs. D.*

To Broil Shad.

Clean, wash, and split the shad, and wipe it dry.

Sprinkle with pepper and salt, and place it over a clear, slow fire, with the skin down so as to retain the juice; put on a clean gridiron, rubbed with lard. Turn it when nearly done; take up, and season with a generous piece of butter, salt, and pepper to taste.—*Mrs. S.*

POTTED SHAD.

Cut the fish as for frying; pack in a stone jar with layers of mixed spices, seasoning with salt; after the jar is filled, pour vinegar over; cover tightly with a cloth. Put the jar in a large pot of water and boil until the fish is thoroughly done.

A nice relish for tea.—*Mrs. C. L. T.*

TO BARBECUE A SHAD.

Split the back of the fish, pepper and salt it, and put on the gridiron with the skin down.

Baste the upper side of the fish with butter; brown a little piece of butter with a small quantity of flour, and when brown add pepper, salt, and a little water.

Dish in a tureen.—*Mrs. J. W. S.*

SCOLLOPED STURGEON.

Four pounds sturgeon, boiled; when cold, pick to pieces and then wash and squeeze out the water. Make a mayonnaise dressing, using celery, cayenne pepper instead of black pepper, and salt. Serve on white lettuce leaves.—*Mrs. R. R.*

STURGEON CUTLET.

Remove all the fat from the fish; cut it into steak pieces. Beat up the yolks of eggs enough to moisten the pieces well; dip them into the beaten egg. Have ready a dish of grated bread crumbs (stale bread is best), then roll them in the bread crumbs and pepper them well.

Prepare a vessel of melted lard, have it boiling hot, but not burnt; lay in the pieces of fish and cover with a lid. Turn them over as they brown and remove the lid when they are nearly done.—*Mrs. Dr. P. C.*

STURGEON OR DRUM.

Slice it like beefsteak, and roll in a thin egg batter, and fry in hot lard.

Chopped parsley and black pepper may be added, if liked.—*Mrs. D., Suffolk.*

BAKED STURGEON.

Wash the skin *well*, put in a pan and bake for three-quarters of an hour. Then take it out on a dish; pierce it with a knife in several places. Make a stuffing of pot-meat, bread crumbs, onions, parsley, thyme, pepper, and salt, all chopped well together. Stuff the holes with the mixture and put the rest in the gravy; return to the pan and bake until done.—*Mrs. D.*

TO FRY PERCH.

Sprinkle with salt and dredge with flour; after a while dredge with flour the other side. When the lard boils hard, skim it well and put in the fish. Serve hot.—*Mrs. W.*

TO FRY TROUT.

Split the fish down the back, insert a thin slice of fat pork. Squeeze lemon juice over it and fry brown.—*Mrs. J. I., La.*

BOILED COD-FISH.

Boil over a slow fire and skim frequently. Season with salt. Garnish with parsley and rings of hard boiled eggs, and serve with butter and egg-sauce.

COD-FISH BALLS.

One-fourth fish, to three-fourths potatoes, eggs enough to moisten. Season with pepper and salt, and fry brown.

Nantucket Cod-fish.

Cut the thick part out of a firm, white dried codfish, and soak it over night, then cut into very small pieces and parboil for a few minutes, changing the water until the fish remains but slightly salted. Drain off the water, leaving the fish in the saucepan. Pour over a little more milk than will cover it; when it becomes heated, add a little butter and pepper, thicken with flour stirred smooth in milk. Stir constantly for a few minutes.

To Dress Salt Cod-fish.

Take one-third of a large fish; soak it from three to four hours; next, boiling it till thoroughly done, pick the meat fine, taking out all the bones. Then add:

3 hard-boiled eggs, chopped fine.
3 to 4 Irish potatoes, boiled and mashed.

Mix all well together in a stewpan, with—

1 teacup of hot water.
Salt and mustard to the taste.

Boil half an hour, and add a liberal supply of butter just before serving. If preferred, the salt and mustard need not be put in until during the cooking.—*Mrs. A. C.*

Boiled Mackerel.

Well wash the fish, put it into nearly boiling water with one tablespoonful salt in it; boil up quickly, then let it simmer gently for a quarter of an hour, and if the fish be very large, a few minutes longer. Serve in a hot dish.—*Mrs. B.*

To Broil Mackerel.

If the mackerel is fresh, after it is nicely scaled and cleaned, dry it; pepper and salt and broil it on a gridiron; baste it with fresh butter. After it is broiled, put it on a hot dish, pour melted butter over it, and serve. If the fish is salt, pour boiling water over it, soak it several hours; butter and pepper, and broil; serve in the same way as the fresh.—*Mrs. R.*

To Cook Salt Mackerel.

Soak the fish over night in fresh water. In the morning drain off the water and place on a gridiron to broil, dressing with hot butter.—*Mrs. T.*

Baked Salmon.

When washed and dried, sprinkle over pepper and salt. Have ready in a baking-pan a small grating; lay the fish on this, with bits of butter over it; set in a hot oven, basting often and freely with butter. When nicely browned, butter a sheet of white paper and lay over it, to prevent its getting too dry; when done and tender, place on a hot dish. Add to the gravy one teacupful milk, one tablespoonful pepper vinegar, pepper, salt, and a mashed Irish potato smoothly mixed in; boil, and pour over the fish. Sift over all browned cracker. Garnish with bleached tops of celery and curled parsley alternately.—*Mrs. T.*

Boiled Salmon.

After the fish has been cleaned and washed, dry it and sew it up in a cloth; lay it in a fish-kettle, cover with warm water, and simmer until done and tender. Meanwhile have ready in a saucepan one pint cream, two tablespoonfuls fresh butter, salt, pepper, minced parsley, and thyme; let it boil up once, not too quickly. Take the fish from the kettle, carefully unwrap it, lay it for a moment on a folded napkin to dry. Have ready a hot dish, lay the fish on it carefully, without breaking it, pour over the cream. Slice some hard-boiled eggs, and lay over the fish alternately with sliced lemon. Border the edges of the dish with curled parsley.—*Mrs. S. T.*

Salmon Steak.

When well dried, pepper and salt, sift over powdered cracker, and lay upon a gridiron, which has been first greased with butter or lard, over hot coals. As soon as the side next to the fire is brown, turn it by carefully slipping under it a batter-cake turner and holding the fish on it with the other hand, lest it should break. When both sides are of a light brown, lay in a hot dish; pepper and salt again; pour over melted butter; place the cover on, and serve.—*Mrs. T.*

Pickled Salmon.

Soak the salmon twenty-four hours, changing the water. Put it in boiling water, with a little vinegar. When done and cold, boil your vinegar with spice and pour on the fish.—*Mrs. A. P.*

German Fish Stew.

Put the fish in a kettle to boil. Stew together in a saucepan one onion chopped fine and a wine-glass of sweet oil; when well done, pour them in with the fish. Then mix yolks of three eggs, juice of two lemons strained, one tablespoonful sifted flour. Beat these well together, and pour upon the fish when nearly done. Then add ginger, pepper, and salt to taste; stew three or four minutes, after mixing all the ingredients. Oysters may be cooked by the same receipt, only substituting one quart oysters for the fish.—*Mrs. A. D.*

GAME.

Haunch of Venison.

Rub the venison over with pepper, salt, and butter. Repeat the rubbing. After it has been put in the oven, put in as much cold water as will prevent burning and draw the gravy. Stick five or six cloves in different parts of the venison. Add enough water to make sufficient gravy. Just before dinner, put in a glass of red wine and a lump of butter rolled in flour, and let it stew a little longer.—*Mrs. T.*

Venison Haunch.

Prepare the venison as you would mutton.

Put in a baking-pan, lard with a little bacon, add a pint of water, a gill of red wine, salt, and a little cayenne pepper. Bake quickly, and serve with or without gravy.

Stewed Venison.

Cut in tolerably thick slices. Put in an oven with two spoonfuls of water and a piece of lard. Cook till nearly done, then pour off the gravy and baste it well with a large spoonful of butter, pepper, and salt.

Stewed Venison.

Slice cold venison in a chafing dish and add—

    A cup of water.
    A small teacup of red wine.
    A small teacup of currant jelly.
    A tablespoonful of butter.
    A teaspoonful of made mustard.
    A little yellow pickle.
    A little chopped celery.
    A little mushroom catsup.
    Salt and cayenne pepper to the taste.

The same receipt will answer for cold mutton.—*Mrs. R. L. O.*

To Barbecue Squirrel.

Put some slices of fat bacon in an oven. Lay the squirrels on them and lay two slices of bacon on the top. Put them in the oven and let them cook until done. Lay them on a dish and set near the fire. Take out the bacon, sprinkle one spoonful of flour in the gravy and let it brown. Then pour in one teacup of water, one tablespoonful of butter, and some tomato or walnut catsup. Let it cool, and then pour it over the squirrel.

Roast Rabbit.

Stew the rabbit. After boiling the haslet and liver, stew them with parsley, thyme, celery-seed, butter, salt, and pepper, for gravy. Soak a piece of loaf bread, a short time, in water. Mix with it the yolk of an egg and some butter, for stuffing; then soak it in milk and cream. Sprinkle the inside of the rabbit with salt and pepper, fill it with the above dressing, sew it up, and roast or bake quickly.—*Mrs. B.*

Barbecued Rabbit.

Lay the rabbit in salt and water half an hour, scald with boiling water, wipe dry, grease with butter, and sprinkle with pepper and a little salt. Lay it on the gridiron, turning often so that it may cook through and through, without becoming hard and dry. When brown, lay on a hot dish, butter plentifully on both sides, and add a little salt and pepper. Set in the oven, while preparing four teaspoonfuls of vinegar, one of made mustard, and one of currant jelly or brown sugar. Pour this over the rabbit, rubbing it in, then pour over the gravy and serve hot.—*Mrs. T.*

Stewed Rabbit.

Cut up the rabbit and wash it. Put it in a stewpan and season it with salt and pepper. Pour in half a pint of water, and when this has nearly stewed away, add half a pint of Port wine, two or three blades of mace, and a tablespoonful of flour, mixed with a quarter of a pound of butter. Let it stew gently till quite tender, and then serve hot.—*Mrs. C. C.*

Stewed Rabbit.

Cut a rabbit into eight pieces. After soaking in salt and water, put it in a stewpan, with a slice of pork or bacon, and with more than enough water to cover it. When nearly done, take out the pieces, strain the water in which they have boiled, and return all to the stewpan, with a teacup of milk, a little pepper, salt, chopped onion and parsley. After this boils up, stir in a heaping tablespoonful of butter, in which a tablespoonful of flour has been rubbed. Let it boil up once more; then serve in a covered dish, with four hard-boiled eggs sliced over it, and grated bread crumbs. The same receipt will answer for squirrel.—*Mrs. T.*

Wild Turkey.

If the turkey is old, after it is dressed wash it inside thoroughly with soda and water. Rinse it and plunge it into a pot of boiling water for five minutes. Make a stuffing of bits of pork, beef, or any other cold meat, plenty of chopped celery, stewed giblets, hard-boiled eggs, pounded cracker, pepper, and salt, and a heaping spoonful of butter. Work this well and fill the turkey. With another large spoonful of butter grease the bird, and then sprinkle salt and pepper over it. Lay in a pan, with a pint of stock or broth in which any kind of meat has been boiled. Place in a hot oven. When it begins to brown, dredge with flour and baste, turning often, so that each part may be equally browned. Put a buttered sheet of paper over the breast, to prevent dryness. When thoroughly done, lay on a dish, brown some crackers, pound and sift over it, and serve with celery or oyster sauce.—*Mrs. T.*

A Simpler Way to Prepare Wild Turkey.

Prepare the turkey as usual, rub the inside with salt and cayenne pepper, and put in the baking-pan, with water enough to make gravy. Cut up the gizzard and liver with a lump of butter and a spoonful of cream. Mix with the gravy and serve hot

To Roast Wild Fowl in a Stove.

Put them on a rack above a pan, so that the gravy will drip through. This makes them as delicate as if roasted on a spit. If roasted in a pan, they will be exceedingly greasy and have the *stovey* taste to which so many persons object.—*Mrs. J. W. S.*

Wild Goose.

After the goose is dressed, soak it several hours in salt and water. Put a small onion inside and plunge it into boiling water for twenty minutes. Stuff with chopped celery, chopped eggs, mashed potatoes, bits of fat pork or other cold meat; a little butter; raw turnip grated; a tablespoonful of pepper vinegar; a little chopped onion; pepper and salt to the taste.

A teacup of stock or broth must be put in the pan with the fowl. Butter it, dredge with flour, and baste often. Pin a buttered paper over the breast to prevent its becoming hard. Serve with mushroom or celery sauce, or, for a simpler taste, serve merely with its own gravy.—*Mrs. T.*

Wild Goose.

Put a small onion inside, a slice of pork, pepper, salt, and a spoonful of red wine.

Lay in a pan with water enough to make gravy. Dredge with flour, and baste with butter frequently. Cook quickly and serve with gravy made as for wild turkey.

Wild Duck.

When the duck is ready dressed, put in it a small onion, pepper, salt, and a spoonful of red wine. Lay in a pan with water enough to make the gravy. Cook in fifteen or twenty minutes, if the fire is brisk. Serve with gravy made as for wild turkey.

Canvas-back ducks are cooked in the same way, only you leave on their heads and do not use onion with them.—*Mrs. R. L. O.*

To Cook Wild Duck for Breakfast.

Split open in the back, put in a pan with a little water, butter, pepper and salt, and cook till tender. Baste with flour. If for dinner, cook whole.—*Mrs. J. L. C.*

TO BROIL PARTRIDGES.

Place them in salt and water, an hour or two before broiling. When taken out, wipe them dry, and rub them all over with fresh butter, pepper and salt. First broil the under or split side on the gridiron, over bright, clear coals, turning until the upper side is of a fine, light brown. It must be cooked principally from the under side. When done, rub well again with fresh butter and if not ready to serve them immediately, put them in a large shallow tin bucket, cover it and set it over a pot or kettle of boiling water, which will keep them hot without making them hard or dry and will give time for the many "last things" to be done before serving a meal. When served, sift over them powdered cracker, first browned.—*Mrs. T.*

TO ROAST PARTRIDGES.

Clean the birds as for stuffing. Rub with butter, salt and pepper. Put in sheets of letter paper and allow to cook in this way.—*Mrs. W. C.*

TO COOK PARTRIDGES AND PHEASANTS.

Place them in a steamer, over a pot of boiling water, till tender.

Have ready a saucepan of large fresh oysters, scalded just enough to make them plump and seasoned with pepper-sauce, butter, and a little salt. Rub the cavity of the birds with salt and pepper, fill with oysters and sew up. Broil till a light brown. Place on a hot dish and sift over them browned cracker. Add a large tablespoonful of butter and one of pounded cracker to the oyster liquor. Boil it up once and pour into the dish, but not over the birds.—*Mrs. T.*

TO BROIL PIGEONS.

Pigeons may be broiled the same as chickens, only cover the

breast with slices of bacon. When nearly done, remove the bacon, dredge with flour and baste with butter. They will be done in half an hour.

STEWED PIGEONS.

The pigeons must be seasoned with pepper, salt, cloves, mace and sweet herbs. Wrap the seasoning up in a piece of butter and put it in the pigeon. Then tie up the neck and vest and half roast the pigeons. Then put them in a stewpan with a quart of good gravy, a little white wine, some pickled mushrooms, a few peppercorns, three or four blades of mace, a bit of lemon peel, a bit of onion and a bunch of sweet herbs. Stew until done, then thicken with butter and yolks of eggs. Garnish with lemon.

PIGEON PIE.

Take six young pigeons. After they are drawn, trussed, and singed, stuff them with the chopped livers mixed with parsley, salt, pepper, and a small piece of butter. Cover the bottom of the dish with rather small pieces of beef. On the beef, place a thin layer of chopped parsley and mushrooms, seasoned with pepper and salt. Over this place the pigeons, between each putting the yolk of a hard-boiled egg. Add some brown sauce or gravy. Cover with puff paste and bake the pie for an hour and a half.—*Mrs. C. C.*

TO DRESS REED BIRDS.

Pick open and carefully wash one dozen or more birds. Place them between the folds of a towel, and with a rolling-pin mash the bones quite flat. Season with salt and a little cayenne and black pepper. Either fry or broil on a gridiron made for broiling oysters. This must be done over a clear fire. When done, season, put a lump of butter on each bird and serve hot.—*Mrs. A. M. D.*

TO COOK SORA, ORTOLANS, AND OTHER SMALL BIRDS.

Prepare as you would a chicken for roasting. Lay in a pan

and pour boiling water over them or, if convenient, steam them. Scald a few large fresh oysters till just plump, season them with cayenne pepper, salt and butter. Pour into the cavity of each bird a few drops of pepper-sauce and then put a large oyster in each. Broil a short time, frequently turning that they may not become dry. If not ready to serve them as soon as they are done, lay in a tin bucket, butter them and sprinkle them again with black pepper, cover the bucket and set it over boiling water till wanted. When laid in the dish, sift browned cracker over the birds, and pour gravy into the dish.— Mrs. T.

To Cook Sora, Ortolans, and Other Small Birds.

After they are split open in the back and dressed, lay them in weak salt and water for a short time. Then lay them on a board and roll with a rolling-pin to flatten the breastbone. Put butter, pepper, and salt on them. Lay them on a gridiron and broil slowly. When just done, add more butter and pepper, lay in a flat tin bucket, which set over a vessel of boiling water to keep the birds hot, juicy, and tender till wanted.— Mrs. T.

Sora, Ortolans, Robins, and Other Small Birds.

They should be carefully cleaned, buttered, sprinkled with pepper and salt, and broiled. When they are served, butter them again. If you like, serve each bird on a piece of toast, and pour over them a sauce of red wine, mushroom catsup, salt, cayenne pepper, and celery.

MEATS.

All meats are better in winter for being kept several weeks, and it is well, in summer, to keep them as long as you can without danger of their being tainted. If it is not in your power to keep meat in an ice-house, in summer, keep it in a cool dark cellar, wrapped around with wet cloths, on top of which lay boughs of elderberry. The evaporation from the cloth will keep the meat cool and the elderberry will keep off insects.

If you should unfortunately be obliged to use stale meat or poultry, rub it in and out with soda, before washing it. Tough meats and poultry are rendered more tender by putting a little vinegar or a few slices of lemon in the water in which they are boiled. The use of an acid will save time and fuel in cooking them and will render them more tender and digestible.

If possible, keep the meat so clean that it will not be necessary to wash it, as water extracts the juices. When it is frozen, lay it in cold water to thaw, and then cook quickly, to prevent its losing its moisture and sweetness.

In roasting or boiling, use but little salt at first, as it hardens meat to do otherwise. In roasting, baste frequently, to prevent the meat from hardening on the outside, and try to preserve the juices. If possible, roast the meat on a spit before a large, open fire, after using salt, pepper, butter or lard, and dredging with flour. Where an open fire-place cannot be obtained, however, the meat may be well roasted in a stove or range. Mutton, pork, shote and veal should be well done, but beef should be cooked rare.

In boiling, put on salt meat in cold water, but fresh meat in hot. Remember also that salt meat requires more water and a longer time to cook than fresh. Boil slowly, removing the scum that rises when it begins to simmer. Keep a tea-kettle of boiling water at hand to replenish the water in the pot, as it boils away. Do not let the meat boil too hard or too long, as this will toughen it and extract the juices. Add salt to fresh meat, just before it is done.

Lardering beef, veal, and poultry is a great improvement, keeping it moist whilst cooking and adding richness to the flavor. Lardering consists in introducing slips of clear fat bacon or salt pork, into the surface of meat, by means of a pin, sharp at one end and cleft into four divisions at the other. This pin may be obtained at any hardware store.

As the housekeeper is sometimes hurried in preparing a dish, it will save time and trouble for her to keep on hand a bottle of meat-flavoring compounded of the following ingredients.

2 chopped onions.
3 pods of red pepper (chopped).
2 tablespoonfuls brown sugar.
1 tablespoonful celery seed.
1 tablespoonful ground mustard.
1 teaspoonful turmeric.
1 teaspoonful black pepper.
1 teaspoonful salt.

Put all in a quart bottle and fill it up with cider vinegar. A tablespoonful of this mixed in a stew, steak, or gravy, will impart not only a fine flavor, but a rich color. Keeping this mixture on hand will obviate the necessity of the housekeeper looking through various spice boxes and packages to get together the requisite ingredients for flavoring, and will thus save her time and trouble.

How to Select Meats.

Good and wholesome meat should be neither of a pale rosy or pink color, nor of a deep purple. The first denotes the diseased condition, the last proves the animal has died a natural death. Good meat has more of a marble look, in consequence of the branching of the veins which surround the adipose cells. The fat, especially of the inner organs, is always firm and suety and never moist, while in general the fat from diseased cattle is flabby and watery and more often resembles jelly or boiled parchment. Wholesome meat will always show itself firm and elastic to the touch, and exibit no dampness, while bad meat will appear soft and moist, in fact, often more wet, so that the liquid substance runs out of the blood when pressed hard.

Good meat has very little smell and diffuses a certain medicinal odor. This can be distinctly proved by cutting the meat through with a knife and smelling the blade or pouring water over it. Lastly, bad meat has the peculiarity that it shrinks considerably in the boiling, wholesome meat rather swells and does not lose an ounce in weight.

Observations on Pork, Curing Bacon, etc.

Hogs weighing from 150 to 200 pounds are the most suitable size for family use. They should not exceed twelve months in age, as they are much more tender from being young. They should be well kept and should be corn-fed several weeks before being killed. After being properly dressed, they should hang long enough to get rid of the animal heat. When they are ready to be cut up, they should be divided into nine principal parts, two hams, two shoulders, two middlings, the head or face, jowl and chine. The hog is laid on its back to be cut up. The head is cut off just below the ears, then it is split down on each side of the backbone, which is the chine. This is divided into three pieces, the upper portion being a choice piece to be eaten cold. The fat portion may be cut off to make lard. Each half should then first have the leaf fat taken out, which is done by cutting the thin skin between it and the ribs, when it is easily pulled out. Just under this, the next thing to be removed is the mousepiece or tenderloin, lying along the edge, from which the backbone was removed, commencing at the point of the ham. This is considered the most delicate part and is used to make the nicest sausage. Just under this tenderloin are some short ribs about three inches long, running up from the point of the ham which are known as the griskin. This is removed by a sharp knife being run under it, taking care to cut it smooth and not too thick. When broiled, it is as nice as a partridge.

The ribs are next taken out of the shoulder and middling, though some persons prefer leaving them in the middling. In this case seven should be taken from the shoulder, by a sharp knife cutting close to the ribs, which make a delicious broil. Then cut off the ham as near the bone as possible, in a half circle. The shoulder is then cut square across just behind the leg. The feet are then chopped off with a sharp axe or cleaver. From the shoulder, they should be cut off leaving a stump of about two inches. From the ham, they should be cut off at the joint, as smoothly as possible, and then you may proceed to salt the meat.

In order to impart redness to the hams, rub on each a teaspoonful of pulverized saltpetre before salting. If the weather is very cold, warm the salt before applying it. First rub the skin side well with salt and then the fleshy side, using for the purpose a shoe-sole or leather glove. No more salt should be used than a sufficiency to preserve the meat, as an excess hardens the meat. A bushel of salt is sufficient for a thousand pounds of meat. For the chine and ribs a very light sprinkling of salt will suffice.

The meat as salted should be packed with the skin side down, where it should remain from four to six weeks, according to the weather. If the weather is mild, four weeks will answer. Should the weather be very cold and the pork in an exposed place, it will freeze, and the salt, failing to penetrate the meat, will be apt to injure it.

After it has taken salt sufficiently, the old Virginia mode is to break the bulk, shake off the salt, rub the joint pieces (hams and shoulders) with good, green-wood ashes (hickory preferred). Then rebulk it and let it remain two weeks longer, when it should be hung up with the joints down and the other pieces may be hung up for smoking at the same time. It is not necessary that the smoke-house should be very tight, but it is important that the pork should not be very close to the fire.

A smothered fire made of small billets of wood or chips (hickory preferred), or of corn cobs, should be made up three times a day till the middle of March or first of April, when the joint pieces should be taken down and packed in hickory or other green-wood ashes, as in salt, where they will remain all the summer without danger of bugs interfering with them.

This recipe has been obtained from an old Virginia family, famous for their skill in this department of housekeeping. This mode of curing makes the best bacon in the world, far superior to what are generally called Virginia cured hams.

Shoat (which I must explain to the uninitiated is a term applied in the South to a young pig past the age when it may be cooked whole) should be kept up and fattened on buttermilk, several weeks before being killed, as this makes the flesh extremely delicate. It is best killed when between two and three months old. It should then be divided into four quarters. It is more delicate and wholesome eaten cold.

Pork Steak.

Remove the skin, beat without breaking into holes; scald with boiling water, wipe dry and broil. When brown lay in a hot dish. Sprinkle over pepper, salt, a little sage, chopped onion, and parsley; then butter profusely.

Grate over all hard biscuit or crackers that have been browned and serve.—*Mrs. S. T.*

Spare-ribs.

Pork chop and pork cutlet may be cooked in the same way, omitting the onion if not liked.—*Mrs T.*

Pork Spare-rib.

With stuffing of sage and onions, roasted spare-rib, done over the potatoes, affords a good substitute for goose.

Spare-ribs.

Always parboil spare-ribs: then broil with pepper and salt cut in pieces three or four bones each.—*Mrs. W.*

Spare-Ribs.

Cut them into pieces of two or three ribs each; put them

into a covered stewpan and boil or stew until perfectly done. Just before you take them out, add salt, pepper, and minced parsley.

Put on the cover and simmer until well seasoned.

Take them out of the pan, drain and dry them. For one moment let them scorch on a gridiron over a bed of hot coals; lay on a hot dish; butter each one; pepper added; sift over browned cracker and serve.—*Mrs. S. T.*

To Cook Spare-ribs and Griskin or Short-ribs.

Put them on in a small quantity of water and boil for fifteen or twenty minutes. Gash them with a knife; sprinkle with pepper and put them on a hot gridiron as near the fire as possible; broil quickly, but not too brown. Have some butter melted and pour over the meat and shut it up in the dish. These are good for breakfast.—*Mrs. P. W.*

To Cook Backbone or Chine.

Cut the chine in three pieces; the large end must be about a foot long, the remainder cut in half. Put it in a pot of water and boil for two hours; then put it in a pan, baste and set it in the stove to brown. Peel some Irish potatoes and put them in the pot; boil till done, mash them up and season with pepper, a little salt, and some of the gravy dripping out of the chine while baking; spread them in the dish, then lay the chine on top. The largest piece is generally put aside to eat cold, and is very nice. Turnips are good, cooked in the same way as potatoes, with the chine.

The chine and ham of a hog are nice, corned like beef.—*Mrs. P. W.*

Backbone Pie.

Take the smallest end of the backbone, cut in pieces two or three inches long; put in water and boil until done. Make nice rich pastry as for chicken pie; line the sides of a baking dish with the pastry, put in the bones, adding some water in which they were boiled; also salt, butter, and pepper to taste, with bits of pastry.

Cover top of baking-dish with pastry; put in stove and brown nicely.—*Mrs. G. B.*

To Cook a Ham of Pork.

Wash off the salt and put it in a pot of water; boil from four to six hours, according to size. Do not take off the skin, as it preserves the juice and is much better cold. It is also nice to slice and broil with pepper and butter over it.—*Mrs. P. W.*

Leg of Pork Stuffed.

Make deep incisions in the meat parallel to the bone, trim it so as to leave the skin longer than the flesh; then boil some potatoes, and when they are done, mash them with a piece of butter, cayenne pepper and salt, an onion finely chopped, and a little rubbed sage.

With this dressing fill the incisions, draw the skin down and skewer it over to keep the dressing from falling out. Season the outside of the meat with salt, cayenne pepper and sage.

Roast it slowly; when done, pour the gravy in a pan, skim off the fat and add some browned flour wet in a little cold water, and boil up once.

Serve with apple or cranberry sauce.—*Mrs. A. M. D.*

To Dress Chine.

Rub the large end with salt and saltpetre, and it will keep some time, or you may boil it fresh. Cut the bones of the other end apart, sprinkle with flour and a little salt: add one teacup of water, and stew.

It will make two large dishes.—*Mrs. W.*

Roast Chine.

Chine should always be parboiled and stewed before roasting, to take away the gross taste which the melted fat frying from it gives. After this lay in the pan with one pint water in which it was boiled, from which all the fat has been skimmed. Put in this several whole leaves of sage, to be removed before serving—just to get the flavor; minced onion, and parsley.

Baste and brown quickly that it may not dry.

This is only stewed chine browned.—*Mrs. S. T.*

Pork Royal.

Take a piece of shoulder of fresh pork, fill with grated bread and the crust soaked, pepper, salt, onion, sage and thyme: a bit of butter and lard. Place in a pan with some water; when about half done, place around it some large apples; when done, place your pork on a dish, with the apples round it; put flour and water on your pan, flour browned, some thyme and sage; boil, strain through a very small colander over your pork and apples.

Seasoning for Sausage.

18 pounds meat.
9 pounds back fat.
2 ounces sage.
4 ounces black pepper.
12 ounces salt. —*Mrs. J. P.*

Excellent Recipe for Sausage.

12 pounds of the lean of the chine.
6 pounds " " fat.
5 tablespoonfuls salt.
6 " sage.
2 " thyme.
5 " pepper.
3 " sweet marjoram.

Mix well together.—*Mrs. S. M.*

Sausage Meat.

25 pounds lean pieces cut from the shoulder and tenderloin.

15 pounds fat from the back of the chine.

1 pound salt; a half pound of black pepper.

4 ounces allspice.

1 ounce sage.

Cut the fat in small pieces and then chop it; chop the lean very fine: mix all together, kneading in the seasoning. Press it down in small pots and pour melted lard over the top.—*Mrs. J. D.*

Sweetbread of Hog.

This nice morsel is between the maw and ruffle piece inside of the hog. Put them in soak for a day; parboil them and then gash them and stew them in pepper, butter, one teacup of milk and a little vinegar.

Or they are very nice fried or broiled.—*Mrs. P. W.*

Souse Cheese.

Lay the meat in cold water as cut from the hog. Let it stand three or four days, shifting the water each day. Scrape it and let it stand a day or two longer, changing the water often, and if it should turn warm, pour a little salt in the water. The oftener it is scraped, the whiter will be the souse. Boil in plenty of water to cover it, replenishing when needed. When tender enough, put it in milk-warm water, and when cold in salt water. Boil the head until the bones will almost fall out. Clean one dozen or more ears and boil also; while hot, chop very fine, and season with pepper and salt.

Put in a mold or bowl with a weight on top. The feet may be soused whole, or cut up with the head and ears; but it is not so nice. Clean them by dipping in boiling water and scraping; do not hold them to the fire to singe off the hair. One head and one dozen ears will make a good-sized cheese.—*Mrs. W.*

To Make Souse from Hog's Feet.

As soon as the hog is cleaned, cut off the feet and throw them in a tub of cold water with a handful of salt; let them remain covered in water until you are ready to clean them, which should be done as soon as possible, as they will be much whiter. To get the hoof off, put the feet in hot water (not above the hoof); as soon as they get hot enough, slip a knife between the foot and hoof, and slip it off; then scrape the foot nicely, and throw into a tub of clear water; do this for several days. When you have scraped and changed the water for a week, then wash them clean and put them on to boil. First put them in a clean pot with a thin gruel made of corn meal; boil until half done. Wash them off, and put on in clear hot water, and boil till done, then take them up and throw them into a firkin of clean salt and water; keep closely covered to prevent them from molding. They are now ready to fry, which should be done by splitting the foot in half and fried in egg batter.—*Mrs. P. W.*

To Cure Lard.

As soon as it is taken from the hog, cut in small pieces, wash clean, press out the water, and put in the pot to boil, with one gallon of water to a vessel holding four gallons. Boil briskly until nearly done, or until the cracklins begin to brown, then cook slowly to prevent burning. The cracklins should be of a light brown and crisp, and will sink to the bottom when done. This is Leaf Lard.

The fat off of the backbone is also very nice, done in the same way, and does not require soaking, unless bloody. The fat from the entrails can also be made into nice lard by soaking for a day or two in fresh water, changing it frequently, and throwing a handful of salt in the tub of water to draw out the blood and impurities. When ready to render, wash in warm water twice and boil in more water than you do for leaf lard. The cracklins will not become crisp, but remain soft, and will sink to the bottom; they are used for making soap.

Virginia Mode of Curing Hams.

Put one teaspoonful saltpetre on the fleshy side of each ham.

Salt *not too heavily* for five weeks; if the weather is freezing cold, six weeks; then brush the hams well, and rub them with hickory ashes; let them lie for one week, then hang and smoke them for six weeks with green hickory chips. After brushing, pack them in hickory ashes in a bulk.—*Mrs. P. C. M.*

To Cure Bacon.

Pack the meat in salt and allow it to remain five weeks. Then take the hams up, wash off, and wipe dry. Have some sacks made of about seven-eighths shirting, large enough to hold the hams and tie above the hock. Make a pot of sizing of equal portions of flour and corn meal, boil until thick, and dip each sack until the outside is well coated with sizing. Put the hams in bags, and tie tight with a strong twine and hang by the same in the smoke-house.

Curing Bacon.

One peck salt to five hundred pounds pork. To five gallons water:

>4 pounds salt.
>1 pound sugar.
>1 pint molasses.
>1 teaspoonful saltpetre.

Mix, and after sprinkling the fleshy side of the ham with the salt, pack in a tight barrel. Hams first, then shoulders, middlings. Pour over the brine; leave the meat in brine from four to seven weeks.—*Mrs. Dr. J.*

For Curing Hams.

For five hundred pounds hams.

>1 peck and 1½ gallons fine Liverpool salt.
>1¾ pounds saltpetre.
>1 quart hickory ashes well sifted.
>1 quart molasses.

2 teacups cayenne pepper.
1 teacup black pepper.

Mix these ingredients well together in a large tub, rub it into each ham with a brick, or something rough to get it in well. Pack in a tight, clean tub and weigh down. Let the hams remain six weeks; then take them out and rub each one on the fleshy side with one tablespoonful black pepper to avoid skippers. Hang in the meat house, and smoke with green hickory for from ten to twelve hours a day for six weeks, not suffering the wood to blaze. On the 1st of April, take them down and pack in any coal ashes or pine ashes well slaked. Strong ashes will rot into the meat.—*Mrs. R. M.*

An Improvement to Hams.

Sometimes very good bacon is found to be of a bad color when cooked. This may be remedied by keeping it in ashes (hickory is best) for a few weeks before using. Must then be hung up, with ashes adhering, until needed. This also prevents skippers.—*Mrs. S. T.*

To Boil a Ham Weighing Ten Pounds.

Let it soak for twenty-four hours, changing the water two or three times. Boil it slowly eight or ten hours: when done, put it into a dish, as nearly as possible the shape of a ham, taking care first to take out the bone—turn the rind down. When cold, turn it out into a large dish, garnish with jelly and ornamental paper. Serve with the rind on. To be eaten cold.— *Mrs. W. C. R.*

To Boil Ham.

Put in the water one pint vinegar, a bay leaf, a little thyme, and parsley.

Boil slowly for two hours, if it weighs ten pounds; then bake. Soak all hams twenty-four hours before cooking.— *Mrs. M.*

To Boil Ham.

The day before you wish to boil a ham, scrape, wash and wipe it dry, and put it in the sun. At night put it into water and soak till next morning. Then lay it with the skin down in a boiler of cold water, and boil slowly for five hours. If the ham is large, boil six hours. When perfectly done and tender, set the boiler aside, with the ham and liquor undisturbed, until cold. Then take off the skin, sprinkle black pepper over thickly, and sift over crackers first browned and pounded; for special occasions, place at equal distances over the ham, scraped horseradish in lozenge shape, and edged with curled parsley. This mode keeps the ham juicy.—*Mrs. S. T.*

BAKED HAM.

First of all, soak an old ham overnight, having first washed and scraped it. Next morning put in a boiler of milk-warm water with the skin side down. Boil slowly for four or five hours, according to size, and if a very large ham, six hours. When done, set aside, the boiler with the ham and liquor in it, to remain until cold; when the skin must be taken off, and it must be trimmed of a nice shape. Sprinkle over two tablespoonfuls black pepper. Lay the ham on a grating or twist in the baking-pan, in which pour a pint of water, and set it in a hot oven. This mode prevents the frying so disagreeable to the taste. After the ham is heated through, and the pepper strikes in, sift over cracker; return to the oven and brown, then decorate with scraped horseradish and parsley, and serve.—*Mrs. S. T.*

BAKED HAM OR TONGUES.

Boil the ham and grate some powdered cracker thickly over it; first rubbing it with beaten yolk of egg. Bake with butter. Lay slices of currant jelly around the tongue, and garnish the ham with parsley.—*Mrs. R.*

Baked Ham.

Most persons boil ham, but it is much better if baked properly. Soak it for an hour in clean water and wipe dry; next spread it all over with a thin batter, put it into a deep dish with sticks under it to keep it out of the gravy. When it is fully done, take off the skin and batter crusted upon the flesh side and set it away to cool.—*Mrs. B. J. B.*

STUFFED AND BAKED HAM.

After your ham is boiled, take the skin off. Take pepper, allspice, cloves and mace, well pounded; add a little bread crumbs, and a little brown sugar; mix with a little butter and water.

Gash your ham and take out plugs; fill in with the mixture. Rub the ham with an egg beaten, and grate on bread crumbs and white sugar.

Put in the oven and brown.—*Mrs. D. R.*

TO STUFF FRESH CURED HAM.

Boil the ham.

Take one-half pound grated cracker or bread.

½ pound butter.

1 teaspoonful spice.

1 teaspoonful cloves.

1 teaspoonful nutmeg.

1 teaspoonful ginger.

1 teaspoonful mace.

3 spoonfuls sugar.

Celery-seed or celery.

6 eggs, beaten light.

1 spoonful mustard.

Mix all well together and moisten with cream, if too stiff. Whilst the ham is hot, make holes to the bone and fill with this mixture. Put in the stove to brown.

SPICED HAM.

Salt the hams for two days; put them in a keg and for each ham add:

½ cup molasses.
1 tablespoonful spice.
1 tablespoonful black pepper.
A pinch of saltpetre.

Let them stand four days, turning each day, then hang them up.—*Mrs. D. R.*

BROILED HAM.

To have this dish in a perfection, ham must first be soaked, then boiled nearly done, and set aside to take slices from, as wanted. Cut rather thin, lay on a gridiron over hot coals; when hot through, lay on a dish, and pepper well. Pour over fresh butter melted, and serve. If a raw ham is used, the slices must be cut thicker, dropped in a pan of boiling water for a few minutes, then broiled as above.—*Mrs. S. T.*

FRIED HAM.

The slices are always taken from a raw ham, but are most delicate when first simmered a short time: five minutes in a stewpan, dried with a clean cloth and put in a hot frying-pan, first removing the skin. The pan must be hot enough to scorch and brown both ham and gravy quickly. Lay the slices on a hot dish, pour into the gravy half a teacup new milk, pepper, and minced parsley; boil up and serve.—*Mrs. S. T.*

SHOULDER OF BACON.

This piece is not used until cured or smoked, it is then boiled with cabbage or salad, as you would the middling. It is inferior to the ham or middling.—*Mrs. P. W.*

BACON AND GREENS.

The middling is generally used for this purpose: cut a piece about a foot square, boil three hours.

Take a good head of cabbage, cut, quarter, and wash clean; press the water out as dry as you can. Boil them one or two hours with half a pod of red pepper; put them on a dish and the middling on top. You can fry the cabbage next day, and make a savory dish, but it does not suit dyspeptics. The thin part of the middling is used for frying, and is called "breakfast bacon."—*Mrs. P. W.*

Fried Bacon.

Dip the ham or slices of middling in bread crumbs. Put in a frying-pan with chopped parsley and pepper. Just before taking off the fire, pour to the gravy a cup of cream.—*Mrs. W.*

Jowl and Turnip Salad.

This is an old Virginia dish, and much used in the spring of the year.

The jowl, which must have been well smoked, must be washed clean, and boiled for three hours. Put in the salad, and boil half an hour; if you boil too long, it will turn yellow. It is also good broiled for breakfast with pepper and butter over it.

The jaw-bone should be removed before sending to the table; this is easily done by running a knife around the lip and under the tongue. The jowl and salad should always be served with fresh poached eggs.—*Mrs. P. W.*

Pickled Pork Equal to Fresh.

Let the meat cool thoroughly; cut into pieces four to six inches wide, weigh them and pack them as tight as possible in a barrel, salting very slightly. Cover the meat with brine made as strong as possible. Pour off a gallon of brine and mix with it one tablespoonful saltpetre for every 100 pounds meat and return it to the barrel. Let it stand one month, then take out the meat, let it drain twelve hours. Put the brine in an iron kettle, and one quart treacle or two pounds sugar, and boil until perfectly clear. When it is cold, return the meat to the barrel and pour on the brine. Weight it down and keep it covered close, and you will have the sweetest meat you ever tasted.

How to Cook Salt Pork.

Many people do not relish salt pork fried, but it is quite good to soak it in milk two or three hours, then roll in Indian meal and fry to a light brown. This makes a good dish wich mashed turnips, or raw onions cut in vinegar; another way is to soak it over night in skimmed milk and bake like fresh pork; it is almost as good as fresh roast pork.

Ham Toast.

Mince about one pint boiled lean ham.

Add the yolks of three eggs well beaten, two tablespoonfuls cream, and a little cayenne pepper.

Stir all on the fire until it thickens, and spread on hot toast with the crust cut off.—*Mrs. J. T. B.*

Ham Toast.

Chop very fine two spoonfuls of lean ham that has been cooked; take two spoonfuls veal gravy; a few bread crumbs.

Put all together in a stewpan and heat it. Have ready a toast buttered, spread the above upon it, strew a few bread crumbs over it and brown it before the fire.—*Mrs. S.*

Ham Relish.

Cut a slice of dressed ham, season it highly with cayenne pepper and broil it brown; then spread mustard over it, squeeze on it a little lemon juice, and serve quickly.

Potted Tongue or Ham.

Remove all skin, gristle, and outside parts from one pound of the lean of cold boiled tongue or ham.

Pound it in a mortar to a smooth paste with either one

quarter pound of the fat, or with two ounces fresh butter, Season with cayenne, pounded mace and allspice.

Press it well into pots and cover with clarified butter or fat.

To Roast Shoat.

The hind-quarter is considered best. Cut off the foot, leaving the hock quite short. Wash well and put into boiling water; simmer until done, adding salt and pepper just before lifting from the kettle; salt put in sooner hardens and toughens. Place the meat in a baking-pan and score across, in the direction in which it is to be carved. Skim several ladlefuls from the top of the kettle and pour over; after this has dried off, sprinkle over a little salt and pepper, cover with an egg beaten stiff, sift over powdered cracker, and set to brown. Lay around sweet potatoes first parboiled, then cut in thick slices. Serve with minced parsley and thyme, both on the meat and in the gravy.—*Mrs. S. T.*

To Roast a Fore Quarter of Shoat.

Put it on in hot water, boil for half an hour; take it out, put in a pan, gash it across with a sharp knife, in diamond shapes, grease it with lard and dredge with flour, pepper and a little salt. Peel some good Irish potatoes, lay them around the pan and set in the stove to brown, basting frequently. This meat should be cooked done, as it is not good the least rare. Grate some bread crumbs over it and serve.—*Mrs. P. W.*

To Barbecue Shoat.

Lay the shoat in water till ready for use; if small, it will cook in an hour. Put in the oven with two spoonfuls of water, a piece of lard, and dredge with flour. When ready for use, pour in half a teacup of walnut catsup, and, if not fat, a piece of butter.

Shoat Jowl.

The upper half of the head is what is generally used for what is called "The Pig's-head Stew." Another nice dish may be made of the under jaw or jowl by parboiling until the jawbone can be taken out; always adding pepper and salt just before it is done. When perfectly tender, score across; pepper and salt again, cover with beaten egg, then with cracker. Set in a pan with some of the water in which it was boiled. Put in a hot oven and brown.—*Mrs. S. T.*

Roast Pig.

When roasted whole, a pig should not be under four nor over six weeks old. In town, the butcher prepares for roasting, but it is well to know, in the country, how this may be done. As soon as the pig is killed, throw it into a tub of cold water, to make it tender; as soon as cold, take it by the hind leg, and plunge into scalding, not boiling water (as the last cooks the skin so that the hair can with difficulty be removed), shake it about until the hair can be removed by the handful. When all that is possible has been taken off in this way, rub from the tail up to the end of the nose with a coarse cloth. Take off the hoofs, scrape and wash the ears and nose until perfectly clean. The nicest way to dress it is to hang it by the hind legs, open and take out the entrails; wash well with water, with a little soda dissolved in it; rinse again and again, and leave hanging an hour. Wrap in a coarse cloth wrung out of cold water and lay on ice or in a cool cellar until next morning, when, if the weather is warm, it must be cooked. It should never be used the same day that it is killed.

First prepare the stuffing of the liver, heart and haslets of the pig, stewed, seasoned, and chopped. Mix with these an equal quantity of boiled potatoes mashed; add a large spoonful of butter, with some hard-boiled eggs, parsley and thyme, chopped fine, pepper and salt.

Scald the pig on the inside, dry it and rub with pepper and

salt, fill and sew up. Bend the fore legs under the body, the hind legs forward, under the pig, and skewer to keep in position. Place in a large baking-pan, pour over one quart of boiling water. Have a lump of fresh butter tied up in a clean rag; rub it all over the pig, then sprinkle over pepper and salt, putting some in the pan with a bunch of herbs; invert over it a baking-pan while it simmers, and steam until entirely done. Underdone pork, shoat, or pig, is both unpalatable and unwholesome. Remove the pan, rub over with the butter and baste often. When of a fine brown, cover the edges of a large dish with a deep fringe of curled parsley; first sift over the pig powdered cracker, then place it, kneeling, in the green bed. Place in its mouth an orange or a red apple; and, if eaten hot, serve with the gravy in a tureen or sauce-boat. It is much nicer cold; served with little mounds of grated horseradish amongst the parsley.—*Mrs. S. T.*

To Stew Pig's Head and Jowl.

Clean the head and feet; take out the bone above the nose; cut off the ears, clean them nicely. Separate the jowl from the head; take care of the brains to add to the stew. Put the head, jowl, feet and part of the liver in water sufficient to keep well covered; boil until quite done. Split the feet to put on the dish; hash the head and liver; but do not spoil the jowl, which must be put in the middle of the dish and surrounded with the feet and hash. Put all of the hash, jowl and feet in the pot and season with a cup of cream, a lump of butter, pepper and salt, a tablespoonful walnut catsup, an onion chopped fine, a stalk of celery.

A teaspoonful mustard improves it.

Stew half an hour; thicken the gravy with grated bread.— *Mrs. P. W.*

Shoat's Head.

Get a shoat's head and clean it nicely. Boil and chop in pieces. Season with:

2 tablespoonfuls tomato catsup.
2 tablespoonfuls walnut catsup.
2 cups water.
A little flour.
1 large spoonful butter.
Pepper and salt.

Have two or three hard-boiled eggs, cut them in half and lay on the top of the head; set it in the oven to bake.

Veal or mutton head, can be cooked in the same way, but are not so nice.—*Mrs. R.*

Shoat's Head, to Stew.

Clean the head and feet; and put them on to parboil with the liver. Then split up the head, through the nose, taking out the bones. Cut the meat from the feet and chop up with the liver, season this with pepper and salt.

Lay the head open and fill it with this mince and the yolks of some hard-boiled eggs: if this does not fill the head, add some grated bread crumbs or crackers and butter.

Sew up the head and bind it with thread; put it in the pot with the water it has been parboiled in and let it stew slowly. Take up the head, and add to the gravy a lump of butter, rolled in flour, some browning and some walnut catsup. Pour this over the head, which should be brown. If the shoat is not very small, use bread and butter instead of the liver.—*Mrs. R.*

To Hash Pig's Head.

Take head, feet, and haslet of pig; boil them until done, then cut them up fine, taking out the bones.

Add black pepper, salt, a little sage.
2 onions chopped fine.
A little red pepp
1 teaspoonful mace.
1 teaspoonful cloves.

Put it back in the same vessel with liquor and cook till

done, then thicken with a little flour. Add two hard-boiled eggs and one cup walnut catsup.—*Mrs. Dr. J.*

BEEF AND VEAL.

In selecting beef, see that the flesh is firm and of a clear red, and the fat of a yellowish white. In buying a quarter of beef, it is better to have it cut up by the butcher, if you are living in town. The hind quarter is considered better, and sells higher than the fore quarter. If a roasting piece is desired, the sirloin from the hind quarter is usually preferred. It is not generally known, however, that the second cut of the rib-roast from the fore quarter is the finest roast from the beef.

When the bone has been removed, and the meat skewered in the shape of a round, by the butcher, it is well to roast it on a spit before an open fire. If the latter cannot be obtained, however, plunge the beef for a moment in boiling water, then rub well with salt and pepper, dredge with flour, and place on a little grate or trivet which will readily go in a baking-pan. In this pour about a pint of the water in which the beef was scalded. Place it in a very hot oven, with an inverted tin plate on top of the roast. Remove this plate often to baste the meat. When nearly done, which will be in about two hours for a roast of six pounds, baste several times and bake a nice brown. Season the gravy with minced onion, parsley and thyme, add a little salt and pepper and a tablespoonful of the meat flavoring of which a receipt was given in the general directions about meat. Serve the gravy in a sauce-tureen, so that each person may choose whether to eat the beef with gravy or with the juice that escapes from the meat while it is being carved. The latter mixed with grated horseradish is preferred to gravy by some persons.

BEEF AND VEAL. 137

Every portion of the beef, from head to feet is useful and delicious when properly prepared.

The rounds and rump pieces are generally used for beef à la mode.

Fresh beef from the ribs, boiled with turnips, is considered a nice dish by some persons.

For steak, nothing is so nice as tenderloin or porter-house steak. I take this occasion to protest against the unwholesome custom of frying steak in lard. When inconvenient to broil, it may be deliciously cooked by being first beaten till tender, then laid in a hot frying-pan, closely covered, and cooked without lard or butter, in its own juices. When scorched brown on both sides, but not hard, remove the pan from the fire, pepper and salt the steak, and put a large tablespoonful of fresh butter on it. Press this in with a knife and fork, turning the steak, so that each side may absorb the butter. Serve on a hot dish. The whole process will not consume five minutes. Some persons think it best to add the salt after the steak is done, though many good housekeepers salt and pepper the steak before before broiling it. Beefsteak should be cooked rare; it is a great mistake to cook it till hard and indigestible.

The parts most suitable for soup are the head, neck, shank, and all the unsightly parts. After the bones are broken and the meat boiled from them, the liquor is used for soup, while the meat, picked or cut to pieces, will make an excellent stew seasoned with potatoes, turnips, sweet herbs, one tablespoonful of butter and the same of meat flavoring.

It is well always to keep brine on hand for corning beef. All the parts not desirable for roast or steak had better be corned.

The beef, after being dressed, should be hung up by the hind legs, with a smooth, round piece of timber sufficiently strong to hold the weight, passed through the legs at the hock, or run between the tendon and bone, with short pegs to keep the legs stretched apart. Then with a sharp axe, standing behind the suspended beef, split it down the backbone, severing it in half. Then pass a knife through the ribs, leaving two or three short ribs on the hind-quarter. Sever the backbone with an axe. Then cut with a sharp knife straight across the parallel line with the spinal bone, which piece must be divided into two pieces, the sirloin and steak. Then take off two rounds, or three, according to the size of the animal, cutting with a sharp knife, and cutting the bone with a meat saw or axe, as near the joints as possible, which leaves the shin-bone.

The fore quarter then is divided into four pieces, after taking off the shoulder, which may be divided into three or more pieces.

The loin of veal is the nicest part, and is always roasted.

The fillets and knuckles may be stewed and roasted.

The latter is nicest for soup.

The breast may be stewed or roasted.

The cutlets are nicest from the legs or fillet.

The head is a dish for soup, stew or pie.

Sweetbreads from the throat make a delicious dish, much prized by epicureans.

The feet, boiled till the bones drop out, make a delightful dish, fried in batter, while the water in which they are boiled makes excellent jelly.

Veal, to be eaten in its perfection, should be killed when from four to six weeks old.

BEEF.

The sirloin, or fore and middle ribs, are best for roasting.

The steaks are best cut from the ribs, or the inner part of the sirloin; shank, tail and head make nice soup.—*Mrs. W.*

TO ROAST BEEF.

Lay the meat on some sticks in a dripping-pan or other vessel, so that it will not touch the water which it is necessary to have in the bottom. Season with salt and pepper, and put in the oven three or four hours before it is wanted for the table. Baste it often with the water in the bottom of the pan, renewing it as often as it gets low. This makes sweet, juicy roast beef. The great secret of it is, not to have the meat touch the water in the bottom of the pan, and to baste it often. Tough, unpromising pieces of beef are best cooked by steaming them an hour and a half or so and then putting them in the oven and roasting as much longer.

Crackers, first browned and then pounded, should always be kept to sift over roast meats: and curled parsley to garnish with. Grated horseradish is also excellent with the roast. —*Mrs. S. T.*

Rib Roast of Beef.

Get, from the butcher, a rib-roast—the second cut is best—and get him to take out the bones, and roll and skewer it: if this is not convenient, it can be done at home with a sharp knife. Before roasting, take out the wooden skewers put in at market, unroll, season well with salt and pepper and anything else liked, and roll again tightly, fastening securely with the iron skewer pins. Put it in a pan on a little iron griddle or trivet, made for the purpose to keep it just over the pint of water in the pan. Pepper and salt freely, dredge with flour and baste. Some persons like half a teacup of pepper vinegar, poured over just before it is done; and minced onion, thyme and parsley added to the gravy, which should be brown.—*Mrs. B.*

To Roast Beef.

The sirloin is the nicest for the purpose.

Plunge the beef in boiling water and boil for thirty minutes: then put it in the stove-pan; skim the top of the water in which it has been boiled, and baste the roast, after dredging it with flour; pepper and salt to taste. Baste frequently, and roast till done.—*Mrs. P. W.*

Beef à la Mode.

Take, from a round of fresh beef, the bone; beat the meat all over slightly to make tender. Grate a loaf of bread, mix with it equal quantities of—

Thyme and parsley, rubbed fine.
1 onion.
The marrow from the bone.
¼ pound suet.
Pepper and salt, cloves and nutmeg to the taste.

Mix these ingredients with three eggs well beaten: fill the place from whence came the bone, and what is left rub all over the round; fasten well with a tape, tied round to keep in shape. Cover the pan with slices of bacon, lay the beef upon them, baste with butter: pour in the pan a pint of water. Cover closely and stew gently for six hours; when thoroughly done, take out the beef, skim the fat from the gravy, strain into a saucepan, set it on the stove and stir into it one teacup Port wine. Let it come to a boil and send to the table in a sauce tureen. You may, for supper, dish cold: dress with vegetable flowers, whites of eggs boiled hard and chopped fine.—*Mrs. J. W. S.*

Beef à la Mode.

Take a round or a rump piece of beef, take out the bone, the gristle and all the tough pieces about the edges. Fill the cavities from which the bone was taken, with suet, and fat salt pork.

Press this so as to make it perfectly round, pass around a coarse, strong piece of cloth, so as to hold it firmly in shape. If the round is six inches thick, the cloth must be six inches wide, leaving the top and bottom open. With a larding needle, fill this thickly with strips of fat pork, running through from top to bottom and about one inch apart each way. Set this in a baking-pan, pour over:

1 teacup boiling water,
1 teacup boiling vinegar; **mixed.**

Add to this one heaping tablespoonful brown sugar and a bunch of herbs.

Sprinkle over the beef liberally with salt and black pepper; chop one small onion fine, and lay over top of the beef. Simmer this for two or three hours, basting frequently and keeping an inverted tin plate over the beef except when basting. If the gravy stews down too much, add stock or broth of any kind. Turn it over, and let the top be at the bottom. When it is done and tender, skim the fat from the gravy. Pour over:

  2 tablespoonfuls celery vinegar.
  2 tablespoonfuls pepper.
  2 tablespoonfuls made mustard.
  1 wineglassful acid fruit jelly.

Simmer and bake for two hours longer, frequently basting, that it may be soft and seasoned through and through. Take the beef from the pan and remove the cloth; place in a large flat dish, pour over the gravy, and over this one teacup of mushroom sauce. Sift finely powdered cracker over the top and garnish with grated or scraped horseradish and parsley.—*Mrs. S. T.*

Beef à la Mode.

To 10 pounds of beef, 4 onions chopped up.
1 tablespoonful allspice, 1 teaspoonful mace.
Red pepper and salt to the taste.
1 pint strong vinegar.

Rub the beef in the mixture for three or four days, then cook, with all these ingredients. The H piece is generally the part taken for this purpose.—*Mrs. M. B.*

BOILED BEEF AND TURNIPS.

The brisket or breast of beef is nicest for boiling. Keep sufficiently covered in water, boiling three hours, or until tender.

Peel and slice half a dozen turnips and put with beef, boiling until soft enough to mash with a spoon, which will require about thirty minutes. Dress with one teacup of milk, pepper and salt to the taste.

Stew together a short time and put in bottom of dish with beef on the top.—*Mrs. P. W.*

To Collar Beef.

Take a flank of fresh beef, stew it with pepper, salt, allspice, saltpetre, thyme, and sage.

Then roll as hard as you can, and wind a string around it; then boil till done. It must be served up cold, cut in slices.—*Mrs. M. P.*

Rolled Beefsteak.

Beat a large tender steak thoroughly and carefully.

Sprinkle over salt, pepper, sage, minced onion, minced parsley, and bits of butter.

Have ready some mealy Irish potatoes mashed fine, and seasoned with a little butter and salt. Spread over all, and roll up tightly: fasten the ends and sides securely with skewer pins. Place in a pan with such broth or gravy as may be on hand; if none, two teacups of boiling water, and one small minced onion, pepper, salt, and one slice of pork.

Simmer and baste as you would a roast duck. Sift over it browned cracker, pounded fine. Very nice.—*Mrs. S. T.*

Beefsteak Broiled.

Cut the steak one-half inch thick; it should then be beaten with a steak beater or pestle. The griddle should be hot and on the coals: place the steak on the griddle, and as soon as seared, turn it; when both sides are seared, place it in a pan, season it with pepper, salt, and butter: repeat this for every piece of steak, and place in the pan, which should be kept closely covered without being on the fire. If your heat is sufficient, from three to five minutes is sufficient to cook.—*Mrs. P. W.*

Broiled Steak.

A porter-house steak is considered, by some persons, best, others prefer the tenderloin. Beat either tender, and place on a gridiron over coals, frequently turning. Have ready a hot dish, place the steak on it, pepper and salt well, then with a knife and fork profusely butter, with one large tablespoonful fresh butter, turning and pressing it so as to absorb the butter; pepper again and set the dish over boiling water until wanted, when it will be found tender and juicy, if not cooked too long on a gridiron. One tablespoonful pepper vinegar gives this the taste of venison, and to this may be added one tablespoonful made mustard, for those who like highly seasoned food.—*Mrs. S. T.*

How to Cook Beefsteak.

Take a thin, long-handled frying-pan, put it on the stove and heat it quite hot. In this put the pieces of steak previously pounded, but do not put a particle of butter in the frying-pan and do not salt the steak. Allow the steak to merely glaze over and then turn it quickly to the other side, turning it several times in this manner, until it is done. Four minutes is sufficient for cooking. When done, lay it on the platter, previously warmed; butter and salt, and set a moment in the hot oven. Allow the steak to heat but a moment on each side; this helps it to retain all its sweet juices, and putting on the salt at the last monent, after it is on the platter, draws out its juices.— *Mrs. S. T.*

Beefsteak Fried with Onions.

Prepare the steak as for broiling, pepper and roll in flour and fry in lard; remove the steak from the pan when done; add to the gravy one chopped onion, pepper, salt, one-half teacup water, and a little mustard.

Cook a few minutes, put the steak in the gravy—let it remain a short time: send to the table hot.—*Mrs. P. W.*

To Fry Steak.

Hunt up all the pickle and take from each one teacup vinegar, lay the steak in a deep dish, pour over the vinegar and let it stand one hour. Take a clean frying-pan, throw in one ounce butter, and some of the vinegar from the dish, sufficient to stew the steak. If managed properly, when done it will be imbedded in a thick gravy. Put the steak in a hot dish, before the fire; into the pan, put one spoonful black pepper, one or two of catsup, and one of raw mustard.—*Mrs. S.*

Fried Steak.

Get from the butcher a tenderloin or porter-house steak. Do not wash it, but be careful to lay it on a clean block and beat it well, but not into holes, nor so as to look ragged. Sprinkle over pepper and salt, then dredge with flour on both sides.

Have ready a hot frying-pan, lay in the steak and cover closely. The juice of the meat will be sufficient to cook it. Turn often, as the pan must be hot enough to scorch and make the steak and gravy brown.

Before it gets hard or overdone, butter liberally; place in a hot dish. Pepper again, and, if preferred, pour over first one tablespoonful pepper vinegar, then one tablespoonful made mustard, and turn in over all the hot gravy. Sift powered cracker over and serve.—*Mrs. S. T.*

Frizzled Beef.

Shred some dried beef, parboil it until it is sufficiently freshened, drain off the water and add enough boiling water to cover it. Rub equal quantities of butter and flour together until smooth, then add to the beef. Beat up three eggs, yolks and whites together, stir these in with a little pepper, a couple of minutes before taking from the fire. This is to be served hot on toast.—*Mrs. F.*

Fricasséed Beef.

Take any piece of beef from the fore quarter, such as is generally used for corning, and cook it tender in just water enough to have it all evaporate in cooking. When about half done, put in salt enough to season well, and half teaspoonful pepper. If the water should not boil away soon enough, turn it off, and let the beef fry fifteen minutes—it is better than the best roast beef. Take two tablespoonfuls flour, adding the fat—when mixed, pour on the hot juice of the meat. Serve with apple sauce.—*Mrs. D.*

Beef Stew.

This is best when made of slices cut from an underdone roast, and simmered in any liquor in which meat has been boiled, but if none is at hand, use water instead—just covering the beef.

To a half dozen slices of the usual size, add:

2 tablespoonfuls pepper vinegar.

1 tablespoonful of made mustard.

1 tablespoonful of acid fruit jelly.

1 tablespoonful of butter.

1 teaspoonful salt.

1 teaspoonful celery-seed.

1 saltspoonful black pepper.

1 raw turnip, grated or scraped fine.

1 mashed Irish potato.

Add minced onion and parsley.

Boil up and serve.

Cold beefsteak or mutton chops, which are always unfit to appear upon the table a second time, are delicious cut up in small pieces and mixed or stewed separately in this way.—*Mrs. S. T.*

To Stew a Rump of Beef.

Stuff the beef with shallots, thyme, parsley, chopped fine, slips of bacon, pepper, salt and allspice. Then lay it in a pot with water sufficient to keep it from burning before it is done.

Thicken the gravy with burnt flour and butter, and when it is served up, pour a little wine over it and strew the top with allspice.—*Mrs. M. P.*

Lebanon Stew.

Take scraps of raw beef, such as are not fit for boiling, cut very fine, picking out all the strings, and put into a kettle, and more than cover with cold water. Let it boil several hours, or until the water is nearly all gone. Season with butter, pepper and salt. It is rich and needs but little seasoning. Serve hot, as you would hash.—*Mrs. S. T.*

Beef Collaps.

1½ pounds lean beef, chopped fine.
1 tablespoonful lard.
1 tablespoonful of butter.
With enough water to cook it.

After being well cooked, thicken gravy, and season with vinegar and pepper.—*Mrs. H. D.*

To Stew Beef Tongue.

Put a fresh tongue in water sufficient to cover it, and let it simmer six or seven hours. Skim the gravy well. Half an hour before dishing it, add one-half wineglassful wine, one-half wineglassful walnut catsup, a little mace, and a few cloves to the gravy, and stew awhile together.—*Mrs. S. T.*

Tongue à la Terrapin.

Take a freshly salted tongue and boil tender; take out, and split it, stick a few cloves in, cut up a small onion, put in some sticks of mace, and a little brown flour.

Have water enough in a stewpan to cover the tongue; mix in the ingredients, before putting in the tongue. Three hardboiled eggs chopped up fine and put in the stew. Add a glass of wine just before taking up. Send to the table hot, garnished with hard boiled eggs cut in rings.—*Mrs. L. C.*

Tongue Toast.

Take cold tongue that has been well boiled, mince fine, mix it well with cream or a little milk, if there is no cream. Add the beaten yolk of one egg and give it a simmer over the fire. Toast nicely some thin slices of stale bread and, having buttered, lay them in a flat dish, that has been heated, then cover the toast with the tongue and serve up directly.—*Mrs. S.*

To Roast an Ox Heart.

Wash it well and clean all the blood carefully from the pipes; parboil it ten or fifteen minutes in boiling water; drain and put in a stuffing which has been made of bread crumbs, minced suet or butter, thyme or parsley, salt, pepper, and nutmeg.

Put it down to roast while hot, baste it well with butter, and just before serving, stir one tablespoonful currant jelly into the gravy. To roast, allow twenty minutes to every pound.—*Mrs. A. M. D.*

Beef Heart.

Parboil the heart until nearly tender, then gash and stuff with rich stuffing of loaf bread, seasoned with onion, salt, pepper, and sage. Then put in a pan and bake, turning it several times. Baste with gravy whilst baking.—*Mrs. J. H.*

Stewed Kidneys.

Soak the kidneys for several hours, put them on to boil until tender. Roll them in flour, add a lump of butter the size of an egg, two spoonfuls catsup—any kind will answer, though walnut is the best; pepper and salt to the taste. Stew them until well seasoned.—*Mrs. P. W.*

To Stew Beef Kidneys.

Cut into pieces and stew in water, with a nice addition of

savory herbs, pepper and salt, and a handful flour to thicken the gravy; flavor and color the latter with burnt sugar.—*Mrs. H.*

KIDNEYS FRIED.

After plunging in boiling water, cut them in thin slices and fry in hot butter; add pepper, salt, and toss them for a few minutes in rich brown gravy.—*Mrs. M.*

BEEF KIDNEY, TO FRY.

Trim and cut the kidney in slices; season them with salt and pepper, and dredge well with flour; fry on both sides, and when done, lift them out, empty the pan and make a gravy for them with a small piece of butter, one dessertspoonful flour, pepper, salt, and a cup of boiling water. Shake these around and give them a minute's simmering; add a little tomato or mushroom catsup, lemon juice, vinegar, or any good sauce to give it a flavor. Minced herbs are to many tastes an improvement to this dish, to which a small quantity of onion may be added when it is liked.—*Mrs. A. M. D.*

KIDNEYS GRILLED.

Prepare them as for stewing, cut each kidney in half and dip them in egg beaten up with salt and pepper; bread-crumb them, dip them in melted butter, bread-crumb them again, then grill before a slow fire; serve with Worcestershire or some other sauce.—*Mrs. K.*

BROILED KIDNEYS.

Plunge some kidneys in boiling water; open them down the centre, but do not separate them; peel and pass a skewer across them to keep them open; pepper, salt, and dip them in melted butter.

Broil them over a clear fire on both sides, doing the cut side first; remove the skewer, have ready some maître d'hote sauce, viz.: butter beaten up with chopped parsley, salt and pepper, and a little lemon juice. Put a small piece in the hollow of each kidney and serve hot.—*Mrs. P.*

Beef's Liver.

Skin the liver, cut in slices and lay in salt water, as soon as it comes from market. Fry in lard with pepper, very brown. Season to taste.—*Mrs. C.*

To Fry Liver.

The slices must be cut thin, as they require some time to fry; brown both sides; when taken up, add butter and salt to taste. Fry in hot lard.—*Mrs. P. W.*

Beef Liver with Onions.

Slice the liver rather thin, and throw into salt and water. Meantime slice the onions and put into a deep frying-pan, just covered with water, and boil until done, keeping it closely covered. When the water has all boiled away, put in a heaping spoonful of sweet lard, and fry until the onions are a light brown. Take them up in a deep plate; set them on the back of the stove or range to keep hot, and fry the liver in the same pan, adding more lard if there is not enough. Season all with salt and pepper, cutting the liver in slices suitable to help one person. Make a little mound of fried onions on each piece, grate pounded cracker on the top, and serve.—*Mrs. S. T.*

Dried Liver for Relish.

Salt the liver well for four days; hang to smoke and dry. Cut in very thin slices, and broil in pepper and butter.— *Mrs. W.*

Fried Liver.

Cut the slices thin, scald them for some minutes, put them in a pan with hot lard, and fry slowly till browned on both sides; add a little salt and pepper. Take up the liver, and pour into the pan half a teacup of water; let it boil a few minutes; put the liver back, stir it up, and cover it up for a short time to keep it from being hard.

Kidneys can be cooked the same way, excepting you must add some butter, as they are very dry.—*Mrs. P. W.*

To Stew Brains.

Have them thoroughly soaked in salt water to get the blood out. Put them in a stewpan with water enough to cover them; boil half an hour, pour off the water, and add one teacup of cream or milk, salt, pepper, and butter the size of an egg. Boil well together for ten minutes, when put into the dish. Add one tablespoonful vinegar.—*Mrs. P. W.*

To Dress Brains.

Lay in salt and water, then either scramble like eggs, or beat the yolks of eggs with a little flour; dip the brains in and fry them.—*Mrs. W.*

To Fry Beef Brains.

Pour over the brains salt water, let them remain for an hour, changing the water to draw the blood out, then pour over them some boiling water and remove the skin. Beat up two eggs, and make a batter with a little flour, bread crumbs and crackers. Season with pepper and salt. Fry in hot lard.—*Mrs. P. W.*

To Fry Brains.

Soak the brains for several hours in weak salt water to get out the blood; drain and put them in a saucepan and pour very little boiling water on; simmer a few minutes. Handle them lightly, and arrange so as to form round cakes, without breaking. Pepper them and use very little salt; brains require very little salt. Have ready a beaten egg, and cover the top of the cakes with it, using a spoon to put it on. Sift over grated cracker and fry in hot lard; serve the other side the same way. Keep closely covered while frying.—*Mrs. S. T.*

Brain Croquettes.

Wash the brains of three heads very thoroughly, until they are free from membraneous matter and perfectly white. Then scramble with three eggs. When cold, roll into egg-shaped balls, with floured hands; dip in beaten egg, then in cracker or stale bread crumbs, and fry in lard.—*Mrs. R. L.*

To Prepare Tripe.

Empty the contents of the stomach of a fat beef; put it in boiling water, one piece at a time, to prevent getting too hot. Scrape with a sharp knife, then put it in a vessel of cold water with salt; wash thoroughly, and change the salt water every day for four or five consecutive days; when perfectly white, boil in a very clean vessel of salt water. Then put it in vinegar until you wish to use it. Cut it in pieces of three or four inches square, and fry in egg batter.—*Mrs. J. H.*

Tripe.

The moment the tripe is taken out, wash it thoroughly in many cold waters. (If you have quick-lime, sift it over the dark inner coat, and instantly scrape off the coat.) Cut it in four parts. Have ready boiling water, dip and scrape until it becomes quite white. Prepare weak brine with a considerable mixture of meal; let it soak a day. Continue to shift it every day, and every other day scrape it; this must be done for a week, and then make nice gruel, in which it must be well boiled, first tying it up in a cloth. When boiled, take it out of the cloth, and lay it in a weak brine for a night, after which it may be put with the feet.—*Mrs. R.*

Beef Tripe.

Clean the tripe carefully. Soak several days in salt water, then in clear water, changing several times. Cut in slices, boil perfectly done, dip in a batter of egg (beaten light), milk and flour, or sift meal over it. Fry or broil. Season with pepper and salt.

To Fry Tripe.

Cut the tripe after it has been boiled, into strips about four inches wide and six long. Make a batter with two eggs, one teacup of flour and a little milk. Pepper the tripe and roll it in the batter. Fry in a pan of hot lard; as soon as one side is done, turn it over on the other side.—*Mrs. P. W.*

Gravy for Roast Beef.

When the joint is done to a turn, dish it and place before the fire; then carefully remove the fat from the dripping-pan, and pour the gravy into the dish, not over the meat, as is the custom of inexperienced cooks, who, moreover, ruthlessly drown it with a cupful of boiling water or highly flavored made-gravy. This is an error, for there is always a sufficient quantity of natural gravy in good meat to render the use of foreign sauces superfluous.—*Mrs. P.*

Brown Gravy.

Take the gravy that drips from the meat; add a little water, one spoonful butter, a little flour, a little pepper and a little salt. Stew all together.—*Miss E. P.*

Bologna Sausage.

Take ten pounds of beef, and four pounds pork, two-thirds lean and one-third fat; chop very fine and mix well together. Season with six ounces fine salt, one ounce black pepper, one-half ounce cayenne pepper, and sage to the taste.—*Mrs. Dr. S.*

Beef Sausage.

Take tough beef and run it through a sausage machine. Form the pulp into shapes an inch thick, and the size of a common beefsteak. Season to the taste.—*Mrs. C.*

Cow Heél.

As soon as the beef is killed, throw the feet in cold water, and let them remain during the night. In the morning, put them into a pot of cold water and let them boil until you find you can easily take off the hair and the hoof with a knife; take care as the water boils away to replenish with boiling water. Have ready strong brine, not boiled nor strong enough to bear an egg, and the moment the feet are stripped, throw them in. Let them stand one night and in the morning pour the brine from them and put to them a fresh brine, with a small quantity of vinegar. In a day or two, they are fit for use.—*Mrs. R.*

Cow Heel Fried.

Buy the feet prepared at the butchers; boil well done. Season with salt and pepper.

Have ready an egg batter; fry brown, and serve hot. A nice breakfast dish.—*Mrs. R. L. O.*

To Fry Beef Heel.

Have a batter made of eggs, flour, etc., as for tripe. Split the feet into convenient shapes and fry in hot lard. Pour some vinegar over them while frying.—*Mrs. P. W.*

Daube Froide.

Take a beef shin, chop in several places to break the bone, keep it cooking in just water enough to prevent burning, till it falls to pieces.

Then after taking out the bones, season with one heaping teaspoonful flour rubbed into one tablespoonful butter, red and black pepper, salt and celery seed.

Stew it long enough to cook the flour. Pour into a deep dish, cover with a plate, and put weights on it to press it. Eat cold, as souse.—*Mrs. C. M. A.*

A French Dish.

To two beef feet, put four gallons water; set on the fire at eight o'clock in the morning. When the bones have dropped off add the half of one large onion, two red peppers, and one sprig parsley, all chopped fine.

Take another pot, put in two gallons water, in which cut up one-half gallon nice pieces of beef, half an onion, one red pepper, parsley, all chopped fine, and salt. When all has boiled to pieces, put all together and let it boil half an hour. Press as souse cheese.—*Mrs. T.*

Brine for Beef.

9 quarts salt.
18 gallons water.
2 pounds brown sugar.
½ pound saltpetre.

Boil and skim well. Let the beef get thoroughly cold, and let as much as possible of the blood be drained out before putting it in the brine. It may sometimes be necessary, in the course of a few months, that the brine be boiled and skimmed a second time.

This quantity will suffice for about half of an ordinary sized beef.—*Mrs. A. C.*

To Corn Beef.

For every hundred pounds of beef, take:

6 pounds salt.
2 pounds brown sugar.
2 ounces saltpetre.
3 or 4 ounces soda.
1 ounce red pepper.

The whole to be dissolved in four gallons of water. The beef must be closely packed in a barrel, and the mixture poured over so as to cover it. Let it stand a week or ten days, or longer if the weather is cold; then pour off the brine, boil it, and skim off the blood. Let it cool, and pour back on the beef. Warranted to keep.—*Mrs. Dr. S.*

To Corn Beef Tongues and Beef.

One tablespoonful saltpetre to each tongue or piece of beef; rub this in first, then a plenty of salt. Pack down in salt; after it has remained ten or twelve days, put this, with a few pods of red pepper cut up fine, in a brine of only salt and water, which has been boiled, strained, and cooled, and strong enough to bear an egg. Wash a rock clean and place on the beef or tongues, to keep them under the brine. This will keep an indefinite length of time. Fit for use in two weeks.—*Mrs. S. T.*

To Corn Beef or Pork.

50 pounds meat.
4½ pounds salt.
1½ pounds brown sugar.
½ pound saltpetre.
1 quart molasses.

Mix well, boil and skim. When milk-warm, pour it over the meat with a ladle. The beef must be soaked in clear water and wiped dry, before putting in the brine. It will be ready for use in a few weeks. Should the brine mould, skim and boil again. Keep the meat under the brine.—*Mrs. P. W.*

To Pickle Tongue.

Rub it well with salt and leave it alone four or five hours; pour off the foul brine; take two ounces saltpetre beaten fine, and rub it all over the tongue; then mix one-quarter of a pound brown sugar and one ounce sal-prunella (the bay salt and sal prunella beat very fine), and rub it well over the tongue. Let it lie in the pickle three or four days; make a brine of one gallon water with common salt strong enough to bear an egg, a half-pound brown sugar, two ounces saltpetre, and one-quarter of a pound bay salt. Boil one quarter of an hour, skimming well; when cold put in the tongue; let it lie in the pickle fourteen days, turning it every day. When ready to use take it out of the pickle, or hang it in wood smoke to dry.—*Mrs A. M. D.*

To Corn Beef.

One tablespoonful saltpetre to each piece of beef, well rubbed in. Then rub in as much salt as it will take. Let it stand ten or twelve days, and then put it in strong brine. Will be ready for use in a week.—*Mrs. Col. A. F*

Corned Beef.

Having a quarter of beef cut into proper size and shape for nice roasting pieces, put it in a barrel of weak brine and let it remain four days. Then make a brine that will bear an egg, to which add:

½ pound saltpetre.
3 pounds brown sugar.

Transfer the beef to this barrel, cover closely, and let it remain a week. Put a weight on the meat to insure its being kept under the brine. Beef thus prepared in January will keep well through the month of March, improving with the lapse of time. It is best served cold. A valuable receipt for country housekeepers.—*Mrs. Wm. A. S.*

Hunter's Beef, or Spiced Round.

To a round of beef weighing twenty-four pounds, take.

3 ounces saltpetre.
3 ounces coarsest sugar.
1 ounce cloves.
1 nutmeg.
½ ounce allspice.
3 handfuls salt.

Beat all into the finest powder; allow the beef to hang three or four days; remove the bone, then rub the spices well into it, continuing to do so every two or three days, for two or three weeks.

When to be dressed, dip it in cold water, to take off the

loose spices, bind it up tightly and put into a pan with a teacupful water at the bottom. Sprinkle the top of the meat with suet, cover it over with a thick batter, and brown paper over it. Bake five hours.—*Mrs. T. C.*

HUNTER'S ROUND, OR SPICED BEEF.

To a round of beef that weighs twenty-five pounds, take the following:

>3 ounces saltpetre.
>1 ounce cloves.
>1 ounce nutmeg.
>1 ounce allspice.
>1 pint salt.

Let the round of beef hang in a cool, dry place twenty-four hours. Take out the bone, and fill the space with suet and spices mixed. Rub the above ingredients all over the *round ;* put in a wooden box or tub, turn it over occasionally and rub a small quantity of salt on it. Let it remain three weeks. Then make a stiff paste of flour and water, cover the *round* with it and set in the oven. Bake three hours slowly. Remove the paste when cold, and trim neatly the rough outside, and slice horizontally. Served only when cold.—*Mrs. W. A. S.*

TO SPICE A ROUND OF BEEF.

Take three tablespoonfuls saltpetre, four tablespoonfuls brown sugar, with which rub your beef well. Two teacups of salt, one teacup of cloves, one teacup of allspice (the spice must be ground fine). Rub the beef with these ingredients. Put it into a tub as near the size of the beef as possible; turn it every day in the pickle it makes. In about four weeks it will be ready for use. For thirty pounds use two pounds beef suet. When cooked place sticks across the bottom of the pot to prevent its burning.—*Mrs. R. L. P.*

SPICED BEEF.

Take eight or ten pounds of the thin flank, remove any gristle, skin or bones; rub it over with half ounce saltpetre, half ounce bay salt, then rub it well in with a mixture of spices, the the following proportions being used:

> 1 ounce black pepper.
> 1 ounce allspice.
> ½ ounce ground ginger.
> ¼ ounce cloves.
> ⅛ ounce mace.

Use only as much as will suffice to rub the beef all over; then add three ounces common salt, and quarter of a pound coarse sugar.

Let the beef remain a fortnight in this pickle, turning it and rubbing it every day: then take it out, cover it with the spices and chopped sweet herbs, roll it very tight, tie it with tape, put it into a pan with half-pint water, and half-pound suet.

Bake it after the bread has been drawn, for six hours; put a heavy weight upon it, and when cold take off the tape.

To Cook a Corned Round of Beef.

Wash it clean of the brine, sew it in a coarse towel and boil six to eight hours. Do not remove the towel until next day; it is nicer to put it in a round mould and gives it a good shape. When perfectly cold, trim nicely and cut it across the grain.—*Mrs. P. W.*

To Cook Corned Beef-Tongue, etc.

If the beef has been in brine long or has been dried, it must be soaked in cold water twelve hours before boiling. If freshly cured it is unnecessary. The beef should be put on in a large pot of water early in the morning and simmer for hours. Set the pot at the back of the range or stove, where it will gently boil during the preparation of dinner. When it first commences to boil, take off the scum. After it is thoroughly done, take off the boiler or pot. Set away with the beef under the liquor to remain until next day, when it will be found juicy and tender. With a sharp knife carefully trim, and garnish with scraped horseradish and curled parsley.—*Mrs. S. T.*

How to Cook Corned Beef.

The flank is a nice piece to corn; though an ugly piece of meat, it can be made a nice and delicious dish. Wash the flank clean, roll it up as tight as you can, and tie it with strong cord in three places; then sew it up in a coarse towel and put it on and boil from five to six hours, according to size; take it out of the pot, but do not undo it, put it on a dish or pan and put a weight on it; let it stand until next day, then remove the cloth and strings; trim it, and you have a nice dish.—*Mrs. P. W.*

Smoked Beef.

To a piece of beef weighing about twelve or fourteen pounds, you rub in the following:

1 pint salt.
1 cup brown sugar.
1 cup molasses.
½ teaspoonful pounded saltpetre.

Rub this well on the beef and turn it several times. At the end of ten days drain it, rub bran on it, hang it up and smoke for several days.—*Mrs. H. T.*

To Cure Beef for Drying.

This recipe keeps the meat moist, so that it has none of that toughness dried beef mostly has when a little old. To every twenty-eight or thirty pounds, allow one tablespoonful saltpetre, one quart fine salt, mixed with molasses until the color is about that of light brown sugar; rub the pieces of meat with the mixture, and when done, let all stick to it that will. Pack in a keg or half-barrel, that the pickle may cover the meat, and let it remain forty-eight hours; at the end of that time, enough pickle will be formed to cover it. Take it out and hang in a suitable place for drying. Allow all the mixture to adhere to the meat that will.—*Mrs. A. M. D.*

To Cure Beef Ham.

Divide the ham into three parts; rub on half-pint molasses; let it remain in this molasses a day and two nights, turning it over occasionally during the time. Rub on then one handful salt and put it back in the vessel with the molasses; turn it over, morning and night for ten days. Hang it up to dry for one week, then smoke a little. It is an excellent plan, after sufficiently smoked, to put each piece of beef in a bag, to protect from insects, and keep hanging till used.—*Miss K. W.*

To Dry Beef and Tongue.

The best pieces are the brisket, the round and rib pieces that are used for roasting. Put about the middle of February in brine. Rub first with salt, and let them lie for a fortnight, then throw them in brine and let them lay there three weeks, take them out and wipe dry: rub them over with bran and hang in a cool place and dark, not letting them touch anything. Should there come a wet season, put them in the sun to dry a little.—*Mrs. R.*

Stewed Loin of Veal.

Take part of a loin of veal, the chump end will do. Put it into a large, thick, well-tinned iron saucepan, or into a stew-pan, add about two ounces of butter, and shake it over a moderate fire until it begins to brown; flour the veal well over, lay it in a saucepan, and when it is of a fine, equal light brown, pour gradually in veal broth, gravy or boiling water, to nearly half its depth; add a little salt, one or two sliced carrots, a small onion, or more when the flavor is liked, and one bunch parsley.

Stew the veal very softly for an hour or rather more, then turn it and let it stew for nearly or quite another hour or longer, should it not appear perfectly done. A longer time must be allowed when the meat is more than middling size. Dish the joint; skim all the fat from the gravy and strain it over the meat, or keep the joint hot while it is rapidly reduced to a richer consistency.—*Mrs. J.*

Veal Chops.

First beat until tender, then lay the chops in a pan, pour in just enough boiling water to barely cover them. Cover closely and simmer till tender, sprinkling over after they are nearly done, with a little pepper and salt. Lift from the pan, dry with a clean towel, butter them, then cover with beaten egg, and sift on cracker crumbs. Lay on a baking dish or pan and set in the stove to brown. Garnish and serve.—*Mrs. S. T.*

Roast Veal.

Plunge into boiling water, dry with a clean cloth; rub well with pepper and salt, then with butter. Dredge with flour, and put into a pan with two teacups of boiling water, a slice of bacon or pork, minced onion and parsley, pepper and salt. Set in a hot oven; simmer, baste and brown. Veal is longer cooking than lamb. When a light brown, with a pin, stick on a buttered paper to prevent dryness. Thicken the gravy with brown flour, if brown gravy is wanted, but always with mashed Irish potato if white gravy is desired.—*Mrs. S. T.*

Veal Steak.

First beat until it is tender, then without washing lay on a gridiron over coals; turn over it a tin plate to prevent hardness and dryness. Turn the steak, and when well done, with a knife and fork press it and turn it in a pan or plate of hot melted butter. After putting in plate of hot butter and letting it absorb as much of the butter as possible, lay it on a dish, pepper and salt it plentifully, and pour over the melted butter. (Set in the oven a few minutes, but not long enough for the butter to fry, which is ruinous to the flavor of steaks, game, etc.) When done, sift over grated cracker. Garnish with parsley and serve hot.—*Mrs. S. T.*

VEAL CUTLET.

Cut the veal as if for steak or frying, put lard or butter in the pan, and let it be hot. Beat up an egg on a plate and have flour on another; dip the pieces first in the egg, then in the flour, on both sides, and lay in the pan and fry until done, turning it carefully once. This makes an excellent dish if well prepared. This way is superior to batter.—*Mrs. D.*

Veal Cutlet.

Cut it in pieces the size of your hand, and lay in salt water some little time. Take out and wipe dry. Put a small piece of lard in the pan and sprinkle the cutlet with a very little flour, pepper, and salt. Fry until nearly done. When it begins to brown, pour off the lard, and pour in a little water, one large spoonful butter, and a little celery-seed. Turn it over frequently.—*Mrs. W.*

Veal Cutlets.

Trim smoothly and beat till tender, sprinkle over pepper and salt; then with a spoon spread over an egg beaten till thick, and cover thickly with pounded cracker.

Have some hot lard ready in the frying-pan, put the cutlets on to fry, with the prepared side down; when of a light yellow brown, dress the other side the same way and fry, keeping closely covered. When they are perfectly done (veal should never be rare), place in a hot dish; pour one teacup o milk, one small piece of butter, pepper, salt, and minced onion and parsley into the pan, stirring constantly. When it boils up, pour into the dish and garnish with parsley. Always sift browned cracker over such dishes.—*Mrs. S. T.*

Cold Veal Dressed with White Sauce.

Boil one pint milk and thicken it a little with one teaspoonful flour, wet with cold water. When well boiled, put in very thin slices of veal, and simmer slowly for fifteen minutes.

Have the yolk of an egg well beaten up, and add to the meat, also a piece of butter.

Let it boil up once, stirring all the time, and serve it on toasted slices of bread. A few slices of bacon, cut thin and fried to a crisp, make a good relish with this dish.—*Mrs. G. P.*

Minced Veal.

Cut some slices of cold veal into small bits or dice; take the cold gravy and add to it a half-pint of boiling water, one teaspoonful tomato or walnut catsup, the grated peel of one lemon, pepper and salt.

Simmer it with the meat slowly for half an hour; then add half a teaspoonful flour made into a thin batter and pour it into the gravy, stirring it rapidly. Boil for ten minutes; turn in one-half cupful cream, or same quantity of milk with a small piece of butter; let it boil up. Serve on a hot platter garnished with sippets of fried bread.—*Mrs. P.*

Veal Loaf.

2 pounds chopped veal.
½ pound chopped pork.
3 tablespoonfuls powdered cracker.
1 tablespoonful sage.
2 tablespoonfuls butter.
1 teaspoonful black pepper.
1 teaspoonful mace.
Salt to taste.
1 egg well beaten and mixed in the ingredients.

Make up into a loaf or pone, and bake slowly three and a half hours. This is an excellent dish to use with lettuce, etc.

in the spring or early autumn, when game is out of season. It is best to be made the day before using.—*Mrs. R. R.*

Veal Loaf.

Two and a half pounds meat taken from fillet or shoulder, or wherever the meat is free from fat. Take out all the little white, fibrous or sinewy particles, and chop very finely, almost to a paste. Mix in rolled cracker crumbs with one egg to hold it together, a little butter, red and black pepper, and salt to taste.

Form into a small loaf; dredge with the cracker crumbs, and put several little pieces of butter over the outside. Set this loaf uncooked, with about one quart water or some broth, in a pan; put it in the oven and baste constantly for two hours, and when taken out to cool, pour any remaining liquid over the loaf. It ought to cut in slices and be quite compact—no caverns in the inside of the loaf.—*Mrs. G. P.*

Veal Cake.

Take one and a half pounds veal, and half a pound of bacon, stew together with very little water, a little salt and pepper, thyme and parsley.

When the veal is tender, cut into small square pieces, as also the bacon.

Boil four eggs hard and slice them up, and chop some raw parsley fine.

Take a mould or small bowl, lay the slices of egg in a kind of pattern prettily at the bottom of it. Sprinkle the parsley between the slices. Add veal, bacon, and more egg alternately, pepper and salt to taste, and a little grated lemon-peel, also some more parsley, and so on until the bowl is nearly full. Fill up with the gravy the veal was boiled in, which ought to be very rich. Let it stand until quite cold, then turn out on a flat dish. The slices cut firmer and more solid when the cake is made the day beforehand, which it is best to do if the weather permits —*Mrs. R. P.*

Sweetbreads.

Three good throat sweetbreads will make a dish. Blanch them well and lay in cold water, then take out and dry well. Add egg, bread crumbs, and herbs.

Put on a dish and brown in an oven. Eat with mushroom or tomato sauce.—*Mrs. R.*

Sweetbreads.

Soak, and put in boiling water for ten minutes.

Stew in cold water to blanch them.

They may be cut in slices or in dice and put in fricassee or meats, or ragoûts, or used as a separate dish.—*Mrs. W.*

Sweetbreads.

Lay them in salt and water, after washing; parboil until done; drain, dry, and split in half. Rub with butter, pepper and salt. Dip in one egg beaten stiff. Sift over pounded cracker.

Butter a baking-dish, lay them in, and set in a hot oven to brown, or fry until a light brown.—*Mrs. S. T.*

Calves' Feet dressed as Terrapins.

Boil eight feet until the meat leaves the bones, then remove them. Put them in a pan with one-half pint of the rich gravy in which they are boiled, and add two large spoonfuls butter.

Rub the yolks of three hard-boiled eggs with a small teaspoonful mustard, a very little cayenne, and salt to the taste.

When well mixed with the egg, stir all together into the feet or gravy. Let it simmer ten minutes, and just before dishing add two wineglasses of good cooking wine and simmer again before serving.—*Mrs. M. E. L. W.*

Calf's Liver Broiled.

Cut the liver in thin slices, wash it and let it stand in salt and water half an hour to draw out the blood. Parboil in

To Fry Calf's Liver.

Cut in thin slices. Season with pepper and salt, sweet herbs, and parsley.

Dredge with flour and fry brown with lard. Have it thoroughly done, but it must not be hard; keep covered while frying.—*Mrs. R.*

Calf's Liver Fried.

A calf's liver, as white as can be procured, flour, one bunch savory herbs, including parsley, juice of a lemon; pepper and salt to taste, a little water.

Cut the liver into slices of a good and equal shape. Dip them in flour and fry brown. Place on a hot dish and keep before the fire while you prepare the gravy. Mince the herbs fine and put into the frying-pan with a little more butter; add the other ingredients with one teaspoonful flour. Simmer gently until the herbs are done, and pour over the liver.—*Mrs. A. M. D.*

Bewitched Liver.

3 pounds calf's liver, chopped fine.
¼ pound salt pork.
1 cup grated bread crumbs.
2 eggs well beaten.
2 teaspoonfuls salt.
2 teaspoonfuls black pepper.
½ teaspoonful red pepper.

Mix all well together, and put into a tin mould; set it in a pot of cold water and let it boil two hours. Then set the mould in a cool oven to dry off a little; when thoroughly cold turn it out.—*Mrs. J. H.*

Simple Way of Cooking Liver.

Wash calf's liver and heart thoroughly; chop them fine as

[page begins:] fresh salt and water, and broil, basting frequently in butter. Lay on a hot dish with a lump of butter.—*Mrs. A. M. D.*

possible, after they have been boiled till very tender; then add pepper and salt, and one tablespoonful flour, straining into it a little of the water.—*Mrs. J. P. H.*

CALF'S BRAINS.

Beat up the brains with a little lemon-peel cut fine, a little nutmeg grated, a little mace beaten, thyme and parsley

Shred fine the yolk of an egg, and dredge with flour. Fry in little flat cakes and lay on top of the baked head.

If for soup, mix in one-half the brains with the soup while the soup is boiling, and make the other in cakes and lay together with forcemeat balls in the soup.—*Mrs. R.*

CALF'S HEAD.

Split the head, take out the brains, boil till it will fall to pieces. Cut it up fine and season with pepper, salt and nutmeg to the taste; add one-quarter pound of butter, wineglassful wine, and the brains, which are not to be boiled with the head. Put in a dish and bake with or without paste.—*Mrs. J. D.*

BAKED CALF'S HEAD.

Boil until tender, then cut into pieces and put into a deep dish with pepper, salt, a few cloves, mace, a little thyme.

A spoonful butter with flour, well mixed through the meat, a layer of bread crumbs on top. Then add a wineglass of wine and fill up the dish with the water the head was boiled in, and bake three-quarters of an hour. Garnish with forcemeat balls and rings of hard-boiled eggs, just before sending to the table. —*Miss N.*

VEAL DAUBE.

After the head of a calf is skinned and the feet prepared by taking off the hoofs, scraping, etc., throw them into cold water for twenty-four hours. Put them in a boiler of cold water, and simmer until the flesh leaves the bones and there is but little water left.

Throw in salt, pepper, minced onion, parsley, and thyme; take the meat and bones out. Beat up two eggs until light, add two tablespoonfuls cold water, then the liquor from the boiler. Stir all together, boil up and strain on the meat from the head, which must first be cut up or picked fine and chopped with six hard-boiled eggs, and seasoned to the taste with the juice of one lemon and wineglass of jelly. This is set aside in a mould or bowl and eaten cold with garnish of scraped horseradish and parsley. The calves' feet make another good dish by drying first, then dipping in batter made of an egg, one spoonful of flour, one small teacupful milk, with a little salt, and frying.—*Mrs. S. T.*

MUTTON AND LAMB.

When the weather will admit of it, mutton is better for being kept a few days before cooking. The saddle, which is considered the finest piece, consists of the back or loin and upper part of the hind legs. In getting this nice roast, however, you spoil the hind quarter, as the saddle takes some of the nicest parts of this and leaves it too dry to cook by itself. The hind quarter and loin together make a very nice dish—the latter being fat and juicy.

The fore quarter is sometimes cut by taking off the shoulder and taking the rib-piece, making a piece called the brisket or breast, and many persons esteem this the choicest part of the mutton. The ribs cut next to the back are used for mutton chops.

When you have a large supply of mutton on hand, it is well to put the hind quarters in brine, as you can thus corn them as nicely as beef. As mutton spoils easily, this plan is very advisable.

Whilst boiled mutton is very nice, lamb is spoiled by this mode of cooking. If lamb is to be roasted, it should be covered with the caul, as the fat, dripping from this, will preserve the moisture of the meat.

In carving the fore quarter of lamb, first take off the shoulder and then cut the ribs in strips.

Lamb is seldom cut except in quarters, and when nicely cooked there is nothing better. It should be four months old before being eaten. The season for lamb is from May to August, whilst that for mutton is from August to Christmas.

To Roast Mutton.

The hind quarter is the nicest part of the mutton to roast, and requires longer to cook than lamb. Put it in a pot of boiling water and let it simmer one hour. Lift it into a baking-pan, rub with salt and pepper (too much salt makes the meat tough). Rub over it a little lard and then dredge with flour: skim off the top of the water and pour over it. Set it in a hot oven, basting frequently to prevent it from being hard and dry; roast till thoroughly done. This is nice to set aside for a cold dish, garnished with horseradish and eaten with currant jelly.—*Mrs. P. W.*

Roast Leg of Mutton.

Choose young and tender mutton. Take off the shank—wash it well; let it lie fifteen or twenty minutes in salt water to take the blood out. Rub with little salt and pepper well. Lay on a grate, which will go nicely in a baking-pan, over one pint boiling water; break the bones of the shank in the water, adding more pepper and salt. Set it in a very hot oven, and baste frequently to prevent it from being hard and dry. When it is of a light brown, cover with sheets of buttered paper. Place it on a dish; add minced parsley to the gravy, which should be brown. Cover the roast with grated brown cracker and garnish at intervals with chopped parsley; pour the gravy in the dish, not over it. Mutton should always be perfectly done.—*Mrs. S. T.*

Roast Saddle of Mutton.

Trim the joint carefully, roast it at a brisk, clear fire; baste frequently, and when done dredge it plentifully with salt, and serve with the gravy well freed from fat.

To Boil a Leg of Mutton.

Make a paste of flour quite plain, mixed stiff with water, roll out as for a meat pudding; break and turn in the shank bone; then cover the leg of mutton carefully with the paste; tie up tight in a well-floured cloth. Have ready sufficient boiling water, place in the joint, allow ten minutes for checking the boiling, and twenty minutes for each pound of meat. Carefully remove the paste, which can be done by one cut longitudinally and one cut across. Strain the gravy and serve as usual.

Boiled Leg of Mutton.

Dip a cloth in hot water, tie up the mutton and put in boiling water. Boil slowly for two hours, or longer, if not kept constantly boiling.—*Mrs. R.*

Broiled Mutton.

After a leg of mutton has been washed and wiped dry, place in a cloth that has been dipped in boiling water. Roll it up, pin and tie securely; put in a pot of boiling water. Let it simmer several hours, removing the scum that rises when it first begins to boil. If a small leg of mutton, it will require a shorter time to cook than a large one. Just before it is done, add enough salt to season it properly, half an onion, and one heaping teaspoonful of black pepper. When this has properly seasoned the meat, take from the fire, unwrap and drain. Serve with drawn butter, adding capers or nasturtium seed, or if you have neither, use chopped sour pickle instead. Mutton should always be served with caper sauce, if possible.—*Mrs. S. T.*

To Cook a Saddle of Mutton.

Meats are all better for being kept a day or two before cooking, particularly mutton. If the mutton be tender, do not boil it, but put it in a pan of water, set it on the stove, and cook slowly, basting constantly with the gravy or water in the pan; with pepper and salt to taste. Just before it is done, put some scraped horseradish over it, and garnish the dish with the same; add a little ground mustard and grated bread or cracker; pour the gravy over it, and grate bread over, and set aside to cool. This is for cold mutton. All meats are better for roasting before a fire than in a stove.—*Mrs. P. W.*

Saddle of Mutton.

This should be covered with paper, and carefully roasted or baked. Season with a little pepper and salt; garnish with horseradish.

Iced Saddle of Mutton.

Reserve the drippings from the meat when it is roasting. After the saddle is nicely cooked, let it get cold. Then take the white part of the gravy and melt it to the consistency of cream. Pour this over the saddle until it is covered with a white coat; if it appears rough, warm an iron spoon and pass over it until it is smooth. Place it on a dish, and dress the dish all round with vegetable flowers and curled parsley, using the parsley to ornament the saddle also.—*Mrs. Judge S.*

To Corn Mutton.

Mutton being less apt to keep than other meat, it is well, when you have an over-supply, to corn it exactly as you would corn beef.—*Miss R. S.*

Shoulder of Mutton Corned.

Take a small shoulder of mutton, rub it with

2 ounces salt.
2 ounces sugar.
½ ounce saltpetre.

After twenty-four hours, rub it again with the pickle; next day boil this in paste like the leg of mutton. Serve smothered in onion sauce.

Mutton Chop.

Get from your butcher nicely shaped mutton chops, not too long. Put them into a pan with pepper and salt, and barely enough water to cover them.

Cover close and simmer till done; drain, wipe dry; pepper, salt and butter them; with a spoon, cover with an egg beaten stiff. Sift over pounded crackers. Put in a pan and set in an oven to brown.—*Mrs. S. T.*

Mutton Chops dressed with Tomatoes.

Place in a pan tomatoes peeled and chopped; season with butter, pepper, sugar, and salt.

Take from your gridiron some nicely broiled mutton chops; put into a pan, cover close, and simmer for fifteen minutes. Lay the chops on a hot dish, put on a little butter, pepper and salt.

With a spoon, cover each chop with tomatoes. Sift over pounded cracker and serve.—*Mrs. S. T.*

Mutton Chop.

Cut the steaks; pepper and salt them. Broil them lightly on both sides; take them off the gridiron, lay them on a spider. Slice up one large onion and stew until it becomes tender; put a layer between each chop and stew until they become tender. Take out the steaks, cover them closely or tilt the gravy to the side of the vessel, till it is brown; stir in a lump of butter.—*Mrs. A. P.*

Mutton Chop.

Mushroom catsup is a nice flavoring. Put pepper and salt on the chops and lay them in melted butter; when they have imbibed sufficient, take out and cover with grated bread crumbs and broil.—*Mrs. R.*

Broiled Mutton Chops.

Beat the mutton chops till tender; then trim, making them of uniform size and shape; pour on them boiling water. Let them remain in it a minute, dry them and rub with pepper, salt, and fresh butter. Lay on a gridiron over hot coals, always remembering to cover them while broiling. Turn them, and as soon as nicely browned place in a hot dish, pepper again, pour over them melted butter, and serve.—*Mrs. S. T.*

Mutton Stew.

Cut slices of rare mutton and put on to stew in a little water; when nearly done put in—

    1 teacup of sweet pickle vinegar.
    3 large spoonfuls jelly.
    A little salt.
    1 teaspoonful mustard.
    ½ teacup of walnut catsup.
    Butter size of an egg.

Stew slowly a short time.—*Mrs. F. D.*

Mutton Stew.

Slice cold mutton or lamb, lay it in a baking dish; put in—
1 teaspoonful black pepper.
1 teaspoonful red pepper.
1 teaspoonful celery-seed, pounded.

Rather more than 1 teaspoonful each of pounded cloves, cinnamon and mace.

1 teacup of yellow pickle vinegar.
1 glassful wine.

Slice up a little yellow pickled cucumber, sugar to taste, one-quarter pound butter, one roll of light bread broken in small pieces or cut in little slices, and toasted before used.

In preparing this dish put a layer of the meat and seasonings alternately.

The peppers, celery-seed, cloves, cinnamon, and mace must all be pounded fine.—*Mrs. C.*

GRILLED SLICES OF MUTTON.

Cut some rather thick slices of underdone cold mutton, score them well and rub in plentifully some common mustard, salt, and cayenne pepper; then broil them over a clear fire, and serve with onion sauce.

SHEEP'S TONGUES.

Boil them till the skin can be taken off; split them, and put them into a stew-pan, with some gravy, parsley, mushrooms, and one minced shallot, and some butter, some pepper, and salt.

Stew till tender, and strain the gravy over them; or they may be glazed and served with the gravy under them. Sheep's tongues may also be skinned, larded, braised, and glazed; and served with onion sauce.

TO ROAST LAMB.

The hind quarter is the nicest piece for roasting. Drop it in a pot of boiling water; boil half an hour, put it in a pan, dredge it with lard, pepper, flour, a little salt; skim the top of the water in which it is boiled, and pour over it; as soon as the gravy accumulates in the pan keep it basted frequently to prevent it from being hard and dry. Lamb should be cooked done to be good.—*Mrs. P. W.*

TO GRILL A SHOULDER OF LAMB.

Half boil it, score and cover it with egg, crumbs, and parsley seasoned as for cutlets. Broil it over a very clear, slow fire, or put it in a Dutch oven to brown it; serve with any sauce that is liked. A breast of lamb is often grilled in the same way.

LAMB'S HEAD TO FRICASSEE.

Parboil the head and haslet (the liver excepted): cut the meat in slices from the head; slice the heart, tongue, etc., and fricassee as for chicken. Have the liver fried in slices with the sweetbreads and slices of bacon and bunches of parsley. Pour the fricassee into the dish, and garnish with the fried pieces.—*Mrs. R.*

LAMB'S HEAD.

Boil the head and liver, but so as not to let the liver be too much done. Take up the head, split it through the bone, which must remain with the meat on. Cut the meat across and across with a knife, grate some nutmeg on it and lay it on a dish before a good fire; then throw over it some grated bread crumbs, some sweet herbs, some allspice, a little lemon peel chopped fine, a very little pepper and salt. Baste it with butter, and dredge a little flour over it.

Just as it is done, take one-half the liver, the lights, the meat, the tongue; chop them small with six or eight spoonfuls water or gravy. First shake some flour over the meat and stew it together; then put in the gravy or water, a good piece of butter rolled in a little flour, pepper and salt, and what runs from the head in the dish. Simmer all together a few minutes, and add half a spoonful of vinegar; pour it on the head. Lay the head on the centre of the mince-meat; have ready the other half of liver, cut in pieces and fried quickly with slices of bacon and lemon; lay these around the dish and serve.—*Mrs. T.*

DECORATIONS AND GARNISHES FOR COLD MEATS AND SALADS.

The day before giving a dinner or evening entertainment, gather up medium and small sized pure white and yellow turnips, carrots, red and pink beets, the different colored radishes. From these the most beautiful flowers can be cut; camellias, roses, dahlias, tulips, tuberoses, etc. No explicit directions can be given except, first, smoothly to pare each vegetable, taking care not to keep them too near the fire, which will cause them to wilt and lose the waxy freshness which makes them so beautiful. Each flower may be laid on a cluster of green leaves or curled parsley, and over the cold meats, and around the edge of the dish.

The cutting of these flowers makes a charming and interesting pastime for the young members of the family, in the evening before.—*Mrs. C. G.*

POULTRY.

In summer, kill and dress the poultry the day beforehand, except chicken for frying, which is not good unless killed the same day it is eaten.

The best way to kill a fowl is to tie it by its legs, hang it up, and then cut off its neck. In this way, it dies more quickly, suffers less, and bleeds more freely.

It is best to pick fowls dry; though, if you are pressed for time, you may facilitate the picking of chickens, as well as of partridges and other small birds, by putting them first into water, hot, but not boiling. Then take off the feathers carefully, so as not to break the skin. Never scald a turkey, duck or goose, however, before picking.

To draw the crop, split the skin of all poultry on the back of the neck. Pull the neck upward and the skin downward, and the crop can be easily pulled out. Then cut off the neck close to the body, leaving the skin to skewer at the back of the neck after the dressing has been put in. Make an incision under the rump lengthwise, sufficient to allow the entrails to be easily removed. Be careful not to break the gall, and to preserve the liver whole. Cut open the gizzard, take out the inner skin, and wash both carefully. Wash the bird inside several times, the last time with salt and water. Some persons object to using water inside or outside, but I consider it more cleanly to wash the bird first and then wipe it dry with a clean towel. It should then be hung with the neck downwards till ready to cook.

The head, neck, and feet, after being nicely washed and the bones in them broken, should be stewed in the gravy, as they make it much richer.

It is said that throwing chickens into cold water immediately after they have finished bleeding, and allowing them to remain there ten or fifteen minutes, will make them deliciously tender, which can be accounted for scientifically. Frozen fowls or game should be thawed gradually, by being laid in cold water. If cooked without being thawed, it will require double time, and they will not be tender nor high-flavored.

The tests by which you may tell the age of a turkey are these. An old turkey has rough and red legs, and if a gobbler, long spurs, while young turkeys have black legs, and if gobblers, small spurs. The fatter they are and the broader their breasts, the better. When dressed, the skin should be a yellowish white, and, if tender, you may easily rip it with a pin. If, when you bend back the wings, the sinews give and crack, this is another test of the turkey being young, and the same test will apply to other fowls. The bill and feet of an old goose are red and hairy. A young goose has pen feathers and its flesh is whiter than that of an old one.

If young, the lower part of a hen's legs and feet are soft and smooth, while a young cock has small spurs. When dressed, the flesh should be white and the fat a pale yellow. Turn the wing back, and if the sinews snap it is a sign the chicken is young.

A few words on the subject of carving may not be out of place here. A sharp knife, with a thin and well tempered blade is essential to good carving. In carving a turkey, cut off first the wing nearest to you, then the leg and second joint, then slice the breast till a rounded, ivory-shaped piece appears. Insert the knife between that and the bone, and separate them. This part is the nicest bit of the breast. Next comes the merry-thought. After this, turn over the bird a little, and just below the breast you will find the oyster, which you will separate as you did the inner breast. The side bone lies beside the rump, and the desired morsel can be taken out without separating the whole bone. Proceed with the other side in the same way. The fork need not be removed during the whole process.

Chicken and partridges are carved in the same way.

Roast Turkey.

Wash nicely in and out. Plunge into boiling water ten minutes. Have ready a dressing of

> Bread crumbs.
> Hard boiled eggs, chopped fine.
> 1 tablespoonful butter.
> Minced parsley, thyme and celery.

After rubbing the cavity well with salt and pepper and putting in a slice of pork or bacon, fill with the above dressing. Do the same also to the crop, so as to make the turkey look plump. Rub the turkey well with butter and sprinkle salt and pepper over it. Dredge with flour. Lay in the pan with a slice of pork or bacon and a pint of boiling water. Lay the liver and gizzard in the pan with it. Put in a hot oven, basting and turning frequently till every part is a beautiful brown. When the meat is amber color, pin a buttered sheet of writing paper over it to keep it from becoming hard and dry. Cook three or four hours. Season the gravy with minced parsley and celery and serve with cranberry sauce.—*Mrs. S. T.*

Roast Turkey.

Wash the turkey thoroughly inside and out, having removed

the insides. Make a dressing of bread soaked in cold water, drained and mashed fine, a small piece of melted butter or salt pork chopped, pepper and salt, sweet herbs, a hard boiled egg, chopped fine.

Any kind of cooked meat is good, minced fine and added to the dressing. The body and crop must be filled with the dressing and sewed up. The giblets ought to be boiled tender, if they are to be used. Use the water in which they are boiled, for gravy, adding a little of the turkey drippings, seasoning with pepper, salt, and sweet herbs, and thickening with a little flour and water, mixed smoothly. Place where it will boil.

When the fowl is put on to roast, put a little water into the dripping-pan. At first it should be roasted slowly and basted frequently. Tie up the wings and legs before roasting, and rub on a little butter and salt. Serve with drawn butter.—*Mrs. W.*

Roast Turkey.

Put the gizzard, heart and liver in cold water and boil till tender. When done, chop fine and add stale bread, grated, salt and pepper, sweet herbs, if liked, two eggs well beaten.

Fill the turkey with this dressing, sew the openings, drawing the skin tightly together. Put a little butter over the turkey and lay it upon the grate of your meat-pan. Cover the bottom of the pan well with boiling water. In half an hour, baste the turkey by pouring over it the gravy that has begun to form in the pan. Repeat this basting every fifteen minutes. In an oven of average temperature, a twelve-pound turkey will require at least three hours' cooking.—*Mrs. A. D.*

ROAST TURKEY, WITH TRUFFLES.

Truffles must be peeled, chopped and pounded in a mortar; one and a half pound will do for one turkey. Rasp the same amount of fat bacon and mix with the truffles and stuff the turkey with it. This dressing is usually placed in the turkey two days beforehand, to impart its flavor to the fowl. Lay thin slices of fat bacon over the breast of the turkey, cover it with half a sheet of white paper, and roast two hours. Chestnuts dressed in the same way as truffles are found an excellent substitute.—*Mrs. S. G.*

Boiled Turkey.

Wash well with cold water, then put on in milk-warm water, either tied in a coarse cloth dredged with flour or with a half-pound of rice in the water. Keep well under water, and boil slowly three hours, adding salt just before it is done. When perfectly done and tender, take out of the pot, sprinkle in the cavity a little pepper and salt, and fill with oysters stewed just enough to plump them, and season, with butter, pepper, salt and vinegar. Place in a dish and set in a steamer to keep hot. Strain the liquor in which the oysters were scalded, add drawn butter, chopped celery, parsley and thyme; pour over the turkey, and serve. If not convenient to use oysters, use egg and butter sauce. Garnish with sliced lemons.—*Mrs. S. T.*

Boiled Turkey.

Prepare the turkey as for roasting. Tie it in a cloth or boil rice in the pot with it, if you wish it to look white. It is improved by boiling a pound or two of salt pork with it. If soup is made of the liquor, let it stand till next day and skim the fat. Season after heating.—*Mrs. W.*

To Steam a Turkey.

Rub butter, pepper and salt inside the turkey after it has been well washed, fill with oysters, sew up, lay in a dish and set in a steamer placed over boiling water. Cover closely and steam from two hours to two and a half. Take up, strain the gravy which will be found in the dish. Have an oyster sauce ready, prepared like stewed oysters, and pour into it this gravy thickened with a little butter and flour. Let it come to a boil and whiten with a little boiled cream. Pour this over the steamed turkey and send to the table hot. Garnish with sliced lemons.—*Mrs. S. T.*

Turkey Hash.

Cut up the meat very fine. Stew the bones in a little water, then stir into this water the meat, adding a large tablespoonful butter, a cup of cream, salt and pepper, a little chopped parsley, thyme or celery (or else a very few celery-seeds). Stew all together.—*Mrs. R.*

Devilled Turkey.

Place the legs and wings (jointed) on a gridiron. Broil slowly. Have ready a sauce made of—

1 tablespoonful pepper vinegar.
1 tablespoonful made mustard.
1 tablespoonful celery sauce.
1 tablespoonful acid fruit jelly.
A little salt and pepper.

Lay the broiled turkey on a hot dish. Pour the dressing and sift pounded cracker over it.—*Mrs. S. T.*

Potato Stuffing for Turkeys and other Fowls.

Mash smoothly six good-sized boiled Irish potatoes. Chop a small onion very fine and fry a light brown, in a frying-pan, with a dessertspoonful lard. Then add the potatoes with salt and pepper, and a lump of butter as large as a walnut. To this add one well beaten egg, stirring till perfectly dry. If for geese or ducks, add a little sifted sage and a small quantity of red pepper.—*Mrs. McG.*

Boned Turkey.

The turkey must be full grown, moderately fat, and picked dry. Do not remove the entrails. Cut off the neck about one inch from the body. Take off the wings above the second joint and cut off the legs as usual. With a sharp pointed knife, split the skin from the end of the neck to the rump. Run the knife between the bones and flesh on one side, till you come to

BONED TURKEY.

where the wing and leg join the body. Twist the wing and raise it, cracking the joint. Separate it from the body. Then proceed with the leg in the same way, on the same side. Run the knife between the bones and flesh till you reach the breast bone. Repeat this on the other side. Take out the craw. Carefully run a sharp knife under the rump, detaching it from the bone without cutting the skin, as it must come off with the flesh. Hold the turkey by the neck and pull the skin carefully down, until the upper part of the breast bone is uncovered. Cut the flesh from the bone on both sides, till the end of the bone is nearly reached. The turkey must now be laid on the back and held by the neck, the front of the turkey being toward you. Take hold of the skin of the neck with the left hand, pulling downwards with a knife in the right hand, separate the skin from the end of the bone. The whole of the turkey is now detached from the carcass. Lay it on a table with the skin down. Pull the bones from the wings and legs, first running the knife around so as to leave the flesh. Pull out all the tendons of the legs. Push them and the wings inside. Cut off the ring under the rump. All this must be done slowly and carefully. Have ready a half-dozen slices of salt pork, and a salad made of shoat, veal or lamb, chopped and seasoned, as turkey salad, with celery, etc. Mix with this salad three or four large Irish potatoes, boiled and mashed, with a spoonful of butter. Now lay the turkey on the table, inside up and the neck from you; pepper and salt it; lay three or four slices of pork on it, then a layer of the salad; pork again and salad alternately until filled; draw the two sides together and sew it up, giving it as near as possible its proper shape. Sew it up carefully in a cloth, place in a kettle of the proper shape, cover with boiling water, adding the broken bones, three pounds fresh lean beef, parsley, thyme, onions and two dozen whole black peppercorns, with salt to the taste. Simmer three hours, then take it from the water and remove the towel. Carefully remove all discolorations and settlings of the water from the turkey. Scald a clean cloth, wrap it up again; place it on its back, put a dish over it with a weight on it and set it in a cool place till next day. Unwrap and remove the twine with which it was sewed. Glaze it with a little meat jelly; just before the jelly congeals sift over a little cracker browned and pounded; decorate with meat jelly and serve. Directions for preparing meat jelly follow.—*Mrs. S. T.*

Meat Jelly for Boned Turkey.

As soon as the water in which the turkey was boiled is cold, take off all the fat and strain it, put it in a porcelain-lined kettle; two ounces gelatine, three eggs, with shells, a wine-glass of sherry, port or madeira wine; stir well. Add one quart of the strained liquor; beat rapidly with an egg-beater, put it on the fire and stir until it boils. Simmer ten or fifteen minutes. Sprinkle in a pinch of turmeric and strain just as any other jelly. When congealed break it up and place around the turkey. Cut some in thick slices and in fanciful shapes with paste cutters. Place some of these lozenges over the turkey and border the edges of the dish with them.—*Mrs. S. T.*

Chickens.

These, whether for boiling or roasting, should have a dressing prepared as for turkeys. Six spoonfuls of rice boiled with the chickens will cause them to look white. If the water is cold when they are put in, they will be less liable to break. They are improved by boiling a little salt pork with them. If not thus boiled, they will need salt.

For broiling, chickens should be split, the inwards taken out, and the chickens then washed. Broil very slowly till done, placing the bony side down; then turn it and brown the other side. Forty minutes is the medium time for broiling a chicken.

For roast hicken, boil the gizzard and liver by themselves, and use the water for gravy.—*Mrs. Col. W.*

Roast Chicken.

Chicken should never be cooked the same day it is killed. Wash well with cold water, then pour boiling water over it and into the cavity. Rub the latter with salt and pepper, and fill with a dressing made of bread soaked in water and squeezed out, a tablespoonful butter, a little salt, pepper and parsley.

Rub the chicken well with butter. Sprinkle pepper and salt over it and dredge with flour. Lay it into a pan with a slice of pork or bacon and a pint of water. Let it simmer slowly two hours, basting and dredging frequently. Turn the chicken so each part may be equally browned. Add chopped thyme and parsley to the gravy.

Some persons think ground ginger a more delicate flavoring for the dressing than pepper.—*Mrs. S. T.*

To Boil Chicken.

Never boil the same day the chicken is killed. Soak them overnight in weak salt and water. Place in a kettle of water, with a handful of rice and a little milk to make the chicken white. Simmer slowly two or three hours, removing the scum that rises when the chicken first begins to boil. Keep under the water, with an inverted deep plate. Just before taking off the fire, add salt to the taste. Lay on a hot dish near the fire. Skim off the fat from the top of the liquor, strain it and add chopped celery, parsley and thyme, drawn butter, a little pepper and salt, or, if preferred, six hard-boiled eggs chopped fine.—*Mrs. S. T.*

To Steam Chicken.

Soak two hours, in salt and water, a fat young pullet. Drain and dry. Rub in the cavity a little salt and pepper and a large lump of butter. Fill with large, plump oysters, seasoned with pepper and salt, and sew up. Lay the chicken on a dish or pan, and set it inside a steamer, which close and keep over boiling water four hours. When thoroughly done, lay on a dish and pour over it drawn butter or celery sauce. Garnish with curled parsley, and serve.—*Mrs. S. T.*

SMOTHERED CHICKEN.

Kill the day before it is smothered. Split open the back, as if to broil. When ready to cook, wipe dry with a clean towel, rub well with butter and sprinkle with pepper and salt. Put in a pan with a slice of bacon or pork and a pint of water. Simmer an hour or more, basting frequently. When thoroughly done, place on a hot dish.

Stir into the gravy remaining on the fire a beaten egg, mixing it carefully. Pour this into the dish, but not on the chicken. Sift over it cracker, first browned and then pounded. Garnish with parsley, and serve.—*Mrs. S. T.*

STEWED CHICKEN.

Cut up the chicken as if to fry, adding the prepared head and feet. Soak in weak salt and water. If for dinner, do this immediately after breakfast.

An hour and a half before dinner, put in a saucepan, covering well with water. Let it simmer slowly for one hour. Take it out with a fork and lay in a bowl. Add a teacup milk and half a teaspoonful black pepper to the liquor. Let it boil up and strain on the chicken. Rinse the saucepan and return all to the fire. Beat one egg with a tablespoonful of flour and one of milk until quite smooth. Mince some parsley, thyme, and a very little onion, and stir all into the saucepan. Then put in a tablespoonful of butter. Stir around and pour into a dish in which small pieces of toast have been neatly arranged. Garnish with curled parsley.—*Mrs. S. T.*

Stewed Chicken.

Cut up and lay in salt and water. Put them in water enough to cover them, with some slices of middling. Let them boil till nearly done. Then put in the dumplings, made like biscuit but rolled thin, and let them boil till done. Roll a piece of butter in flour, with pepper, salt, chopped parsley and celery, or a little celery-seed. When the gravy is thick enough, pour in a teacup of cream or milk, and let it boil up once. Take off the fire and serve hot.—*Mrs. Col. W.*

Fried Chicken.

This dish is best when the chicken is killed the same day it is fried. Cut off the wings and legs, cut the breast in two, and also the back. Wash well and throw in weak salt and water, to extract the blood. Let it remain for half an hour or more. Take from the water, drain and dry with a clean towel, half an hour before dinner. Lay on a dish, sprinkle a little salt over it, and sift flour thickly first on one side and then on the other, letting it remain long enough for the flour to stick well. Have ready on the frying-pan some hot lard, in which lay each piece carefully, not forgetting the liver and gizzard. Cover closely and fry till a fine amber color. Then turn over each piece and cover well again, taking care to have the chicken well done, yet not scorched. Take the chicken up and lay in a hot dish near the fire. Pour into the gravy a teacup of milk, a teaspoonful of butter, a saltspoon of salt, and one of pepper. Let it boil up and pour into the dish, but not over the chicken. Put curled parsley round the edge of the dish and serve.—*Mrs. S. T.*

Fried Chicken.

Kill the chicken the night before, if you can, and lay on ice, or else kill early in the morning. When ready, wipe dry, flour it, add pepper and salt, and fry in a little lard. When nearly done, pour off the lard, add one-half teacup water, large spoonful butter, and some chopped parsley. Brown nicely and serve. Meal mush fried is nice with the chicken.—*Mrs. Col. W.*

To Dress Chickens with Tomatoes.

Fry till a light brown. Then add some tomatoes, cut in

small pieces, with the juice. Strain the tomatoes from the seed, season them with salt, pepper, a little sugar, and let them stew.—*Mrs. J. B. D.*

To Fricassee Chicken.

Wash and joint the chicken; place the pieces in a stew-pan with the skin side down. Sprinkle salt and pepper on each piece. Add three or four slices of pork, stew till tender, take them out and thicken the liquor with flour, and add a piece of butter the size of a hen's egg. Replace the chicken in the pan and let it stew five minutes longer. When it is taken up, soak in the gravy some pieces of toast, put them on plates and lay the chicken on the toast, pouring the gravy over it. To brown the chicken, stew till tender, without the pork; brown the pork, take that up, then put in the chicken and fry a light brown.—*Mrs. Col. W.*

To Broil Chicken.

Kill the chicken the day before using, split open in the back, nicely clean, and, if the weather is warm, slightly sprinkle with salt. If for breakfast, half an hour before press between the folds of a clean towel till dry, grease well with fresh butter, sprinkle with pepper and salt and lay on a gridiron, over hot coals, with the inside of the chicken down. Let it cook principally from this side, but turn often till the outside of the chicken is of a bright, yellow brown. When thoroughly done, pour over it melted butter, sprinkle pepper, and sift pounded or grated cracker.—*Mrs. S. T.*

Chicken Pie.

Cut up the chicken and place in a deep oven with one large spoonful of lard. Let it brown a little and add one onion, parsley, thyme, sage and black pepper, to suit the taste. Pour on it a cupful boiling water, stir well and let it simmer till well cooked. Just before taking from the fire, rub together:

1 cup cream.
1 spoonful butter.

Yolks of 2 hard-boiled eggs.

1 grated nutmeg and other spices to the taste.

Stir well and pour in a pan lined with a paste.—*Mrs. A. C.*

Chicken Pie.

Make into a paste one quart of flour with the weight of four eggs in butter and a large spoonful of lard. Put the paste in a deep dish, lining the bottom and side with chicken interspersed with layers of very thin bacon. Add some large crumbs, some pepper, and a quarter-pound butter. Fill the dish with cold water, and yolks of four or six hard-boiled eggs, then dredge with flour and put on the top crust. Let it bake gradually. It will take two hours to bake.—*Mrs. Col. W.*

CHICKEN PUDDING.

Cut up the chicken and stew it a little, after which lay the pieces in a buttered dish with a few bits of butter, a little pepper and salt, and a little of the water in which the chicken was stewed.

Make a batter of one quart milk, five eggs, a little salt. Pour this batter over the chicken, and bake half an hour.—*Mrs. A. B.*

Chicken Pudding.

10 eggs beaten very light.

1 quart rich milk.

¼ pound melted butter.

Pepper and salt to the taste.

Stir in enough flour to make a thin, good batter. Put four young chickens, nicely prepared and jointed, in a saucepan, with some salt and water and a bundle of thyme or parsley. Boil till nicely done, then take up the chickens and put in the batter. Put all in a deep dish and bake. Serve with gravy in a boat.—*Mrs. Dr. C.*

CHICKEN PUDDING WITH POTATOES.

Cut up a young chicken as if to fry, and parboil it. Boil and mash Irish potatoes. Beat up three or four eggs, add to the potatoes, and thin with milk. Season with butter, pepper and salt, stir in the chicken, and bake it.

Boiled rice is a good substitute for potatoes.—*Mrs. E. W.*

N. B.—Most of the recipes given for turkey apply to peafowl, and most of those given for chicken may be used for guinea fowl.—*Mrs. S. T.*

To Roast Goose.

A goose must never be eaten the same day it is killed. If the weather is cold, it should be kept a week before using. Before cooking let it lie several hours in weak salt and water, to remove the strong taste. Then plunge it in boiling water, for five minutes, if old. Fill the goose with a dressing made of:

Mealy Irish potatoes, boiled and mashed fine.

A small lump of butter.

A little salt or fresh pork chopped fine.

A little minced onion.

Parsley, thyme, and a pinch of chopped or powdered sage.

Grease with sweet lard or butter. Lay in a pan with the giblets, neck, etc. Pour in two teacups of boiling water, set in a hot oven, and baste frequently. Turn so that every part may be equally browned. Serve with gravy or onion sauce.

The above recipe will answer equally as well for duck.—*Mrs. S. T.*

Devilled Goose.

Plunge the goose into a pot of boiling water and let it remain half an hour. Fill with a stuffing made of:

Mashed Irish potatoes, a heaping tablespoonful butter, minced onions, sage, parsley and thyme, half a teaspoonful black pepper.

Place it in a pan with a slice of fat pork and a pint of broth or liquor in which any kind of meat has been boiled.

Mix two tablespoonfuls pepper vinegar, celery vinegar, made

mustard, and one of acid fruit jelly. Butter the breast of the goose and pour this mixture over it, adding salt and pepper to the taste.

Place in a hot oven, dredge with flour and baste frequently till done; when serve with its own gravy. This receipt will answer equally as well for wild goose.—*Mrs. S. T.*

To Prepare Young Ducks.

Kill and hang to drain. Plunge, one at a time, in boiling water, then immediately in cold water, which makes them easier to pick. Kill some days before using, or if obliged to use them the same day as killed, they are better roasted.—*Mrs. R.*

To Stew Ducks.

Truss the ducks and stuff them with bread, butter, and onion. Flour them and brown them in lard. Have prepared slips of bacon, giblets, onion, water, pepper, salt, and a little clove or mace, if you like. Put in the ducks and let them stew gently but constantly for two hours. Then add the juice of green grapes or of a lemon, or else a little lemon pickle. Flour the ducks each time you turn them, and thicken with butter rolled in flour.—*Mrs. Col. W.*

SALADS.

In making salads, be careful to add the vinegar last. Where oil cannot be obtained, fresh butter, drawn or melted, is an excellent substitute and is indeed preferred to oil by some persons, epicureans to the contrary notwithstanding. Always use good cider vinegar in making salads, as chemical vinegar is sometimes very unwholesome. Much depends on the rotation in which you mix the ingredients for a salad, so I would call particular attention to the directions given on this point on the subsequent pages.

Oyster Salad.

½ gallon fresh oysters.
The yolks of four hard-boiled eggs.
1 raw egg, well whipped.
2 large spoonfuls salad oil or melted butter.
2 teaspoonfuls salt.
2 teaspoonfuls black pepper.
2 teaspoonfuls made mustard.
1 teacup good vinegar.
2 good sized pickled cucumbers, cut up fine.
Nearly as much celery as oysters, cut up into small dice.

Drain the liquor from the oysters and throw them into some hot vinegar on the fire; let them remain until they are *plump*, not cooked. Then put them at once into clear cold water; this gives them a nice plump look and they will not then shrink and look small. Drain the water from them and set them away in a cool place, and prepare your dressing. Mash the yolks as fine as you can and rub into it the salt, pepper, and mustard, then rub the oil in, a few drops at a time. When it is all smooth, add the beaten egg, and then the vinegar, a spoonful at a time. Set aside. Mix oysters, celery, and pickle, tossing up well with a silver fork. Sprinkle in salt to your taste. Then pour dressing over all.—*Mrs. E. P. G.*

Salmon and Lobster Salad.

If the salmon salad is made of the fish preserved in cans, drain it from the oil and mince the meat fine. Cut up one third as much lettuce or celery.

For one box of salmon, boil four eggs hard; lay them in cold water a few minutes, shell and separate the whites from the yolks; lay the whites aside. Mash the yolks smooth with two tablespoonfuls sweet olive oil or one teacup sweet rich milk or cream. The oil makes the smoothest and best paste. Dissolve in one teacup vinegar,

>   1 tablespoonful sugar.
>   1 teaspoonful salt.
>   2 or more teaspoonfuls fine mustard.
>   Pepper to the taste.

Mix this with the paste and toss lightly over the meat with a silver fork. Ornament the dish in which it is served with the green leaves of the celery, or with curled parsley and the whites of eggs cut in rings.

Lobster salad is prepared in the same way. Take the nicest parts of the lobster.—*Mrs. C. C.*

LOBSTER SALAD.

Chop up one can of lobsters; cut in small pieces as much celery. Then cream with one teacup butter, one tablespoonful mustard, one tablespoonful sugar, one teaspoonful salt, and yolks of four hard boiled eggs, rubbed smooth; stir in five tablespoonfuls pepper vinegar (simply pepper steeped in vinegar and sweetened with a little sugar), and pour the mixture over the lobster and celery.—*Mrs. S. T.*

FISH SALAD.

Boil four flounders, or any medium sized fish; when done, take off the skin and pick out the bones, then shred very fine. Add pepper and salt, one tablespoonful mixed mustard, a half cup vinegar, and half a pound butter, and mix all well with the fish. Put into shallow pans, set in the oven and bake ten minutes. When cold put over it a little Worcestershire sauce, and sherry wine.—*Miss F. N.*

TERRAPIN SALAD.

Boil them until the shells will come off easily and the nails pull out; then cut into small pieces and carefully remove the sand-bag and gall.

TURKEY SALAD.

To three good sized terrapins, take six hard-boiled eggs; remove the yolks and rub into a powder with half a pound sweet butter. When creamy and light, add one teaspoonful flour. Put this with the meat into a saucepan; season with cayenne pepper and salt, and let it boil for one or two minutes. Just before taking from the fire, add wine to taste, and if desired, a little mace.

Be careful to remove the skin from the legs.—*Mrs. A. M. D.*

TURKEY SALAD.

Mince the turkey very fine. Have ready the following mixture, for a large company.

Twelve or fourteen eggs boiled hard; mash the yolks smooth with one spoonful water; add to it pepper, salt, and mustard to the taste. Two teaspoonfuls celery-seed, one teacup of fresh melted butter or fine olive oil, and pour in strong vinegar to the taste.

Mix the turkey and celery, and pour over the mixture just before eating.—*Mrs. F. C. W.*

Turkey Salad.

Remove the skin and fat from a turkey; mince the meat fine.

    Mince 2 or 3 slices lean ham.

    2 or 3 bunches celery.

    3 or 4 apples.

    3 or 4 cucumber pickles; mix well together.

Prepare a dressing of the yolks of four eggs, rubbed in a little thick cream.

        4 tablespoonfuls butter.

        2 teaspoonfuls black pepper.

        2 teaspoonfuls salt.

        2 teaspoonfuls of mustard.

        Vinegar to the taste.

—*Mrs. Dr. S.*

Turkey Salad.

Boil two turkeys till well done, pick out all the bones, skin and fat, and cut up the balance in small pieces.

Boil one dozen eggs hard, let them cool, then separate the yolks and whites, mash the yolks fine, chop the whites very fine and set them to one side.

Have a large flat dish, in which put four large spoonfuls mixed mustard; pour in a little oil, and with a fork rub it in till smooth, then a little vinegar, in which has been melted two full tablespoonfuls of salt, then oil, and alternately put in oil and vinegar, each time rubbing it in till well mixed. When you have mixed a whole bottle of oil and one pint vinegar till it is as smooth as butter, add one heaping teaspoonful cayenne pepper, three teaspoonfuls celery-seed rubbed fine in a mortar, and one large mango cut fine, put in stuffing and all.

Have ready as much celery as you have fowl, cut fine, mix meat and celery carefully together, and pour the dressing over all.—*Mrs. E. I.*

Chicken Salad.

One large chicken boiled; when cold remove the skin and chop into a dish, over which throw a towel slightly dipped in cold water to keep the meat moist. When the celery is cut, put between clean cloths to dry.

Take one tablespoonful best mustard, the yolk of one raw egg, which drop into a dish large enough to hold all the dressing; beat well for ten minutes and slowly add to the mustard one tablespoonful vinegar.

When well mixed add three-eighths bottle of oil, a drop at a time, always stirring the same way.

Rub the yolks of six hard-boiled eggs very smooth and stir in half a teacup of vinegar. Pour this mixture to the mustard, oil, etc., stirring together as lightly as possible.

Add to the chicken one pint chopped celery, a little yellow pickle, and half a loaf of stale bread crumbs, and the oil taken from the water in which the chicken has boiled. Salt and pepper to taste.

Pour on the dressing just before serving. If the salad is kept too cool the dressing will curdle.—*Mrs. E.*

Chicken Salad.

The meat of 2 boiled fowls chopped very fine.
2 or 3 heads of cabbage cut fine.
1 cup olive oil.
½ pint vinegar.
Yolks of 9 hard-boiled eggs.
1 gill made mustard.
1 small teaspoonful black pepper.
1 small teaspoonful salt.

Mix smoothly with the oil and then add the vinegar.—*Miss N.*

Chicken Salad for Thirty-five People.

Yolks of 4 eggs beaten lightly.
¼ box of mixed mustard, and salt to the taste.

Add slowly, beating all the time, one large sized bottle of best salad oil. Lastly, add two-thirds teacup of vinegar.—*Mrs. C. C. McP.*

Chicken Salad.

1 head cabbage.
2 heads celery.
2 chickens finely minced.
10 eggs.
3 small cucumber pickles.
1 tablespoonful mustard.
A little cayenne pepper.
½ cup butter; ½ cup cream.
1 onion.
1 teaspoonful sugar.

Boil the eggs hard, mash the yolks, put in the seasoning with a little vinegar.

Chop up the whites of the eggs, the pickle, chicken, cabbage and celery—then mix. If liked, add a little olive oil.—*Mrs. O. B.*

Chicken Salad.

Boil a chicken; while warm, mince it, taking out the bones. Put it in a stewpan with boiling water. Then stir together until smooth, one quarter of a pound butter, one teaspoonful flour and yolk of one raw egg; all of which add to the chicken one half at a time, stirring all well together.

Season with salt and pepper.

Let it simmer ten minutes; then add half a gill of Madeira wine, and send to the table while hot.—*Mrs. P.*

CELERY SALAD.

2 boiled eggs.
1 raw egg.
2 tablespoonfuls melted butter, or 1 of oil.
1 tablespoonful sugar.
1 teaspoonful mustard.
½ teaspoonful salt.
½ teaspoonful pepper.
½ teacup vinegar.

Rub the yolks of eggs smooth, then add the oil, mustard, etc., the vinegar last. Cut the celery into pieces half an inch long. Set all in a cool place.

Just before serving sprinkle over a little salt and black pepper, then pour over the dressing.

If you have any cold fowl, chicken, or turkey left from dinner, chop it up and mix it with some of the above—equal proportions of both—and it will make a delicious salad; or a few oysters left in the tureen will be a great addition to the celery salad.—*Mrs. S. T.*

Tomato Salad.

8 large tomatoes.
1 tablespoonful made mustard.
1 tablespoonful salad oil.
2 tablespoonfuls white sugar.
4 hard-boiled eggs.
1 raw egg beaten.
2 teaspoonfuls salt.
1 saltspoon nearly full cayenne pepper.
¾ teacup vinegar.

First rub the yolks of eggs smooth, adding mustard, oil, sugar, salt, pepper and beaten raw egg—then the vinegar. The tomatoes should be peeled and sliced and set in the refrigerator—the dressing also.

Just before serving, cover the tomatoes with ice broken up; sprinkle over a little salt and pour over the dressing.—*Mrs. S. T.*

A Salad of Turnips.

Scrape six common sized turnips.
Add 2 cups of sugar.
1 or more cups vinegar.
Mustard, celery-seed, and pepper to taste.

—*Mrs. G. A. B.*

Potato Salad.

Boil your potatoes very carefully; or, rather, steam them until very dry and mealy; cut in slices and prepare a dressing of egg, onion, mustard, oil, pepper, salt, and vinegar, and pour over them.— *W. S. S.*

Veal and Potato Salad.

Take equal proportions of cold veal and boiled Irish potatoes.

Shred the veal and cut up the potatoes. Season with a little butter or oil, vinegar, salt, pepper, celery, and mustard.—*Mrs. R.*

Irish Potato Salad.

Cut ten or twelve cold boiled potatoes into small pieces. Put into a salad bowl with—

    4 tablespoonfuls vinegar.
    4 tablespoonfuls best salad oil.
    1 teaspoonful minced parsley.
    Pepper and salt to taste.

Stir all well that they may be thoroughly mixed; it should be made several hours before putting on the table.

Throw in bits of pickle, cold fowl, a garnish of grated cracker, and hard-boiled eggs.—*Mrs. C. V. McG., Alabama.*

Potato Salad.

To one quart potatoes mashed fine and rubbed through a colander:

    1 tablespoonful fresh butter.
    1 teaspoonful salt.
    1 teacupful rich milk.

Cream all together and beat until light.

Rub the yolks of three hard-boiled eggs with—

    2 teaspoonfuls mustard.
    2 teaspoonfuls sugar.
    1 teaspoonful pepper.
    1 teaspoonful salt.
    Enough pepper vinegar to moisten.

Then chop the whites of the eggs very fine and mix in.

Put a layer of the potatoes in the salad-bowl and with a spoon put the dressing over in spots. Another layer of potatoes, then the dressing, and so on, putting the dressing on top. Garnish with curled parsley, and serve.—*Mrs. S. T.*

Lettuce Salad.

Take two large lettuces, after removing the outer leaves and rinsing the rest in cold water, cut lengthwise in four or six pieces, rub into a bowl and sprinkle over them—

COLD SLAW.

1 teaspoonful salt.
½ teaspoonful pepper.
3 ounces salad oil.
2 ounces English, or 1 ounce French vinegar.

Stir the salad lightly in the bowl until well mixed. Tarragon and chevies, or a little water or mustard cress.—*Mrs. R.*

SLAW.

Chop fine one head of cabbage put in a pan.
1 cup cream.
1½ teaspoonful mustard.
1 teaspoonful salt.
1 tablespoonful butter.
1 tablespoonful sugar.
And yolk of one egg, beaten light.

When boiled add one-half cup of strong vinegar; stir well and pour over the cabbage.—*Mrs. E. T.*

COLD SLAW.

Wash well and shred fine, a firm white cabbage.
Boil one teacup vinegar.
One tablespoonful butter in a little flour, stir this in the vinegar.

Beat the yolks of four eggs till light and stir also in the mixture, just before taking from the fire.

Add mustard, pepper, and salt, to the butter and flour, before putting in the vinegar.

Pour all, when hot, over the cabbage and set away to cool.—*Mrs. M. C.*

Cold Slaw.

Wash your cabbage and lay in cold water some hours. Have a seasoning of egg, mustard, oil, pepper, salt, celery-seed, and vinegar, and pour over it. In winter the slaw will keep a day or two.—*Mrs. W.*

Lettuce Dressed.

Take well headed lettuce, chop it fine and pour over a dressing made of salt and pepper, mustard, hard-boiled egg, and olive oil.

Cream the yolk of the egg and mustard together with a little oil, until quite smooth. Add vinegar if desired.—*Mrs. R.*

Lettuce Dressed.

Lettuce chopped fine.
½ cup vinegar.
½ cup ice-water.
1 tablespoonful white sugar.
1 teaspoonful salt.
1 saltspoonful cayenne.
2 hard-boiled eggs, chopped.
1 onion chopped.
1 tablespoonful made mustard.
1 tablespoonful of olive oil.—*Mrs. S. T.*

SAUCES.

Sauce for Salad or Fish.

Yolks of two hard-boiled eggs, mashed well with mixed mustard, pepper, salt, three tablespoonfuls salad oil, three of vinegar and one of tomato capsup.—*Mrs. J. H. F.*

Fish Sauce.

Six hard-boiled eggs, chopped and stirred into two cups of drawn butter.

Let it simmer, then add one tablespoonful of pepper-sauce, two tablespoonfuls minced parsley, a little thyme, and salt to the taste.

Pour over the fish and slice a lemon over all.—*Mrs. S. T.*

Sauce for Fish.

Yolks of three eggs, one tablespoonful vinegar, half a tablespoonful fresh butter, a little salt.

To be stirred over a slow fire till it thickens, it must only be warm or it will curdle and spoil.—*Mrs. S.*

Sauce for Cod's Head.

Take a lobster, stick a skewer through the tail, to keep the water out; throw a handful of salt in the water. When it boils put in the lobster and boil half an hour; pick off the spawns, if any, and pound them very fine in a marble mortar and put them in one-half pound drawn butter. Take the meat out of the lobster, pull it in bits and put it in your butter; add:

1 spoonful walnut catsup.
1 slice of lemon.
1 or 2 slices horseradish.
A little pounded mace.
Salt and cayenne pepper.

Boil them one minute; then take out the lemon and horseradish, and serve it up in the sauce-boat.—*Mrs. R.*

Dutch Sauce for Fish.

½ teaspoonful flour.
2 ounces butter.
4 tablespoonfuls vinegar.
Yolks of two eggs.
Juice of half a lemon.
Salt to the taste.

Put all the ingredients, except the lemon juice, into a stewpan; set it over the fire and keep constantly stirring. When it is sufficiently thick, take it off, as it should not boil. If, however, it happens to curdle, strain the sauce through a taminy, add the lemon juice, and serve. Tarragon vinegar may be used instead of plain, and by many is considered far preferable. — *Mrs. C.*

Maître d'Hôte Sauce.

It is nothing more than butter-sauce made thus:
Add to one teacup drawn butter, the juice of one-half lemon.
2 teaspoonfuls chopped parsley.
A little minced onion and thyme.
Cayenne pepper and salt to taste.

Beat with an egg-whip while simmering. Good for almost any dish of fish or meat.—*Mrs. S. T.*

Fish Sauce.

3 tablespoonfuls butter.
1 wineglassful vinegar.
2 wineglassfuls tomato or mushroom catsup.

Pepper, salt, and mustard to the taste. Stew till well mixed.—*Mrs. J. D.*

Anchovy Sauce.

Soak eight anchovies in cold water, for several hours; cut up and stew in a very little water for twenty minutes; strain into one teacup drawn butter.

Pour all in a saucepan and set it on the fire. Beat it up until it comes to a boil; pour into a sauce tureen. Add a little cayenne pepper; one squeeze of lemon.—*Mrs. S. T.*

Horseradish Sauce.

Grate one teacupful horseradish.
1 tablespoonful ground mustard.
1 tablespoonful sugar.
4 tablespoonfuls vinegar, or olive oil if preferred.
Pepper and salt.
1 teaspoonful turmeric.—*Mrs. J. H. T.*

Celery sauce is good made in the same way, by adding butter instead of oil, and celery instead of horseradish.—*Mrs. P. W.*

Mushroom Sauce, for Fried or Broiled Fish.

Get fine-grown fresh gathered mushrooms; break them up and sprinkle salt over them. Let them lie for the juice to run out, stirring them often. When the juice has been extracted, strain it, boil well with a little ginger and pepper.

Do not season much, as it is the mushroom flavor to be desired. You can add seasoning as required; all necessary to keep it is enough salt and pepper.

This makes a nice flavoring for any sauce or gravy mixed with soy or lemon pickle.—*Mrs. C. C.*

Pepper Vinegar.

Fill a quart bottle with small peppers, either green or ripe; put in two tablespoonfuls sugar, and fill with good cider vinegar.

Invaluable in seasoning sauces, and good to eat with fish or meat. If small peppers cannot be obtained, cut up large pods instead.—*Mrs. S. T.*

Tomato Sauce.

Scald and peel six large ripe tomatoes; chop them up and stew slowly. Cream one tablespoonful butter, one tablespoonful sugar, one tablespoonful flour, together.

When the tomatoes are thoroughly done, and reduced to a fine pulp, add pepper and salt.

Stir the butter, sugar, and flour in. Let boil up and serve.—*Mrs. S. T.*

Mushroom Sauce.

Roll a piece of butter as large as an egg into one heaping easpoonful sifted flour; stir in two tablespoonfuls warm water; et it simmer. Pour in one teacup cream, and stir; throw in one pint young mushrooms, washed, picked, and skinned; add pepper, salt, another small piece of butter.

Let it boil up once, shaking the pan well, and serve.—*Mrs. S. T.*

Onion Sauce.

Boil four or five large white onions in salt and water; change the water, then drain them. Chop fine and boil with one teacup new milk, salt, pepper, and one tablespoonful pepper sauce. Add drawn butter and serve.—*Mrs. S. T.*

Nasturtium Sauce.

This is made by stirring into one teacup drawn butter, three tablespoonfuls pickled nasturtiums, adding a little salt and pepper. Simmer gently and serve.—*Mrs. S. T.*

Apple Sauce.

Pare and slice some tart apples; stew until tender in a very little water, then reduce to a smooth pulp. Stir in sugar and butter to the taste, a squeeze of lemon juice, and a little nutmeg.—*Mrs. S. T.*

Mint Sauce.

3 tablespoonfuls vinegar.
2 tablespoonfuls mint.
1 tablespoonful powdered sugar.
1 saltspoonful salt.

Mix ten minutes before using.—*Mrs. S. T.*

Sauces especially suitable for Fowls, though they may be used for any kind of Meats.

White Sauce for Fowls.

Take the neck, gizzard, liver, and feet of fowls, with a piece of mutton or veal, if you have any, and boil in one quart water with a few whole peppers, and salt, till reduced to one pint; then thicken with a quarter pound butter mixed with flour and boil it five or six minutes.

Mix the yolks of two eggs with one teacup good cream; put it in the saucepan, shaking over the fire till done.—*Mrs. Dr. S*

Sauce for Boiled Poultry.

One stick of white, blanched celery, chopped very small; put it in a saucepan with one quart milk and a few black peppercorns; let it boil gently, till reduced to one pint. Keep stirring the celery up with the milk until it is in a pulp. Thicken the whole with the yolk of one fresh egg well beaten, and half a teacup of fresh cream.—*Mrs. S.*

Celery Sauce.

Chop celery into pieces half an inch long, enough to fill one pint measure, and stew in a small quantity of water till tender. Add one tablespoonful pepper vinegar, a little salt and pepper; pour in one teacup cream or milk, then add a sufficient quantity of drawn butter.—*Mrs. S. T.*

Egg Sauce.

Cut up six hard-boiled eggs, with salt and pepper to taste.

Stir in a sufficient quantity of drawn butter, adding, just as you serve, minced onion, parsley, and thyme.—*Mrs. S. T.*

Asparagus Sauce.

Parboil one bunch of asparagus, first scraping. When nearly done, drain and cut in small pieces. Stew in a teacup of milk, with pepper and salt. When done pour into drawn butter, and serve.—*Mrs. S. T.*

Oyster Sauce.

Scald one pint large fresh oysters, just enough to plump them; adding one tablespoonful pepper vinegar, a little black pepper and salt.

Pour into a sufficient quantity of drawn butter and serve.—*Mrs. S. T.*

Drawn Butter.

Take one-quarter pound of best fresh butter, cut it up and mix with it two teaspoonfuls flour; when thoroughly mixed, put it into a saucepan and add to it four tablespoonfuls cold water.

Cover the pan and set it in a kettle of boiling water, shake it round continually, always moving it the same way. When the butter is entirely melted and begins to simmer, then let it rest until it boils up. In melting butter for pudding, some substitute milk for water.—*Mrs. Dr. S.*

Drawn Butter.

Cream together one-quarter pound fresh butter, with two heaping teaspoonfuls sifted flour; add to this six teaspoonfuls water.

Put it in a small tin saucepan and set it in a vessel of boiling water, until it begins to simmer, shaking it often.—*Mrs. S. T.*

Drawn Butter.

Rub a piece of butter in a little flour, add two or three tablespoonfuls boiling water.

Shake continually over the fire without letting it boil, till it thickens.—*Mrs. P. W.*

CRANBERRY SAUCE.

Stew two quarts cranberries; putting only water enough to keep from sticking to the bottom of kettle. Keep covered until nearly done, then stir in one quart white sugar, and boil until thick. The color is finer when the sugar is added just before the sauce is done.—*Mrs. S. T.*

MUSHROOM SAUCE.

Wash and pick one pint young mushrooms, rub them with salt to take off the tender skin. Put them in a saucepan with a little salt, nutmeg, one blade of mace, one pint cream, lump of butter rubbed in flour.

Boil them up and stir till done, then pour it round the chickens. Garnish with lemon.—*Mrs. C. C*

SALAD DRESSINGS.

Take the yolk of one raw egg; add to that one-half tablespoonful of either dry or thickly mixed mustard, salt and pepper to your taste.

When well mixed together, add sweet oil in *very* small quantities, at a time, stirring briskly until it is very thick. Then add a little vinegar, but not sufficient to make the dressing thin. These are the proportions for the yolk of one raw egg, sufficient for four people. The quantity of eggs, mustard, etc., must be increased in proportion to the quantity of dressing needed.—*Mrs. McK.*

Salad Dressing.

Beat two eggs. Add butter size of half an egg.
½ teaspoonful mustard rubbed smooth in a little water.
4 tablespoonfuls vinegar.
½ teacupful boiling water.

Set it in a bowl on top of the tea-kettle and stir until as thick as cream.—*Mrs. W. H. M.*

Dressing.

To one tumblerful vinegar, warmed in a stewpan, add four beaten eggs; stir for a few minutes till cooked like boiled custard. Then throw in:

A teaspoonful of salt.
1 teaspoonful of sugar.
1 teaspoonful of mustard.
1 teaspoonful of pepper.
A lump of butter size of half an egg, instead of oil.

Stir well and pour out. Will keep for weeks. Good for chicken salad.—*Mrs. W.*

Dressing for Salad.

Turkey is more economical and better for salad than chicken To one turkey, weighing about nine pounds, allow nine eggs:

DRESSING FOR CHICKEN SALAD.

7 hard-boiled eggs.
2 raw eggs, yolks and whites beaten separately.
To each egg allow 2 tablespoonfuls salad oil, perfectly pure and sweet.
1 saltspoonful salt.
1 saltspoonful made mustard.
2 saltspoonfuls cayenne pepper to the whole amount.
Celery to the taste.
Lettuce leaves, if in season, using only the heart.
The juice of 2 lemons.
This will last a week.—*Mrs. A. M. D.*

DRESSING FOR CHICKEN SALAD.

To four chickens, the yolks of twelve eggs mashed very smooth with:

1 raw egg beaten light.
½ teacup of mustard.
½ teaspoonful red pepper.
1 teacup salad oil.
1 cup of vinegar.
1 quart of cut celery.
Salt to the taste.

—*Mrs. J. W.*

LETTUCE DRESSING.

1 raw egg.
1 tablespoonful sugar.
1 teaspoonful salt.
½ teaspoonful mustard.
A little cayenne pepper (never use black pepper on lettuce).
2 tablespoonfuls best olive oil.
1 tablespoonful vinegar.

—*Miss R. S.*

DRESSING FOR CABBAGE.

The yolk of an egg.
1 teaspoonful salt.

1 teaspoonful mustard.
2 teaspoonfuls sugar, mashed smooth.
1 cup of cream.
Vinegar to your taste.

—*Mrs. E. C G.*

Sana Mayonnaise.

The yolks (raw) of two eggs.

Stir in oil, a drop at a time, until it begins to thicken, and then pour it in slowly still, but in greater quantities, stirring continually. Add cayenne pepper, salt, and vinegar to the taste.

If mustard is liked in the sauce, it must be mixed with the yolks of the eggs before dropping the oil.

This sauce should be nearly as thick as soft butter. It makes a delicious dressing for lettuce, celery, cold poultry or game; and also for cold boiled fish or pickled salmon. If used with the latter, the salmon should be placed in the centre of the dish and covered thickly with sauce.

Boiled chestnuts, peeled, small pickled onions, sliced cucumbers, lettuce, etc., are a great addition, and should be used to dress or garnish the dish, but not be mixed with the salmon.— *Mrs. E. P., Cin.*

Salad for Slaw.

3 eggs well beaten.
Nearly a cup of sugar.
1 tablespoonful butter.
1 tablespoonful mustard.
Pepper and salt to your taste.
Tumbler of milk.
Tumbler of vinegar.

Stir well over the fire until as thick as custard. Let it cool and pour over cabbage.—*Mrs. R. A.*

Dressing for Cold Slaw.

1 cup of vinegar.
2 eggs well beaten.
1 teaspoonful salt.
1 teaspoonful mustard.
1 tablespoonful sugar.
1 tablespoonful butter.
A little black pepper.

Mix together the butter, salt, pepper, sugar, mustard; add the eggs last.

Have the vinegar boiling and pour it on, stirring all the time. Then pour it back in the saucepan and boil a few minutes. Pour on the slaw when cold.—*Miss N.*

Lettuce Dressing.

Yolks of 4 eggs.
1 teacup milk.
1 teacup vinegar.
4 tablespoonfuls oil or melted butter.

After mixing all well together, except the vinegar, let it come to a boil. When cold, beat well, add the vinegar, salt, pepper, and made mustard to suit the taste. Keep corked in a bottle.—*Mrs. A. M. D.*

Salad Dressing.

Put one tumbler vinegar, and one lump butter, size of an egg, on to boil.

Beat up the yolks of three or four eggs, and pour the boiling vinegar over them, stirring all the time; return it to the fire and continue to stir, until it thickens like custard. When it is perfectly cold add one tumblerful cream, into which has been mixed one tablespoonful salt, one tablespoonful mustard, two spoonfuls sugar, and one spoonful bruised celery-seed.

Bottle the dressing and it will keep for a month.—*Mrs. P.*

Celery Dressing.

2 tablespoonfuls butter.
2 beaten eggs.
1 teaspoonful salt.
1 teaspoonful mixed mustard.
1 cup vinegar.
1 cup fresh milk or cream.

Boil and use cold.—*Mrs. I. D.*

To Dress Celery.

Beat light the yolk of one egg; add:
2 tablespoonfuls cream.
1 tablespoonful white sugar.
3 tablespoonfuls vinegar.
1 teaspoonful olive oil.
1 teaspoonful mustard.
1 teaspoonful salt.

—*Mrs. Dr. S.*

BRUNSWICK STEWS, GUMBO, AND SIDE DISHES.

Brunswick Stew.

A twenty-five cent shank of beef.
A five-cent loaf of bread—square loaf, as it has more crumb, and the crust is not used.
1 quart potatoes cooked and mashed.
1 quart cooked butter-beans.
1 quart raw corn.
1½ quart raw tomatoes peeled and chopped.

If served at two o'clock, put on the shank as for soup, at the earliest possible hour; then about twelve o'clock take the shank out of the soup and shred and cut all of the meat as fine as you can, carefully taking out bone and gristle, and then return it to the soup-pot and add all of the vegetables; the bread and two slices of middling are an improvement to it.

Season with salt and pepper to the taste; and when ready to serve, drop into the tureen two or three tablespoonfuls butter.

This makes a tureen and about a vegetable-dish full.—*Mrs. R. P.*

Brunswick Stew.

About four hours before dinner, put on two or three slices of bacon, two squirrels or chickens, one onion sliced, in one gallon water. Stew some time, then add one quart peeled tomatoes, two ears of grated corn, three Irish potatoes sliced, and one handful butter-beans, and part pod of red pepper.

Stew altogether about one hour, till you can take out the bones. When done, put in one spoonful bread crumbs and one large spoonful butter.—*Mrs. M. M. D.*

Brunswick Stew.

Take one chicken or two squirrels, cut them up and put one-half gallon water to them. Let it stew until the bones can be removed. Add one-half dozen large tomatoes, one-half pint butter-beans, and corn cut from half a dozen ears, salt, pepper, and butter as seasoning.—*Mrs. I. H.*

Brunswick Stew.

Take two chickens or three or four squirrels, let them boil in water. Cook one pint butter-beans, and one quart tomatoes; cook with the meat. When done, add one dozen ears corn, one dozen large tomatoes, and one pound butter.

Take out the chicken, cut it into small pieces and put back; cook until it is well done and thick enough to be eaten with a fork.

Season with pepper and salt.—*Mrs. R.*

Gumbo.

Put one tablespoonful lard into a pan. Slice two onions and fry them in it a few minutes. Have ready a chicken cut up, and fry it in the lard till it slightly browns, also one or two slices of bacon or pork, and three or four bunches parsley cut up.

Have a heaping plateful of ochra cut up; put that in the pan and let it wilt a few minutes (you must stir it), then add three or four tomatoes cut up. Then put the whole into a stewpan, pour hot water to it, not quite as much as for soup. Let it boil until quite thick. Season with pepper and salt, also red or green pod pepper.

It must be dished like soup and eaten with rice; the rice to be boiled dry and served in a vegetable dish; put one or two spoonfuls in a plate and pour the gumbo over it.—*Mrs. G.*

Gumbo.

Cut up two chickens, fry slightly with a little onion, and a few slices pickled pork.

Put in three or four quarts boiling water, together with pepper and salt, eighteen okras, one-half peck cut up tomatoes.

Stew one hour and a half.—*Mrs. D. R.*

Gumbo.

Take one chicken, frying size, cut up in hot lard; add one quart ochra chopped fine, and one good sized onion chopped fine, when the chicken begins to brown, stirring all the time until it ceases to rope and is a nice brown.

Then put it into a deep vessel and pour on enough boiling water to make soup for ten or twelve persons, adding two or three tomatoes, skinned and sliced, two ears of tender corn, salt, and black and red pepper to the taste.

Let the whole boil one hour.

Boil rice very dry and serve with it.—*Mrs. P McG.*

Gumbo Filit à la Creole.

Put into a deep pot one tablespoonful lard, when hot put in one tablespoonful flour, stir in until brown, then slice one large onion and fry it till brown; skim out the onion and do not put it back until a chicken cut up in small pieces has been fried. Stir it all the time. Have a kettle of boiling water near by; pour one or two cups of water on the chicken, stir well and let it simmer slowly. Add:

10 allspice.
8 cloves.
Red and black pepper.
Parsley and thyme if you like it.

Put in two quarts of water, boiling, and let it boil gently two hours. Have ready the liquor from one quart oysters, put that in with the water; put the oysters in later, allowing them time to cook. When ready to serve stir in one tablespoonful filit, boil up once. To be eaten with rice cooked dry.

N. B. *Filit* is only pulverized sassafras leaves, dried and sifted; you can make it yourself.—*Mrs. S., La.*

Veal Pâtés.

3½ pounds leg of veal.
¼ pound salt pork.
6 soda crackers rolled and sifted.
1 tablespoonful salt.
1 tablespoonful black pepper.
1 nutmeg.
2 eggs well beaten.
Butter the size of an egg.

Hash veal and pork together, cutting very fine. Then mix seasoning very thoroughly and form into oval shapes. Put a small piece of butter and bread crumbs over the top, while in the baking dish; half a teacup water, and baste frequently while baking. In moulding it and when mixing it keep wetting the hands in cold water, also wet the dish when you begin moulding it in shape.—*Mrs. J. P. H.*

HASHED MUTTON.

Cut cold mutton into very thin slices, and make a gravy by boiling the bones for two hours with a little onion, pepper and salt.

Strain this gravy and thicken it with a little flour, adding a small amount of tomato or mushroom gravy to flavor it, and a small piece of butter. When the gravy is of a proper consistency, put in the slices of mutton, and let it simmer slowly for ten minutes. Serve on a platter with parsley and sippets of bread.

Hashed Mutton.

Fry in a saucepan three small onions, and three small slices of bacon or ham, until they are brown; then add a little more than half a pint water, and thicken it with flour. Next strain it and add it to the meat with a little sauce; pepper and salt to the taste.

It will take about an hour to hash.

MUTTON HASH.

Cut the meat up fine, putting the bones on to stew in water; then take out the bones and put in the hash, with pepper, salt and gravy left from the day before.

Let these stew at least half an hour. Put in one large tablespoonful browned flour. Add—

6 tablespoonfuls red wine.
1 tablespoonful walnut catsup.
1 tablespoonful tomato catsup.
A lump of butter rolled in a little flour.

If a small dish, proportion the seasoning.

Beef, goose, and duck hash can be made the same way.—*Mrs. R.*

Hotch Potch.

During the summer season get lamb chops, which half fry. Cut up cabbage, lettuce, turnips, onions and any other vegetables, which boil, with seasoning of pepper, salt, etc.; one hour before dinner, put in the lamb chops, with some green peas; boil the potatoes separately.

Scotch Broth.

3 pounds of the scrag end of a neck of mutton.
1 onion.
1 small turnip.
A little parsley.
A little thyme.

Put the mutton in the pan and cover with two quarts cold water, add the vegetables and not quite one teacup rice; one small carrot and a little celery added will give a nice flavor.

When it boils, skim carefully, cover the pan, and let it simmer for two hours. Of course, the vegetables must be cut small.

Meat Loaf.

Chop fine whatever cold meat you may have, fat and lean together; add pepper and salt, one finely chopped onion, two slices of bread which have been soaked in milk, and one egg.

Mix well together and bake in a form. This makes an admirable tea or breakfast dish.—*Mrs. J.*

Black Stew.

Take any kind of fresh meat that has been boiled or roasted, cut up enough to make a dish; put one tablespoonful currant jelly, one tablespoonful of wine, one large spoonful butter, one-half onion chopped, pepper and salt.

Stir all together fifteen minutes. Pickle cut up is an improvement, and brown sugar can be used instead of currant jelly.— *Mrs J. T.*

A nice Side-dish.

Make a mince meat of turkey; after it is stewed put boiled

rice around the dish and set it in an oven to brown. Then garnish with hard boiled eggs.—*Mrs. E. I.*

MEAT CROQUETTES.

Any nice cold meat when nicely minced will make good croquettes, especially veal. Take about one-quarter loaf bread, well soaked in water and squeezed dry; mix with the minced meat about one dessertspoonful chopped parsley, one dessertspoonful ground ginger, three eggs, a pinch of ground mace, pepper and salt, roll them into egg-shaped balls; have ready two or three eggs well beaten, in one plate, and flour in another; first roll in the flour, then in the egg, fry in boiling drippings; serve hot.—*Mrs. T.*

CROQUETTES.

Take cold fowl or fresh meat of any kind, with slices of fat ham; chop together very fine, add one-half as much stale bread grated, salt and pepper, grated nutmeg, one tablespoonful catsup, one teaspoonful made mustard, and lump of butter size of an egg. Mix well together till it resembles sausage meat; mould them into cakes, dip into well beaten yolk of an egg, cover thickly with grated bread. Fry a light brown.—*Mrs. F. D.*

Croquettes.

Boil or roast a turkey, chop the meat as fine as possible. Mix eight beaten eggs with the meat, add one quart of milk, one-quarter pound butter, salt and pepper, a little mace.

Stew all together for a few minutes, then take it off to cool and make into little cone shapes. Roll each one into pounded crackers and drop in boiling lard till a light brown.—*Mrs. M. E. L. W., Md.*

CHICKEN CROQUETTES.

Cold chicken, chopped parsley, a little cream, grated crackers, lemon flavoring, salt and pepper. Cut chicken very fine and season with salt and pepper; add chopped parsley, moisten with cream sufficient to make paste; mould in a wineglass with grated cracker or bread crumbs on outside. Fry quickly in hot lard. Brown lightly. Lemon flavoring can be added at will.—*Mrs. G. P.*

POTATO CROQUETTES.

Peel, boil, and mash one quart potatoes, mix with yolks of four eggs and some milk.

Set on the fire, stir two minutes; set on a dish to cool or leave overnight. In the morning add a little milk, mix thoroughly, roll in bread crumbs; divide in cakes and fry in lard. Take off when done; drain, dish, and serve immediately.—*Mrs. E.*

CROQUETTE BALLS.

Chop up one quart of any cold meat very fine, to which add one pint stale bread. Mix up one egg, mustard, pepper, salt and butter, and pour over the bread and meat; roll into balls, which must be rolled into the white of an egg, then into bread crumbs, and bake a nice brown. This is a nice side-dish for breakfast or tea.—*Mrs. S. G.*

CROQUETTES.

Have some nice pieces of veal or fowl, chopped fine, season with nutmeg, pepper and salt to your taste.

Boil one-half pint milk with one small garlic. Thicken with two tablespoonfuls flour, and one tablespoonful butter.

Let it remain till thoroughly done; stir in the meat and then form the croquettes. Roll in bread crumbs, then the yolk of an egg, then in bread crumbs, and fry a nice brown.—*Miss E. P.*

Croquettes.

Take cold meat or fresh meat, with grated ham, fat and lean, chopped very fine—add one-half as much stale bread grated, salt, pepper, and nutmeg, one tablespoonful catsup, a lump of butter.

Knead all well together—if not soft enough add cream or

gravy. Make in cakes the shape of a pear; dip them in the yolk of an egg beaten, roll in dried bread crumbs, and fry a light brown.—*Miss M. C. L.*

SAUSAGE CROQUETTES.

2 pounds of meat.
4 eggs.
1 cup butter.
1 cup milk.

Add powdered cracker or stale bread crumbs sufficient to thicken, while on the fire. Roll in oblong shapes and fry in lard. Roll the balls in cracker dust before frying.—*Mrs. R. K. M.*

SAUSAGE CROQUETTES.

One pound sausage meat, two eggs, well beaten, and bread crumbs well minced.

Make the meat into cakes, then roll in the beaten egg, and afterwards in bread crumbs. Fry in pan and serve hot. Cold ham served in the same way is delicious; mince it very fine.—*Mrs. G.*

FORCEMEAT BALLS.

One pound of fresh suet, one ounce ready dressed veal, or chicken chopped fine, bread crumbs, a little shallot or onion, salt and pepper (white), nutmeg; parsley and thyme, finely shred.

Beat as many eggs, yolks and whites separately, as will make the above ingredients into a moist paste; roll into small balls, and fry in boiling lard. When of a light brown, take out with a perforated skimmer. Forcemeat balls made in this way are remarkably light, but being somewhat greasy, some persons prefer them with less suet and eggs.—*Mrs. A. M. D.*

MINCE WITH BREAD CRUMBS.

Chop up any kind of cold meat very fine, place in a baking dish a layer of bread crumbs, seasoned with lump of butter, black pepper, and salt.

Then a layer of minced meat, and so on with alternate layers, till the dish is filled. Pour over all a cup of rich cream, and be sure to have enough lumps of butter to make it rich. Bake until it is a good brown on top.—*Mrs. C. M. A.*

MINCE WITH POTATOES.

Chop fine any cold meat; parboil enough Irish potatoes to be two-thirds as many as there is chopped meat. Mix all together with one raw egg, one onion, black pepper, and salt.

Fry with butter, either in large or small cakes in a pan, the cakes rather larger than sausages. If you have cold ham, it is an advantage to add some of it to the mince; and the whole is very nice made of cold pickled beef.—*Mrs. C. M. A.*

POT POURRI.

Take any kind of fresh meat chopped fine, and put into a stewpan with a little warm water, pepper and salt, and chopped onion. Cook twenty minutes; then put into a baking-dish with an equal quantity of bread crumbs, and pour over a cup of sweet cream. Bake to a light brown.—*Mrs. F. D.*

HASH.

One and one-half teacup of boiling water must be poured into a saucepan, mix one heaping spoonful flour with one tablespoonful cold water, stir it in and boil three minutes. Then add two teaspoonfuls salt, half a small teaspoonful pepper, and butter size of an egg.

After removing all tough, gristly pieces from the cold cooked meat, chop it fine with some boiled potatoes. Put them in the dressing, heat through, then serve. It injures meat to cook it *again*, making it hard and unpalatable. Should you have any cold gravy left, use it; in that case you will require less butter, salt and pepper. You can serve it with buttered toast underneath, or you may set it into the oven to brown on top, or drop eggs into a skillet of boiling salt water, and when cooked, place on top of hash.—*Mrs. J.*

CASSA ROLLS.

Boil some Irish potatoes until quite done, mash them smooth and add an equal quantity of salt meat chopped fine. Mix with this several well beaten eggs, one spoonful butter, some pepper and salt.

Bake in little cakes like potato cakes.—*Mrs. F. D.*

RAGOUT SOUSE.

Split four feet once, fry with one or two dozen large oysters, a light brown. Lay them in a stewpan over the liquor from the oysters, or some beef or veal gravy; add one large spoonful butter rolled in flour, one dozen allspice, beaten, one glass red wine, one glass walnut catsup, and pepper.

Stew gently until dinner, skimming off any grease. Garnish with hard-boiled eggs. Mace or cloves may be used instead of allspice.—*Mrs. B.*

BREAKFAST DISH.

Take the remnant of any cold meats, either boiled or roasted. Prepare it, as if for chicken salad, in fine shreds. Mix with potatoes mashed fine, and add two well-beaten eggs.

Season with butter, pepper, and other spices if you like.

Make it into a loaf and bake it brown, or fry it in cakes if preferred.—*Mrs. J. F. G.*

MOCK TERRAPIN.

Mince cold veal very fine, sprinkle with salt and cayenne. Mash the yolks of three hard-boiled eggs, three tablespoonfuls cooking wine, three tablespoonfuls cream or milk, a little nutmeg and a little mixed mustard, a large lump of butter with a little flour rubbed in.

Let all steam five minutes, and serve hot on toast.

A nice relish for breakfast or lunch.—*Miss E. S.. La.*

Breakfast Dish.

One pound pork sausage, one tablespoonful pounded crackers, two well beaten eggs. Work thoroughly together, and make into cakes. These will be rather soft, but dropping each one into a plate of pounded or grated cracker will enable you to handle them. Put into a hot frying-pan. No lard is to be used, but keep the pan covered while frying.—*Miss E.*

Baked Hash.

Take cold beef or veal, chop the meat very fine, put it in a pan with some water; add salt, pepper, butter and bread crumbs to taste. Season with a little chopped onion, parsley and thyme, all minced fine, half a cup milk or cream with one egg beaten. Grate some crumbs over the top, and bake till brown.—*Mrs. J. H. F.*

Sandwiches.

Grate one quarter pound cold ham in a bowl, with one tablespoonful chopped pickle, one teaspoonful mustard, a little black pepper, six dessertspoonfuls butter; put in a bowl and stir quickly until a cream.

Add the ham and seasoning, mix all together well. Have slices of light bread and spread the mixture on each side of each slice.

Cold grated tongue, instead of ham, is very nice spread on the inside of biscuit.

Sandwiches.

Mince ham and tongue together, and spread between buttered bread. Add a little French mustard to the mince if liked.—*Mrs. R.*

Pillau.

Take cold fresh meat, either chicken or veal, and cut it up quite small after taking off the outer skin either fat or gristle. Mix it well with some cold rice, then stir this in a batter made of two eggs well beaten, and about one quart milk. Season with salt, pepper, and butter.

Bake in a deep dish.—*Mrs. A. B.*

Calf's Head Pudding.

Skin the head, take out the brains. Thoroughly wash, then soak the head one night to extract the blood. Put on in cold water and boil five or six hours, or until the bones are ready to drop out. Pick it very fine, taking all the bones out; then add the liquor in which it was boiled, one tablespoonful butter, four eggs well beaten; one small piece of lemon or pickle; one onion, if liked; pepper and salt

Lay the brains all over the top and bake. Bread crumbs are an improvement. The liquor seasoned makes excellent soup.— *Miss F. E.*

Liver Pudding.

Take two hog's heads, clean nicely; two livers, two lights, and cut all the good part off half a dozen milts; half a dozen sweet-breads; half a dozen kidneys, split open.

Put all together in a tub of salt and water; let them soak all night; take them out next morning, put them in a kettle with two slices of fat pork. Let all boil until done, then take it up and let it cool a little and grind it in a sausage mill, and while grinding, skim some of the grease off of the kettle and pour it into the mill. After it is ground, season with black pepper, salt, and onions chopped fine, to suit the taste.

If it is not rich enough, boil more middling or pork and mix with the meat; if stuffed, boil again a few minutes.

Pig's Head Pudding.

Boil head and liver until perfectly done, cut up as for hash. Put it on again in warm water and season highly with butter, pepper, salt, and a little chopped onion.

After well seasoned, put in a baking-dish with one egg beaten light. Bake two hours, and lay over hard-boiled eggs sliced, and strips of pastry across the top.

Calf's Head Pudding can be made in the same way.—*Mrs. Col. S.*

POTATO PIE.

The remains of cold mutton, either roasted or boiled, cut into nice slices, three hard-boiled eggs, also sliced, and two or three potatoes, seasoning of pepper, salt, and pounded mace to your taste.

All laid alternately in a baking-dish and filled nearly up with any gravy or stock at hand; cover with a potato crust, full two inches thick, and bake until the potatoes are a nice brown color. If the potatoes are scratched over with a fork, it gives them a pretty, rough appearance. To make the crust, boil and mash the potatoes with a little butter and milk and a small quantity of salt.—*Mrs. R. P.*

A NICE PIE.

One pound steak, three soft crackers rolled, one small piece of butter, two tablespoonfuls of water, salt and pepper. Bake in a deep pan.—*Mrs. R.*

POTATO PIE.

A savory potato pie is made thus: A layer of mashed potatoes placed in a pie dish and then slices of any cold meat (if chicken or veal, slices of tongue or ham may be added), and herbs, pepper and salt, sprinkled over to taste. Continue these layers alternately till the dish is full; the potatoes must well cover the top, which should have some butter added, and be brushed over with the yolk of an egg, and put into the oven till done through. A little butter on each layer is needed if the meat is not fat, and it should not be too fat.—*Mrs. S.*

CRUMB PIE.

Mince any cold meat very finely, season it to taste, and put it into a pie dish; have some finely grated bread crumbs, with a little salt, pepper, and nutmeg; and pour into the dish any gravy that is at hand. Cover over with a thick layer of bread crumbs and put small pieces of butter over top. Place in the oven till a fine brown. Send to the table hot.—*Mrs. W.*

HAGGIS.

Cut cold beef in pieces and mix with mashed potatoes; fill a baking-dish and season with butter, pepper, and salt. Bake and serve hot.

COLD CHICKEN WITH VINEGAR.

Cut up the chicken in fine pieces and crack the bones. Season with salt and pepper; put it in a deep baking plate with a lump of butter, and one tablespoonful vinegar. Cover it with hot water. Put a plate over it and stew on a stove or over hot embers. Add one heaping teacup chopped celery to the mixture before cooking.—*Mrs. A. P.*

DEVILLED COLD CHICKEN.

Take the legs and wings of any cold fowl.
Dress with pepper, salt, mustard, and butter; then broil.

GIBLET PIE.

Made as chicken pie, adding livers of chicken or pigeon, which have been boiled in the water left from cooking; celery and sweet herbs. Season with mushroom or walnut catsup.—*Mrs. T.*

SQUAB PIE.

After the squabs are picked and drawn as a large fowl is for roasting, wash them and put them in a saucepan with a close cover. They should be covered with boiling water and boiled slowly till tender, when a little salt and an onion clove should be added. Then take them out, drain and dry, and put in each squab a teaspoonful of butter, a little pepper, salt, minced parsley and thyme. Then put into the cavity of each squab, a hard-boiled egg. Lay them in a large, round, earthen baking dish, three or four inches deep. Strain over them the liquor in which they were simmered. Add a tablespoonful of butter and a teacup of milk or cream. Sift in two tablespoonfuls of cracker crumbs not browned, a tablespoonful of minced parsley and thyme, and a little salt. Put in a few slips of pastry. Cover with a rich crust and bake.

The same recipe will answer for robins, except that the eggs must be chopped, instead of being placed whole in the cavity of the bird.—*Mrs. S. T.*

BEEF CAKES.

Chop pieces of roast beef very fine. Mix up grated bread crumbs, chopped onions, and parsley; season with pepper and salt, moisten with a little dripping or catsup.

Cold ham or tongue may be added to improve it.

Make in broad, flat cakes, and spread a coat of mashed potatoes on the top and bottom of each. Lay a piece of butter on every cake and put it in an oven to brown.

Other cold meats may be prepared in the same way for a breakfast dish.—*Mrs. D.*

FISH AND POTATOES.

Boil salmon or other fish; mash up boiled Irish potatoes; chop yolks of hard boiled eggs.

Mix all together with butter; make very hot, and keep it so at table.—*Mrs. R.*

BEEFSTEAK AND POTATOES.

Cut up in a stewpan, with cold water, and stew till well cooked, the steak you will use; mash some potatoes with creamed butter, pepper and salt.

Line a baking dish with it and put in the steak, seasoning with butter, pepper, and salt. Bake a little while.

Bacon Fraise.

Take a nice piece of middling about six inches square, pare off the skin and cut in small square pieces, then fry it. Make a batter of three pints flour, five eggs, one handful parsley, chopped fine. Beat all light and fry with bacon. Serve hot. This will make two dishes.—*Mrs. M. D.*

Italian manner of Cooking Macaroni.

One and a half pound macaroni, parboiled with a little salt, and one clove garlic. One pound of beef chopped fine, lean and fat stewed with one pint tomatoes.

Alternate layers of macaroni and the stewed beef with grated cheese. Add cayenne pepper, salt, butter, and a little wine.

A thick layer of grated cracker crumbs and cheese on top. Serve with a stand of grated Stilton cheese.—*Mrs. R. R.*

Macaroni.

Break into pieces one inch long and put in the dish you wish to fill, filling it only one-third full. Wash well and boil in a covered stewpan until soft and tender, drain off all the water; cover with this the bottom of a baking dish. Sprinkle over pepper and salt, grated cracker, bits of butter and grated cheese; then another layer of macaroni, etc., in the same order. When the dish is filled, pour over fresh milk until all is barely covered. Sift over pounded cracker and set in the oven. If it becomes too brown, sift over more cracker before serving.—*Mrs. S. T.*

Macaroni.

Boil one-half pound macaroni in water, with salt, one small onion and two blades mace.

Put in one sweetbread, chopped fine, or the same amount of fresh veal, the nice part being taken.

Boil till tender before taking it up, drain off the water and add one large spoonful butter, one-half pint milk, a quantity of grated cheese; one teaspoonful mustard; two teaspoonfuls black pepper, one pint skinned tomatoes, salt to the taste; one egg, beaten up, is a great improvement.

Butter a deep dish and bake the macaroni a light brown. Have it served with a small bowl of grated cheese, of the best quality, so that each one may add what they like.—*Mrs. M. C.*

Macaroni.

Parboil enough macaroni to make a dish; lay alternate layers of macaroni, and grated cheese. Season with salt, pepper, and butter; add three eggs, well beaten, and enough milk to fill a dish. Sprinkle bread crumbs over top and bake. —*Mrs. R. A.*

Macaroni.

To one and one-half pound macaroni, add one pound beef, chopped fine. Make a stew of the beef with one quart water, one clove of garlic, catsup, tomato, or walnut, to suit the taste, one dessertspoonful currant jelly, salt and pepper.

Boil the macaroni; put in a pan a layer of macaroni and a layer of cheese, with plenty of butter, using quarter of a pound of butter for the dish.

Then pour the stew over the top, and bake fifteen minutes.— *Miss M. B. B.*

To Boil Hominy.

Take two quarts of hominy, wash through several waters until the water is clear; put it on to boil in a pot half full of water, with a plate turned down in the bottom of the pot to prevent its burning. Boil for six hours—do not stir it; when done, take off the vessel and set it aside in a cool place. When it is ready to fry, put a little lard in the pan, let it get hot, and mash in the hominy; then add a little salt. Put it in the pan and press down; let it fry till brown, turning it upside down on the dish.—*Mrs. P. W.*

Hominy Croquettes.

To one cup cold boiled hominy, add two teaspoonfuls melted

butter, and stir it well, adding by degrees one cup milk, till all is made in a soft light paste; adding one well-beaten egg.

Roll into oval balls with floured hands; dip in beaten egg, then roll in cracker crumbs and fry in hot lard.—*Mrs. M*.

Fried Hominy.

Warm the boiled hominy; add a piece of butter, a little salt half a pint cream, two eggs, and flour enough to stiffen the mixture. Fry like mashed potatoes.—*Mrs. E*.

To Boil Hominy.

Soak in hot water the overnight. Next morning wash out in two waters and boil thoroughly. A little milk added to the water whitens and seasons it.—*Mrs. W*.

To Stew, Fry, or Broil Mushrooms.

After you have peeled them, sprinkle with salt and pepper and put them in a stewpan with a little water and lump of butter. Let them boil fast for ten minutes and stir in a thickening of flour and cream. They may be broiled on a gridiron, and seasoned with butter. Fry them also in butter. The large mushrooms are used for the two latter modes of cooking them. —*Mrs. C. C.*

Sweetbread and Mushroom Pâtés.

Ten sweetbreads, parboiled, skinned and all the fat removed; cut into small pieces. Add one even teaspoonful salt, one can of French mushrooms. Slice thin, add to juice one teaspoonful salt, one teaspoonful pepper, one saltspoonful powdered mace, lump of butter size of guinea egg.

Simmer slowly twenty minutes. Add sweetbreads dredged with one heaping spoonful corn starch, well mixed in the sweetbread. Let it boil up once, stirring to prevent sticking. Serve in puff paste shapes, hot. A little chopped parsley may be added —*Mrs. R. R.*

To Stew Mushrooms.

One pint mushroom buttons, three ounces fresh butter, pepper and salt to taste, lemon juice, one teaspoonful flour, cream or milk a little nutmeg.

Pare the mushrooms, put them into a basin of water with a little lemon juice. Take them from the water, put into a stewpan, with the above ingredients. Cover the pan closely and let them stew gently twenty minutes. If the mushrooms are not perfectly tender, stew them five minutes longer; remove every particle of butter which may be floating on top, and serve.—*Mrs. C. C.*

Broiled Mushrooms.

Cleanse the large mushrooms by wiping with flannel and a little salt. Cut off stalks and peel the tops; broil them over a clear fire, turning them once. Arrange on a hot dish. Put a small piece of butter on each mushroom, season with pepper and salt; squeeze over them a little lemon juice. Place before the fire, and when the butter is melted, serve quickly.—*Mrs. C. C.*

Fondée.

2 ounces butter.
4 ounces bread crumbs.
8 ounces cheese.
1 cup sweet milk.
3 eggs.

Cut the butter and cheese into small pieces and place them in a large bowl with the bread; on this pour scalding milk, after which add the yolks well beaten, also a little salt. Mix well together, cover and place on the back of the range, stirring occasionally, till all is dissolved; when add the whites beaten to a stiff froth. Place in a buttered pie-plate and bake in a quick oven for twenty minutes. Serve as soon as taken from the stove. Mustard is considered by some an improvement.—*Mrs. H. H. S.*

Welsh Rarebit.

Cut up cheese fine and place in a saucepan with a little butter, add one or two spoonfuls beer, and boil till the cheese is well dissolved. Cut a slice of bread, pour on the cheese; season with pepper, salt, and catsup.—*Mrs. S.*

Rice and Egg Pâtés.

Mix cold rice with well-beaten eggs, season with pepper, and salt.

Then cook like scrambled egg; don't let the rice burn.

Tongue and Prunes.

Get a fresh beef tongue, parboil and skin it. Add one pound prunes, one pound raisins, one-quarter pound sugar, spices to the taste.

Let it stew until perfectly well cooked.

When nearly done, add one lemon.—*Miss M. B. B.*

To Stew Dried Apples, Peaches, Quinces, or Pears.

Take three pounds of dried fruit; wash it in lukewarm water, through three or four waters, rubbing it hard. Pour on this five quarts boiling water; boil at least three hours. Just before taking from the fire, add two teacups nice brown sugar. Do not stir, except occasionally, to prevent sticking to the bottom. Try to cook the pieces of fruit separate, except the apples, which run through a colander and season with nutmeg. The other fruits need no seasoning.—*Mrs. S. T.*

Fried Apples.

Slice apples without peeling; cut and fry some thin slices of breakfast bacon until thoroughly done; remove the slices from the vessel, adding water to the gravy left. Put in apples and fry until done, sweetening to taste.—*Mrs. G. B.*

Spiced Apples.

8 pounds apples pared.
4 pounds sugar.
1 quart vinegar.
1 ounce stick cinnamon.
½ ounce cloves.

Boil the sugar, vinegar, and spices together; put in the apples when boiling, and let them remain until tender; then take them out and put them in a jar; boil the syrup down, and pour over them.

Stewed Prunes.

Immediately after breakfast, wash two pounds prunes in several waters, rubbing them in the hands.

Put in a preserving kettle with one gallon boiling water. Simmer three or four hours. Add two teacups light brown sugar and boil till the syrup is thick. Keep closely covered and do not stir, so each prune may be stewed whole. Put in a shallow bowl and set to cool. This amount will make two dishes.

Excellent side dish for winter or spring.—*Mrs. S. T.*

EGGS.

Properly cooked, eggs are very wholesome and nutritious diet. Always be certain, however, that they are fresh, before attempting to make a dish of them. Some persons use Krepp's family egg-tester, to ascertain if an egg is sound. Full directions, as to the mode of using it, accompany the egg tester; so it is unnecessary to give them here. A simple mode of testing the soundness of an egg, is to put it in water; and if fresh it will sink to the bottom.

BOILED EGGS.

Let the water be boiling when you put the eggs in it, and let the eggs boil three minutes after putting them in.—*Mrs. S. T.*

SOFT-BOILED EGGS.

Put the eggs in a large tin cup or any tin vessel convenient. Pour boiling water over them, and let them remain near the fire, five minutes. Do not let them boil. Eggs cooked thus are slightly jellied throughout. They can be kept hot without becoming hard.—*Mrs. S. T.*

SCRAMBLED EGGS.

Beat four eggs very light. Add a teacup milk, thickened with a teaspoonful flour. Have the pan very hot, put in a tablespoonful butter, pour in the eggs, and scramble quickly.—*Mrs. E.*

Scrambled Eggs.

Wash the pan with hot water and soap. Wipe dry. Grease with a little lard. Break into this the eggs, adding a lump of butter and a little salt. Stir till done.—*Mrs. P.*

EGGS FOR BREAKFAST.

Heat in the oven a common white dish, large enough to hold the number of eggs to be cooked, allowing plenty of room for each. Melt in it a small piece of butter, break the eggs, one at a time, carefully in a saucer, and slip them in the hot dish. Sprinkle over them pepper and salt, and let them cook four or five minutes. It is a great improvement to allow to every two eggs a tablespoonful of cream, adding it when the eggs are first put in.—*Mrs. A. M. D.*

EGG CUPS—A BREAKFAST DISH.

Boil some eggs perfectly hard. Halve them, take out the yolks, which mix smoothly with some finely chopped or ground ham or fowl, salt and pepper, and a few spoonfuls melted butter or salad oil. Cut a piece off the bottom of each white half, to make them stand, and fill each with a chopped mixture. Make a sauce of sweet cream, boiled within an inner saucepan, and pour over the eggs. Decorate the edges of the dish with sprigs of curled parsley.—*Mrs. A. M. D.*

OMELETTE.

Break six eggs in a pan, beat them well together, add half a gill of milk, pepper and salt to suit the taste, and a few sprigs of parsley chopped fine. Beat all well together. Have the cooking-pan hot enough to brown the butter. Put in half a tablespoonful of butter. Pour the mixture in the pan or skillet to cook. When sufficiently done, roll with a spoon and turn into the dish.—*Miss E. P.*

Omelette.

Boil one pint milk in a shallow vessel.

Beat up four eggs very light; add salt, pepper, and a little flour, making it of the consistency of paste. Put this into the boiling milk. Have a pan well buttered, into which turn the mixture, and set inside an oven to bake a light brown. Serve immediately.—*Mrs. J. D.*

Omelette.

6 eggs beaten very light.
2 ounces butter.
Salt and pepper to the taste.
Chopped parsley or celery.

Fry a light brown in a well buttered pan. Some minced ham or oysters improve the flavor.—*Mrs. R.*

Omelette.

4 eggs beaten separately.
3 tablespoonfuls cream.
Salt and pepper to the taste.

—*Mrs. G. W. P.*

OMELETTE SOUFFLÉ.

Six eggs, whites and yolks beaten separately and very light. Put on the stove a teacup milk with a piece of butter in it the size of a walnut. When the butter is melted, mix in one tablespoonful corn starch. Mix this with the yolks, add salt to the taste, then stir in slowly the whites. Bake in a buttered pudding dish, fifteen minutes, in a quick oven.—*Mrs. M. E. L. W.*

MOCK OMELETTE.

Two cups bread crumbs soaked all night in one and one-half cup milk. Add, next morning, three eggs, whites lightly stirred in; pepper, one teaspoonful salt.—*Mrs. E. W.*

HAM OMELETTE.

1 ounce minced ham.
A little pepper.
Eggs beaten very light and fried in lard.

—*Miss E. W.*

CHEESE OMELETTE.

3 eggs beaten to a thick froth.
½ teacup grated cracker.
3 tablespoonfuls grated cheese.

Cook in a frying-pan with butter.
Some persons add chopped thyme and parsley.—*Mrs. P.*

GERMAN OMELETTE.

3 eggs (yolks and whites beaten separately).

Mix thoroughly one-half teacup milk and one teaspoonful of flour. Then add it to the yolks (well beaten) together with a little salt. Pour this mixture into a moderately hot pan, greased with butter. When this is nearly done (which will be in about five minutes), add the whites, stiffly frothed and slightly salted, spreading them over the whole surface. Run a knife carefully around the edges, and turn into a heated dish when done.

It is an improvement to mix one-third of the frothed whites with the yolks before pouring into the pan.—*Mrs. M. C. C.*

POACHED EGGS.

Let the eggs be perfectly fresh, and the pan at least two inches deep in boiling water. Break the eggs carefully, just over the water or in a spoon, so that they may be slipped into the water with their shape preserved. Take them up in a large perforated spoon, cover with fresh melted butter and sprinkle with salt—never pepper, as some persons do not use it, and it mars the appearance of the dish.—*Mrs. S. T.*

EGGS WITH TOAST. (*A Spring Dish.*)

Cut bread in squares, and toast a light brown. Poach eggs nicely, place each one on a piece of toast. Pour melted butter over them, and serve.—*Mrs. S. T.*

RUMBLE EGGS.

Beat up three eggs with two ounces fresh butter or well washed salt butter. Add a teaspoonful cream or new milk. Put all in a saucepan and stir over the fire five minutes. When it rises up, dish it immediately on toast.—*Mrs. S.*

HAM AND EGGS.

Slice the ham rather thick. Fry in a hot pan. Before it becomes hard, take from the pan and lay in a dish over a vessel of hot water.

Let the pan remain on the fire, so as to keep the ham gravy hot, that it may cook the eggs nicely when dropped into it. Break the eggs carefully, drop them in whole, and do not let them touch each other. Cook a light brown, not allowing the yolks to get hard. Lay an egg on each slice of meat.
Mrs. S. T.

Ham and Egg Pudding. (*A Spring Dish.*)

6 eggs beaten very light.
A light pint of flour.
A pint of milk.
A small piece of butter.
Salt and pepper to the taste.

Sprinkle some slices of boiled ham (both fat and lean) with pepper, and lay them across a deep dish that has been greased. Then pour the pudding batter over the bacon and bake quickly. *Mrs. V. P. M.*

Eggs à la Crème.

Six eggs boiled hard and chopped fine, and stale bread. Put in a dish alternate layers of chopped egg and grated bread. When the dish is full, pour on one pint boiling milk seasoned with salt, pepper, and one tablespoonful butter. Bake a light brown.—*Miss N.*

Baked Eggs for Dinner.

Have ready eight or ten hard-boiled eggs, a cup of light grated bread crumbs, butter, pepper and salt. Place in a buttered pudding dish a layer of sliced eggs, dotted with bits of butter, and sprinkled with salt and pepper; next a layer of bread crumbs, and so on to the top, being careful to let the top layer be of bread crumbs.—*Mrs. A. M. D.*

Egg Pie.

Take six hard-boiled eggs, slice, season with salt, pepper, and butter, bake in a paste, top and bottom.

Stuffed Eggs.

Boil six eggs very hard. Peel them, and after having sliced a bit off of each end to make them stand well, cut in halves and extract the yolks. Rub up the yolks with a pinch of pepper and salt, melted butter, bread crumbs, and finely chopped celery. Fill in the whites nicely, stand on end in the pan, lay bits of butter on each egg and bake.—*Mrs. D. P.*

VEGETABLES.

If possible, use vegetables gathered early in the morning, with the dew on them. It is even better to gather them late the evening before, with the evening dew on them (setting them in the ice-house or some cool place), than to gather them after the morning sun has grown hot. If you are living in the city, get your vegetables from market as early in the morning as possible.

As soon as gathered or brought from market, all vegetables should be carefully picked over, washed, placed in fresh water, and set in a cool place till the cook is ready to put them on for dinner.

Put them on in water neither cold nor boiling hot. The slow heating that takes place when you put them on in cold water deprives them of their flavor, to some extent, whilst too rapid heating toughens the vegetable fibre.

Just before they are thoroughly done and tender, add sufficient salt to season them. Do not stir them and mutilate them with a spoon, but turn them into a colander and drain. Place them in a hot dish and put a large tablespoonful of fresh butter over them.

In cooking dried peas and beans, as well as corn, put up in brine, always soak them the overnight. These vegetables should first be parboiled, whether they are to be used for soup or for side dishes.

To Boil Green Peas.

Early in the morning, either buy the peas from market or have them gathered in your garden, while the dew is on them. Shell and lay in cold water till half an hour before dinner. Then put in boiling water and boil steadily a half hour. Add a little salt, just before taking from the fire. Drain, add a heaping tablespoonful fresh butter and put in a covered dish.—*Mrs. S. T.*

To Cook Asparagus.

As soon as you get the asparagus from market or your garden, throw into salt and water, after scraping the outer skin and tying up in bunches. Put on to boil one hour before dinner. After boiling thirty minutes, drain, cut in pieces half an inch long, and put in the saucepan with enough milk to cover them. Just before serving, add one tablespoonful fresh butter, in which one teaspoonful flour has been rubbed. Season with salt and pepper.—*Mrs. S. T.*

To Cook Asparagus.

Wash well, scrape, cut off the tough end, tie up in bunches and put in boiling water with a spoonful of salt. Boil thirty minutes or till tender. Lay it on slices of toast in a dish, pour melted butter over it, and serve hot.—*Mrs. P. W.*

To Boil Beets.

Wash them. Do not break or cut the roots. Leave an inch of the tops, so that the color and juice cannot escape. Boil hard for two hours. When tender, slice them, sprinkling over them sugar, then butter and salt to the taste. Sugar is the greatest improvement.—*Mrs. S. T.*

To Bake Onions.

Boil six onions in water, or milk and water with a seasoning of pepper and salt. When done enough to mash, take them off, mash them with butter, grate bread crumbs over them and set them to bake. Or place them whole in the baking dish with butter and bread crumbs.

To Cook Onions.

Boil till tender, in milk and water. Pour melted butter over them, and serve; or chop up and stew with a little milk, butter, and salt.

To Fry Onions.

Wash and slice them. Chop fine, put in a frying-pan and cover with water. Simmer till the water is dried up, then fry brown, with a large slice of fat pork. Add pepper and salt.— *Mrs. S. T.*

To Dress Raw Onions.

Slice and chop fine, and put in weak salt and water till just before dinner. Then drain off and dress with half a teacup vinegar, two tablespoonfuls pepper vinegar, two tablespoonfuls made mustard, two tablespoonfuls white sugar, one tablespoonful salt.

Lay a large lump of ice on top, and garnish with curled parsley; which, eaten after onions, is said to remove the scent from the breath.—*Mrs. S. T.*

Radishes.

As soon as taken from the ground, put in cold water. Then put red and white radishes alternately in a dish of fanciful design, ornamenting with curled parsley, in the centre and around the edges.—*Mrs. S. T.*

Celery.

Wash carefully and put in cold water to keep crisp till dinner. Remove all the green, as nothing is so ornamental as the pure white leaves of bleached celery. If the ends of the stalks have been broken, split and curl them.—*Mrs. S. T.*

To Boil Snaps.

Early in the morning, string round, tender snaps. Throw into water and set in a cool place, till an hour before dinner, when they must be drained and thrown into a pot where the bacon is boiling.—*Mrs. S. T.*

To Boil Snaps Without Bacon.

Prepare as above directed. Boil an hour in hot water, adding a little salt, just before they are done. Drain and serve with pepper, fresh butter and a little cream.—*Mrs. S. T.*

To Stew Cymlings (*or Squash, as it is sometimes called*).

Peel and boil till tender. Run through a colander. To a pint of pulp, add one half pint rich milk, a heaping tablespoonful fresh butter and a little salt. Stew till thick like marmalade. Pepper freely, pour over it, if convenient, half teacup cream, and serve.—*Mrs. S. T.*

TO FRY CYMLINGS.

Steam or boil the cymlings (unpeeled), till tender. When cool, slice and butter them, sprinkle pepper and salt and pour over them a spoonful of eggs, lightly, beaten. Sift over it cracker, pounded fine, and fry a light yellow brown. Take from the frying pan, prepare the other side the same way. Return to the pan and fry it a pale brown.—*Mrs. S. T.*

CYMLINGS FRIED WITH BACON.

Fry some slices of fat bacon in a pan. Remove the bacon when done and keep hot. Fry in the gravy some cymlings that have been boiled tender and cut in slices. While frying, mash fine with a large spoon, and add pepper and salt. Fry brown, and serve with the bacon, if you like.—*Mrs. G. B.*

CYMLING FRITTERS.

After boiling and running through a colander, mix with an egg, season with salt, pepper, and butter, make into cakes and fry a light brown.

CYMLING PUDDING.

Boil young cymlings, mash and run through a colander. Add one teacup of milk, three eggs, a large lump of butter, pepper and salt.

Put in a buttered deep dish, and bake a light brown. For a change, you might line the dish with thin slices of buttered bread, pour in the cymling batter and put some pieces of butter and grated cracker on top.—*Mrs. M. C. C.*

TO BOIL GREEN CORN.

Strip off the outer shucks, leaving only the thin white ones. Cut off the ends. Throw into boiling water. Boil an hour.

Strip off the silk with the shuck. Cut from the cob while hot. Sprinkle over salt, add a tablespoonful fresh butter and serve hot.—*Mrs. S. T.*

Corn Pudding.

1 pint milk.
3 eggs, whites and yolks beaten separately.
3 tablespoonfuls melted butter.
1 dessertspoonful white sugar.
1 heaping teaspoonful cornstarch or flour.
1 teaspoonful salt.
6 ears of corn.

With a sharp knife, slit each row of corn in the centre. Then shave in thinnest slices. Add the corn to the yolks of the eggs, next the butter, cornstarch, sugar, and salt, then the milk, gradually, and last of all the whites. Bake in a hot oven. As soon as a light brown on top, cover with a buttered paper. Grate cracker or bread crumbs over it and serve.—*Mrs. S. T.*

Corn Pudding.

One dozen large ears corn. Cut off the top of the grain, scrape with a knife, so as to get the heart of the grain without the husk. Season with a teacup of cream, a large tablespoonful butter, salt and pepper to the taste. Bake in a dish.—*Mrs. Dr. E.*

Corn Fritters.

3 dozen ears corn.
6 eggs, beaten well.
3 tablespoonfuls flour
Salt to the taste.

Grate the corn, add to it the flour, and gradually mix with the eggs. Beat all hard together. Drop in oval shapes, three inches long, into a pan, in which fry them brown, in equal parts of lard and butter. A batter cake-turner is convenient for turning them.—*Mrs. Dr. J.*

Corn Fritters.

8 large ears of corn, cut three times (not grated).

2 eggs.

1 teacup sweet milk (or more, if the corn is not juicy).

2 teaspoonfuls flour.

Salt and pepper to taste.

Make the mixture the consistency of a soft batter, and fry in lard or butter.—*Mrs. A. W.*

CORN FRITTERS FOR BREAKFAST.

Make a batter as you would for fritters, put in pepper, salt, lard, or butter, add to a quart of batter, a pint of corn, cut from the cob, and fry.—*Mrs. A. P.*

BAKED TOMATOES.

1 quart peeled and sliced tomatoes (not scalded).

1 cup sugar.

1 tablespoonful butter.

1 dessertspoonful salt.

1 teaspoonful black pepper.

1 roll of bread.

Spread a layer of tomatoes on the bottom of an earthen (never a tin) baking dish. Put over it half the sugar, butter, pepper and salt, and crumble half the roll over it in small bits. Then spread another layer of tomato, sugar, etc., ending with the remaining half of the roll. Grate cracker or hard brown biscuit on top, and serve.—*Mrs. S. T.*

Baked Tomatoes.

Scald and peel the tomatoes, or else peel thin with a sharp knife, without scalding. Cut in small pieces, season with a little sugar, salt, pepper, and finely minced onion. Grease a baking dish and line it with thin slices of light bread buttered. Pour the tomatoes in the dish, crumming up a little light bread on them. Spread on top a layer of heavily buttered light bread, and bake.—*Mrs. M. C. C.*

STEWED TOMATOES.

Peel and chop tomatoes till you have a quart. Add one teacup brown sugar, one teacup butter, one teacup bread crumbs. One tablespoonful salt; one teaspoonful black pepper.

Stew till free from lumps and perfectly done. Pour in a deep dish, sift powdered crackers over it, and serve.—*Mrs. S. T.*

Stewed Tomatoes.

Scald and peel the tomatoes, chop fine, season with salt, pepper, onion, and a little sugar. Put in some pieces of buttered light bread, cut up very fine. Add a lump of butter, and stew in a saucepan.—*Mrs. V. P. M.*

TOMATO OMELETTE.

Peel and chop fine one quart of tomatoes, add salt and pepper, a little onion minced fine, a half teacup grated bread. Beat five eggs to a foam, stir into the tomatoes and turn the mixture into a hot pan, greased with butter, stir rapidly till it begins to thicken. Let it brown a few minutes on the bottom, then fold it half over and serve hot. This dish may be made of canned tomatoes, when fresh cannot be obtained.—*Mrs. I. G.*

FRIED TOMATOES.

Slice tomatoes one-quarter inch thick. Put them in a skillet in which a spoonful of nice lard has been melted. After getting hot, the skins of the tomatoes may be removed: Sprinkle with salt and pepper, take the tomatoes out, thicken the gravy with a teacup cream in which a teaspoonful flour has been stirred. Put the tomatoes in a dish and pour the gravy over them. Serve hot.—*Mrs. C. L. T.*

ROPA VIGA.

Select fine ripe tomatoes. Pour boiling water over them so

as to remove the skins readily. Put them in a pan of melted butter, with some pepper and salt. Shred cold meat or fowl over them. Fry sufficiently, and serve hot.—*Mrs. A. D.*

Tomato Toast.

Put some canned tomatoes in a frying pan with a little butter and salt. Cook lightly and pour over slices of toasted bread, buttered and softened with cream.—*Mrs. Dr. G.*

To dress Raw Tomatoes.

Slice a plateful large fresh tomatoes. Pour over them a dressing made of the yolk of one egg and olive oil, creamed smoothly together; salt and pepper to the taste; one teaspoonful prepared mustard, a little vinegar. If you like, you may add sugar.—*Mrs. R. L. O.*

To dress Raw Tomatoes.

Peel and cut in thick slices six large ripe tomatoes which have been kept on ice. Put a layer into a salad bowl, sprinkle with salt, pepper, and powdered sugar. Put in another layer, and so on, till all the tomatoes are disposed of. Pour over the top a teacup of weak vinegar. Cover the top with ice, and set in the refrigerator ten minutes before serving.—*Mrs. S. T.*

Lima Beans.

Shell and throw into cold water. Put in boiling water an hour before dinner; add some salt; when tender, drain off the water and add a tablespoonful fresh butter. Beans are seldom cooked enough.—*Mrs. S. T.*

Lima Beans.

Shell and lay in cold water. Boil thoroughly, and then stew a little with butter, pepper, salt, and cream.—*Mrs. R.*

Succotash.

1 pint shelled Lima beans.

1 quart green corn, cut from the cob.

1 quart tomatoes, prepared and seasoned as for baking.

Boil the corn and beans together till done, then drain off the water and pour in a cup of milk, a tablespoonful of butter, and salt to the taste. Let it boil up, and then pour in the tomatoes. Let all simmer an hour. Baked or stewed dishes should have cracker or brown biscuit grated on top, before sending to the table.—*Mrs. S. T.*

To Fry Cucumbers.

Peel, cut lengthwise in thick slices and lay in water till just before dinner. Wipe dry, sprinkle with pepper and salt, dip in beaten egg, sift over pounded cracker and fry with the cover on till light brown. Prepare exactly as egg-plant.—*Mrs. S. T.*

To Dress Cucumbers Raw.

Gather early in the morning, peel, lay in cold water till just before dinner. Then drain, slice as thin as possible into ice water, which drain and then fill a dish with alternate layers of sliced cucumber and thinly sliced white onion, sprinkled with salt and pepper. Pour a cup of weak vinegar over it and lay a lump of ice on top.—*Mrs. S. T.*

Okra.

Boil young okra till tender, in salt and water. Drain, add half a teacup of cream, and a heaping tablespoonful butter. Let it boil up, turn it out in a dish, sprinkle salt and pepper over it and serve hot.

To Boil Irish Potatoes.

Old potatoes must be nicely peeled and dropped in boiling water, covered with a lid and boiled hard half an hour. Then drain off the water and set by the fire. This makes them mealy.—*Mrs. S. T.*

CREAMED POTATOES.

Peel and boil white mealy potatoes, till perfectly done. Take out one at a time from the saucepan, which must be left on the fire. With a large spoon, mash perfectly fine; add salt, a heaping tablespoonful butter and a teacup rich milk. Stir rapidly ten or fifteen minutes and send hot to the table. It is much lighter when well creamed and beaten.—*Mrs. S. T.*

POTATO SNOW.

Peel and boil in a saucepan, six large mealy white potatoes. Add a little salt to the water. Take them out one by one, leaving the saucepan on the fire. Rub through a sieve into a deep dish, letting it fall in a mound. Do not touch with a spoon or the hand. Have a sauce-boat of melted butter to serve with it at table.—*Mrs. S. T.*

IRISH POTATO CHIPS.

Shave the raw potatoes with a cabbage cutter. Drop the pieces, one at a time, into boiling lard, and fry a rich brown. Sprinkle a little salt over them.—*Mrs. R. L. O.*

TO FRY SLICED POTATOES.

Peel and slice thin. Dry well in a cloth. Fry in lard, stirring till crisp. Take up and lay on a sieve to drain. Sprinkle a little salt over them.—*Mrs. R.*

POTATO CAKES.

Mash potatoes, just boiled. Add salt, pepper, butter, and cream, make into cakes, and fry brown on both sides.—*Mrs. P. W.*

POTATO PUDDING.

May be made by putting potatoes prepared exactly as above directed, in a pudding dish, and baking.—*Mrs. S. T.*

POTATO HASH.

Cut cold boiled potatoes in slices. Put in a pan with boiling water, adding pepper, salt, and butter. Stew till thick, and serve.—*Mrs. Dr. G.*

To Boil Sweet Potatoes.

Boil large, smooth potatoes till quite done. Peel and slice lengthwise. Pour melted butter over them. Some persons like a dressing of pepper, salt, butter, and cream. Others prefer butter, sifted sugar, and grated nutmeg.

To Fry Sweet Potatoes.

Parboil and cut in thick slices, sprinkling over them pepper, salt, and sugar. Fry with a slice of fat pork. Take from the pan, sift over them pounded cracker, and serve.—*Mrs. S. T.*

To Cook Inferior Sweet Potatoes.

Boil till nearly done. Cut in thick slices; put a layer in the bottom of a baking dish. Put pepper, salt, sugar, bits of butter, and a teaspoonful vinegar on this layer, and so on till the dish is filled, leaving a layer of seasoning for the top. Pour over it a teacup rich milk. Put a tin plate on top and bake a few minutes. Put grated cracker, on top.—*Mrs. S. T.*

To Dress Yams.

Steam them till done, peel and slice them. Put in a buttered baking-dish a layer of yam, on which put sugar and some lumps of butter. Fill up the dish in this way, and when full, pour over it milk or cream, and bake brown.—*Mrs. Dr. P. C.*

To Stew Egg-plants.

Put them on whole in a plenty of water, and let them simmer till tender. Then take off the skin and divide them. Mash them well in a deep dish, adding a large spoonful butter and some grated bread crumbs. Grate bread crumbs on top, and brown it.

Purple egg-plants are best.—*Mrs. M.*

To Fry Egg-plant.

Cut the egg-plant in thick slices, carefully paring each piece. Throw it in salt and water, and let it remain there several hours. Take from the water, drain and wipe. Then butter the slices of egg-plant, dip in beaten egg, then in grated cracker, and fry a light brown. Pepper, grate more cracker over them, and serve.—*Mrs. S. T.*

Egg-plant Pudding.

Quarter the egg-plant and lay it in salt and water the overnight, to extract the bitterness. The next day, parboil, peel and chop fine, and add bread crumbs (one teacup to a pint of egg-plant), eggs (two to a pint of egg-plant), salt, pepper, and butter to taste; enough milk to make a good batter.

Bake in an earthen dish twenty minutes.—*Mrs. R. L. O.*

To Bake Egg-plant.

Parboil the egg-plant. Take out the meat and mix it with butter, pepper, salt, and bread crumbs. Fill the hulls with this mixture and bake a dark brown. Cucumbers may be prepared by the same recipe.

Burr Artichokes.

Strip off the coarse outer leaves, cut the stalk, and lay several hours in cold water. Then put in boiling water, with their leaves downward. Keep covered with a plate. Boil steadily two or three hours. Serve with butter, pepper, salt, mustard, and vinegar.—*Mrs. R.*

To Stew Parsnips.

Peel and slice parsnips. Boil them in a covered vessel with slices of nice pork, until done, adding salt and pepper to taste. —*Mrs. G. B.*

To Fry Parsnips.

Peel and parboil the parsnips. Slice lengthwise, and fry with fat pork, sprinkling over them salt, pepper, and sugar. Grate bread crumbs over it and serve. Salsify may be cooked the same way.—*Mrs. S. T.*

To Cook Parsnips.

Boil the parsnips till thoroughly done. Serve with salt, pepper, butter, and cream; or mash the parsnips, mix with an egg batter, and season as before.

To Cook Salsify.

Wash, trim, scrape the roots and cut them up fine. Boil till tender, mash and season with pepper, salt, bread crumbs, butter, and milk. Put in a dish and bake brown.—*Mrs. A. P.*

To Stew Salsify.

Scrape and throw at once in water to prevent from turning dark. Boil till tender in a closely covered vessel. Drain off the water and cut the salsify in pieces half an inch long. Throw in a saucepan with

1 teacup vinegar.
1 teacup water.
1 tablespoonful sugar.
1 tablespoonful butter.
Salt and pepper to taste.

Just before serving, add the yolk of an egg, beaten up and mixed with a little water. The seasoning above given is for one quart salsify.—*Mrs. S. T.*

Another Way to Stew Salsify.

Prepare the salsify exactly as in the foregoing recipe. Boil till tender, drain and cut in pieces, half an inch long, and then stew in milk. Just before serving, add a tablespoonful of butter, rolled in a teaspoonful flour. Let it boil up once. Pepper and salt it, grate cracker over it and serve.—*Mrs. S. T.*

To Fry Salsify.

Prepare as for stewing. When perfectly tender, run through a colander. Add grated cracker, two eggs, well beaten, one tablespoonful vinegar, one tablespoonful butter, one teaspoonful salt, one teaspoonful sugar, a little pepper. Make into oval cakes, roll in grated cracker, and fry a light brown.—*Mrs. S. T.*

To Boil Cabbage with Bacon.

Quarter a head of hard white cabbage, examine for insects, lay in salt and water several hours. An hour before dinner, drain and put in a pot in which bacon has been boiling—a pod of red pepper boiled with it will make it more wholesome and improve the flavor of both bacon and cabbage.—*Mrs. S. T.*

Cabbage Boiled without Bacon.

Prepare exactly as directed in the foregoing recipe.

Boil an hour in a large pot of boiling water. Drain, chop fine, add a tablespoonful butter, the same of cream, the same of pepper-vinegar, and salt and pepper to your taste.—*Mrs. S. T.*

Cabbage Pudding.

Boil nice, hard, white cabbage with good bacon.

When thoroughly done, chop fine and add a large lump or butter, one teacup rich milk, three eggs beaten light, two teaspoonfuls mixed mustard; pepper and salt to the taste.

Pour in a buttered deep dish; put on top dusted pepper, bits of fresh butter, and grated cracker or stale bread.

Bake a light brown.—*Mrs. M. C. C.*

Cabbage Pudding.

Boil the cabbage till tender, chop fine and add four eggs, well beaten, one pound bread crumbs, one teacup melted butter, milk enough to make it as thick as mush, salt and pepper to the taste. Bake in a dish till the eggs and milk are cooked.—*Mrs. McD.*

Warm Slaw.

Cut the cabbage very fine and sprinkle over it a tablespoonful flour. Put a piece of butter, the size of an egg, in the oven to melt. Salt and pepper the cabbage and put it in the oven with the butter. Mix half a teacup of cream with the same quantity of vinegar, pour it over the cabbage and heat thoroughly.—*Mrs. S. G.*

Warm Slaw.

Cut the cabbage (hard red is best) as for cold slaw. Put in a saucepan one-quarter pound butter, two gills water, three gills vinegar, one teaspoonful salt, and a little cayenne pepper. If you like, add a garlic, minced fine. When this mixture has come to a boil, pour it boiling hot over the cabbage, and cover it five or ten minutes, when it will be ready for use.

Warm Slaw.

Wash the cabbage, cut fine and put on the fire with enough water to keep it from burning.

When sufficiently tender, have ready a dressing made of vinegar, pepper, salt, mustard, a spoonful of butter rolled in flour, and beaten eggs, all thoroughly mixed. Stir this quickly in the cabbage and let it boil up.—*Mrs. Col. W.*

Fried Cabbage.

Reserve some cabbage from dinner. Set it away till next morning. Chop fine, season with pepper and salt, and fry brown with a slice of fat bacon.

Cauliflower.

Remove the outside leaves. Cut in four parts, tie them together, put in boiling water and let them simmer till the stalk is thoroughly tender, keeping it covered with water, and removing the scum. Boil two hours, drain well and serve with melted butter. You may cook broccoli by the same recipe, except that you cut it in two pieces instead of four.—*Mrs. R.*

Spinach.

Pick and soak several hours in cold water. Drain and shake

each bunch. Throw in boiling water and boil till tender. Take up with a perforated skimmer. Put in a saucepan with a heaping tablespoonful butter; pepper and salt to taste. Stir in three hard-boiled eggs, chopped up. Let it simmer, stirring frequently. Put in a deep dish and cover with nicely poached eggs, buttered, peppered, and salted. Sea-kale may be prepared by the same recipe.—*Mrs. S. T.*

Turnip Salad.

Pick early in the morning. Wash one peck and put in cold water. Have ready a pot of boiling water in which a piece of bacon has boiled several hours, and the amount of water become much reduced. Take out the bacon, put in the salad, put the bacon back on top of the salad, and boil till very tender. Dip from the pot with a perforated skimmer, lay in a deep dish, skim the fat from the liquor and pour over the salad. Cover with nicely poached eggs. Cover and send to the table hot. Any other kind of salad might be cooked by this recipe.— *Mrs. S. T.*

Turnips.

Boil and mash through a colander. Season with a cup cream, spoonful butter, pepper, and salt, and stew quite dry. Then you may bake them.—*Mrs. Col. W.*

To Stew Turnips.

Peel five or six turnips and put on to boil, adding a little salt to the water. When thoroughly done, mash fine through a colander, season with a teacup of cream, or milk, a tablespoonful butter, red and black pepper, and a little more salt, if needed. Stew two or three minutes. Cabbage prepared the same way is very nice.—*Mrs. C. M. A.*

Resipee for Cukin Kon-feel Pees.

Gether your pees 'bout sun-down. The folrin day, 'bout leven o'clock, gowge out your pees with your thum nale, like gowgin out a man's eye-ball at a kote house. Rense your pees, parbile them, then fry 'em with som several slices uv streekt middlin, incouragin uv the gravy to seep out and intermarry with your pees. When modritly brown, but not scorcht, empty intoo a dish. Mash 'em gently with a spune, mix with raw tomarters sprinkled with a little brown shugar and the immortal dish ar quite ready. Eat a hepe. Eat mo and mo. It is good for your genral helth uv mind and body. It fattens you up, makes you sassy, goes throo and throo your very soul. But why don't you eat? Eat on. By Jings. Eat. *Stop!* Never, while thar is a pee in the dish.—*Mozis Addums.*

Cornfield or Black Eye Peas.

Shell early in the morning, throw into water till an hour before dinner, when put into boiling water, covering close while cooking. Add a little salt, just before taking from the fire. Drain and serve with a large spoonful fresh butter, or put in a pan with a slice of fat meat, and simmer a few minutes. Dried peas must be soaked overnight, and cooked twice as long as fresh.—*Mrs. S. T.*

To Boil Dried Peas.

Soak in boiling water the night before. Then next day parboil and drain. Put in fresh water with a piece of middling or ham, and boil till tender.—*Mrs. Col. W.*

To Boil Dried Lima, or other Beans.

Soak overnight. Next morning, soak in fresh water till two hours before dinner, when boil steadily in a covered saucepan two hours. Drain and add a large spoonful fresh butter, and a little salt.—*Mrs. S. T.*

Corn Put up in Brine.

Late as possible in the fall prepare tender roasting ears for winter use. Strip off the outer shuck, leaving the inner, silky ones next to the grain. Have ready a nice clean wooden firkin or tub, properly scalded and sunned. Sprinkle salt over the bottom. Pack closely with corn. Wash a large flat rock and lay on the top, when nearly full. Pour strong brine over the corn, covering it well. The day before using, strip off the shuck and silk, place in a bucket of cold water (renewing the water once, or twice), and let it stand till ready to use it. Two ears soaked thus, and shaved into a pot of soup with other vegetables, will impart a delicious flavor.—*Mrs. S. T.*

PICKLES AND CATSUPS.

For pickles and catsups, use the best cider vinegar, it being not only more wholesome than other kinds of vinegar, but the only sort that will keep pickles or catsup for any length of time.

In making catsup, or in scalding pickles in vinegar, if a brass kettle is used, it must be scoured with sand and ashes, washed and wiped dry, and then scoured with vinegar and salt. By attending to these directions, the brass kettle may be safely used —though the pickles or catsup must be poured from it the instant it is taken from the fire, or they will canker.

In making pickles, it is a good rule to allow two pounds of sugar to each gallon of vinegar for sour pickle, though a larger proportion must be allowed for sweet pickle.

Vinegar for pickling should be spiced and set to sun from spring to autumn. Never put pickle in a jar that has been used for butter or lard. Examine often to see if the pickle is well covered with vinegar, and if any of it has turned soft, remove it. Keep it in a dry, airy closet, and be careful not to let it freeze. Pickle is generally considered best when from six months to a year old. Some housekeepers use the same vinegar (with a slight addition) from year to year, by draining the pickle as they take it out of the jar.

Pickle Vinegar.

2 gallons cider vinegar.
4 ounces white pepper, beaten.
4 ounces whole allspice.
4 ounces mustard-seed.
2 ounces ground mustard.
2 ounces of mace.
2 ounces of turmeric.
2 ounces of white ginger.
2 ounces of garlic.
2 ounces of horseradish.
2 gills of celery-seed.
2 sliced lemons.
5 pounds of sugar.

This ought to be prepared several months before using, and always kept on hand ready for use.—*Mrs. S. T.*

Pickle Vinegar.

2 gallons vinegar.
1 pint black mustard-seed.
4 ounces ginger.
3 ounces allspice.
1 ounce cloves.
4 ounces whole black pepper.
1 ounce celery-seed.
3 pounds brown sugar.
2 handfuls scraped horseradish.
1 handful garlic.
3 sliced lemons.

Make in May, and sun all summer.—*Mrs. D. R.*

Vinegar for Pickles.

2 gallons vinegar.
1 cup bruised ginger.
1 cup black mustard-seed.

YELLOW PICKLE VINEGAR.

1 cup garlic.
½ cup black pepper.
1 cup celery-seed.
½ cup of mace.
½ cup of cloves.
½ cup of turmeric.
2 pounds brown sugar.
1 pod red pepper.
1 handful horseradish. —*Mrs. P. W.*

Cucumbers (sliced), snaps, gherkins, muskmelons, cabbage, onions, or anything to be put into the spiced vinegar, must be previously boiled tender in strong vinegar and salt—well pressed out—and then put into the pickle vinegar, will soon be ready for use.—*Mrs. J. J. C.*

YELLOW PICKLE VINEGAR.

2 gallons of pure cider vinegar.
1 pint black mustard-seed.
1 pint white mustard-seed.
2 ounces ground mustard.
4 ounces white ginger.
3 ounces pepper.
3 ounces allspice.
1 ounce mace.
1 ounce cloves.
2 ounces turmeric.
1 large handful horseradish.
1 handful garlic.
1 spoonful salt.
1 gill celery-seed.
6 lemons.
5 pounds sugar.

The liquid should be mixed in the spring, and set in the sun —*Mrs. T. M. C.*

Ingredients to One Gallon Green Pickle.

3 pounds of sugar.
½ ounce of mace, full weight, and beaten.
½ ounce of black pepper, full weight, and beaten.
1 ounce ginger, light weight, and beaten.
¼ ounce allspice, light weight.
⅛ ounce cloves, light weight.
½ tablespoonful salt, light weight.
½ ounce celery-seed, light weight.
2¼ ounces cinnamon, beaten.—*Mrs. Dr. P. C.*

Preparing Pickles.

Vegetables for pickle should be kept in cold and strong brine till they turn yellow: then put vine-leaves in the bottom of the kettle, then a layer of vegetables and a layer of leaves till full. Pour on them, boiling salt and water and let them boil until a bright green. Take them, while hot, and place in weak vinegar for a whole week. Then add them to the spiced vinegar. Afterwards rub on them a little turmeric. Prepare the spiced vinegar in May, and expose to the sun every day for some time. —*Mrs. R.*

Yellow Pickle.

2 gallons vinegar.
2 pounds sugar.
1 ounce turmeri
3 ounces allspice
1 ounce cloves.
1 ounce mace.
1 pint mustard-seed.
2 tablespoonfuls celery-seed.

Pound all together and stir into the hot cider vinegar for several minutes. Prepare your vegetables by quartering the cabbage and scalding them in brine; cover them and leave until cold; squeeze dry and hang in the sun; when bleached, throw in plain vinegar, then into the spiced vinegar.—*Mrs. P.*

Yellow Pickle.

2½ gallons vinegar.
7 pounds sugar.
1 pound white mustard-seed.
1 bottle mustard.
1 pound white ginger.
½ pound white pepper.
½ pound turmeric.
2 ounces nutmeg.
2 ounces allspice.
2 ounces cloves.
2 ounces celery-seed.

Pound them all before putting in the vinegar, add one pound scraped horseradish, half-dozen lemons sliced.

Scald two dozen onions, sprinkle them with salt, and let them stand a day; drain off the water and wash well with the vinegar. Add them to your spiced vinegar. Cut your cabbage and scald them in strong salt water till you can run a straw through them; drain them for a day and put into plain vinegar for two weeks; let them drain again a day or two before putting into the prepared vinegar. Put two tablespoonfuls turmeric in the plain vinegar to turn the cabbage yellow.—*Mrs. J. T. A.*

Yellow Pickle.

One peck cabbage cut up. Lay in a jar, sprinkling with salt; leave it twenty-four hours; squeeze out and put in a kettle with half a dozen onions chopped, cover with vinegar, add one ounce turmeric, and boil one hour. Then add:

2 pounds brown sugar.
½ ounce mace.
½ ounce allspice.
½ ounce cloves.

4 tablespoonfuls mixed mustard.
1 teacup black peppercorn.
4 tablespoonfuls ground ginger.
2 tablespoonfuls celery-seed.

Boil till clear.—*Mrs. S. B.*

Yellow Pickle.

2 gallons cider vinegar.
4 ounces beaten white pepper.
4 ounces whole allspice.
4 ounces white mustard-seed.
4 ounces black mustard-seed.
2 ounces mace.
2 ounces turmeric.
2 ounces white ginger.
2 ounces ground mustard.
3 ounces garlic.
3 ounces horseradish.
2 gills celery-seed.
4 sliced lemons.
5 pounds brown sugar.

Should be prepared months before using. Cabbage to be pickled should be boiled or scalded in salt and water until the leaves can be turned back so as to sprinkle salt between them; then must be dried in the sun. Shake all the salt out when dry, and soak in plain vinegar, with a little turmeric sprinkled on each layer of cabbage. After ten days, drain them and put in the spiced vinegar.—*Mrs. S. T.*

YELLOW PICKLED CABBAGE.

1 ounce turmeric.
1 gill black pepper.
1 gill celery-seed.
A few cloves.
A few pieces of ginger.

A QUICK WAY TO MAKE YELLOW PICKLE.

4 tablespoonfuls made mustard.
½ ounce mace.
2 pounds sugar.
1 tablespoonful allspice.

Take one peck of quartered cabbage; slice them and put a layer of cabbage and one of salt; let it remain over night. In the morning squeeze them and put on the fire with four chopped onions, and cover with vinegar; boil for an hour, then add the spices mentioned above, and let it boil an hour longer; when cold it is ready for use.—*Mrs. W. H. M.*

A QUICK WAY TO MAKE YELLOW PICKLE.

Two gallons chopped cabbage, sprinkle one handful salt through it, and let stand over night. Squeeze it out dry and put into a kettle. Add one ounce of celery-seed, one ounce of turmeric, one quarter-pound of mustard-seed, (black and white mixed), five pounds brown sugar, with vinegar enough to cover the whole well.

Boil until the cabbage is tender. Put it in stone jars and keep it closely covered. It is fit for use the day after it is made.—*Mrs. J. C. W.*

YELLOW PICKLE.

2 ounces black mustard-seed.
2 ounces white mustard-seed.
2 ounces celery-seed.
1 ounce coriander.
1 ounce white pepper.
1 ounce green ginger.
2 ounces turmeric.
1 pound brown sugar.

Put these in one and one-half gallons best cider vinegar, and set in the sun. This can be prepared during the winter, if you choose. Quarter your cabbages (small heads about the size of a large apple are best), and put in a tub. Make a strong brine, boil and pour over while hot. Let them stand twenty-four hours and then repeat. On the third day spread them on a board or table, salt them slightly, and let them stand in the hot sun four days, taking care that no dew shall fall on them. Put in a jar, and pour on your prepared vinegar boiling hot. This pickle will not be ready for the table till it has softened and absorbed the vinegar. You can judge of this by your taste. To make quick pickle by this recipe, you simply salt your cabbage for one night, pouring off in the morning the water drawn out by the salt. Then put in the kettle with the spices and vinegar, and boil until a straw will go through.—*Mrs. J. B. D.*

Cabbage Pickle for Present Use.

Boil the cabbage in salt and water till tender; lay them on dishes, drain or press them in a towel.

Boil together two gallons strong vinegar.

1 pint white mustard-seed.

4 ounces ginger.

3 ounces black pepper.

3 ounces allspice.

1 ounce mace.

1 ounce cloves.

1 ounce turmeric.

1 large handful horseradish.

1 large handful garlic.

1 ounce celery-seed.

2 pounds brown sugar.

Pour it over the cabbage boiling hot. If you have no garlic, use one pint onions chopped fine.—*Mrs. H.*

Cut Cabbage Pickle.

Fill the jar with cut cabbage. To every gallon of cabbage put one handful horseradish.

3 tablespoonfuls black pepper.

½ tablespoonful red pepper.

CHOPPED CABBAGE PICKLE.

   3 tablespoonfuls coriander-seed.
   3 tablespoonfuls celery-seed.
   2 tablespoonfuls mace.
   2 tablespoonfuls allspice.
   1 dozen cloves.
   ½ teacup made mustard.
   4 tablespoonfuls white mustard-seed.
   1 pound sugar.
   4 or 5 sliced onions.

Salt your cabbage first as for slaw, and let it stand two or three hours. Put in a porcelain kettle and cover with weak vinegar; put turmeric enough to color, boil it till tender, then drain off the weak vinegar, and cover it with strong cider vinegar, and mix the spices well through it; add three or more tablespoonfuls turmeric, and boil the whole fifteen minutes very hard. When cold, it is ready for use.—*Mrs. S. M.*

CHOPPED CABBAGE PICKLE.

Cut the cabbage as for slaw, pour over it enough boiling brine to cover it. Chop and scald a few onions in the same way, cover both, and leave twenty-four hours; then squeeze in a cloth until free from brine. If it should taste very salt, soak in clear water for a few hours and squeeze again. Loosen and mix the cabbage and onions thoroughly. To one-half gallon cabbage put:

   1 small cut onion.
   1 pound brown sugar.
   1 small box mustard.
   ½ pound white mustard-seed.
   1 small cup grated horseradish.
   ½ ounce mace.
   1 tablespoonful ground black pepper.
   2 ounces celery-seed.
   1 ounce turmeric.

Chopped celery and nasturtiums, if they can be had. Mix

all, and cover with cold vinegar. If necessary, add more vinegar after it has stood awhile.—*Mrs. C. N.*

GREEN PICKLE.

Put the pickles in a strong brine, strong enough to bear an egg. Three weeks is long enough for them to remain in brine, if you wish to make your pickle early in the fall; but they will keep several months, indeed all the winter, by having them always well covered with the brine.

When ready to make your pickle, drain off *every drop* of brine, and pour boiling water over the pickles. Repeat this for three mornings in succession. Then pour off this last water, and soak the pickles two days in cold water, changing the water each morning. Next, pouring off this water, scald the pickles *three* mornings in weak vinegar, weakening the vinegar by putting two quarts of water to one of vinegar. This is the time for greening the pickles, by putting in the jar or keg a layer of pickle, then sprinkling in a little powdered alum, and so on, till the vessel is filled; then pouring on the weakened vinegar. Only use the alum the first morning; but the other mornings pour off the vinegar and pour on a fresh quantity. All this is necessary, if you wish to have pickle perfectly free from the brine, and in a condition to keep. Fill your jars with the pickle thus prepared, and pour over them the best of vinegar, after seasoning it and letting it boil a few minutes. Seasoning to one gallon vinegar:

        3 pounds brown sugar.
        1 tablespoonful allspice.
        1 tablespoonful of cinnamon.
        1 tablespoonful of ginger.
        1 tablespoonful of black pepper, all pounded.
        20 drops oil of cloves, or 3 ounces of cloves.
        1 ounce celery-seed.
        1 pod red pepper.
        2 tablespoonfuls grated horseradish.—*Mrs. C.*

Green Pickles.

Put the pickle in strong brine for two days; then boil the brine and pour it over them hot. Repeat this twice. Then pour over them boiling vinegar and water mixed, three successive times, at intervals of two days. For a three-gallon jar take:

1 teacup black pepper.
1 teacup allspice.
½ teacup of ginger.
½ teacup of mace.
½ teacup of cloves, all beaten, but not fine.
2 heads of cabbage chopped fine.
2 teacups horseradish.
8 onions chopped fine.
1 quart mustard seed.

Take half of the beaten spices and mix with the latter ingredients, also three cups of brown sugar; stuff the mangoes with this. Add the rest to the vinegar with five pounds of sugar, and pour on the pickle hot.

This makes very superior pickle.—*Miss S. S. V.*

Green Pickle [3 gallons].

2 ounces mace.
½ pound ginger, scalded and sliced.
2 ounces cloves.
2 ounces cinnamon.
2 ounces long pepper.
2 ounces black pepper.
2 ounces allspice.
1 ounce nutmeg.
¼ pound horseradish scraped, sliced, but not *dried*.
1 ounce turmeric.
4 ounces black mustard-seed.
1 ounce coriander-seed.

2 ounces garlic, or onion.
2 pounds brown sugar.

Prepare the cucumbers as follows : gather cucumbers, snaps, etc., and put them in a large stone jar, pouring over them a strong brine which has been boiled and skimmed—hot, but not boiling; cover with an old table-cloth to keep the steam in. Let them stand about a week, then take and soak twenty-four hours in cold water. Next put them in a large kettle lined with grape leaves, and fill, covering with weak vinegar. Sprinkle in a dessertspoonful of powdered alum, and cover with grape leaves, setting on the stove until a beautiful bright green. Put in a jar and pour this vinegar over them and let them stand until next day; then dry the pickles with a cloth, and have ready the jar, putting in a layer of the pickles with a layer of the seasoning before mentioned; fill with strong cider vinegar. Tie up closely, and keep in a warm, dry place.

The spices must be bruised or beaten tolerately fine before putting with pickles; and a little salad oil added is an improvement.—*Mrs. P. McG.*

CUCUMBERS OR OTHER SMALL PICKLES.

2 gallons vinegar.
3 tablespoonfuls ginger.
2 tablespoonfuls celery-seed.
1 tablespoonful cinnamon.
2 tablespoonfuls turmeric.
1 tablespoonful horseradish.
1 tablespoonful garlic.
2 tablespoonfuls pepper.
1 teaspoonful cloves.
1 teaspoonful of mace.
1 teaspoonful of allspice; all the spices must be pulverized.

Add the garlic and horseradish when cold. Add two pounds sugar, which must be boiled in the vinegar and poured over the spices. One teaspoonful red pepper will improve it. Boil the vegetables in plain vinegar before putting in the spiced vinegar.

Gherkins and snaps are made in the same way as cucumbers.—*Mrs. S.*

PICKLED CUCUMBERS.

½ gallon vinegar.
3 pounds brown sugar.
2 tablespoonfuls cloves.
2 tablespoonfuls allspice.
2 tablespoonfuls mustard.
2 tablespoonfuls celery.
1 tablespoonful white ginger.
1 tablespoonful cinnamon.
1 tablespoonful black pepper.
2 pods green pepper.
4 lemons sliced.
A little horseradish.
12 onions, and as many cucumbers as the vinegar will well cover.

Boil all together until the cucumbers are tender, and they will be ready for use in a week or so. To green the fruit: line your brass kettle with grape-leaves, and then pour weak vinegar on the cucumbers, cover with leaves, and boil a little while.—*Mrs. E. I.*

CUCUMBER PICKLE.

2 gallons good vinegar.
1 cup bruised ginger.
1 cup mustard-seed.
1 cup garlic.
2 onions chopped fine.
½ teacup black pepper.
1 teacup celery-seed.
½ ounce mace.
½ ounce cloves.
½ ounce turmeric.

1 pod red pepper.
1 handful horseradish.
3 pounds brown sugar.

After greening the cucumbers, put them in plain vinegar for a few days. Then boil the spices in one gallon of the vinegar, and pour it over the pickle boiling hot. Do this twice; it will be ready for use in a week.—*Mrs. P. W.*

Boiled Cucumber Pickle.

Take fresh cucumbers (size for eating), put them in brine for a few days; take them out, and put them in vinegar to soak for two days. Then wipe them dry, cut them in pieces one inch thick. Make a seasoning of a mixture of allspice, cloves, mace, nutmeg, and whole black pepper, about two ounces to seventy-five cucumbers. Add celery-seed, and onion chopped fine.

Take a large stone jar, put a layer of cucumber and a layer of the mixture, with plenty of brown sugar (about eight pounds to a large jar). In this way fill the jar, then cover it with strong vinegar: tie the mouth up securely, put the jar in a pot of cold water, and boil until the cucumber is tender, and they will be ready for use in a few days.—*Mrs. C. C. McP.*

Pickled Cucumbers.

Put them in a wooden or stone vessel, pour over strong salt and water boiling hot, put a weight on to keep them under the pickle. After three days, pour it off, boil, and turn it over again: let stand three days again; then take them out and let them he one night in plain cold water; next day put them over the fire, but do not let them boil, allowing one tablespoonful alum to one gallon vinegar; mace, cinnamon, peppercorns, white and black mustard-seed and grated horseradish, one tablespoonful each to every gallon vinegar, and one teaspoonful turmeric, and two and one-half pounds sugar. Fold a double piece of linen, and a soft, thick brown paper, and tie the jars tight; throw in the vinegar and keep in a dry place. A bladder and linen cloth are nice to be over the pots.—*Mrs. G. P.*

Sweet Cucumber Pickle.

Slice cucumbers and soak in brine a week; then soak in salt water until the salt is extracted sufficiently. Boil in strong alum water half an hour, then in ginger tea half an hour. Make a syrup of one quart good vinegar, one pint water, three pounds sugar, to four pounds cucumbers; season with mace, cinnamon, cloves, and celery-seed. Put in the cucumbers and boil till the syrup is thick enough. Add some sliced ginger.— *Mrs. S. M.*

Cucumber Sweet Pickle.

First lay the cucumbers in salt and water for one week or ten days; next cut them in slices quarter of an inch thick. Then soak out the salt and boil them in alum water half an hour, and afterwards in ginger tea for one hour. Then make a syrup of one pint water, one quart vinegar, three pounds sugar to every four pounds cucumbers. Flavor with cloves, mace, and cinnamon. Boil all together until the syrup is sufficiently thickened. —*Mrs. A. C.*

To Pickle Ripe Cucumbers.

Take them yellow, but not too ripe, scrape the seeds well out; lay them in salt and water twenty-four hours, then make syrup same as for peaches; in a week scald the vinegar again. —*Mrs. C.*

Green Tomato Pickle.

Slice green tomatoes and onions; sprinkle each layer with salt; let them stand until next day, then press all the juice out, and season very highly with red and black pepper, celery, mustard seed, a little turmeric, and some sugar; cover with vinegar, and cook until tender.—*Mrs. M. D.*

Green Tomato Pickle.

Slice and chop green tomatoes, until you have one gallon

Chop one dozen large onions. Mix and sprinkle four large spoonfuls of salt upon them, let it stand one night; next day drain off all the water, and have one quart strong vinegar, two pounds sugar, spices and pepper to your taste. Put in the vinegar, and put with the tomatoes in a porcelain kettle; boil half an hour. Place in the jar for keeping and cover closely. Three or four days afterwards, boil again for a few minutes and put away for use.—*Mrs. L. P.*

Green Tomato Pickle.

One peck tomatoes sliced.
One dozen onions.

Sprinkle with salt, and lay by twenty-four hours; then drain them.

>3 pounds sugar to one gallon vinegar.
>$1\frac{1}{2}$ ounces ground pepper.
>1 ounce whole cloves.
>1 ounce mustard-seed.
>1 ounce allspice.
>1 cup mustard, mixed.

Put all in a kettle, with vinegar enough to cover; boil till tender.—*Mrs. S. B.*

TO MAKE GREEN TOMATO SAUCE.

>16 pounds tomatoes.
>7 pints good cider vinegar.
>4 pounds brown sugar.
>$\frac{1}{2}$ pint celery-seed.
>$\frac{1}{2}$ pint mustard-seed.
>$1\frac{1}{2}$ pints onions, cut fine.
>1 teacup ground mustard.
>$\frac{1}{2}$ ounce mace.
>2 ounces cinnamon.
>1 ounce allspice.

½ ounce cloves.
¼ pound black pepper.

Put all of the spices in the vinegar, and boil one hour. Then put in the tomatoes, which you must slice the night before, and put one layer of salt and one of tomatoes. Drain the water off, and boil the tomatoes in the spiced vinegar till done.—*Mrs. Dr. S.*

GREEN TOMATO SAUCE.

Peel and slice the tomatoes. To two gallons add:

5 tablespoonfuls ground mustard.
2½ tablespoonfuls ground black pepper.
2 tablespoonfuls ground allspice.
2 tablespoonfuls ground cloves.
3 gills white mustard-seed.
1 gill celery-seed.
1 gill salt.
1 pint onions, chopped fine.
2 quarts brown sugar.
2 quarts vinegar.

Beat all the spices, except the mustard-seed, and boil together until thick as marmalade.—*Mrs. S. T.*

Green Tomato Sauce.

2 gallons tomatoes, sliced.
3 tablespoonfuls salt.
3 gills of mustard-seed, whole.
2½ tablespoonfuls pepper.
1½ tablespoonfuls allspice.
3 tablespoonfuls mustard, beaten smooth.
1 teaspoonful cloves.
1 teaspoonful cinnamon.
1 teaspoonful celery-seed.
1 pint onions, chopped fine.
1 quart sugar.
2½ quarts vinegar.

Mix thoroughly and boil till done.—*Mrs. P. McG.*

Sweet Tomato Pickle.

Peel small tomatoes with a sharp knife; scald in strong ginger tea until clear. To four pounds tomatoes, two pounds sugar, not quite one quart vinegar; cinnamon, mace, nutmeg, to taste.

Scald the tomatoes and pour on boiling hot.—*Mrs. J. H. F.*

Sweet Tomato Pickle.

Boil green tomatoes in strong ginger tea for ten minutes. Then take out, and to every two pounds add one quart of vinegar, one pound sugar, cinnamon, cloves and mace to your taste.—*Mrs. P.*

Sweet Tomato Pickle.

Slice one gallon green tomatoes, and put a handful salt to each layer of tomatoes. Let them stand twelve hours, then drain off the liquor, and add to them two green peppers, and from two to four onions, sliced; take two quarts vinegar, half a pint molasses, two tablespoonfuls mustard, one teaspoonful allspice, and one of cloves; heat it until it begins to boil, then put in tomatoes, onions, and peppers; let them boil ten minutes: pour into a stone jar, and seal tight. In a fortnight they will be ready for use.—*Mrs. Dr. P. C.*

To make Piccalilli.

To one-half bushel nicely chopped tomatoes, which must be squeezed dry, add two dozen onions, chopped fine, one dozen green peppers, chopped, one box ground mustard, one large root horseradish, nearly one pint salt, four tablespoonfuls ground cloves, four tablespoonfuls allspice.

Mix thoroughly in a stone jar and cover with vinegar, making a hole in the centre to let the vinegar to the bottom.—*Mrs. B.*

Ripe Tomato Pickle.

Puncture the tomato with a thorn or straw. Put a layer of tomatoes, with onions cut up. Sprinkle salt on them, then put another layer of tomatoes and onions, with salt sprinkled over them. When you have filled the jar or vessel with tomatoes, let them remain about a week, then lay them in dishes to drain. Give each tomato a gentle squeeze, to get the salt water out. Put them in a jar and cover with strong vinegar. Boil a small quantity of vinegar with pepper, horseradish, and such other spices as you like, and pour it over the tomatoes. To two gallons of tomatoes, use a box of mustard dissolved in the vinegar.—*Mrs. C. C.*

Tomato Marmalade or Sauce for Meats.

Scald and peel fully ripe tomatoes, then cut them up, if large. To twelve pounds add six pounds sugar, one tablespoonful beaten cloves, one tablespoonful spice and one tablespoonful cinnamon.

Boil all in a kettle until the syrup becomes the thickness of molasses. Then add one quart of strong vinegar and boil for ten minutes. Put away in quart jars —*Mrs. McG.*

Hyden Salad.

1 gallon cabbage.
½ gallon green tomatoes.
¼ gallon onions,—all chopped fine.
4 tablespoonfuls salt.
2 tablespoonfuls ginger.
2 tablespoonfuls cloves.
1 tablespoonful cinnamon.
2 tablespoonfuls mustard.
1½ pounds brown sugar.
Plenty of celery-seed.
½ gallon strong vinegar.

Boil the whole one-half hour.—*Mrs. H. D.*

Hyden Salad.

Cut one gallon cabbage as for slaw, one-half gallon green tomatoes. Cut up one pint green pepper, taking out the seed carefully and cutting up the pod (do not use the seed), one quart onions cut up, and the water pressed from them and thrown away.

Mix all these, and sprinkle through them 2 tablespoonfuls salt, and let them stand over night. Then take:

    2 pounds sugar.
    3 large spoonfuls ginger.
    3 large spoonfuls turmeric.
    3 spoonfuls celery-seed.
    3 spoonfuls ground mustard.
    2 spoonfuls allspice.
    2 spoonfuls cinnamon.
    1 spoonful cloves.
    1 spoonful mace.

Beat all fine, and mix with the salad; pour over the whole three quarts good vinegar, and simmer for twenty minutes. Ready for use very soon, and very good.—*Mrs. C. M. A.*

Hyden Salad.

    1 gallon cabbage, chopped fine.
    ½ gallon green tomatoes, chopped fine.
    ½ pint green pepper, chopped fine.
    1 pint onions, chopped fine.

Sprinkle salt, and let it stand overnight; next morning, pour boiling water over, and squeeze dry. Take:

    2 ounces ginger.
    4 tablespoonfuls ground mustard.
    1 ounce cinnamon.
    1 ounce cloves.
    2 ounces turmeric.
    1 ounce celery-seed.
    2 pounds sugar.
    2 spoonfuls salt.
    ½ gallon vinegar. Boil ten minutes.—*Mrs. H.*

Hyden Salad.

Cut up fine, 1 gallon cabbage.

½ gallon green tomatoes.

½ pint green pepper.

1 quart onions minced, the juice thrown away.

Add to all these:

> 4 tablespoonfuls ground mustard.
>
> 2 tablespoonfuls ginger.
>
> 1 tablespoonful cinnamon.
>
> 1 tablespoonful cloves.
>
> 2 ounces of turmeric.
>
> 1 ounce celery-seed.
>
> 2 pounds sugar.
>
> 2 tablespoonfuls salt.

Mix all well together, add one-half gallon good vinegar, and boil slowly twenty minutes. Take the seed out of the green pepper. Make late in the summer.—*Mrs. R.*

Hyden Salad.

1 gallon of finely chopped cabbage.

1½ gallon green tomatoes.

1 pint green peppers—½ pint will do.

1 quart onions.

½ pint horseradish.

1 pound sugar.

½ gallon vinegar.

4 tablespoonfuls ground mustard.

2 tablespoonfuls ginger.

1 tablespoonful cloves.

1 tablespoonful cinnamon.

1 tablespoonful celery-seed.

2 spoonfuls salt.

Beat the spice well, mix all together well, and boil fifteen minutes.

Black peppers can be used instead of the green, one tablespoonful ground.—*Mrs. E. C. G.*

OIL MANGOES.

1 pound race ginger, well soaked, beaten and dried.
1 pound horseradish.
1 pound white mustard-seed.
1 pound black mustard-seed.
2 ounces ground mustard.
2 ounces black pepper.
2 ounces turmeric.
2 ounces cloves.
½ ounce mace.
1 ounce celery-seed.
2 pounds sugar.

Beat the ingredients together in a mortar, and mix the mustard with as much olive oil as will make a paste. Then after the mangoes have been in brine two weeks, and greened as you would cucumbers, stuff them; if any filling is left, sprinkle between the layers in the jar. Pour over as much boiling vinegar as will cover them.—*Mrs. T. C.*

TO MAKE OIL MANGOES.

Put the mangoes in strong brine for five days. Wash them, and remove the seed.

Stuffing for the same.

1½ pound white mustard-seed.
¼ pound pounded ginger.
⅛ pound black pepper, pounded.
4 tablespoonfuls celery-seed.
3 ounces mace.

Mix these ingredients with as little oil as possible, stuff the mangoes with it, adding scraped horseradish and one blade of garlic. Pour cold vinegar over them, and one pound salt. Press the mangoes under the vinegar, and watch them closely. It is well to scald the vinegar in the spring.—*Mrs. H. T.*

To Green Mangoes.

After taking them from the brine, lay them in a kettle with grape-vine leaves between each layer of mangoes; a little alum sprinkled on each layer. Let them simmer all day, changing the leaves if necessary. If not green enough, put them on the second day.—*Mrs. E.*

Mangoes.

To a three-gallon jar of mangoes prepared for the vinegar, take:

1 teacup black pepper.
1 ounce allspice.
½ ounce ginger.
½ ounce mace.
½ ounce cloves, beat well, but not fine.
Take one head of raw cabbage.
8 onions.
2 teacups of horseradish.
1 quart of mustard-seed.

Take half the beaten spices, and mix with the latter ingredients, also three cups of brown sugar; besides, put one teaspoonful brown sugar in each mango before you put in the stuffing.

It takes five pounds of sugar for a three-gallon jar. The balance of the sugar mix with the spice and vinegar enough to cover the pickle.—*Mrs. H. C.*

Stuffing for Sixty Mangoes.

1 pound black mustard-seed.
1 pound white mustard-seed.
2 pounds chopped onion.
1 ounce mace.

PEACH MANGOES.

    1 ounce nutmeg.
    2 handfuls black pepper.
    1 ounce turmeric, well mixed with cold water.
    Pound the mace, nutmeg, and pepper.
    1 cup sweet oil.
    ½ pound English mustard.
    4 pounds brown sugar.

Mix all these well together, throwing in little bits of mango or cucumbers.

PEACH MANGOES.

Pour boiling salt water over the peaches—let them stand two days; take them out and slit them on one side, and put them in turmeric vinegar for two days. Extract the seed, stuff and sew them up, and put in the prepared vinegar. Prepare the stuffing as follows: chop some of the peaches from the turmeric vinegar, add a large quantity of mustard-seed, celery-seed, a good deal of brown sugar—one pound to two and a half pounds peaches; ground ginger, cinnamon, cloves, pepper, turmeric, and any other spices, if you like. Onions chopped fine. Vinegar to be seasoned the same way; and any of the stuffing left may be put in the vinegar.—*Mrs. C. C.*

Peach Mangoes.

Remove the stones from large white Heath peaches by cutting in halves. Stuff them with white mustard-seed, a little pounded mace, turmeric, and celery-seed. Sew them up, and drop them in with the yellow cabbage.—*Mrs. H. T.*

Peach Mangoes.

Pour boiling salt water over the peaches, let them stand two days; then take them out, slit them on the side, and put them in turmeric vinegar for two days or longer. Take them out, extract the seed, stuff them, sew them up, and put into the prepared vinegar. To prepare the stuffing:

Chop up some of the peaches, add a large quantity of white

mustard-seed, a good deal of brown sugar, some ground ginger, cinnamon, cloves, pepper, turmeric, celery-seed, also a great deal of chopped onion. Vinegar, seasoned with same ingredients. Quantity of spices can be regulated by your taste.—*Miss S.*

Peach Mangoes.

Take large plum peaches, sufficient quantity to fill the jar. Peel nicely, and take out the stones. Have ready the stuffing in proportion to the peaches. Mince fine some soft peaches, preserved orange peel, preserved ginger, coriander-seed, celery-seed, a small quantity mace, cinnamon, candied strawberries, if you have them, and pickled cherries. Sew the peaches up, after stuffing them, and fill the jar. Then to every pound coffee sugar add one-half pint vinegar, allowing the above quantity to two pounds fruit. Make a syrup of the sugar and vinegar, and pour on the peaches, boiling-hot Repeat this for three mornings; the fourth morning put them all on together, and boil a short time; add a few spices, cinnamon, and ginger to the syrup when you make it. They will be ready for use in a few weeks.—*Mrs. R.*

Pepper Mangoes.

With a sharp knife take the cap out of the pod, then scrape out the seed. Lay the pods in weak salt and water for one hour.

Take hard cabbage, chop them very fine, and to every quart of cabbage, add

1 tablespoonful salt.
1 tablespoonful pulverized black pepper.
2 tablespoonfuls white mustard-seed.
1 teaspoonful ground mustard.

Mix all this well together, drain the peppers, and stuff them with the mixture, and replace the cap.

Pack them closely in a stone jar, with the small end downwards. Do this until the jar is filled; then pour on them strong cold vinegar. They are ready for use in three weeks. You can use spices and sugar, if preferred.—*Mrs. W. A. S.*

To Pickle Walnuts.

After the walnuts have been in brine six weeks, scrape and wipe them with a coarse towel. Put them in plain vinegar, and let them remain for a week or two. Drain them well—place in a jar, and pour over them vinegar spiced and prepared as for yellow pickles, omitting the turmeric and lemons, and using black pepper instead of white.—*Mrs. S. T.*

Walnut Pickle.

The walnuts must be quite green and tender. First soak them in fresh water, then rub off with a coarse towel. The walnuts must be kept in brine a week, and then soaked in clear water for several hours. Boil them in vinegar a little while— this time put water in the vinegar; then put them in good strong vinegar, a portion of which must be boiled and poured over them four successive mornings. Season with cinnamon, mace, cloves, and add two pounds sugar to one gallon vinegar, or in proportion to quantity of pickle.—*Mrs. C. C.*

Walnut Pickle.

Gather the nuts about the 10th or 20th of June, when they are sufficiently tender to be pierced with a pin; pour boiling salt water on, and let them be covered with it nine days, changing it every third day. Put them on dishes to air, until they are black; then soak out the salt, and put them in weak vinegar for a day or two; put into the jar, and pour on hot the following pickled vinegar:

7 ounces ginger.
7 ounces of garlic.
7 ounces of salt.
7 ounces of horseradish.
½ ounce red pepper.

½ ounce of orange peel.
½ ounce of mace.
½ ounce of cloves, all boiled in 1 gallon strong vinegar.
1 ounce black pepper also.—*Mrs. J. H. F.*

Walnut Pickle.

Put the walnuts in salt water for five or six weeks; then in fresh water for twenty-four hours; boil in weak vinegar and water until soft enough to run a straw through. Then rub them with a coarse towel; make a strong liquor of vinegar, horseradish, garlic, and mace; pour on, and leave them till ready for use, in two or three weeks.—*Mrs. T.*

To Pickle Martinas.

Take one gallon pot full of martinas. Make a brine strong enough to bear an egg; keep them covered for ten days. Take them out and wash them in cold water, then put them in cold vinegar. Let them remain for ten days; drain them, and put them in the jar intended for use. In half a gallon of vinegar scald a large handful of horseradish, scraped fine.

A cupful black pepper.
1 cupful ginger.
½ cupful black mustard-seed.
3 tablespoonfuls of beaten cloves.
3 onions sliced fine.
1 pod red pepper.
3 pounds brown sugar.

Pour them over the pickle, and fill with cold vinegar.—*Mrs. S. D.*

Pickled Martinas.

Put three gallons of martinas in very strong brine, keep covered for ten days, then wash them in cold water, and put them in vinegar to stand ten more days; then drain and put them in the jar intended for them. In three pints of vinegar, scald:

A large handful of scraped horseradish.
1 cup allspice.
½ cup black pepper.
1 cup of ginger.
½ cup of black mustard.
3 large spoonfuls of cloves, all beaten.
3 onions sliced.
1 pod red pepper.
3 pounds brown sugar.

Pour it over the martinas, and fill up with cold vinegar.—*Miss E. T.*

To Pickle Martinas.

Put the martinas in a strong brine of salt and water, let them remain a week or ten days. Then wash them, and put them in cold vinegar, to soak the salt and greenish taste out of them. When ready to pickle, lay them out to drain; scald the following ingredients in a gallon of vinegar, and pour over them in a jar; if not full, fill up with cold vinegar.

1 large handful of sliced horseradish.
1 teacup of allspice.
½ cup of black pepper.
½ cup of mustard-seed (black).
2 tablespoonfuls cloves.
2 pounds brown sugar.
3 or four onions, sliced.

The spices to be beaten, but not too fine. This quantity fills a two-gallon jar.—*Mrs. J. J. M.*

Chow-Chow Pickle.

½ peck green tomatoes.
2 large cabbages.
15 onions.
25 cucumbers.
1 plate horseradish.
¼ pound mustard-seed.

CHOW-CHOW.

1 ounce celery-seed.
2 ounces ground pepper.
2 ounces turmeric.
½ ounce cinnamon.

Cut the onions, tomatoes, cucumbers and cabbage in small pieces; pack them down overnight in salt, lightly; in the morning pour off the brine, and put them to soak in weak vinegar two days; drain again, and mix the spices. Boil half a gallon vinegar and three pounds sugar, and pour over them hot. Mix two boxes ground seed.—*Mrs. R. A.*

Chow-Chow.

½ peck onions.
½ peck green tomatoes.
5 dozen cucumbers.

Slice all very fine, and put in a few whole cucumbers, one pint small red and green peppers; sprinkle one pint salt over them, and let them stand all night; then add:

1 ounce mace.
1 ounce white mustard-seed.
1 ounce celery-seed.
1 ounce turmeric.
1 ounce whole cloves.
3 tablespoonfuls ground mustard.
2 pounds brown sugar.
1 stalk horseradish, grated fine.

Cover all with one gallon and one pint of strong vinegar, and boil thirty minutes.—*Miss E. T.*

Chow-Chow.

½ peck onions.
½ peck green tomatoes.
3 dozen large cucumbers.
4 large green peppers.
½ pint small peppers, red and green.

Sprinkle one pint salt on, and let them stand all night; the cucumbers not peeled, but sliced one inch thick, the onions also sliced. In the morning drain off the brine, and add to the pickles:

    1 ounce mace.
    1 ounce black pepper.
    1 ounce white mustard-seed.
    1 ounce turmeric.
    ½ ounce cloves.
    ½ ounce celery-seed.
    3 tablespoonfuls made mustard.
    2 pounds brown sugar.
    With a little horseradish.

Cover with vinegar, and boil till tender, a half-hour or more When cold, ready for use.—*Mrs. C. N.*

Chow-Chow Pickle.

    1 gallon chopped cabbage.
    4 onions.
    2 pounds brown sugar.
    2 pints strong vinegar.
    2 tablespoonfuls black pepper.
    2 tablespoonfuls of allspice.
    2 tablespoonfuls of celery-seed.
    ½ pint mustard-seed.
    1 tablespoonful ground mustard.

The cabbage and onions must stand in strong salt and water two hours, then place in a brass kettle, with the vinegar and spices, and sugar; boil until syrup is formed. Excellent.—*Mrs. J. H. F.*

Chow-Chow.

The recipe is for one gallon pickle; for more, the quantities must be increased, of course. The ingredients consist of:

    ¼ peck green tomatoes.
    1 large head of cabbage.

LEESBURG CHOW-CHOW.

6 large onions.
1 dozen cucumbers.
½ pint grated horseradish
½ pound white mustard-seed.
½ ounce celery-seed.
A few small onions.
¼ teacup ground pepper.
Turmeric, ground cinnamon.
A little brown sugar.

Cut the cabbage, onions and cucumbers into small pieces, and pack them down in salt one night; then put in vinegar, poured over hot. Do this three mornings. The third morning, mix one box ground mustard with one-quarter pint salad oil. To be mixed in while warm.—*Mrs. O. B.*

LEESBURG CHOW-CHOW.

½ peck green tomatoes.
2 large heads cabbage.
15 large white onions.
25 cucumbers.

Cut these up, and pack in salt for a night. Drain off, and then soak in vinegar and water for two days. Drain again. Mix with this, then:

1 pint grated horseradish.
½ pint small white onions.
½ pound white mustard-seed.
1 ounce celery-seed.
½ teacup ground black pepper.
¼ teacup turmeric.
½ teacup cinnamon.

Pour over one and a half gallons boiling hot vinegar. Boil this vinegar for three mornings; the third morning, mix with two boxes mustard, three pounds brown sugar, and half-pint sweet oil.—*Mrs. J. B. D.*

Sweet Pickle Peaches.

Powder cloves, mace, and allspice, and mix well together.

To every pound fruit add one-quarter pound sugar, one gill vinegar, one teaspoonful of the mixed spices. Boil all together, and when the fruit is done, take from the syrup, and lay on dishes. Let the syrup cook thoroughly. Put the fruit in jars, and pour on the syrup. Cover when cool.—*Mrs. D. R.*

To Pickle Peaches.

1 pound peaches.
½ pound sugar.
1 pint vinegar.

Mace, cloves, cinnamon; boil the ingredients every day, for six days, and pour over the peaches.—*Mrs. F. D. G.*

Spiced Peaches.

Take nine pounds ripe peaches, rub them with a coarse towel, and halve them. Put four pounds sugar and one pint good vinegar in the kettle with cloves, cinnamon, and mace. When the syrup is formed, throw in the peaches a few at a time; when clear, take them out and put in more. Boil the syrup till quite rich; pour it over the peaches.

Cherries can be pickled in the same way.—*Mrs. C. C.*

Peaches to Pickle.

Make a syrup with one quart vinegar and three pounds sugar; peel the peaches and put them in the vinegar, and let boil very little. Take out the fruit, and let the vinegar boil half an hour, adding cinnamon, cloves, and allspice.—*Mrs. A. H.*

Pickled Peaches.

Take peaches pretty ripe, but not mellow; wipe with flannel as smooth as possible; stick a few cloves in each one. One pound sugar to one pint vinegar. Allow three pounds sugar and three pints vinegar to one pan peaches. Scald the vinegar, then put on the peaches; boil till nearly soft, then take out and boil the vinegar a little longer, and pour over the fruit.—*Mrs. G. P.*

Pickled Peaches.

Put the peaches in strong brine, and let them remain three or four days; take them out, and wipe them dry; put them in a pot with allspice, pepper, ginger, and horseradish; boil some turmeric in your vinegar. Pour it on hot.—*Miss E. T.*

PEACH, PEAR, QUINCE AND APPLE PICKLE.

1 pound fruit.
½ pound sugar
½ pint vinegar.

Dissolve sugar and vinegar together; put a small quantity of fruit; boil until you can stick a straw through it. Season with cinnamon and mace. Rescald the vinegar, and pour over the fruit for nine mornings.—*Mrs. Dr. J.*

SWEET PICKLE. (*Honolulu Melon.*)

4 pints vinegar, very clear.
4 pints sugar
1 ounce cloves.
1 ounce cinnamon.

Put all to boil, then drop in the melons, as much as the vinegar will cover, and boil fifteen minutes. Put them in jars, and every day, for two or three days, pour off the vinegar, boil it over, and pour on the pickles until they seem done.—*Mrs. M. W. T.*

CANTALOUPE PICKLE.

Cut up ripe melons into small square pieces, peel and scrape out the soft pulp and seeds, soak one night in alum water, and then boil in strong ginger tea. Then to each pound of fruit add three-quarters of a pound loaf sugar, mace, cinnamon, and white ginger to the taste, and cover with best cider vinegar Boil till it can be pierced with a straw, then set aside, and the next day pour off, and boil the syrup until it thickens a little, and return to the fruit boiling-hot.—*Mrs. F. F. F.*

Cantaloupe Pickle.

Pare and cut in small pieces, cover with vinegar; pour off and measure, and to each pint put three-quarters of a pound brown sugar cloves and mace to your taste.

Boil the syrup, put in the fruit and boil until clear; then take out the fruit, boil a few minutes longer, and pour it on the pickles, hot. When cold, it is ready for use.—*Mrs. E. I.*

Cantaloupe Pickle.

Take four or five cantaloupes, quarter, and cover with vinegar; to stand twenty-four hours. Then measure off the vinegar, leaving out one quart. To each quart, add three pounds brown sugar, cinnamon, cloves, and mace to the taste. Place the spiced vinegar over the fire, and when it has boiled awhile, drop in the fruit, cooking it thirty or forty minutes.—*Mrs. R. P.*

RIPE MUSKMELON PICKLES.

Take hard melons, after they are sufficiently ripe to be well flavored. Slice them lengthwise, scrape out the seed, and lay the melon in salt over night; wash and wipe dry, put them in alum water one hour, wash and wipe them again; cut them in slices and pack in jars. Pour over them a syrup of vinegar seasoned with cinnamon and cloves; put three or four pounds of sugar to one gallon vinegar, and boil until it is right thick.—*Mrs. A. C.*

SWEET WATERMELON PICKLE.

Trim the rinds nicely, being careful to cut off the hard coating with the outer green. Weigh ten pounds rind and throw it in a kettle, and cover with soft water; let this boil gently for half an hour, take it off and lay it on dishes to drain. Next morning put one quart vinegar, three pounds brown sugar, one ounce cinnamon, one ounce mace, the white of one egg well beaten and thrown on top of the liquid (to clear it as you would jelly), three teaspoonfuls turmeric, all together in a kettle, and boil for a few minutes; skim off what rises as scum with the egg. Throw in the rind, and boil for twenty minutes. The peel of two fresh lemons will give a nice flavor, though not at all necessary.—*Mrs. L. W. C.*

WATERMELON PICKLE.

4 pounds watermelon rind.
2 pounds sugar.
1 pint vinegar.
Mace, cloves, cinnamon, and ginger to the taste.

Peel the rind and cut in pieces; boil in ginger tea till clear, then throw in cold water overnight. Next morning make a syrup and preserve the rind; just before taking off the fire, pour in the vinegar.—*Mrs. A. T.*

WATERMELON RIND PICKLE.

Ten pounds melon, boil in water until tender. Drain the water off. Make a syrup of two pounds sugar, one quart vinegar, one-half ounce cloves, one ounce cinnamon; boil all this and pour over rind boiling-hot; drain off the syrup and let it come to a boil; then pour it over the melons.—*Mrs. C. C. McP.*

PICKLE OF WATERMELON RIND.

Cut in pieces and soak the rind in weak salt and water for twenty-four hours—of course having first peeled off the outside. To seven pounds rind put three pounds sugar; scald well in ginger tea, and make a syrup of the sugar and vinegar, enough to cover the rind. Season the syrup with mace and ginger, and boil the rind in it till tender. A delicious pickle.—*Mrs. Dr. P. C.*

PICKLED PLUMS.

7 pounds sweet blue plums.
4 pounds brown sugar.

2 ounces stick cinnamon.
2 ounces whole cloves.
1 quart vinegar.

Put a layer of plums and spice alternately; scald the vinegar and sugar together; pour it on the plums; repeat for two or three days, the last time scalding plums and syrup together.—*Mrs. W.*

To Pickle Damsons.

Take seven pounds damsons, wash and wipe them dry, three pounds sugar, one-half ounce cinnamon, half-ounce mace, half-ounce cloves, half-ounce allspice.

With one quart strong vinegar and the sugar make a syrup, and pour it over the fruit boiling-hot. Let it stand twenty-four hours; repeat the boiling next day, and let it remain twenty-four hours longer; then put all on the fire together and cook till the fruit is done.—*Miss D. D.*

Sweet Pickle.

Boil in three quarts of vinegar four or five pounds sugar, one ounce cinnamon, one ounce allspice, one ounce mace, one-half ounce cloves, and pour all over fourteen pounds damsons or peeled peaches.—*Mrs. O. B.*

German Pickle.

½ pound white sugar.
1 pound damsons.
1 pint vinegar.
1 teaspoonful cloves.
A few sticks of cinnamon.

Make a syrup with vinegar, sugar and spices, then drop in a few of the damsons at a time. Scald them until the skins crack, laying each quantity in a dish till all are done. Fill the jars three-fourths full, and pour in the syrup.—*Mrs. R. L. P.*

Damson Pickle.

7 pounds fruit.
1 ounce cinnamon.
1 ounce cloves.
1 ounce mace.
1 ounce celery-seed.
3 pounds brown sugar.

Spices to be beaten fine; put them in the jar, sprinkling the spice through in layers. Boil one quart vinegar with the sugar, and pour over the fruit and spices. Repeat the scalding of the vinegar for four days.—*Mrs. C. N.*

Composition Pickle.

1 gallon chopped cabbage,
½ gallon green tomatoes, sliced,
½ gallon cucumbers,
1 quart onions,

all finely chopped. Let them stew several hours, then drair off the water. Add:

4 tablespoonfuls ground mustard.
2 tablespoonfuls ginger.
1 ounce cloves.
2 ounces turmeric.
2 ounces celery seed.
2 pounds brown sugar.
2 spoonfuls salt.
½ gallon strong vinegar; boil twenty minutes.—*Mrs. C. C.*

Ragout Pickle.

2 gallons chopped cabbage.
2 gallons green or ripe tomatoes.
5 tablespoons of mustard, ground.
3 gills mustard-seed.
2 tablespoonfuls allspice.

2 teaspoonfuls cloves.
1 gill salt.
1 pint chopped onions.
1 pound brown sugar.
Some chopped celery, or celery-seed.
3 quarts good cider vinegar.

Boil all well together, and it is ready for use.—*Miss E. T.*

Kentucky Pickle.

Take green tomatoes, cabbage, and onions, about equal quantities—grind them in a sausage machine. Salt, and put the mixture in a bag, and let it hang all night or until the juice has run from it—then season with red and black pepper, mustard-seed, celery-seed, cloves, sugar.

Pack in jars, and cover with strong cold vinegar.—*Mrs. M. D.*

French Pickles.

1 peck green tomatoes.
¼ peck onions.
¼ pound white mustard-seed.
1 ounce allspice.
1 ounce cloves.
1 bottle mixed mustard.
2 tablespoonfuls black pepper.
1 tablespoonful cayenne.
1 ounce celery-seed.
1 pound brown sugar.

Slice the tomatoes and lay them in salt for twelve hours; pour off the brine.

Slice the onions, and put a layer of onions, tomatoes, spices and sugar into a bell-metal kettle, until the ingredients are all in. Pour in vinegar until well covered, and boil for one hour.—*Mrs. Dr. S.*

French Pickle.

1 gallon cabbage.
½ gallon green tomatoes.

1 quart onions.
6 pods green pepper, without the seed.
3 tablespoonfuls ground mustard, or seed.
1 tablespoonful ginger.
1 tablespoonful horseradish.
1 tablespoonful cinnamon.
1 tablespoonful cloves.
2 tablespoonfuls salt.
1 tablespoonful celery.
¼ pound sugar.
½ gallon vinegar.

Chop up cabbage, tomatoes, onions, and pepper; sprinkle salt over it, and let it stand an hour or so, and pour off the liquor. Add spices and vinegar, boil all together until you can stick a straw through the cabbage and tomatoes. This, as you see, will only make a small quantity when boiled down.—*Mrs. M. McN.*

Spanish Pickle.

4 dozen large cucumbers.
4 large green peppers.
½ peck onions.
½ peck green tomatoes.

Slice the whole, and sprinkle over with one pint salt, allow them to remain over night, then drain them. Put the whole into a preserving kettle, and add the following ingredients: sliced horseradish according to your judgment, one ounce mace, one ounce white pepper, one ounce turmeric, one ounce white mustard-seed, half an ounce cloves, half an ounce celery-seed, four tablespoonfuls of dry mustard, one and a half pounds brown sugar. Cover the whole with vinegar, and boil it one hour.—*Mrs. J. J. M.*

Onion Pickle.

Peel and scald the onions in strong salt water twenty-five or thirty minutes; take them out and lay on dishes in the sun, a day or two, then put them in vinegar prepared as for cabbage pickle.—*Mrs. Dr. J.*

Pickled Onions.

Pour boiling water over the onions and let them stand until the brine gets cooled; then change the brine for nine mornings, warming it every day. The ninth day put them in fresh water, and let them soak one day and night. Then put the spices and vinegar on the fire, and let them come to a boil, and drop in the onions in a few minutes; add sugar to your taste.—*Mrs. A. H.*

Lemon Pickle.

Rasp the lemons a little and nick them at one end; lay them in a dish with very dry salt, let them be near the fire, and covered. They must stand seven or eight days, then put in fresh salt, and remain the same time; then wash them well, and pour on boiling vinegar, grated nutmeg, mace, and whole pepper. Whenever the salt becomes damp, it must be taken out and dried. The lemons will not be tender for nearly a year. The time to pickle them is about February.—*Mrs. A.*

Pickling Fifty Lemons.

Grate off the yellow rind, cut off the end, and pack in salt for eight days. Set them in a hot oven, in dishes; turning until the salt candies on them. Place them in a pot and pour on two gallons vinegar (boiling) to which has been added two pounds white mustard-seed, two tablespoonfuls mace, one pound ginger, four tablespoonfuls celery-seed, one pound black pepper, two pounds sugar, one handful horseradish scraped.

All the spices, except mustard-seed, must be pulverized.—*Mrs. H. P. C.*

Apple Pickle.

3 pounds apples.
2 pounds sugar.
1 pint vinegar.

1 teaspoonful mace.
1 tablespoonful beaten cinnamon.
1 dozen cloves.
2 teaspoonfuls allspice.
1 tablespoonful beaten ginger.
1 tablespoonful celery-seed.

Boil until the apples are perfectly clear.—*Mrs. J. A. S.*

Cherry Pickle.

Pick firm, ripe, short-stem cherries, and lay them in a stone jar, with the stems on. Put into a kettle vinegar, sweetened to your taste, allspice, mace, cloves, and cinnamon.

Put on the fire until it is scalding hot, then pour over the cherries, and let them stand until next day, when the vinegar must be poured off them into the kettle again, and scalded as before, and poured on the cherries. Repeat this for nine mornings, and your pickle is ready for use.—*Mrs. C.*

Pickled Blackberries.

One pound sugar, one pint vinegar, one teaspoonful powdered cinnamon, one teaspoonful allspice, one teaspoonful cloves, one teaspoonful nutmeg. Boil all together, gently, fifteen minutes, then add four quarts blackberries, and scald (but not boil) ten minutes more. The spices can be omitted, if preferred.—*Mrs. W.*

Tomato Catsup.

Take sound, ripe tomatoes, grate them on a coarse grater, then strain through a wire sieve, throwing away the skins and seed. Then put the liquid in a cotton bag and let it drip for twenty-four hours. Take the residuum and thin to the proper consistency with vinegar. Then season it to your taste with garlic, salt, pepper, and spices.—*Mrs. A. A.*

Tomato Catsup.

One-half bushel tomatoes stewed sufficiently to be strained

through a colander; to every gallon of pulp add three quarts strong vinegar, two tablespoonfuls salt, four tablespoonfuls grated horseradish, one pound brown sugar, three large onions chopped fine, one tablespoonful black pepper. Boil till quite thick.—*Mrs. C. B.*

Cold Tomato Catsup.

½ peck ripe tomatoes.
½ gallon vinegar.
1 teacup salt.
1 teacup mustard, ground fine.
4 pods red pepper.
3 tablespoonfuls black pepper.
A handful celery-seed.
1 cup horseradish.

All of the ingredients must be cut fine, and mixed cold. Put in bottles, cork, and seal tight. It is better kept awhile.— *Mrs. P.*

Tomato Catsup.

1 gallon pulp of tomatoes.
1 tablespoonful ginger.
2 tablespoonfuls cloves.
1 tablespoonful black pepper.
2 tablespoonfuls grated horseradish.
2 tablespoonfuls salt.
⅔ gallon vinegar.

Boil all well together, then add three pounds sugar, and boil awhile.—*Mrs. M. S. C.*

Tomato Catsup.

Put into a preserving kettle about one pint water, fill up the kettle with ripe red tomatoes, previously washed and picked, with the skins on, cover closely, and set on a hot fire; frequently stirring that they may not stick to the bottom. Boil about one hour. Turn into a wooden tray; when cool enough, rub through a coarse sieve, through which neither skin nor seed can pass. Measure five quarts of this pulp, and boil until very thick, then add two tablespoonfuls horseradish, two tablespoonfuls white mustard-seed, two tablespoonfuls celery-seed, two tablespoonfuls black pepper beaten fine, two or three races of ginger beaten fine, three or four onions chopped fine, a little garlic, one nutmeg, salt and sugar to the taste.

Stir all in, and let it come to a boil. Pour in one quart strong cider vinegar. Let it boil up once more, and take off the fire. Bottle, cork, and seal.—*Mrs. S. T.*

Cucumber Catsup.

Pare and grate the cucumbers. To one quart of cucumbers add three large onions grated, one teaspoonful salt, one teaspoonful pepper, and as much vinegar as cucumbers. Exclude the air.—*Mrs. L. P.*

Cucumber Catsup.

Grate three cucumbers; one onion, one pint of vinegar, one tablespoonful black pepper, one tablespoonful salt, one teaspoonful pounded celery-seed.

Put the catsup in bottles, with large mouths; as the cucumber settles, and is hard to get out.—*Mrs. H. T.*

Cucumber Catsup.

Chop three dozen large cucumbers and eight white onions, fine as possible, or grate them. Sprinkle over them three-fourths of a pint of salt, one-half teacup ground pepper; before seasoning, drain off all the water through a sieve; mix well with good vinegar, and bottle.—*Mrs. P. W.*

Cucumber Catsup.

One dozen cucumbers, four large onions, four tablespoonfuls salt, four teaspoonfuls black pepper, one quart strong vinegar. Grate onions and cucumbers.—*Mrs. H. D.*

Walnut Catsup.

To one gallon vinegar:
Add 100 walnuts pounded.
2 tablespoonfuls salt.
A handful horseradish.
1 cup mustard-seed, bruised.
1 pint eschalots, cut fine.
½ pint garlic.
¼ pound allspice.
¼ pound black pepper.
A tablespoonful ginger.

If you like, you can add cloves, mace, sliced ginger, and sliced nutmeg. Put all these in a jug, cork tightly, shake well, and set it out in the sun for five or six days, remembering to shake it well each day. Then boil it for fifteen minutes, and when nearly cool, strain, bottle, and seal the bottles.—*Mrs. A. C.*

Walnut Catsup.

Take forty black walnuts that you can stick a pin through; mash and put them in a gallon of vinegar, boil it down to three quarts and strain it. Then add a few cloves of garlic or onion, with any kind of spice you like, and salt. When cool, bottle it. Have good corks.—*Miss E. T.*

To make Catsup of Walnuts.

Bruise the walnuts (when large enough to pickle) in a mortar; strain off the liquor and let it stand till it be clear; to every quart thus cleared add one ounce of allspice, one ounce black pepper, one ounce ginger bruised fine. Boil the whole about half an hour; then add one pint best vinegar, one ounce salt, eight eschalots, or one ounce horseradish. Let it stand to cool; then strain it again, and bottle for use.—*Mrs. M. P.*

To make Walnut Catsup from the Leaves.

Provide a jar that will hold about three gallons. Mix the following ingredients: common salt one pound, one-half ounce powdered cloves, four ounces powdered ginger, one handful garlic sliced, six pods bruised red pepper, three handfuls horseradish root, sliced. Gather the young leaves from the walnut—cut them small. Put a layer at the bottom of the jar; then sprinkle on some of the ingredients, and so on with alternate layers, until the jar is packed full. Let the whole remain in this state one night. Then fill with boiling vinegar, tie it closely, and let it set in the sun for a fortnight. Then press out the liquor, strain and bottle.—*Mrs. E. W.*

Bay Sauce.

Get young walnut leaves while tender. Make a mixture of the following ingredients: one quart salt, one handful horseradish, one-half dozen onions chopped up, two teaspoonfuls allspice, one tablespoonful black ground pepper.

Put in a layer of the leaves, and then one of the mixture, so on till the jar is nearly filled; cover with good cold vinegar. Put it in the sun for a fortnight, then bottle. It will not be good for use until it is six months old.

This is an excellent sauce for fish. It will improve it to add a tablespoonful of ground ginger.—*Mrs. E. C. G.*

Bay Sauce.

One pound salt, one-half ounce cloves, four ounces ginger, all powdered; three handfuls garlic, three handfuls horseradish scraped fine, six pods of red pepper cut up fine. Gather leaves of black walnut when young, cut them up fine; put a layer of leaves in the bottom of a jar, then one of ingredients (mixed together), until the jar is filled; tie it up closely and set it in the sun for two weeks; then bottle for use. It is not good for six months. Some think two or three large onions an addition.—*Mrs. H. D.*

MUSHROOM CATSUP.

Take the largest mushrooms, cut off the roots, put them in a stone jar, with salt; mash them and cover the jar. Let them stand two days, stirring them several times a day; then strain and boil the liquor, to every quart of which put one teaspoonful whole pepper, cloves, mustard-seed, a little ginger; when cold bottle it, leaving room in each bottle for one teacupful strong vinegar, and one tablespoonful brandy.

Cork and seal.—*Mrs. C.*

Mushroom Sauce.

After peeling, lay them on the oyster broiler and sprinkle with a little salt. Have ready a hot dish with butter, pepper, salt, and cream, and throw the mushrooms into this as they are taken from the broiler. A very nice sauce for steaks.—*Mrs. J. S.*

Mushroom Catsup.

Break one peck large mushrooms into a deep earthen pan. Strew three-quarters pound salt among them, and set them one night in a cool oven, with a fold of cloth or paper over them. Next day strain off the liquor, and to each quart add one ounce black pepper, one-quarter ounce allspice, one-half ounce ginger, two large blades mace.

Boil quickly twenty minutes. When perfectly cold, put into bottles, and cork well, and keep in a cool place.—*Mr. J. B. N.*

Mushroom Catsup.

Pack the mushrooms in layers, with salt, in a jar; let them stand three hours, then pound them in a mortar, return them to the jar and let them remain three or four days, stirring them occasionally.

For every quart of the liquor add, one ounce of pepper, half ounce allspice; set the jar in the kettle of water, and boil four hours, then pour the liquor through a fine sieve, and boil until it is reduced one-half.

Let it cool and bottle.—*Mrs. C. C.*

Horseradish Sauce.

Five tablespoonfuls scraped or grated horseradish, two teaspoonfuls sugar, one teaspoonful salt, half teaspoonful pepper, one tablespoonful mixed mustard, one tablespoonful vinegar, four tablespoonfuls rich sweet cream. Must be prepared just before using.—*Mrs. S. T.*

Horseradish Sauce.

Just before dinner, scrape one teacup of horseradish, add one teaspoonful white sugar, one saltspoonful salt, and pour over two tablespoonfuls good cider vinegar. It is best when just made.

Celery Vinegar.

Pound a gill of celery-seed, put in a bottle and fill with strong vinegar. Shake it every day for two weeks, then strain it, and keep it for use. It will flavor very pleasantly with celery.—*Mrs. Dr. J.*

Celery Vinegar.

Take two gills celery-seed, pound and put it in a celery bottle, and fill it with sharp vinegar. Shake it every day for two weeks; then strain it, and keep it for use. It will impart an agreeable flavor to everything in which celery is used. Mint and thyme may be prepared in the same way, using vinegar or brandy. The herbs should not remain in the liquid more than twenty-four hours. They should be placed in a jar—a handful is enough, and the vinegar or brandy poured over them; take out the herbs next day, and put in fresh. Do this for three days; then strain, cork, and seal.—*Mrs. R.*

Pepper Sauce.

2 dozen peppers.
Twice this quantity of cabbage.
1 root of horseradish, cut up fine.
1 tablespoonful mustard-seed.
1 dessertspoonful cloves.

2 tablesponfuls sugar.

A little mace.

Boil the spices and sugar in two quarts of best cider vinegar, and pour boiling hot over the cabbage and pepper.—*Mrs. W. A. S.*

PEPPER VINEGAR.

One dozen pods red pepper, fully ripe. Take out stems and cut them in two. Add three pints vinegar. Boil down to one quart; strain through a sieve, and bottle for use.—*Mrs. Dr. J.*

RED PEPPER CATSUP.

To four dozen fine ripe bell-peppers add two quarts good vinegar, one quart water, three tablespoonfuls grated horseradish, five onions chopped fine. Boil till soft, and rub through a sieve. Then season to your taste with salt, spice, black and white mustard well beaten; after which boil ten minutes. Add celery-seed if liked, and a pod or more strong pepper, a little sugar. All should be cut up and the seed boiled with it. Bottle and cork tightly.—*Mrs. G. N.*

CAPER SAUCE.

Stir in melted butter two large tablespoonfuls capers, a little vinegar. Nasturtiums pickled, or cucumbers cut very fine will be good substitutes for the capers. For boiled mutton.—*Mrs. R.*

Caper Sauce.

To one cup drawn butter add three tablespoonfuls green pickled capers. If prepared for boiled mutton, use half teacupful of the water in which it was boiled; add salt and cayenne pepper. Let it boil up once and serve.—*Mrs. S. T.*

TARTAN SAUCE.

One mustardspoon of mixed mustard, salt and cayenne to the taste. the latter highly.

Yolk of one raw egg, sweet-oil added very slowly, until the quantity is made that is desired; thin with a little vinegar.

Take two small cucumber pickles, two full teaspoonfuls capers, three small sprigs parsley, and one small shaleot or leek. Chop all fine, and stir into the sauce about an hour before serving. If very thick, add a tablespoonful cold water. This quantity will serve eight persons—is good with trout, veal cutlets, and oysters.—*Miss E. S.*

Morcan's Tartan Sauce.

Put into a bowl one spoonful of dry mustard, two spoonfuls salt, a little cayenne pepper, yolk of one raw egg; mix these together.

Then add, drop by drop, one teacupful sweet-oil; stir until a thick mass. Add a little vinegar. Chop very fine two small cucumber pickles, two teaspoonfuls capers, two sprigs parsley, one leek or small onion, and a little celery; stir all into the dressing. This is delicious with boiled fish, either hot or cold— also cold meats, chicken or turkey.—*Mrs. S.*

Aromatic Mustard.

4 tablespoonfuls ground mustard.

1 tablespoonful flour.

1 tablespoonful sugar.

1 teaspoonful salt.

1 teaspoonful black pepper.

1 teaspoonful cloves.

1 teaspoonful cinnamon.

Mix smoothly with boiling vinegar, add a little salad oil, and let it stand several hours before using. It will keep any length of time.—*Mr. R. H. M.*

To Mix Mustard.

Take half a cup ground mustard, one tablespoonful sugar, four tablespoonfuls vinegar, olive oil, or water, whichever is preferred, one teaspoonful pepper, and one of salt.—*Mrs. P. W.*

CAKE.

Before commencing to make cake, be sure that you have all the ingredients in the house, and all the implements at hand, such as trays, bowls, large dishes, large strong iron spoons, egg-beaters, etc.

Use none but the best family flour in making cake. It is a good plan to sift it before weighing or measuring it, and to let it air and sun several hours before using it; as this makes it much lighter.

It is a great mistake to set aside rancid or indifferent butter for cake-making. The butter used for the purpose should be good and fresh.

Always use granulated sugar or else powdered loaf or cut sugar; as pulverized sugar is apt to have plaster of Paris or other foreign elements in it. Never use brown or even clarified sugar in cake-making, unless it be for gingerbread.

Do not attempt to make cake without fresh eggs. Cream of tartar, soda and yeast powders are poor substitutes for these.

A fresh egg placed in water will sink to the bottom.

In breaking eggs, do not break them over the vessels in which they are to be beaten. Break them, one by one, over a saucer, so that if you come across a defective one, you will not spoil the rest by mixing it with them; whereas, if it is a good one, it will be easy to pour the white from the saucer into the bowl with the rest of the whites, and to add the yolk which you retain in the egg-shell to the other yolks.

The Dover egg-beater saves much time and trouble in beating eggs and will beat the yolks into as stiff a froth as the whites. It is well to have two egg-beaters, one for the yolks and the other for the whites. Eggs well beaten ought to be as stiff as batter. Cool the dishes that you are to use in beating eggs. In summer, keep the eggs on ice before using them, and always try to make the cake before breakfast, or as early in the morning as possible.

Some of the best housewives think it advisable to cream the butter and flour together, and add the sugar to the yolks when these are whipped to a stiff froth, as it produces yellow specks when you add the sugar sooner. The whites must always be added last.

In making fruit cake, prepare the fruit the day before. In winter time, this may be easily and pleasantly done after tea. It requires a longer time to bake fruit cake, than plain. Every housekeeper should have a close cake-box in which to put cake after cooling it and wrapping it in a thick napkin.

WHITE CAKE.

The whites of 20 eggs.
1 pound of flour.
1 pound of butter.
1 pound of almonds.

Use a little more flour, if the almonds are omitted.—*Mrs. Dr. S.*

White Cake.

1 cup of butter.
3 cups of sugar.
1 cup of sweet milk.
The whites of 5 eggs.
3 cups of flour.
3 teaspoonfuls cream of tartar.
1 teaspoonful of soda.—*Mrs. D. C. K.*

SUPERIOR WHITE CAKE.

1 pound sugar.
The whites of 10 eggs.
¾ pound butter.
1 pound of flour.

Flavor with lemon or rose-water, and bake in a my oven.—*Mrs. F. C. W.*

LEIGHTON CAKE.

1 pint butter.
1 pint cream.
2 pints sugar.
4 pints flour.
2 teaspoonfuls essence of almonds.
The whites of 12 eggs.
2 teaspoonfuls yeast powder, mixed in flour.—*Mrs. N.*

WHITE MOUNTAIN CAKE.

4 cups flour.
1 cup butter.
3 cups sugar, creamed with the butter.
1 cup sweet milk.
2 small teaspoonfuls cream of tartar.
1 small teaspoonful of soda.
Whites of 10 eggs beaten very light.

Bake in jelly-cake pans; when cold, make an icing of whites of three eggs and one pound of sugar. Grate cocoanut over each layer of icing.—*Mrs. P. McG.*

White Mountain Cake.

1 pound sugar.
½ pound butter.
¾ pound of flour.
1 large teaspoonful essence of bitter almonds.
Whites of 10 eggs, whipped very stiff.

Cream butter and sugar, put next the eggs, then the flour, lastly the flavoring.—*Mrs. D. C. K.*

White Mountain Cake.

Make four or five thicknesses of cake, as for jelly cake. Grate one large cocoanut. The juice and grated rind of two lemons or oranges. The whites of six eggs beaten very light, with one pound sugar. To this add the milk of one cocoanut, then rind and juice of one orange. Lastly, stir in the cocoanut well, and put between the cakes as you would jelly.—*Mrs. J. L.*

White Mountain Cake.

1 pound flour.
1 pound sugar.
¾ pound butter.
Whites of 16 eggs.
Wine-glass of wine or brandy.
Bake in flat pans.

Grate two cocoanuts. Beat the whites of four or five eggs to a stiff froth, and mix as much sugar as for icing. Stir in the cocoanut; spread between each layer of the cake, as jelly cake. Ice it all, or only on top, or not at all, as you please.—*Mrs. M.*

Mountain Cake.

The whites of 8 eggs.
1 cup of butter.
2 cups of sugar.
3 cups of flour.
½ cup sweet milk.
1 teaspoonful of cream of tartar.
½ teaspoonful of soda.

Mix all the ingredients well, and flavor with lemon. Bake in very shallow pans. Ice each cake separately and cover with jelly; then form a large cake, and ice over.—*Mrs. Dr. S.*

Snow Mountain Cake.

1 cup of butter.
3 cups of sugar, creamed together.
1 cup of sweet cream.
1 teaspoonful cream of tartar and ½ teaspoon of soda, sprinkled in 3½ cups of sifted flour.
Whites of 10 eggs.

Bake in thin cakes as for jelly cakes. Ice and sprinkle each layer with grated cocoanut.

Take the whites of three eggs for the icing, and grate one cocoanut.—*Mrs. C. M. A.*

Snow Cake.

Whites of 10 eggs.
1½ cups of sugar.
1 cup of flour.
2 teaspoons of cream of tartar.
Salt.
Flavoring.

Rub the flour, cream tartar, sugar, and salt, well together. Add the eggs beaten light, and stir only sufficient to mix very lightly.—*Mrs. G. P.*

White Mountain Ash Cake.

1 pound white sugar.
1 teacup of butter.
½ teacup sweet milk.
Whites of 10 eggs.
½ small teaspoonful of soda.
1 teaspoonful cream tartar.
3 cups of flour.
Flavor with vanilla or almond.

Bake in jelly-cake pans, with icing and cocoanut between.

Icing for cake.—One pound fine white sugar, and whites of three eggs.—*Miss E. P.*

Mountain Ash Cake.

The whites of 8 eggs.
1 cup of butter.
2 cups of sugar.
3 cups of flour.
½ cup of sweet milk.

BRIDE'S CAKE.

½ teaspoonful of soda.
1 teaspoonful cream of tartar.

Mix all the ingredients well, and flavor with lemon.

Bake in shallow pans; ice each cake separately and cover with jelly, then form a large cake and ice over.—*Mrs. P.*

BRIDE'S CAKE.

1 pound flour.
¾ pounds sugar.
½ pound butter.
Whites of 14 eggs.

Cream sugar and butter together, and stir in them flour and beaten whites, very little at a time; one and a half pounds fruit, prepared and mixed with batter, will make a nice fruit cake.—*Mrs. H. D.*

Bride's Cake.

Whites of 18 eggs.
1¼ pounds sugar.
1 pound flour.
¾ pound butter.

Cream butter and sugar together; whip the eggs to a stiff froth, then add gradually, flour, butter, sugar.

Season with lemon or brandy. Bake as pound cake.—*Mrs. R. E.*

Bride's Cake.

1½ pounds flour.
1½ pounds sugar.
1⅛ pounds butter.
Whites of 20 eggs.
½ a teaspoon of powdered ammonia dissolved in ½ a wineglass of brandy.

Heavy plain icing. 1½ pound mould.

Insert the ring after the cake is baked.—*Miss S.*

Bride's Cake.

¾ pound flour.
½ pound butter.
14 whites of eggs.
1 pound sugar—beat in the whites.
The acid of 1 green lemon.

Double for one and a half pound cake.—*Mrs. J.*

Silver Cake.

Whites of 8 eggs.
¼ pound of butter.
½ pound of sugar.
¼ and ½ a quarter of a pound of sifted flour, or 6 ounces of flour.

Cream the butter and sugar.—*Mrs. W. C. R.*

Silver Cake.

1 pound powdered sugar
¾ pound flour.
½ pound butter.
Whites of 11 eggs.
1 teaspoonful essence of bitter almond.

Cream the butter, gradually rub in the flour, then the sugar; add the flavoring; last of all, stir in the whites of the eggs beaten to a stiff froth. Flavor the icing with vanilla or bitter almonds.—*Mrs. S. T.*

Silver Cake.

One cup sugar.
½ cup butter.
1½ cups flour.
½ cup of milk.
½ teaspoon of cream tartar, and half as much soda
Whites of 4 eggs.

Beat the butter and eggs to a cream, then add the milk and flour with the soda and cream tartar; whisk the whites of the eggs to a froth, and stir them in gently at the last. Flavor with lemon.—*Mrs. C.*

Gold Cake.

1 pound flour.
1 pound sugar.
¾ pound butter.
Yolks of 11 eggs.
Grated rind of an orange.
Juice of 2 lemons.
1 teaspoonful soda.

Cream the butter well, rub into it the flour. Beat the yolks well, put in the sugar, and beat again; add the orange rind and lemon juice.

Mix all together, and beat for ten minutes. Last of all, sift in the soda, stirring it in well. Requires two hours to bake in one pound cake-mould. Flavor the icing with lemon.—*Mrs. S. T.*

Angel's Cake.

Whites of 8 eggs, well beaten.
1 cup of butter.
2 cups of sugar.
3 cups of flour.
1 teaspoonful cream of tartar.
½ teaspoonful of soda, dissolved in ½ cup of milk.

Mix in this way; add the sugar to the eggs, then the butter well creamed, then the flour and milk alternately. Season to taste. Bake thin, and spread icing between, on the top and sides, sprinkling grated cocoanut over the whole.—*Mrs. C.*

Lady Cake.

1 pound sugar.
½ pound of flour.
6 ounces of butter.
The whites of 14 eggs.

Season with two drops oil of bitter almond.—*Miss S.*

Lady Cake.

The whites of 8 eggs, beaten to a froth.
3 cups flour.
2 cups of sugar.
1 cup of butter, creamed with the sugar.
1 teaspoonful cream of tartar in the flour.
½ teaspoonful of soda in ½ cup sweet milk.

Beat all together, and bake in a mould or small pans. Season to taste. A little whisky or rum improves cake of all kinds.—*Mrs. Dr. C.*

DELICATE CAKE.

2 cups white sugar.
2½ cups corn starch.
8 tablespoonfuls butter.
Whites of 8 eggs.
½ teaspoonful soda, dissolved in milk.
½ teaspoonful cream tartar in corn starch.

Flavor with juice of one lemon.—*Mrs. R. R.*

Delicate Cake.

One pound pulverized white sugar, seven ounces of butter (stirred to a cream).
Whites of 16 eggs, beaten stiff.
Stir in 1 pound of sifted flour.
Flavor to the taste. Bake immediately.—*Mrs. A. H.*

MERRY CHRISTMAS CAKE.

2 cups sugar.
1 cup corn starch.
2 cups flour.
1 cup butter.
½ cup sweet milk.
Whites of 8 eggs.
2 teaspoonfuls baking powder.

Bake in jelly-cake pans. Between each layer when done, on

sides and top, spread icing, with grated cocoanut. A very pretty dish.—*Mrs. McG.*

Corn Starch Cake.

1 cup butter.
2 cups sugar.
1½ cups corn starch.
2 cups flour.
1 cup milk, perfectly sweet.
¼ teaspoonful soda.
½ teaspoonful cream tartar.

Beat the sugar and butter together. Dissolve the soda and corn starch in the milk; put the cream tartar in the flour. Mix these well, and then add the whites of eight eggs well beaten. —*Mrs. S.*

White Fruit Cake.

1 pound sugar.
1 pound flour.
1 pound butter.
1 pound blanched almonds.
3 pounds citron.
1 cocoanut.
Whites of 16 eggs.—*Mrs. Dr. J.*

White Fruit Cake.

1 pound pulverized sugar.
¾ pound butter.
Whites of 12 eggs, beaten very light.
1 pound flour.
2 grated cocoanuts.
2 pounds citron, cut in small pieces.
2 pounds blanched almonds, cut in thin slices.

Bake slowly.

White Fruit Cake.

Whites of 16 eggs, beaten well.
8 ounces butter.
1 pound flour.
1 pound sugar.
1 teacup citron.
1 cup almonds.
3 cups grated cocoanut.

The citron and almonds to be cut and blanched, of course.

White Fruit Cake [superior, tried recipe].

1 pound white sugar.
1 pound flour.
½ pound butter.
Whites of 12 eggs.
2 pounds citron, cut in thin, long strips.
2 pounds almonds, blanched and cut in strips.
1 large cocoanut, grated.

Before the flour is sifted, add to it one teaspoonful of soda, two teaspoonfuls cream tartar. Cream the butter as you do for pound cake, add the sugar, and beat it awhile; then add the whites of eggs, and flour; and after beating the batter sufficiently, add about one-third of the fruit, reserving the rest to add in layers, as you put the batter in the cake-mould. Bake slowly and carefully, as you do other fruit cake.—*Mrs. W.*

BLACK CAKE.

1¼ pounds butter.
1½ pounds sugar.
1½ pounds flour.
1½ dozen eggs.
2 pounds stoned raisins.
2 pounds picked and washed currants.
1 pound sliced citron.
2 tablespoonfuls pulverized cloves.

BLACK CAKE.

2 tablespoonfuls nutmeg.
2 tablespoonfuls mace.
2 tablespoonfuls cinnamon.
1 tablespoonful powdered ginger.
1 teaspoonful salt.
2 wineglasses of brandy.—*Mrs. D.*

Black Cake.

1½ pounds flour.
1½ pounds butter.
1½ pounds sugar.
1 pound citron.
2 pounds beaten raisins
2 pounds sweet raisins, well cut.
2 pounds currants.

The juice and rind of two lemons and two oranges, one teaspoonful of soda; after the beaten fruit is well beaten, add the cut fruit. The citron or orange peel should never be rubbed in flour.—*Mrs. P.*

Black Cake.

Yolks of 24 eggs.
1 pound butter.
1 pound sugar.

Take out a gill of the sugar, and in place put one gill of molasses, one pound flour; out of it take six tablespoonfuls, and in place put five spoonfuls of seconds, and one of corn meal.

4 pounds seedless raisins.
⅛ pound citron.
½ pound currants.
½ pound almonds and palm nuts.
2 ounces grated cocoanut.
2 ounces fine chocolate.
1 tablespoonful finely ground coffee.
1 tablespoonful allspice, mace, and cloves.
1 tablespoonful vanilla.

1 gill blackberry wine, or brandy.
1 teaspoonful soda.
2 teaspoonfuls cream tartar.

Bake the mass six hours very moderately.—*Mrs J.*

Fruit Cake with Spices.

1 pound butter.
1 pound sugar.
1 pound flour.
1 dozen eggs.
Mix as for pound cake.
Add 1 pound almonds.
1 pound raisins.
½ pound citron.
1 ounce mace.
1 ounce cloves.
1 ounce allspice.—*Mrs. A. C.*

Fruit Cake.

2 pounds best stoned raisins.
2 pounds currants.
1 pound citron.
12 eggs.
1 pound fresh butter.
1 pound loaf sugar.
1 pound flour.

Make the batter as you would for nice cake, and before adding the fruit, stir into the batter—

4½ teaspoonfuls cream of tartar.
1¼ teaspoonful soda.
1 large tablespoonful of ground cinnamon.
1 small tablespoonful of white ginger.
4½ nutmegs.
1 tablespoonful of *best* molasses.

Add by degrees the fruit and one-half teacup best brandy; bake slowly five hours. Excellent, and will keep good six months.—*Mrs. F.*

Fruit Cake.

18 eggs.
1½ pounds flour.
1½ pounds sugar.
1½ pounds butter.
2 pounds raisins.
2 pounds currants, washed and picked.
1½ pounds citron.
2 nutmegs.
2 pounds almonds, weighed in shell.
2 tablespoonfuls cinnamon.
2 tablespoonfuls mace.
1 small teaspoonful cloves.
1 small teaspoonful salt.
2 teaspoonfuls ginger.
2 wine-glasses of wine.
1 wine-glass of brandy.
1 teaspoonful soda.
2 teaspoonfuls cream of tartar, in a cup of milk.

Let it rise about three hours, then bake slowly, and let it stand a good while after it is baked, in the oven.—*Mrs. C. B.*

Fruit Cake.

2½ pounds butter.
2¼ pounds flour.
25 eggs.
2½ pounds sugar.
3 pounds citron.
5 pounds currants.
5 pounds raisins.
A large spoonful cinnamon.

1 spoonful mace.
4 nutmegs.
A glass wine.
A glass brandy.

This will make a very large cake.—*Mrs. A. P.*

Fruit Cake.

1½ pound risen dough.
10 eggs.
2 cups butter.
4 cups sugar.
1 cup milk.
1 cup wine, or brandy.
1 light teaspoonful soda.
1 teaspoonful lemon extract.
½ teaspoonful cloves.

Beat these ingredients together and add one pound of stoned raisins, one pound of citron dredged in flour.

If very soft for cake, add a little flour.—*Mrs. J. W.*

RICH FRUIT CAKE.

1 quart of sifted flour.
1 pound of fresh butter, cut up in 1 pound powdered sugar.
12 eggs.
3 pounds of bloom raisins.
1½ pound of Zante currants.
¾ pound of sliced citron.
1 tablespoonful each of mace and cinnamon.
2 nutmegs.
1 large wineglassful Madeira wine.
1 large wineglassful French brandy mixed with the spices.

Beat the butter and sugar together—eggs separately. Flour the fruit well, and add the flour and other ingredients, putting the fruit in last. Bake in a straight side mould, as it turns out easier. One pound of blanched almonds will improve this recipe. Bake until thoroughly done, then ice while warm.—*Mrs. L.*

Fruit Cake.

1 pound sugar.
1 pound flour.
1 pound butter.
2 pounds raisins.
2 pounds currants.
1 pound citron.
2 tablespoonfuls of mace and cinnamon.
2 nutmegs, powdered.
½ pint of brandy and wine, mixed.

Bake in a slow oven. Seedless raisins are best for cake.—*Mrs. F. C. W.*

PINEAPPLE, OR ORANGE CAKE.

1 cup of butter.
3 cups sugar.
5 eggs, beaten separately.
3½ cups flour.
½ cup sweet milk.
2 teaspoonfuls cream of tartar.
1 teaspoonful soda.

Bake in jelly-cake tins, four or five deep. Have ready a thick icing, which put on the cakes as thickly as will stick; spread thickly on that the grated pineapple, or orange, the icing to be flavored with the juice of the fruit and a little tartaric acid.—*Mrs. C. C.*

ORANGE CAKE.

Bake sponge cake in jelly-cake pans, three for each cake. Spread an icing between the cakes, made of whites of three eggs, beaten very light, and one and one-quarter pounds powdered sugar.

The rind and juice of one large, or two small oranges.

The rind and juice of one-half lemon; the other half to be used for the cake.—*Mrs. P. McG.*

Orange Cake.

8 eggs.
1½ pounds sugar.
1½ pounds flour.
¾ pound butter.
1 pint milk.
2 teaspoonfuls cream tartar.
1 teaspoonful soda.

Beat the eggs very light, and mix in the sugar and creamed butter. Pour in half the milk, and dissolve the cream tartar and soda in the other half. Add the sifted flour as quickly as possible after the foaming milk is poured in. Bake in jelly-cake pans.

Take six oranges, grate the peel and squeeze the juice with two pounds pulverized sugar. If you use sweet oranges, add the juice of two lemons. After stirring to a smooth paste, spread between the layers of the cake. Ice, or sprinkle over sugar the last layer on top of the cake.—*Mrs. J. C. W.*

Orange Cake.

First make a sponge cake with twelve eggs, the weight of twelve eggs in sugar, and weight of ten in flour. Then make an icing of the whites of two eggs, the juice of one lemon, and the juice and grated rind of two oranges; add sufficient powdered sugar to make the proper consistency for icing—then put between each cake, and on top of the whole cake.—*Mrs. C. B.*

LEMON CAKE.

1 cupful butter.
3 cupfuls white sugar.
5 eggs beaten separately.

Cream butter and sugar together.

LEMON CAKE—"GEN. ROBERT LEE" CAKE.

1 teaspoonful soda.
1 cup milk.
The juice and grated rind of one lemon.
5 small teacupfuls flour.

Bake in small or shallow tins.—*Mrs. C.*

Lemon Cake.

One cupful of butter, three cupfuls of white sugar, rubbed to a cream.

Stir in the yolks of five eggs well beaten, and one teaspoonful of soda dissolved in a cupful of milk; add the whites, and sift in as lightly as possible four cupfuls of flour. Add the juice and grated peel of one lemon.—*Mrs. Dr. S.*

"ROBERT E. LEE" CAKE.

Twelve eggs, their full weight in sugar, a half-weight in flour. Bake it in pans the thickness of jelly cakes. Take two pounds of nice "A" sugar, squeeze into it the juice of five oranges and three lemons together with the pulp; stir it in the sugar until perfectly smooth; then spread it on the cakes, as you would do jelly, putting one above another till the whole of the sugar is used up. Spread a layer of it on top and on sides.—*Mrs. G.*

"GEN. ROBERT LEE" CAKE.

10 eggs.
1 pound sugar.
½ pound flour.
Rind of 1 lemon, and juice of ½ lemon.

Make exactly like sponge cake, and bake in jelly-cake tins. Then take the whites of two eggs beat to a froth, and add one pound sugar, the grated rind and juice of one orange, or juice of half a lemon. Spread it on the cakes before they are perfectly cold, and place one layer on another. This quantity makes two cakes.—*Mrs. I. H.*

Cocoanut Cake.

1 teacup fresh butter.
3 teacups white sugar.
3½ teacups flour.
Whites of ten eggs.
1 cup sweet milk.
1 light teaspoonful soda.
2 light teaspoonfuls cream of tartar.
A little essence of lemon.

Bake in cakes an inch thick and spread with icing, having grated cocoanut stirred in; pile one on another, allowing a little time for drying off. In making the icing, reserve some plain for the outside of cake. Finish off by sprinkling on the prepared cocoanut.—*Miss P.*

Cocoanut Cake.

Beat to a fine cream three-quarters of a pound of butter and half a pound of sugar. Add gradually eight eggs well beaten, then mixed, one tablespoonful essence of lemon, one small nutmeg, grated; mix all well together, then stir in lightly half a pound flour in turn with half a pound of grated cocoanut. Pour the mixture in a well-buttered pan, and bake quickly.— *Mrs. C. V. McG.*

Mountain Cocoanut Cake.

Cream together one pound sugar, half a pound butter. Beat eight eggs lightly without separating. Stir them gradually into the butter and sugar. Sift in one pound of flour, beat all light, then put in an even teaspoonful of soda dissolved in half a teacupful of sweet milk, two even teaspoonfuls cream of tartar dissolved in the same quantity of milk. Season with lemon or vanilla. For the icing, nine tablespoonfuls of water and one pound sugar; boil until it glistens. Beat the whites of four eggs to a stiff froth, stir into the boiling icing, then add half a pound of grated cocoanut. Spread the icing between the cakes and on the top.—*Miss S.*

Angel's Bread.
A variety of Cocoanut Cake.

1 cup butter.
2 cups sugar.
3 cups flour.
Whites of eight eggs.
½ cup sweet milk.
½ teaspoonful soda, 1 teaspoonful cream of tartar, stirred in the milk.
Flavor with vanilla.
Bake in jelly-cake pans.
1 grated cocoanut.

Spread top and bottom of cake with icing, then put on the cocoanut, and so on till your cake is large as you wish. Ice the whole cake, and sprinkle on cocoanut. Make the icing, three whites to one pound of pulverized sugar, with juice of one lemon.—*Mrs. D. R.*

Clay Cake.

3 cups sugar.
1 cup butter.
4 cups flour.
1 cup sweet milk.
6 eggs.
1 teaspoonful soda in the milk.
1 teaspoonful cream of tartar in the flour.

Flavor with vanilla. Bake it in layers.

Icing for the Cake.—Beat the whites of four eggs into a froth, and add nine teaspoonfuls of pulverized sugar to each egg, flavoring it with vanilla. Then grate up two large cocoanuts, and after icing each layer, sprinkle grated cocoanut on it. Put the layers on each other as in making jelly cake.—*Mrs. I. W.*

Cocoanut Cake.

2 cups powdered sugar.
½ cup butter.
3 eggs.
1 cup milk.
3 cups flour.
2 teaspoonfuls cream of tartar.
1 teaspoonful soda.

Bake in jelly-cake pans.

Filling: one grated cocoanut; to half-pound of this add the whites of three eggs beaten to a froth, one cup of powdered sugar; lay this between the layers of the cake; mix with the other half of the cocoanut four tablespoonfuls powdered sugar, and strew thickly on top of the cake.—*Mrs. D. C. K.*

One, Two, Three, Four Cocoanut Cake.

1 cup butter.
2 cups sugar.
3 cups flour.
Whites of 4 eggs.
1 teaspoonful cream of tartar.
½ teaspoonful soda.
⅓ small cocoanut, stirred in at the last.—*Mrs. D. C. K.*

Cocoanut Cake.

1 teacup of butter.
3 teacups of sugar.
3½ teacups of flour.
Whites of 10 eggs.
½ cup sweet milk, with one teaspoon not quite full of soda.
2 teaspoonfuls cream of tartar.
Essence of lemon.

Beat the eggs very light. Cream the butter, then mix the ingredients gradually. Sift the cream tartar with the flour, and dissolve the soda in the milk, and add to the cake last. Bake in pans; an inch thick when baked. Mix prepared cocoanut with the icing; ice the top of the first cake with the cocoanut icing, dry it slightly; lay another cake on top, and ice again, and continue until the last cake is added, then ice all over. When the last coat of icing is put on, sprinkle the prepared cocoanut all over the cake, to give it a frosted appearance.—*Mrs. M. S. C.*

Chocolate Cake.

1½ pounds grated chocolate.
12 eggs.
1¾ pounds brown sugar.
1 teaspoonful cinnamon.
1 teaspoonful nutmeg.
1 teaspoonful cloves.
A few coriander-seed.

Break the eggs in the sugar and beat them, adding the chocolate by degrees, until well incorporated; then add the spices, all of which must be well powdered. Grease some small tins with lard, and bake quickly.—*Mrs. T.*

Chocolate Cake.

2 cupfuls sugar.
1 cupful butter.
3 cupfuls flour.
¾ cupful sour cream or milk.
3 eggs.
1 teaspoonful cream tartar.
½ teaspoonful soda.

Beat the sugar and butter together; break the eggs into it one at a time; then add the flour, then the sour cream with the soda. Bake in jelly-cake pans.

Filling: two ounces of chocolate, one cupful of sugar, three-quarters cup of sweet milk; boil half-done.—*Mrs. F.*

Chocolate Cake.

3 cupfuls sifted flour.
1½ cupfuls sugar.

CHOCOLATE CAKE.

1 cupful sweet milk.
1 egg.
2 tablespoonfuls butter.
1 teaspoonful soda.
2 teaspoonfuls cream tartar.
1 teaspoonful essence lemon.

Beat the butter and sugar to a cream, then add the milk (in which the soda should be dissolved), next the eggs well beaten, and lastly the essence. Mix two cupfuls of flour, and afterwards the third cupful of flour into which the cream tartar has been stirred. Bake in square, flat pans. Grate three ounces of chocolate, add four tablespoonfuls of milk; warm slowly, and add eight tablespoonfuls of white sugar. Boil three minutes, and pour over top of the cake. If you choose, you can slice open the cake, and put inside of it a custard of one pint of milk, warmed, and two eggs added, with sugar and flour to your taste.—*Mrs. H.*

Chocolate Cake.

2 cupfuls sugar.
1 cupful butter.
Yolks of 5 eggs and whites of 2.
1 cupful milk.
3½ cupfuls flour.
½ teaspoonful soda.
1 teaspoonful cream tartar, sifted in the flour.

Bake in jelly-cake tins.

Filling: whites of three eggs, one and a half cupfuls of sugar, three tablespoonfuls of grated chocolate, one teaspoonful of vanilla. Beat well together; spread on top and between layers of the cake.—*Mrs. K.*

Chocolate Cake.

Cream together one pound sugar, one and a half pounds butter. Beat eight eggs light without separating; stir them gradually into the sugar and butter. Sift in one pound of flour:

beat all light. Then put in an even teaspoonful of soda dissolved in a half-teacupful of sweet milk, two even teaspoonfuls cream tartar dissolved in the same quantity of milk. Season with lemon or vanilla. Bake in jelly pans.

Icing for the same: nine tablespoonfuls of water, one pound of sugar; boil till it glistens.

Beat the whites of four eggs to a stiff froth. Stir them into the boiling icing, then add one-quarter pound grated chocolate.

Spread the icing between the cakes and over the top.—*Miss S.*

Chocolate Jelly Cake.

Make a sponge cake according to old family recipe, bake either in jelly tins or moulds; then slice the cake for the following preparation: one teacupful of milk, half a cake Baker's chocolate, scraped or grated, one egg beaten with sugar enough to make it sweet; flavor with vanilla. Let it boil (stirring all the time) till quite thick. Place it evenly and thickly between the slices of cake. Instead of the sponge cake, some use the ordinary jelly-cake recipe.—*Mrs. B.*

Citron Cake.

12 ounces flour.
12 ounces butter.
10 eggs.
1 pound sugar.
1 pound citron, cut in thin slices.

Mix like a pound cake.—*Mrs. C. L. T.*

Citron Cake.

4 large coffeecups sifted flour.
2¼ cupfuls powdered sugar.
1 cupful butter.
Whites of 10 eggs, beaten to a stiff froth.
Add two tablespoonfuls rose water.

Butter a cake pan, and put alternate layers of batter and citron sliced in long, thin slices.—*Mrs. McG.*

Citron Cake.

1 pound flour.
1 pound sugar.
¾ pound butter.
12 eggs.
2 pounds citron.
2 pounds grated cocoanut.
2 pounds almonds.
1 teaspoonful mace.—*Mrs. M. E.*

Citron Cake.

1 pound of flour.
½ pound of sugar.
¾ pound of butter.
10 or 12 eggs.
2 pounds of citron.
1 cocoanut, grated.

Fruit to be put in last.—*Mrs. Dr. S.*

ALMOND CAKE.

1¼ pounds of sugar.
1¼ pounds of butter.
1 pound of flour.
12 eggs.
1 pound almonds.—*Mrs. B.*

Almond Cake.

12 eggs.
1 pound flour.
1 pound sugar.
1 pound butter.

1 pound almonds (blanched).
1 pound citron.

Blanch the almonds, and slice the citron thin.

One wine-glass of brandy.

Mix like pound cake.—*Mrs. S. T.*

DARK FIG CAKE.

2 cups of sugar.
1 cup of butter.
One cup of cold water, with one teaspoonful of soda dissolved in it.
3 cups of raisins, chopped fine.
Cinnamon and nutmeg.
4 eggs.
1 pound of figs.

Use the figs whole, covering them well with the cake to prevent burning. Bake in layers, frosting between each layer. Make as stiff as pound cake. Cut with a very sharp knife, to prevent crumbling. This recipe makes two loaves.—*Mrs. A. T.*

CURRANT CAKE.

1 cup butter.
2 cups sugar.
½ cup sweet milk.
5 eggs.
4 cups flour.
½ a nutmeg.
3 teaspoonfuls baking powder.

One pound currants washed, dried, and rolled in the flour.—*Mrs. W. L. H.*

POUND CAKE.

1 pound butter.
1 pound flour.
1 pound sugar.
16 eggs, yolks of 4.

After the butter is creamed, work the sugar and butter well before mixing.—*Mrs. M. S. C.*

Pound Cake.

1 pound sugar.
1 pound butter.
1 pound of flour.
12 eggs.

Cream the butter; rub into it gradually the sifted and dried flour. Beat the yolks of ten eggs very light, then add the powdered sugar, beat again, add a wine-glass of brandy or one of good whiskey flavored with nutmeg, or the grated rind of a lemon; mix all together. Stir in the whites of twelve eggs beaten to a stiff froth, just before baking. It will take two hours to bake.—*Mrs. S. T.*

Pound Cake.

1 pound flour.
1 pound of sugar.
¾ pound of butter.
10 eggs.

Cream the butter well with flour; beat the yolks well, and add, by degrees, the butter and flour, and then the whites beaten to a stiff froth. Season with mace and one glass of wine. Bake in cups well greased. For fruit cake add to above, two pounds of raisins, two pounds of currants, one-half a pound of citron, stirred in by degrees. Add nutmeg and cinnamon to the seasoning. One pound of butter, and one dozen eggs for fruit cake.—*Mrs. A. C.*

Pound Cake.

Beat the whites of twelve eggs to a stiff froth. The yolks beat until they look light and white; then beat in one pound of sugar; next add the whites; cream the light pound of butter until it looks frothy; then sift in by degrees one pound of flour and cream them together, and add the other mixture. Put a little powdered mace, if you like, a wine-glass of wine, and the same of brandy.—*Mrs. W.*

VERY DELICATE POUND CAKE.

  16 eggs, 4 yolks.
  1 pound of flour.
  1 pound of sugar.
  ¾ pound of butter.—*Mrs. S. T.*

SUPERIOR POUND CAKE.

 1 pound of white sugar.
 ¾ pound of butter.
 1 pound of flour.
 Whites of 12 eggs, yolks of 9.

Cream the butter; add part of the sugar and yolks, and beat well; then gradually add the whites, and flour and balance of yolks. Beat well, flavor with extract of lemon, and bake in a moderate oven.—*Mrs. F. C. W.*

Pound Cake.

 1 pound flour.
 1 pound sugar.
 ¾ pound butter.
 11 eggs.

Sift and dry the flour, sift the sugar; wash all the salt out of the butter, and squeeze all the water out of it. Cream the butter with half the flour or more; beat the whites and yolks separately, beating rather more than half of the sugar with the yolks; then rub the remaining sugar and flour up together. Mix all these ingredients, part at a time, first one, then another. Beat well, and season with French brandy and lemon, or wine and nutmeg, to your taste.—*Mrs. M.*

BUTTER SPONGE CAKE.

  14 eggs.
  Weight of 14 in sugar.

Weight of 8 in butter.
Weight of 6 in flour.
Juice and grated rind of two lemons.

All the ingredients added to the beaten yolks, and the frothed whites stirred in last.—*Mrs. S. T.*

Butter Sponge Cake.

14 eggs.
Their weight in sugar.
8 in flour.
6 in butter.
The rind of 1, and juice of 2 lemons.

Bake quickly.—*Mrs. S.*

Sponge Cake.

The weight of 1 dozen eggs in sugar.
The weight of 4 eggs in flour.
The juice and rind of 1 lemon.

Beat well, and bake quickly.—*Mrs. McG.*

Confederate Sponge Cake.

1 cupful white sugar.
2 cupfuls sifted flour.
½ cupful cold water.
3 eggs.

One teaspoonful yeast powder in the flour; flavor to the taste. Mix yolks and sugar, then add the water after the whites (beaten to a stiff froth first), then the flour.—*Miss S.*

Sponge Cake.

14 eggs.
Weight of 10 in powdered sugar.
Weight of 6 in flour.
Grated rind and juice of 1 lemon.

Beat the yolks of eight eggs very light, then add the sugar

and beat again. Put in the juice and grated rind of a lemon, then the whites of fourteen eggs beaten to a stiff froth. Beat all together for fifteen minutes without cessation, stirring in the flour last, barely mixing; do not beat it. Pour into buttered moulds or shapes and bake in a hot oven. A large cake will require fully an hour for baking. If it bakes too fast on top, cover with buttered paper.—*Mrs. S. T.*

Sponge Cake. (*Never fails.*)

12 eggs.
Their weight in sugar.
The weight of 7 in flour.
Juice of 1 lemon.
1 tablespoonful good vinegar.

Beat the whites, beat the yolks and sugar; add the whites, beat well; add the flour, and after adding it, do not beat it longer than is required to stir it in; then add the lemon and vinegar, just as you put it in the tins or moulds.

When the cake is hot, *lemon sauce* is nice to eat with it.—*Mrs. K.*

CREAM SPONGE CAKE.

4 eggs, whites and yolks beaten separately.
2 teacupfuls sugar.
1 cupful sweet cream.
2 heaping cupfuls flour.
1 teaspoonful soda.

Two teaspoonfuls cream of tartar, mixed in the flour before it is sifted. Add whites of eggs last thing before the flour, then stir that in gently, without beating. Very nice.—*Mrs. F. C. W.*

EXTRA SPONGE CAKE.

Whites of 14 eggs.
Yolks of only 7.

One pound best white sugar stirred in the yolks after they

are well beaten. Add the whites, and lastly stir in very lightly half a pound of sifted flour. Beat very little after putting in the flour. Bake quickly.—*Mrs. D. C. K.*

Sponge Cake Roll.

6 eggs.
1½ teacups flour.
1 teacup powdered sugar.
Rind and juice of a lemon.

Beat the eggs separately and very light. Do not beat the batter much after adding the flour, which must be done last of all. Get a square baking-pan, butter it, and pour one-half the batter in, reserving the rest for a second layer. Have ready a nice damp towel, lay the cake on it when taken out of the pan; spread over the cake, jam or currant jelly; roll it up whilst damp, and when firmly set put it in a place to dry. It is good eaten with sauce, when for a dinner dish, or it can be cut in slices and eaten as small cakes.—*Mrs. M. C.*

Sponge Roll.

4 cupfuls of sugar.
4 cupfuls of flour.
1 dozen eggs.

Mix as for sponge cake. Bake in thin sheets and spread on stewed apples, or any kind of fruit, a little sweetened; roll the sheets with the top on the outside. Serve with rich wine sauce. —*Mrs. Col. S.*

Jelly for Cake.

1 lemon bruised and strained.
1 cupful sugar.
1 large apple.
1 egg.

Beat the egg and mash the apple fine, grate the lemon peel, then mix all together; put into a can or cup and set into a pot of water. Let boil until it is cooked, and use as you would for common jelly cake.—*Mrs. W. McF.*

Another Filling for Cake.

Dissolve one-half cake of chocolate in one teacup of cream or milk, and let it cool slowly; then take it off the fire and stir in the well-beaten whites of three eggs mixed with one pound of sugar. Let it cool, stirring all the time till you find that it will harden when cool.

Spread between the cakes while it is still soft.—*Mrs. E. C. G.*

Jelly Cake.

Beat 8 eggs very light.
Cream ½ pound butter.
¾ pound flour.
¾ pound sugar well beaten.
1 teaspoonful tartaric acid.
1 teaspoonful of soda.

Stir these in when ready to bake. Bake in thin pans, and put on jelly while warm.—*Mrs. J. L.*

Lemon Jelly Cake.

Bake sponge-cake batter (by recipe given) in jelly-cake pans. Beat with three eggs, two cupfuls sugar, butter size of an egg, melted, and juice and grated rind of two lemons. Stir over a slow fire until it boils, then spread between the layers of cake. Ice with lemon icing, or sift over powdered sugar.—*Mrs. S. T.*

Jelly Cake.

8 eggs.
The weight of 4 in flour.
The weight of 6 in sugar.

To be baked in flat tins.

For the jelly: one-quarter pound butter, one-half pound sugar, yolks of three eggs, juice and grated rind of one lemon.

To be put in a saucepan and allowed to come to a boil. Then the three whites, beaten to a stiff froth, must be stirred in and the saucepan returned to the fire until it boils up. Spread between layers of cake.—*Mrs. E. C. G.*

LEMON JELLY CAKE.

Bake as for the orange cake. For the jelly: take the juice and rind of three lemons, one pound sugar, one-quarter pound butter, six eggs; beat together; scald as you do custard. When cool, it must be thick-spread between the cakes; ice the top.—*Mrs. C. C.*

ROLLED JELLY CAKE.

3 eggs.
1 teacup of sugar.
1 teacup of flour.

Beat the yolks of the eggs till light, then add the sugar; continue beating for some time, then add the whites beaten to a stiff froth; next put in the flour, a little at a time. Bake in a long pan, well greased; when done turn out on bread-board, then cover the top with jelly and roll while warm, and slice as needed.—*Mrs. A. H.*

Rolled Jelly Cake.

1 cupful sugar.
1 tablespoonful of butter.
1½ cupful of flour.
⅔ cupful of milk.
1 egg.

Two teaspoonfuls of baking powder sifted with the flour. Bake in a large sheet, and when done, spread on the jelly and cut the sheets in strips three or four inches wide and roll up. If instead of jelly a sauce is made and spread between the layers of cake, it may be eaten as a cream-pie and furnish a very nice dessert. For the sauce, beat together one egg, one teaspoonful of corn-starch, or one tablespoonful flour and two tablespoonfuls of sugar. Stir into a half-pint of milk and boil until it forms a good custard. Remove from the fire and flavor with vanilla.—*Mrs. M.*

FILLING FOR JELLY CAKE.

Whites of two eggs, beaten to a froth.
2 cupfuls of sugar.
Juice and grated peel of 2 oranges.

Put this between the layers, and on top the cakes.—*Mrs. C. C.*

Oranges cut fine, and sweetened and mixed with grated cocoanut, also chocolate, is used for filling jelly cake. Sponge cake is better than the soda recipe.—*Mrs. C. C.*

MARBLE CAKE.

Weigh and make a pound cake; add a spoonful of yeast, take one-third part of the batter and add to it two teaspoonfuls of cinnamon, two teaspoonfuls of mace, one teaspoonful of cloves, one teaspoonful of nutmeg, finely ground.

Put in your pan, first a layer of the plain batter, then a layer of the spiced, finishing with the plain. The batter will make three layers of plain and two of spiced. It bakes in beautiful layers.—*Mrs. C. L. T.*

MARBLE OR SPICED CAKE.

Make up a pound cake and add two teaspoonfuls of yeast-powder. Take one-third part of the batter and add to it two teaspoonfuls of cinnamon and mace each, one teaspoonful of cloves and allspice each, one nutmeg finely powdered. Then grease a pan and put in first a layer of the plain batter, then the spiced, alternately, till you have it full, finishing with the plain. Bake as a pound cake.—*Mrs. C. V. McG.*

MARBLE CAKE. *Light Part.*

3 cupfuls sugar.
1 cupful butter.

MARBLE CAKE.

1 cupful sour cream.
5 cupfuls flour.
Whites of 8 eggs.
1 teaspoonful soda.

Dark Part.

2 cupfuls brown sugar.
1 cupful molasses.
1 cupful sour cream.
1 cupful butter.
5 cupfuls flour.
1 teaspoonful soda.
Yolks of 8 eggs.
1 whole egg.
1 wine-glassful wine.
Mixed spices.

Put alternately layers of each kind in two-pound moulds

Marble Cake. Light Part.

1 cupful white sugar.
½ cupful butter.
½ cupful buttermilk.
Whites of 3 eggs.
1 teaspoonful cream tartar.
½ teaspoonful soda.
2 cupfuls flour.

Dark Part.

½ cupful brown sugar.
¼ cupful butter.
½ cupful molasses.
½ cupful milk.
½ nutmeg.
1 teaspoonful cinnamon.
½ teaspoonful allspice.
2 cupfuls flour.

½ teaspoonful soda.
1 teaspoonful cream tartar.
Yolks of 3 eggs.

Put in the mould, alternately, tablespoonfuls of light and dark batter.—*Mrs. D. C. K.*

MARBLE OR BISMARCK CAKE.

3 cupfuls white sugar.
1 cupful butter.
1 cupful sour cream, or buttermilk
5 cupfuls flour.
Whites of 8 eggs.
1 small spoonful soda.

This is for the white batter.

Dark Batter.

2 cupfuls coffee sugar.
1 cupful molasses.
1 cupful sour cream.
1 cupful butter.
5 cupfuls flour.
1 teaspoonful soda.
Yolks of 8 eggs, and a whole one.
1 wine-glassful mixed spices, finely powdered.

Put in the pan, in alternate layers of light and dark batter. Bake quickly, like sponge cake. Ice and ornament with chocolate drops. This fills a two-pound mould.

ROSE OR CLOUDED CAKE.

12 eggs, leaving out the whites of 3.
1 pound flour.
1 pound sugar.
¾ pound butter.
2 small teaspoonfuls cream tartar.
2 small teaspoonfuls powdered alum.
1 small teaspoonful soda.

2 small teaspoonfuls cochineal, dissolved in ⅛ cupful boiling water.

Having dissolved the alum, soda, and cream tartar, mix with the cochineal. Stir these ingredients in nearly one-third of the batter. Pour into the cake mould a layer of white batter, and a layer of red batter, alternately, beginning and ending with white; three layers of white and two of red. This is an ornamental cake to cut for baskets.

Spice Cake.

Yolks of 4 eggs.
Mix 2½ teaspoonfuls yeast powder in 2½ cupfuls flour.
1 cupful brown sugar.
½ cupful syrup.
½ cupful butter, must be melted after being measured.
Stir with the sugar 2½ teaspoonfuls powdered cloves.
1 teaspoonful powdered cinnamon.
1 teaspoonful powdered allspice.

The spices must be put in the flour, the syrup added after the sugar and butter are stirred together, then the eggs and milk, and lastly the flour. Mix the above alternately, in your pans, after having them buttered.—*Mrs. W.*

Cream Cake.

2 cupfuls of sugar.
3 cupfuls of flour.
½ cupful of butter.
3 eggs.
1 cupful of sour milk.
1 teaspoonful of soda.
2 teaspoonfuls of cream tartar.

Dissolve the soda in the milk, melt the butter and add it to the eggs. Add the sugar and cream tartar to the flour. Pour it all together in shallow pans that have been well greased. Bake twenty minutes.

While baking the above, get one pint of sweet milk, one cupful of sugar, one cup of flour, butter one-half size of an egg. If you use cream instead of milk, you can omit butter. Break two eggs into the sugar, beat awhile, then add flour and beat thoroughly. Have the milk on the fire, and as soon as it boils, stir the mixture in it, after thinning it with some of the milk until it is like paste; cook until it is like stiff starch. Season freely with vanilla when cold, and spread it between the cakes as jelly cake is made.

Grated cocoanut can be used instead, by preparing as follows: one large cocoanut grated, two pounds of loaf sugar. Pour the milk from the nut on the sugar; boil it two or three minutes, first mixing in the whites of three eggs; if not soft enough, add some sweet milk. Take it off the fire, stir in the grated cocoanut, and spread between the cakes.—*Mrs. J. F. G.*

Cream Cake.

2 cupfuls of sugar.
1 cupful of sweet milk.
3 cupfuls of flour.
2 tablespoonfuls of butter.
4 eggs.
½ teaspoonful of soda.
1 teaspoonful of cream tartar.

Bake in four jelly pans.

CREAM FOR THE SAME.

2 cupfuls of sugar.
½ pint of sweet milk.
⅛ cupful of flour.
1 egg.

Heat the milk to boiling heat, beat the egg and sugar together; take a little milk, and make a smooth paste with the flour, and stir into the sugar and egg, then stir all into the

milk. Let it boil until thick, then spread between cakes.—
Mrs. A. H.

Capital Cake. (*Delicious*.)

1 pound of sugar.
4 cupfuls of flour, after being sifted.
1 cupful of butter.
1 cupful of morning's milk.
6 eggs beaten light.
2 teaspoonfuls of cream tartar, sifted in the flour.
1 teaspoonful of soda dissolved in the milk. Flavor with lemon or nutmeg.—*Mrs. M.*

Cup Cake.

5 cupfuls of flour.
3 cupfuls of sugar.
1½ cupfuls of butter.
As much fruit as you like.
1 teaspoonful of soda dissolved in a cupful of milk.
3 eggs.
1 nutmeg.
1 wine-glass wine and brandy mixed.

Mix as pound cake.—*Mrs. J. W. H.*

Cup Cake.

1 cupful of butter.
2 cupfuls of sugar.
2½ cupfuls of flour.
½ cupful of milk.
5 eggs, beaten separately.
1 teaspoonful yeast powder.—*Miss M. W.*

A Nice Cup Cake.

6 eggs.
4 cupfuls of flour.

A DELICIOUS CAKE—CAKE.

3 cupfuls of sugar.
1 cupful of butter.
1 cupful of milk.
1 teaspoonful cream of tartar.
½ teaspoonful of soda.

Season with mace and nutmeg. Bake in cups or little tin pans.—*Mrs. Wm. C. R.*

A Delicious Cake.

2¼ pounds flour.
2 pounds butter.
24 eggs, yolks and whites.
12 ounces almonds.
2 tablespoonfuls rose water, in which the almonds should be beaten.
2 wine-glasses of French brandy.
2 heaping teaspoonfuls beaten mace, and a butter-plate of preserved lemon-peel.—*L. T.*

Delicious Cake.

2 cupfuls of sugar.
1 cupful of butter.
1 cupful of milk.
3 cupfuls of flour, after being sifted.
3 eggs.
2 tablespoonfuls baking powder.

Bake in jelly-cake pans, and between each layer put fruit jelly, icing of chocolate and cocoanut each. This quantity will bake five thin cakes.—*Mrs. McG.*

Cake.

1 quart of flour, well dried.
1 cupful of butter.
3 cupfuls granulated sugar—it is better than pulverized.
6 eggs, well beaten.

Lemon, or other seasoning.

1 light measure of both Horsford's powders, or, if preferred, a small teaspoonful of soda, and ½ cup of buttermilk.

Cream of tartar takes the place of buttermilk, when used with soda.—*Mrs. A.*

CAKE *with sauce.*)

5 eggs.
1 pound of flour.
¾ pound of sugar.
½ pound butter.
1 cup of cream.
2 teaspoonfuls cream of tartar.
1 teaspoonful of soda.—*Mrs. C. B.*

CAKE THAT CANNOT FAIL.

1 pound sugar.
1 pound flour.
¾ pound butter.
8 eggs.
1 teacup of sweet cream.
2 teaspoonfuls cream of tartar, sifted in the flour.

1 teaspoonful of soda dissolved in a little water, and put in the cream. Bake in pans or cups.—*Mrs. P.*

CUSTARD CAKE.

½ cupful butter.
2 cupfuls sugar.
7 eggs, leaving out 4 yolks.
3 cupfuls flour.
1 cupful of milk.
2 teaspoonfuls baking powder. Bake in shallow pans.

For the custard: one quart of milk, let come to a boil, sweeten it; take the four yolks and three tablespoonfuls of cornstarch, mix with a little of the milk cold, and then stir it gradually into the boiling milk, and continue to stir until done. Add a piece of butter the size of a walnut; flavor with vanilla, and put between the cakes.—*Mrs. C. B.*

Mrs. Galt's Cake.

Whites of 13 eggs, yolks of 3.
¾ pound of butter.
1 pound of flour.
1 pound of sugar. Season to taste.—*Miss E. T.*

Norfolk Cake.

Beat to a cream:
 1 teacup of butter.
 6 eggs.
 3 teacups of sugar.
 1 teacup of cream.
 4 teacups of flour.
 ½ nutmeg.
 1 wine-glass of brandy.
 1 pound raisins.
 1 teaspoonful of soda, dissolved in cream.—*Mrs. Dr. S.*

Kettle Cake.

Have a large, nice brass kettle ready. Set it on a few warm embers, not with any fire; put into the kettle:
 12 eggs.
 1 pound sugar.
 1 pound butter.
 A light pound of flour.
 1 teaspoonful of mace.
 Rind and juice of a large lemon.

Stir all the materials rapidly, and with a strong, large iron spoon or a long butter-ladle. When it is light, which will be in about three-quarters of an hour, put it in a mould and bake as common pound cake. It is good with

2 pounds currants.
2 pounds raisins.
½ pound citron.
1 glass of brandy.—*Mrs. M. C. C.*

PARSON'S CAKE.

5 eggs.
1 large teacupful brown sugar.
4 cupfuls flour.
3 cupfuls molasses.
1½ cupful butter.
Ginger and spice to the taste.
1 teaspoonful soda, dissolved in a little milk. Bake.—*Mrs D. R.*

RISEN CAKE.

1½ pound flour.
1 pound sugar.
9 ounces butter.
3 gills milk.
¼ pint yeast.
4 eggs.

Work the butter and sugar together. Put the yeast in the flour and one-half the butter and sugar the overnight; then mix the milk in, and beat it some time. Set it where it will rise. In the morning, when well risen, mix in the remainder of the butter and sugar, and the eggs, also some currants or raisins, or both, if you wish them, a little nutmeg or mace, and beat all well together for some time. Then put it in the pan and set it to rise again. It must be very light before you put it in the oven. It requires some time to soak.—*Mrs. I. H.*

RUGGLES' CAKE.

6 eggs.
1¼ cupful butter.
3 cupfuls sugar.

4 cupfuls flour.
1 cupful milk.
1 teaspoonful soda.

Season to taste.—*Mrs. R.*

Tipsy Cake.

Soak sponge cake in wine and water. Make a custard of six eggs to one quart of milk, and pour over it. Reserve the whites, beat to stiff froth, to put over last.—*Mrs. Dr. S.*

Velvet Cake.

Half a pound of butter, one pound sugar; creamed together. One teacup of cold water, with a level teaspoonful of soda dissolved in it, and poured in the butter and sugar, two teaspoonfuls cream of tartar, sifted in one pound of flour.

Mix the flour with butter, sugar, and water, and beat well. Take five eggs, beat yolks and whites separately, and then beat them together three minutes. Season as you like, and mix with the batter. Beat considerably and bake half an hour.—*Mrs. A. B.*

Whortleberry Cake.

6 eggs, beaten separately.
1 pound sugar.
½ pound butter.
1 quart flour.
½ pint sifted meal.
1 teaspoonful soda.
A little mace and cinnamon.

After mixing, stir in one quart of the berries, so as not to mash them, having previously dusted them with flour. Mix the soda with one-half pint of cream or milk.—*Mrs. A. P.*

Naples Biscuit.

1 pound flour.
1 pound sugar.

12 whites, and 10 yolks of eggs.

2 glasses wine.

They should gradually harden in the oven till quite crisp, and be frequently turned in the pans.

Icing.

1½ pound sugar.

½ pint water.

Boil until it ropes. Have ready the whites of seven eggs well beaten, pour the syrup into a bowl, and beat until milk-warm. Then put in the eggs, and beat for an hour.—*Mrs. W.*

Hot Icing.

Dissolve one pint powdered sugar in two or three tablespoonfuls water, and boil.

Beat the whites of four eggs to a strong froth; add the hot sugar, stirring in till smooth. Beat about two minutes and flavor to your taste, spread on the cake, and put in a hot place.—*Mrs. P.*

Icing.

Whites of two eggs, beaten to a froth.

One pound of sugar, dissolved and boiled in a small teacup of water.

Then strain the sugar and pour it into the egg, beating it hard until cool.

Add one-half teaspoonful lemon acid.—*L. D. L.*

Boiled Icing.

1½ pound cut sugar, or double refined.

1 teacup of water.

6 whites of eggs.

Boil the sugar to candy height; when nearly cold put in eggs.—*Miss E. P.*

Cold Icing.

Whites of 3 eggs.

1 pound sugar.

Beat very light and season with vanilla or lemon. After beating very lightly, add the white of another egg and it will give a pretty gloss upon the icing.—*Miss E. P.*

ICING FOR CAKE.

Take three pounds cut or best quality of loaf sugar, dissolve it in a small quantity of water, boil to candy height or until it ropes. Have ready the whites of thirteen eggs well beaten. When the sugar is boiled sufficiently, pour it into a deep bowl, occasionally stirring it gently, until you can just bear your finger in it; then add the beaten egg all at once, beating it very hard for half an hour, when it is ready for use. Strain into the icing the juice of one lemon into which the peel has been grated, for half an hour.—*Mrs. F. C. W.*

ICING.

Break into a dish the whites of four eggs. Whip in by degrees one and one-quarter pound of the finest loaf sugar, powdered and sifted. Beat till stiff and smooth, then add the strained juice of a large lemon with a few drops of oil of lemon, and beat again; in all beat half an hour. If too stiff add a little more white of egg. Some persons put it on with a knife, but it is far smoother and more evenly spread over the cake if put on with a large spoon. Dip up a spoonful of the icing and pour it from the spoon over the cake. Pour it over the top of the cake and it will diffuse itself down the sides. To color icing yellow, steep the rind of an orange or lemon in the lemon juice before straining it into the icing. To make it pink, put in strawberry or cranberry juice with the lemon juice.—*Mrs. S. T.*

ICING FOR CAKES.

Whites of six eggs to one pound sugar, or one egg to three teaspoonfuls of sugar.—*Mrs. Dr. J.*

BOILED ICING.

One and one-fourth pound loaf sugar, added to one teacup

of water and boiled to a thick syrup. Then strain it through thin muslin, and, while hot, stir into it the whites of three eggs beaten stiff. Then beat in the strained juice of a lemon and season with a little oil of lemon. If too thin, add a little sugar; if too stiff, add a little more white of egg.—*Mrs. S. T.*

SOFT GINGER CAKE.

1 cupful butter.
1 cupful sugar.
1 cupful molasses.
1 cupful sour cream.
3 eggs.
½ tablespoonful of soda.
2 tablespoonfuls of ginger.

Flour until the spoon will almost stand alone. Cloves and cinnamon to taste. (This is very good.)—*Mrs. J. F.*

SOFT GINGERBREAD.

3 eggs.
1 teacup butter.
½ teacup ginger.
1 teacup molasses.
3 teacups sifted flour.
1 large tablespoonful of ginger.
1 small teaspoonful of soda, dissolved in ½ teacup of sour cream.—*Mrs. McG.*

GINGER LOAF.

6 eggs.
4 cupfuls molasses.
2 cupfuls of butter.
6 cupfuls flour.
1 teaspoonful soda.
1 tablespoonful ginger.
Cinnamon to your taste.—*Mrs. P. W.*

Risen Gingerbread.

2 pounds flour.
1 pound nice brown sugar.
1 pound butter.
6 eggs.
½ pint molasses.
3 ounces ginger.

Bake in a large cake.—*Mrs. A. T.*

Lightened Gingerbread.

1½ pound of flour.
½ pound butter.
½ pound sugar.
6 eggs.
6 races of white ginger.
1 teaspoonful soda.
1 pint molasses.

To be baked in tins or a pan.—*Mrs. I. H.*

Ginger Cup Cake.

3 eggs.
1 cupful molasses.
1 cupful sugar.
1 cupful butter (half lard will answer).
½ teaspoonful soda, dissolved in 1 tablespoonful buttermilk.
1 tablespoonful ground ginger.
2¼ cupfuls flour.

Mix as other cake. Some like allspice.—*Mrs. H. D.*

Molasses Cake.

5 light cupfuls flour.
5 eggs.
2 cupfuls sugar.
2 cupfuls molasses.
1 cupful butter.

1 cupful cream, with one teaspoonful soda.
2 tablespoonfuls cream of tartar.
2 teaspoonfuls ground ginger.

All well beaten together. Bake as pound cake.—*Miss E. T*

Molasses Cake.

1 teaspoonful soda.
1 pound butter.
1 pound sugar.
1 pint molasses.
1 tablespoonful ginger.

enough to make it as thick as ordinary cake.—*Miss*

Molasses Pound Cake.

½ pound butter.
2 cupfuls sugar.
2 cupfuls molasses.
6 cupfuls flour.
1 cupful cream.
4 eggs.

Some cloves and nutmeg; add lemon to taste.

—*Mrs. Dr. S.*

Black, or Molasses Cake.

1 quart flour.
5 eggs.
1 pint molasses.
1 pound butter.
2 tablespoonfuls ginger.
1 teaspoonful soda, dissolved in 1 teacup sour milk.

—*Mrs. T. C.*

SMALL CAKES.

ALBANY CAKES.

1½ pound flour.
1½ pound brown sugar.
1½ pound butter.
1 tablespoonful lard.
4 tablespoonfuls powdered cinnamon.
1 teaspoonful soda, dissolved in a cup of milk.

Roll on extra flour very thin. Dip the face of each cake in granulated sugar. Bake slowly in greased pans.—*Mrs. R. R.*

SCOTCH CAKES. (*Very nice.*)

2 pounds flour.
1¼ pound sugar.
1 pound butter.
6 eggs, beaten together.
3 nutmegs.—*Mrs. P. McG.*

SWEET CRACKERS.

4 eggs.
4 cupfuls sugar.
½ pound butter.
1 teaspoonful soda.
1 cupful sour cream.

Pounded cinnamon and grated nutmeg for flavoring.
Sufficient flour for a soft dough.

Roll thin and cut it with tin shapes, and bake quickly.—*Mrs. S.*

DROP CAKE.

6 eggs.
1 pound sugar.
¾ pound butter.
1 teaspoonful soda, in 1 cupful sour cream.
2 teaspoonfuls cream of tartar, in 1 quart flour.

—*Mrs. S.*

Cream Cakes.

Beat up one egg, add to it half a cupful sugar, half a cupful flour, mixing thoroughly. While this is being done, put on the fire half a pint milk; when it boils, stir in the eggs, sugar, and flour mixture, then add a piece of butter, half the size of an egg. Stir all the time until it is of the desired consistency, which will be in a few minutes. When cold, add, and thoroughly mix, one and one-half teaspoonful vanilla.

For the cake: put one tumblerful of water to boil, and then add one-quarter pound butter; when melted, put in one and one-half tumblerful of flour. Stir in, mixing thoroughly, being careful not to burn it. It is sufficiently cooked by the time it is thoroughly mixed. Remove from the fire, and when cool, stir in five unbeaten eggs, mixing one at a time. It will then be the consistency of stiff paste. Drop on buttered tins, and bake in a quick oven fifteen or twenty minutes. Cut the side and insert the cream.—*Mrs. H. M.*

Marguerites.

Cream together one pound of sugar and one pound of butter very light. Beat the yolks of six eggs, sift one and one-half pound of flour into the eggs, butter, and sugar; one teaspoonful of mixed spices, one-half glassful of rose water. Stir the whole well, and roll it on the board till it is half an inch thick; cut in cakes and bake quickly. When cold, spread the surface of each cake with marmalade. Beat the whites of four eggs light, and add enough powdered sugar to make them as thick as icing. Flavor it with lemon, and put it on top of each cake. Put the cakes in the oven, and as soon as they are of a pale brown, take them out.—*Miss M. C. L.*

Marguerites.

Two pounds of flour, one pound and five ounces of sugar, one pound and five ounces of butter, eight eggs. Rub together the butter and sugar till perfectly light; beat the eggs till very thick, leaving out the whites of six eggs for the icing. Sift the flour into the eggs, butter and sugar, one teaspoonful of mixed spices (cinnamon, mace, and nutmeg), half a glass of rose water. Stir the whole well together, and roll it on your paste-board about half an inch thick; then cut out the cakes and bake them a few minutes. When cold, spread the surface of each cake with marmalade or jam. Beat the whites, left out, very light, and add enough powdered sugar to make them as thick as icing. Season with lemon or vanilla, and with a spoon put it on each cake. Put the cakes in the oven to brown.—*Mrs. H.*

Marguerites, or Jelly Cakes.

Rub together one pound sugar, one pound of butter, till perfectly light. Beat six eggs till very thick, leaving out the whites. Sift one and a half pound of flour into the eggs, butter, and sugar, one teaspoonful of mixed spices (cinnamon, mace, and nutmeg), and half a glass of rose water. Stir the whole well, and roll it on the paste-board about one-quarter inch thick. Then cut out the cakes and bake them a few minutes. When cold, spread the surface of each cake with peach jam or any marmalade. Beat the whites of four eggs very light, and add enough powdered sugar to make them as thick as icing. Flavor it with lemon or rose water and with a spoon put it on each cake, high in the centre. Put the cakes in the oven, and as soon as they are of a pale brown take them out.—*Mrs. I. H.*

Shrewsbury Cake.

1 pound flour.
12 ounces sugar.
12 ounces butter.
2 eggs.

Add two tablespoonfuls rose water, or two teaspoonfuls beaten mace. Roll and bake in tin sheets or in an oven.—*Mrs. T.*

MACAROONS.

Blanch and pound one pound of sweet almonds with a little rose water; whip the whites of seven eggs to a froth; add one pound sugar; beat some time. Add the almonds; mix well. Drop on buttered paper, sift sugar over them, and bake quickly.

JUMBLES.

1 pound flour.
¾ pound butter.
1 pound sugar.
3 eggs. Flavor with mace.

A delicious cake.—*Mrs. A. T.*

JACKSON JUMBLES.

3 teacups sugar.
1 teacup lard.
6 teacups flour.
1 teaspoonful soda in one cup of sour cream.
3 eggs.

The grated rind of one or two lemons, or a little grated nutmeg. Roll out and bake.—*Mrs. H. S.*

JUMBLES.

3 pounds flour.
2 pounds sugar.
1 pound butter.
8 eggs.
1 teaspoonful soda.

A little milk if the eggs are not enough.—*Mrs. M. E.*

Jumbles.

Rub one pound butter into one and a quarter pound flour; beat four eggs with one and a quarter pound sugar, very light; mix well with the flour. Add one nutmeg and a glass of brandy.—*Mrs. J. W.*

Coffee Cake.

1 teacup of molasses.
1 cupful of good liquid coffee.
1 cupful sugar.
1 cupful butter.
4 cupfuls flour.
1 teaspoonful of cinnamon.
1 teaspoonful cloves.
1 teaspoonful cream tartar.
½ teaspoonful soda.
1 pound of raisins.
¼ pound of citron.
3 eggs.
½ wine-glass of brandy.—*Mrs. J. H. F.*

Cinnamon Cakes.

1 pound butter.
2 pounds flour.
1 pound sugar.

Six eggs, leaving out two yolks, which you will beat up with a little rose water, and, with a feather, spread on the cakes; then strew cinnamon and sugar on them, and blanched almonds. Lay them on tins, and bake them in a slow oven.—*Mrs. I. H.*

Cinnamon Cakes.

2 quarts flour.
6 or 8 eggs, the yolks only.
½ pound butter.
¼ pound sugar.
1 spoonful cinnamon.—*Mrs. Dr. R. E.*

Strawberry Cakes.

2 pounds flour.
1 pound loaf sugar.

1 pound butter.
6 eggs.
Mace and a little wine to flavor.

Bake quickly.—*Mrs. A. T.*

HOLMCROFT CAKE.

1 coffee-cup of sugar.
2 tablespoonfuls of butter not melted.
1 teacup of sweet milk.
Whites of 2 eggs, or 1 whole egg.
2 coffee-cups of flour.—*Mrs. N.*

NOTHINGS.

Take one egg, two tablespoonfuls cream, butter the size of a walnut, flour to make the dough very stiff; work it well and roll it very thin. Cut the size of a saucer. Fry in lard and sprinkle with powdered sugar.—*Mrs. T. C.*

SUGAR CAKES.

Mix four cupfuls of sugar with eight cupfuls of flour and one large spoonful of coriander-seed; add one cupful of butter, one cupful of lard, six eggs, two tablespoonfuls of sour cream or milk, one teaspoonful of soda.—*Mrs. Dr. S.*

COOKIES.

3 eggs.
1 cupful of butter or lard.
2 cupfuls of sugar.
6 cupfuls of sifted flour.
1 nutmeg.
1 teaspoonful of soda.
2 teaspoonfuls of cream of tartar, sifted with the flour.

Cream the butter with one cup of the sugar, beat the eggs separately and put into the yolks the remaining cup of sugar; add this to the butter, and put in whites and flour last. Roll thin and bake quickly.—*Mrs. F. F. F.*

Gloucester Cakes.

5 eggs.
1 quart of milk.
1 quart of flour.
A piece of butter the size of an egg.

Beat the eggs very light; mix into them the flour and milk alternately, and beating it until perfectly smooth, add a little salt. Melt the butter and stir it into the batter. Bake in small moulds.—*Mrs. J. D.*

Tea Cakes.

2 quarts of flour.
1 small teacup of lard.
1 small teacup of butter.
3 cupfuls of sugar.
3 eggs.
1 cupful of cream (sour is best).
2 small teaspoonfuls of soda.
1 grated nutmeg.

Roll out half an inch thick, and bake in a moderate oven.—*Mrs. F. C. W.*

Crullers.

2 quarts of flour.
2 cups of sugar.
6 eggs.
2 spoonfuls of soda.
4 spoonfuls cream of tartar.
4 tablespoonfuls of melted butter.
A little salt.

Rub the cream tartar, flour, and sugar together; wet with sweet milk quite soft. Have the lard several inches deep in the pot or pan you cook in, and when boiling lay in enough crullers just to cover the bottom. They must be quite thin, and when brown on the lower side, turn over with a fork. They are more convenient to turn with a hole in the centre.—*Mrs. B.*

Tea Cakes.

2 quarts of flour.
3 cupfuls of sugar.
1 cup of butter.
5 eggs.
1 teaspoonful of soda dissolved in 2 tablespoonfuls of sweet milk.
2 teaspoonfuls cream of tartar.
Season with lemon or nutmeg.—*Mrs. H.*

Delicate Tea Cakes.

Whites of 3 eggs beaten to a froth.
1 cupful of pulverized sugar.
½ cupful of sweet milk.
1 teaspoonful cream of tartar.
½ teaspoonful of soda.
2½ cupfuls of flour.
1 teaspoonful of almonds.
½ cupful of melted butter.—*Mrs. R.*

Tartaric Cakes.

Beat the yolks of three eggs, the whites whipped to a froth, three full cups of brown sugar, half a pound of butter, one spoonful lard, one and a half pound of flour, leaving two spoonfuls to roll with. Mix all well together. Dissolve one teaspoonful soda and three-quarters teaspoonful tartaric acid in a little cream. First mix the soda with the dough, then the acid. Season with mace or wine. They will rise very much.—*Mrs. D.*

A Delicate Cake for Tea.

Beat the yolks and whites of two eggs separately; to the yolks add two coffee-cups of sugar, and two cupfuls of sweet milk; then four tablespoonfuls butter creamed; next the white of the eggs, lastly, four cupfuls of flour with one teaspoonful soda, two teaspoonfuls cream of tartar, sifted in the flour. Bake in shallow pans.—*Mrs. C. V. McG.*

LEMON JUMBLES.

1 egg.
1 teacupful sugar.
½ teacupful of butter.
3 teaspoonfuls milk.
1 teaspoonful cream of tartar.
½ teaspoonful of soda.
2 small lemons; juice of two and grated rind of one.

Mix rather stiff. Roll and cut out with a cake-cutter.—*Mrs. W.*

BONNEFEADAS.

Make a rich paste with one quart flour; roll it out very thin, first dividing it in two pieces, spread it with butter, washed and creamed, "A" sugar, and pulverized cinnamon. Roll it up, cut it in pieces one inch wide; put them in a pan with the whole side down; sprinkle over them sugar, butter, and cinnamon. Bake quickly. Take them out of the pan while hot.—*Mrs. Col. A. L.*

DELICIOUS SMALL CAKES.

Yolks of 6 eggs.
1 light pound flour.
¼ pound butter.
1 spoonful lard.
1 pound sugar.

These cakes are better without soda and of the consistency of Shrewsbury cakes. Beat the whites of three eggs to a strong froth; weigh one pound of the best "A" sugar, put it in a tin can with three wine-glasses of water. Let it boil slowly, till it begins to rope, or rather, when a little of it will cool on a plate, like it would begin to candy. Then pour the boiling sugar gradually to the white of egg; beat it well till it begins to thicken and to cool somewhat, then beat into the icing two tablespoonfuls of powdered cinnamon, and ice over the little cakes, using a stiff feather for the purpose. You can add the other unbeaten whites of eggs, with an addition of sugar, to make more small cakes.—*Mrs. M. C. C.*

WAFERS.

4 ounces butter.
4 ounces sugar.
5 ounces flour.
4 eggs.
1 glass of wine.
A little mace and nutmeg.—*Mrs. Dr. J.*

Wafers.

4 spoonfuls flour.
4 spoonfuls sugar.
4 spoonfuls cream.
1 spoonful butter.
Orange peel, mace, and nutmeg.

Prepare as for pound cake. Bake in wafer irons, rolling them while hot.

DIMPLES.

Beat the whites of three eggs and three-quarters pound of sugar till well mixed. Stir in blanched almonds, cut fine. Drop on tins and bake in a cool oven.—*Mrs. A. C.*

GINGER CAKES.

1 teacup of butter.
1 teacup brown sugar.
1 teacup sour milk.
7 cupfuls flour.

1½ teacup molasses.
1½ teaspoonfuls soda.—*Mrs. C. B.*

GINGER SNAPS.

1 pint of molasses.
1 teacup brown sugar.
1 teacup of butter and lard mixed.

Beat the molasses till it looks light, then put it in the sugar; next pour in the hot butter and lard, one egg beaten light, one teacup ground ginger.

Have the mixture milk-warm; work flour in briskly. Roll them and bake quickly.—*Miss N. S. L.*

GINGER CAKES.

1 dozen eggs.
2 pounds of flour.
1 pound butter.
1 pound sugar.
1 pint molasses.
1 small teacup of ginger.
1 teaspoonful of soda.—*Mrs. Col. S.*

CHEAP GINGER CAKES.

3 pints of flour.
1 large spoonful of lard.
2 large spoonfuls of ginger.
1 dessertspoonful of soda in a pint of molasses.

—*Mrs. H. S.*

GINGER BUNNS.

¾ pound butter, ½ pound sugar, rubbed to a cream.
½ nutmeg.
1 tablespoonful ginger.

Stir all together, then add two eggs well beaten, stir in one pound of flour and moisten with sweet milk, until it can be easily worked. Roll out and bake in quick oven.—*Mrs. H. D.*

Molasses Cakes.

7 cupfuls of flour.
2 cupfuls of molasses.
1 cupful sugar.
1 cupful of butter.
1 cupful of sour milk.
1 even tablespoonful of soda.
2 tablespoonfuls of ginger.

Let the dough be as soft as you can conveniently handle it Bake in a moderately quick oven.—*Mrs. R. L.*

Spice Nuts.

1 pound sugar.
1 pound flour.
1 pint molasses.   Mix well.
¾ pound butter.
3 tablespoonfuls ginger.
1 tablespoonful allspice.
1 tablespoonful cinnamon.

Bake in small drops or cakes.—*Mrs. Dr. J.*

Ginger Snaps.

1 cupful butter.
1 tablespoonful ginger.
1 teaspoonful soda, in 1 pint boiling molasses.

Stir and let it cool; add sifted flour enough to make a dough; roll thin and bake.—*Mrs. S. B.*

Drop Ginger Cakes.

1 pound butter, cream it as for pound cake.
2 packed quarts flour.
1 pound sugar.
1 pint molasses.
5 eggs.
2 tablespoonfuls ginger.—*Mrs. N.*

PUDDINGS.

The directions given for cake apply likewise to puddings. Always beat the whites and yolks of the eggs separately and very light, and add the whites just before baking or boiling. All puddings (except those risen with yeast), should be baked immediately after the ingredients are mixed. Thick yellow earthenware dishes are better than tin for baking puddings, on several accounts. One is that the pudding, to be good, must be baked principally from the bottom, and tin burns more easily than earthenware. Another reason is, that the acids employed in some puddings corrode and discolor tin. Garnish the pudding with sifted white sugar, and with candied or preserved orange or lemon peel.

In boiling a pudding, cold water should never be added. Keep a kettle of hot water to replenish the water in the pot as it boils away. As soon as the pudding is done, remove it from the boiling water. A decrease in heat whilst cooking, makes boiled pudding sodden, and makes baked pudding fall. The best sauce for a boiled pudding is cold sauce made of the frothed whites of eggs, butter, sugar, nutmeg, and a little French brandy, while for a baked pudding, a rich, boiled wine sauce is best.

Plum Pudding.

3 dozen eggs.
3 pounds baker's bread, stale, and grated fine.
3 pounds suet.
3 pounds brown sugar.
1 pound sliced citron.
3 pounds currants.
4 pounds seeded raisins.
$\frac{1}{2}$ ounce nutmeg, and the same of mace, cloves, and cinnamon.
Half pint wine.
Half pint French cooking brandy.

Mix and divide into six parts. Tie each part in a twilled cotton cloth, put them in boiling water, and let them boil four hours. Then hang them in the air to dry a day or two. Keep them in a cool, dry place.

When you wish to use one, it must be boiled an hour before dinner. Serve with rich sauce. It will keep six months or a year.—*Mrs. T. M. C.*

Plum Pudding.

10 eggs.
1 pound chopped suet.
1 pound seeded raisins.
1 pound currants.
1 pound stale bread crumbs.
½ pound citron.
1 nutmeg.
1 wine-glassful wine.
1 wine-glassful brandy.
½ pound brown sugar.

Beat the eggs light, add the sugar and spices, stir in the suet and bread crumbs, add the fruit by degrees, then the wine and brandy. Pour into a well-floured bag, leaving a third as much room as the mixture occupies, for swelling. Put into a pot of boiling water and boil four hours. Dip the bag into cold water when ready to turn out the pudding, to prevent it from sticking.—*Mrs. E. B.*

Plum Pudding.

At sunrise, sift a quart of the best flour; rub into it an Irish potato mashed, free from lumps. Put in it a teaspoonful of salt, and a half teacup of yeast. Add six eggs, beaten separately, and enough water to make a soft dough. Knead half an hour without intermission. In winter, set it in a warm place, in summer set it in a cool place to rise. If dinner is wanted at two o'clock, knead into this at one o'clock, half pound of butter, two pounds of stoned raisins, cut up, and a grated nutmeg. Work very little, just enough to mix. Wet a thick cloth, flour it and tie it loosely that the pudding may have room to rise. Put it in a kettle of milk-warm water, heating slowly until it boils. Boil one hour. Serve with wine sauce.—*Mrs. S. T.*

Rich Plum Pudding.

Nine eggs beaten to a froth.

Add flour sufficient to make a thick batter, free from lumps. Then add one pint of new milk and beat well. Afterwards add the following ingredients, in small quantities at a time, keeping it well stirred.

Two pounds stoned raisins, two pounds currants, well washed, picked, and dried. One-quarter pound bitter almonds, blanched and divided; three-quarters pound brown sugar; three-quarters pound beef suet, chopped fine; one nutmeg, grated fine; one teaspoonful of ground allspice, the same of mace and cinnamon.

This pudding should be mixed several days before cooking, then well beaten, and more milk should be added, if required. Make this into two puddings, put in cotton bags and boil four hours. By changing the bags, and hanging in a cool, dry place, they will keep six months and be the better for it. Steam and serve with sauce made as follows:

One cup of sugar, one of butter. Beat well together. Break an egg in and mix well. Add a tablespoonful of wine or brandy, and serve immediately.—*Mrs. F.*

English Plum Pudding.

1 pound of stale bread grated.
1 pound currants.
1 pound sugar.
1 pound of suet chopped as fine as flour.
¼ of a pound of raisins, and the same of citron.

When ready to boil, wet the above with ten eggs, well beaten, two wine-glasses of wine and the same of brandy. Grate the rinds of two lemons, pare and chop them and beat all well together. Then dip a strong cloth in boiling water and wring it dry. Lay it on a waiter, greasing well with butter. Put it in a large bowl and pour the pudding in, putting two sticks in the cloth across each other, and tying below the sticks. Have the water boiling and throw in the pudding as soon as tied. Put a plate at the bottom of the pot and boil four hours.—*Mrs. Dr. S.*

Christmas Plum Pudding.

Half a loaf of bread (grated).
1 pound currants.
2 pounds stoned raisins.
1 pound chopped suet.
6 eggs, and 2 pieces of citron cut up.

Beat the yolks of the eggs with two cups of flour and some milk, then stir in the other ingredients, adding a little salt and ginger. If too stiff, add more milk. The water must be boiling when the pudding is put in. It will take two hours to cook.—*Mrs. M. E. J. B.*

Plum Pudding.

8 eggs (the yolks and whites beaten very light).
1 pint of suet chopped fine.
1 pint of sweet milk.
1½ pint stoned raisins, rubbed in flour.
1 quart of bread crumbs rubbed till very fine.
Half pint citron sliced thin.
1 teacup of light brown sugar.

Grease and flour your mould, pour your pudding in, boil two hours, and eat with rich boiled sauce, made of sugar, butter, wine, and nutmeg.—*Mrs. B. C. C.*

Recipe for a simpler Plum Pudding.

3 cupfuls flour.
1 cupful raisins.
1 cupful brown sugar.
1 cupful buttermilk.
½ cup molasses.
1 cup of suet, or half a cup of butter.
2 eggs.
1 teaspoonful soda.

Boil and eat with sauce.—*Mrs. E. B.*

Economical Plum Pudding.

4 cupfuls flour.
1½ cup of suet.
1 cupful milk.
2 cupfuls raisins.
1 cupful molasses.
2 eggs, and 1 teaspoonful of soda.

Boil four hours.—*Mrs. L.*

Another Recipe for the Same.

One bowl of raisins, one of currants; one of bread crumbs; one bowl of eggs; one of brown sugar; one of suet; citron at pleasure. Boil four hours.—*Mrs. L.*

Original Pudding.

Reserve a portion of light dough intended for breakfast. Set it in a cool place, and four hours before dinner, roll thin, without kneading. Sprinkle thickly over it, first, a layer of sliced citron, then a layer of seeded raisins. Roll up and lay on a buttered bread-pan till very light. Then either boil in a cloth, prepared by wetting first and then flouring (the pudding being allowed room for rising in this cloth), or set the pan in the stove and bake. In the latter case, after it becomes a light brown, it must be covered with a buttered paper.

Dough for French rolls or muffin bread is especially adapted to this kind of pudding.—*Mrs. S. T.*

STEAMED PUDDING.

½ pound of seeded raisins.
4 eggs.
2 cupfuls of sugar.
3 cupfuls of flour.
1 cupful of sour cream.
1 teaspoonful of soda.
2 teaspoonfuls of cream tartar.

Let it steam two hours. Have the water boiling fast, and don't open till it has boiled two hours.—*Mrs. Dr. J.*

BOILED PUDDING.

One pound of flour, twelve ounces of butter, eight ounces of sugar, twelve ounces of fruit (either dried cherries or two kinds of preserves). A little mace and wine.

Boil like a plum pudding.

SAUCE FOR THE SAME.

One pint of cream, large spoonful of butter, one glass of wine. Season to the taste. Let it cook, but not come to a boil.—*Mrs. A. F.*

Another Sauce.

Cream half a pound of butter; work into it six tablespoonfuls of sugar; beat in one egg, add a wine-glass of wine or brandy, and half a grated nutmeg. Set it on the fire, and as soon as it boils, serve it for the table.—*Mrs. F*

AMHERST PUDDING.

3 cupfuls of flour.
1 cupful of suet.
1 cupful of milk.

1 cupful of molasses.
2 cupfuls of raisins.
1 teaspoonful of salt.
1 teaspoonful of cloves and the same of cinnamon.
½ teaspoonful of soda, dissolved in milk.

To be boiled three hours in a coarse bag, and eaten with wine sauce.—*Mrs. W.*

BOILED PUDDING OF ACID FRUIT.

1 quart of flour (or the weight in stale bread).
2 eggs.
1 pint of milk.
1 teaspoonful of salt.
½ pound of dried fruit.

If apples are used, plump them out by pouring boiling water on them, and let them cool before using them. Season with mace and nutmeg, and eat with sauce.—*Mrs. T.*

CHERRY PUDDING.

3 cupfuls of flour.
2 cupfuls of fruit.
1 cupful of molasses.
1 cupful of milk.
2 teaspoonfuls of cream tartar.
1 teaspoonful of soda, put in the flour.
1 cupful of suet.

Mix well, put in a buttered mould, and boil three hours and a half.—*Miss E. T.*

TROY PUDDING.

1 cupful of milk.
1 cupful of molasses.
½ cupful of currants.
½ cupful of butter.
1 teaspoonful of baking soda, dissolved in the milk.
1 teaspoonful of ginger.
1 teaspoonful of ground cloves.

Enough flour to make it as stiff as soft gingerbread. Put it in a mould, and steam four hours. If no steamer is at hand, tie the mould in a cloth and boil four hours.

Sauce: One egg (frothed), one cupful of powdered sugar, one cupful of cream or milk, boiled with a small piece of butter. Add wine, if you like.—*Mrs. W. C. R.*

Sweet Potato Roll.

Prepare pastry as for cherry roll. Spread it out, and cover it with layers of boiled sweet potatoes, thoroughly mashed. Pour over it melted butter and sugar, highly flavored with lemon. Roll it up, boil in a bag, and serve with butter and sugar sauce.—*Mrs. Dr. J. F. G.*

Boiled Sweetmeat Pudding.

Twelve ounces flour and eight ounces butter rolled in a square sheet of paste. Spread over the whole sweetmeats (or stewed fruit, if more convenient). Roll closely and boil in a cloth. Pour sauce over it.—*Mrs. T.*

Boiled Bread Pudding.

Pour one quart milk over a loaf of grated stale bread. Let it stand till near dinner time. Then beat six eggs very light and add them to the bread and milk, together with a little flour, to make the whole stick. Flour the bag and boil. Eat with sauce.—*Mrs. J. A. B.*

Boiled Bread Pudding. (*Economical.*)

Soak one pound stale bread in enough milk to make a pudding. When soft, beat it up with two eggs and three tablespoonfuls flour. Pour in a large lump of butter, melted. Put in any sort of fruit you like, and then boil.—*Miss E. T.*

Boiled Pudding.

One quart milk, four eggs, lard size of turkey's egg. Flour enough to make a batter for a teacup of fruit.

Boil and eat with sauce.—*Mrs. R.*

Paste for Boiled Dumplings.

One quart flour, three good-sized Irish potatoes (boiled and mashed). One tablespoonful butter, and the same of lard. One teaspoonful soda, and two teaspoonfuls cream of tartar.—*Mrs. E. W.*

Apple Dumplings.

Three pints of flour, one and one-half pint of milk, one large tablespoonful of butter, one egg. As many apples (chopped fine) as the batter will take. Boil two hours in a well-floured cloth.

The water should be boiling when the dumplings are dropped in, and it should be kept boiling all the while, else they will be heavy. Eat with sauce.—*Mrs. G. N.*

Boiled Molasses Pudding.

1 cupful molasses.
1 cupful sweet milk.
4 cupfuls sifted flour.
1 cupful stoned raisins.
½ cupful butter.
1 teaspoonful soda.
1 teaspoonful salt.

Boil or steam in a pudding mould. Eat with wine sauce.—*Mrs. McG.*

Suet Pudding.

1 quart flour.
2 teacups suet, chopped fine.
1 teaspoonful salt.

Mix the suet with two-thirds of the flour, reserving the rest of the flour to roll the dough in. Put in a cloth and boil one hour.—*Mrs. B.*

Suet Pudding.

1 pint milk.
3 eggs, well beaten.

½ pound finely chopped suet.
1 teaspoonful powdered ginger.
1 teaspoonful salt.

Add flour gradually, till you have made it into a thick batter. Boil two or three hours, and serve with hot sauce.—*Mrs. P. W.*

Suet Dumplings.

Rub into one quart flour, one-half pound beef suet, free of skin, and chopped very fine. Add a little salt, one teaspoonful of soda dissolved in buttermilk, one pound fruit, either apples, dried cherries, or dried peaches cut very fine, and sufficient water to make it into dough. Make it into dumplings half an inch thick, boil two or three hours, and eat with a sauce made of butter, sugar, and wine.—*Mrs. G. S.*

Eve's Pudding.

½ pound finely grated bread crumbs.
½ pound finely chopped apples.
4 eggs.
6 ounces sugar.
2 ounces citron, and lemon peel.
½ pound finely chopped suet.
½ pound currants.
A little nutmeg.

Butter the mould well, and boil three hours.—*Mrs. H. T. S.*

Fruit Pudding.

4 eggs.
1 pint milk.
4 tablespoonfuls flour.
1 tablespoonful butter.

Apples or peaches cut in thin slices, and dropped in the batter. Serve with sauce.—*Mrs. Dr. S.*

Baked Peach Dumplings.

Make up one quart of flour as for soda biscuit. Roll like pastry, putting on bits of lard or butter several times. Make out the dough like biscuit, roll thin and on each piece put two or three pieces of canned peaches. (Peach preserves or marmalade would answer also.) Add a teaspoonful of butter, and (if you use canned peaches) a tablespoonful of sugar to each dumpling. Draw the edges firmly together and place them in a deep, large baking-dish. Put sugar and butter between, and pour, over all, the syrup from the can. (Use a three-pound can for this quantity of flour.) Bake quickly and serve with or without sauce. A good substitute for the old-fashioned "pot peach pie." Baked apple dumplings may be made in the same way. —*Mrs. S. T.*

Currant Pudding.

1 pound currants.
1 teaspoonful soda.
1 teaspoonful salt.

Nutmeg to suit the taste. Citron will improve the flavor. Eat with wine sauce.—*Mrs. Dr. E.*

Raspberry Pudding.

One pint flour, six eggs, yolks and whites beaten separately. Mix the eggs with a pint of milk and one cupful of butter. Into this stir the flour. Make the berries very sweet. Mash them and stir them into the batter. Bake in a dish and serve with sauce.—*Mrs. C. C.*

Cherry Pudding.

10 eggs.
1 cupful melted butter.
1 quart milk, make in a thick batter.
1 pound dried cherries (stoned).—*Mrs. Dr. E.*

Apple Pudding.

1 pound apples stewed very dry.
1 pound sugar.
½ pound butter.
Yolks of 7 eggs.
Rind and juice two lemons.

Bake in a paste.—*Mrs. Dr. E.*

Delicious Apple Pudding.

Three eggs, one cupful sugar, one cupful melted butter, one cupful sweet milk, one and one-third cupful of apples, one teaspoonful essence of lemon; baked in pastry. This quantity will make two plates.—*Mrs. M. M. D.*

Apple Pudding.

Boil and strain twelve apples as for sauce. Stir in one-quarter pound butter, and the same of sugar. When cold, add four eggs, well beaten. Pour into a baking-dish thickly strewn with crumbs, and strew crumbs on the top. When done, grate white sugar on top.—*Mrs. M.*

Apple Pudding.

1 quart chopped apples.
1 pint flour.
1 pint new milk.
3 eggs.

Bake quickly after mixing, and eat with sauce.—*Miss E. T.*

Dried Apple Pudding.

Wash ten ounces of apples well in warm water. Boil them in a quart of water. When soft, add ten ounces of sugar, eight ounces of butter, the juice and grated rind of two lemons. When cold and ready to bake, add five beaten eggs. Bake with or without pastry. Ten ounces of apples will make a common sized pudding.—*Mrs. R.*

BAKED APPLE ROLL.

Make a paste, roll out thin. Spread over it apples cut in thin slices. Sprinkle nice sugar, and put bits of butter all over this. Roll it up, place it in a baking-pan. Pour in water and put sugar and butter around it, grating over all a nutmeg. Any other kind of fruit can be made into the same kind of roll. —*Mrs. S. T.*

APPLE MÉRINGUE, *with custard.*

1 quart apple-sauce.
Juice of a lemon.
Whites of 4 eggs.
1 large cup of sugar.

Strain apple-sauce through a colander. Put it in the dish in which it is to be served. Beat the whites to a stiff froth, adding a little sugar. Cover the apples with the frosting. Set in the oven to brown, and eat with whipped cream or soft custard. —*Mrs. G. W. P.*

Apple Méringue.

Stew the apples until well done and smooth. Sweeten to the taste; add the rind of a grated lemon. Beat the whites of five eggs to a stiff froth; add to them a teacup powdered sugar, a little rose water, juice of a lemon, or any seasoning preferred. Put the fruit in a flat dish, and put the egg on with a spoon. Brown a few minutes. Add a little butter to the apples while hot.—*Mrs. C. McG.*

APPLE CUSTARD PUDDING.

Stew six sour apples in half a cup of water. Rub through a sieve and sweeten. Make a custard of three pints milk, six eggs, four tablespoonfuls sugar. Put the apples in a pudding-dish, pour the custard over them, and bake slowly half an hour. —*Mrs. M. B. B.*

APPLE CHARLOTTE.

Equal quantities stewed apples and bread crumbs, one spoonful butter, three eggs beaten up and stirred in at the last, just before baking. Spoonful wine, cinnamon, nutmeg, lemon peel, and plenty of brown sugar. Stir together, and bake quite a long time.—*Mrs. I. H.*

APPLE CUSTARD.

1½ pint stewed apples.
¼ pound sugar.

Set them away til cold.

Beat six eggs very light, and stir in gradually a quart sweet milk. Mix all together, pour in a deep dish, and bake twenty minutes.—*Mrs. F.*

CITRON PUDDING.

Yolks of 8 eggs.
¾ pound sugar.
¼ pound butter (melted).

Two tablespoonfuls of cracker soaked in a teacup of new milk, and made into a paste with a spoon. A glass of wine, a little nutmeg, all well beaten together and poured over sliced citron, laid on a rich paste. After baking it, pour over it the whites beaten to a stiff froth, sweetened with four tablespoonfuls of powdered sugar, and flavored to the taste. Put it in the stove again, and bake a light brown.—*Mrs. S. T.*

Citron Pudding.

Yolks of 12 eggs.
½ pound butter.
1 pound sugar.

Stir in the butter while warming the eggs. Cut the citron in pieces and drop in the mixture. Have a rich paste, and bake in a quick oven.—*Mrs. H.*

ORANGE PUDDING.

Peel and cut five good oranges into thin slices, taking out the seed. Pour over them a coffee-cup of white sugar. Let a pint of milk get boiling hot by setting it in some boiling water. Add yolks of three eggs well beaten, one tablespoonful corn starch, made smooth with a little milk. Stir all the time, and as soon as thickened pour over the fruit. Beat the whites to a stiff froth, adding a tablespoonful of sugar, spread over the top. Set it in the oven a few minutes to harden. Serve either hot or cold.—*Mrs. E. P. G.*

Orange Pudding.

Yolks of 16 eggs.
1 pound powdered sugar.
1 pound butter, creamed.

The rinds of two oranges, grated, and the juice of one lemon. —*Mrs. Dr. T. W.*

Orange Pudding.

Take skin of a large orange, boil it soft, pound it, and add the juice of one orange, with the juice of a lemon, ten eggs, one pound butter, one pound sugar; beat to a cream; add glass of wine, brandy, and rose water.—*Mrs. J. T. G.*

Orange Pudding.

Pare two oranges, beat very fine, and add half a pound of sugar, and half a pound of butter, washed. Beat the yolks of sixteen eggs, and add to them the other ingredients, well mixed and beaten together. Bake in a puff-paste. For eight or ten persons.—*Mrs. F.*

Orange Pudding.

Put two oranges and two lemons into five quarts of water. Boil them till the rinds are tender, then take them out, slice them thin, and take out the seed. Put a pound of sugar into a pint of water. When it boils, slice into it twelve pippins, sliced and cored. Lay in the lemons and oranges; stew them tender. Cover the dish with puff-paste. Put in the fruit care fully, in alternate layers. Pour over the syrup, put some slips of paste across it, and bake it.—*Mrs. E.*

LEMON PUDDING.

½ pound sugar.
¼ pound butter, well creamed.
Yolks of 8 eggs.

Pour this mixture into a rich crust of pastry, after adding the grated rind of two lemons. Then partially bake it. Beat the whites very stiff, and add a spoonful of sugar for each egg Then add the juice of two lemons, pour this méringue over the pudding and brown it quickly.—*Mrs. I. D.*

Lemon Pudding.

½ pound butter.
¾ pound sugar.
6 eggs.
½ pint milk.
3 lemons, juice and rind.—*Miss E. W.*

Lemon Pudding.

6 eggs.
¾ pound sugar.
¼ pound butter.
Juice of two lemons.

Pour on the butter boiling hot.—*Mrs. E. B.*

Lemon Pudding.

6 eggs.
7 tablespoonfuls sugar
1 tablespoonful flour.
1 tablespoonful butter.
1 pint of buttermilk.

Season with extract of lemon, beat well and bake in a crust. —*Mrs. A. C.*

Lemon Méringue.

One pint of bread crumbs soaked in a quart of new milk.
1 cup of sugar.
Yolks of 4 eggs.
Grated rind of 1 lemon.

Beat these ingredients light and bake as custard. Then spread on fruit jelly or stewed apples (fresh). Froth the whites with four tablespoonfuls of sugar and juice of the lemon. Spread over the top and brown.—*Mrs. Col. S.*

Lemon Méringue.

The rind of two small lemons and the juice of one.
2 cupfuls sugar.
½ cup butter.
½ cup cream (or sweet milk).
6 eggs, beaten separately.

Leave out the whites of two eggs, which must be mixed with sugar and put on top of the pudding just before it is done. Bake in a rich paste.—*Mrs. H.*

Almond Pudding.

Blanch a pound of almonds, pound them with rose water to prevent their oiling; mix with them four crackers, pounded, six eggs, a pint of milk or cream, a pound of sugar, half a pound of butter, four tablespoonfuls of wine. Bake on a crust.—*Mrs. Dr. T. W.*

Cocoanut Pudding.

Two grated cocoanuts.
1 pound sugar.
¼ pound butter.
8 eggs, leaving out 4 whites.

Beat the eggs separately and to the yolks add the butter, sugar, cocoanut, and whites. Add a little wine or brandy, if you like. Bake in tins lined with pastry.—*Mrs. D. R.*

Cocoanut Pudding.

One-half pound butter, one-half pound sugar, a whole cocoanut grated, five eggs beaten to a froth, leaving out two whites. Bake in plates with pastry underneath. The oven must not be too hot.—*Mrs. I. H.*

Cocoanut Pudding.

Stir together,

½ pound butter.
½ pound sugar.
A glass of wine.
6 eggs (beaten light).

When all these ingredients have been stirred together till light, add a pound of grated cocoanut, mixed with a little stale cake.—*Mrs. E. T.*

Cocoanut Pudding.

1 pound sugar.
¼ pound butter.
¾ pound grated cocoanut.
½ pint cream.
7 whole eggs, or 9 whites and 2 yolks.
1 lemon.
Half a nutmeg.

Stir butter and sugar as for cake. Beat eggs well. Bake some time.—*Mrs. E. G.*

Cocoanut Pudding.

One grated cocoanut, one pound of sugar, one quarter of a pound of melted butter, and six eggs.—*Mrs. M. S. C.*

CHOCOLATE PUDDING.

Scrape fine three ounces of chocolate. Add to it a teaspoonful of powdered nutmeg and one of cinnamon. Put it in a saucepan, and pour over it a quart of rich milk, stirring it well. Cover it and let it come to a boil. Then remove the lid, stir up the chocolate from the bottom and press out the lumps. When dissolved and smooth, put it on the fire again. Next stir in, gradually and while it is boiling hot, half a pound white sugar. Set it away to cool. Beat six or eight eggs very light. Pour into the pan of chocolate when quite cold. Stir the whole very hard. Put it in an oven and bake well. It will bake best by being put in a pan of boiling water. Eat cold.—*Mrs. J. B. F., Jr.*

Chocolate Pudding.

1 quart milk.
3 eggs.
Sugar to taste.
2 tablespoonfuls corn-starch, dissolved in milk.
4 tablespoonfuls chocolate

Set the milk on the fire, and just before it boils put in the eggs, sugar, and corn-starch. Let it boil about a minute, then take it off the fire and add the chocolate.

CHOCOLATE MÉRINGUE.

One quart milk and yolks of four eggs, made into custard. Three tablespoonfuls powdered chocolate, put into a cup of warm water. One tablespoonful of corn-starch. Sweeten to your taste and let all boil together. Then put it in a baking-dish, and when done, cover with a méringue of the whites of eggs and white sugar. Put in the oven again to brown, a few minutes.—*Mrs. B.*

CAROMEL PUDDING.

Cream together one cupful of butter, and one of sugar. Add five eggs (yolks and whites beaten separately) and one cupful of preserved damsons, removing the seed. Beat all together very light and season with a teaspoonful vanilla. Bake on pastry.—*Mrs. A. D.*

QUEEN OF PUDDINGS.

Take slices of sponge cake and spread with preserves or jelly. Place them in a deep dish. Make a custard with one quart of milk and yolks of four eggs. Sweeten and season to the taste and pour over the cake. Beat the whites stiff, adding five or six spoonfuls of sugar and seasoning with lemon. Spread this over the top of the pudding and bake a very light brown.—*Mrs. M. D.*

Queen of Puddings.

1 pint bread crumbs.
1 quart milk.
1½ cupful of sugar.
Yolks of 4 eggs, well beaten.
1 teacup of butter, well creamed.
Grated rind of one lemon.

Bake until done, but not watery. Whip the whites of the four eggs (above mentioned) very stiff and beat into a teacup of sugar, into which has been strained the juice of the lemon aforesaid. Spread over the top of the pudding, after it has slightly cooked, a layer of jelly or sweetmeats. Then pour over it the dressing of eggs, sugar, and lemon, and set it in the oven to brown.—*Mrs. B. J. B.*

Queen of Puddings.

1½ cupful white sugar.
2 cupfuls fine dry bread crumbs.
Yolks of 5 eggs.
1 tablespoonful of butter, flavored to taste.
1 quart fresh, rich milk.
½ cup jelly or jam.

Rub the butter into a cupful of the sugar, and cream these together, with the yolks beaten very light. The bread crumbs soaked in the milk come next, then the seasoning. Bake this in a large butter dish, but two-thirds full, till the custard is "set." Spread over the top of this a layer of jam or jelly and cover this with a méringue made of the whipped whites and the half cupful of sugar. Bake till the méringue begins to color. - *Mrs. D. C. K.*

Queen of Puddings.

Saturate the crumbs of a loaf of bread with a quart of rich milk. Add to this the yolks of six eggs, two tablespoonfuls of butter, three-quarters pound of sugar. Beat well together, season to taste, and when well stirred, put it on to bake. When nearly done, spread over it a layer of fruit jam or jelly and whites of the eggs well beaten. Sift sugar on top and bake.—*Mrs. J. V. G.*

Méringue Pudding or Queen of Puddings.

Fill a baking dish within one and a half inch of the top with slices of sponge cake, buttered slightly on both sides, scattering between the slices, seeded raisins (about half a pound). Over this pour a custard made of a quart of milk, the yolks of eight eggs, sweetened to the taste.

As soon as it has baked a light brown, make an icing of the eight whites and put it on top. Set again in the oven to brown a little. Eat with sauce of butter and sugar.—*Mrs. R. P.*

Tapioca Pudding.

4 tablespoonfuls of tapioca.
1 quart of milk.
The yolks of 4 eggs.
Whites of 2 eggs.
1 tablespoonful of sugar.

Soak the tapioca over night or several hours in a little water, boil the milk and turn over the tapioca and when it is blood-warm, add the sugar and the eggs well beaten, flavor the pudding with lemon or rose water. Bake it about an hour. After it has cooled a little add the two remaining whites of the eggs and one-half pound of white sugar beaten together for frosting. This serves as sauce for the pudding.—*Mrs. A. B.*

Tapioca Pudding.

Wash a teacup of tapioca in warm water and let it stand half an hour. Then stir in a custard made of a quart of milk, four eggs, a small piece of butter, and sugar to taste. Bake about an hour and a quarter. Stir two separate times from the bottom, whilst baking.—*Mrs. Dr. S.*

Tapioca Pudding with Apples.

Soak a cupful of tapioca in three cupfuls of water, four or five hours, where it will be warm, but not cook. Peel and core six apples and stew till tender. Put them in a pudding-dish, filling the holes (from which the cores were extracted) with sugar and nutmeg or grated lemon peel. Then pour over them the soaked tapioca, slightly sweetened and bake three-quarters of an hour. To be eaten cold with sugar and cream.—*Mrs. E. W.*

Snow Pudding.

Let a box of gelatine stand one hour in a pint of cold water. Then add two pints of boiling water, four cupfuls of crushed sugar, the juice of four lemons and the rind of the same, pared thin. (The latter must, however, be taken out when the pudding begins to congeal.)

Beat the whites of six eggs to a stiff froth, adding two tablespoonfuls of sugar. Then beat all together till it becomes a stiff froth.

Make the six yolks into a custard flavored with vanilla or nutmeg and pour over the pudding after it has been turned out of the mould.—*Mrs. B. J. B.*

Snow Pudding.

Dissolve one-half box gelatine in one pint hot water. Let it stand long enough to cool a little but not to congeal. Then add the whites of three eggs, juice of two lemons and sugar to taste. Beat all to a stiff froth and pour into moulds. Serve with a custard made of the yolks of the eggs and a pint of milk seasoned with vanilla.—*Mrs. Dr. P. C.*

Snow Pudding.

Soak a half box of gelatine in a half pint of cold water, all night. In the morning, add the grated rind of two lemons and the juice of one, three cupfuls of white sugar and a half pint of boiling water. Strain into a deep vessel and add the unbeaten whites of three eggs. Beat constantly for three-quarters of an hour, then set it in a cool place. With the yolks of the eggs, make a pint of custard flavored with vanilla or rose-water, to put around the pudding, when congealed.—*Mrs. A. B.*

Cake Pudding.

Take a moderate sized baking-dish, around which lay small sponge cakes, split and buttered on both sides. Spread them with marmalade or preserves on the inside. Put in the centre of the dish pieces of cake buttered and spread with preserves on both sides. Leave room for a custard, to be made, seasoned and poured over the pudding before baking. Eat hot with hot sauce.—*Mrs. V. R. I.*

Preserve Pudding.

1 cupful preserves.
1 cupful sugar.
Nearly a cupful butter.
5 eggs.

Bake in pastry.—*Mrs. E. B.*

Jelly Roll.

3 eggs.
1 cupful sugar.
1 cupful flour.
1 teaspoonful cream of tartar.
½ teaspoonful soda, dissolved in milk.

Bake in pie-pans, spread with acid jelly, roll up in a compact form.—*Mrs. R.*

Sweetmeat Pudding.

Yolks of 10 eggs.
Whites of 2.
1 pound of sugar.

Half a pound of butter, beaten with the sugar, and poured over pastry, on which is placed a layer of sweetmeats and a layer of some other preserves. Any two kinds of preserves may be used.—*Mrs.* ———.

Sweetmeat Pudding.

½ pound of sugar.
½ pound of butter.
Juice and rind of one lemon.
8 eggs.

Mix the eggs, well beaten, with the sugar. Melt the butter and pour into the mixture. Line a dish with rich pastry, on which lay sweetmeats, damson, or peach preserves, or any other kind that may be convenient. On this, place one layer of the mixture above mentioned, then another of sweetmeats. Put a layer of the mixture on top, and bake.

Cheese-cake Pudding.

Yolks of eight fresh eggs, three-quarters of a pound of good brown sugar, and the same of butter, well creamed together.

Beat the eggs light, mix all the ingredients well; season with nutmeg or extract of lemon; add a tablespoonful of good brandy or rum. Bake in a pastry, in small tins or plates.—*Mrs. Dr. P. C.*

Transparent Pudding.

8 eggs, beaten very light.
½ pound of sugar.
¼ pound of butter.
Nutmeg, mace, or any spice for flavoring.

Put it on the fire in a tin pan, stirring constantly till it begins to thicken. When cool, pour it over a rich paste, and bake over a moderate fire. Add citron, if you like.—*Mrs. Dr. E.*

Transparent Pudding.

¼ pound of sugar.
¼ pound of butter.
Dessertspoonful of rose water.
Stir well till light.

Beat four eggs very light, and add to the other ingredients. Butter the baking-dish, line with stale cake, sliced thin, which you may cover with sweetmeats of any kind. Pour the mixture on, and bake for nearly an hour.—*Mrs. I. H.*

Transparent Pudding.

Yolks of 10 eggs; whites of 2.
1 pound of sugar.
½ pound of butter.
Season with nutmeg.

Make pastry, on which put a layer of citron or any other fruit. Pour the mixture over it and bake. Beat the remaining whites to a froth. Add a teacup of powdered sugar, flavor to taste, and pour over the top of the pudding after baking. Then put it again in the stove, a few minutes, to brown.—*Mrs. E.*

Arrow-root Pudding.

Boil a quart of milk and make it into a thick batter with arrow-root. Add the yolks of six eggs, half a pound of sugar, one-quarter of a pound of butter, half a nutmeg, and a little grated lemon peel. Bake it nicely in a pastry. When done, stick slips of citron all over the top, and pour over it the whites of the six eggs, beaten stiff, sweetened with three or four tablespoonfuls of sugar, and flavored to the taste.—*Mrs. S. T.*

Sago Pudding.

Boil one cupful of sago in a quart of water. Pare apples, put them in a dish and stew a little. Pour the sago over them, and bake thirty minutes. Sweeten and flavor to the taste.—*Mrs. A. B.*

Sago Pudding.

Boil one pint and a half of new milk with four spoonfuls of sago, nicely washed and picked. Sweeten to the taste; flavor with lemon peel, cinnamon, and mace. Mix all, and bake slowly in a paste.—*Mrs. V. P. M.*

Bread Pudding.

Slice some stale bread, omitting the crust. Butter it moderately thick. Butter a deep dish, and cover the bottom with slices of bread, over which put a layer of any kind of preserved fruit. (Acid fruits are best.) Cover all with a light layer of brown sugar. Make a rich custard, allowing four eggs to a pint of milk. Pour it over the pudding, and bake an hour. Grate nutmeg over it, when done.—*Mrs. Col. S.*

Custard Pudding.

Cut thin slices of bread. Butter them, and lay them in a baking-dish. Mix a cold custard of three pints of milk, the yolks of eight or ten eggs, beaten light; sweeten to your taste; pour over the bread; bake, and let it stand to cool. Froth and sweeten the whites, pour them over the top of the pudding, and then put it in the stove a few minutes more to brown on top.—*Mrs. R.*

Sippet Pudding.

Butter a baking-dish, cut slices of light bread very thin, buttering them before cutting. Put them in the dish, strewing over each separate layer, currants, citron, raisins, and sugar. When the dish is full, pour over it an unboiled custard of milk and eggs, sweetened to the taste. Saturate the bread completely with this, then pour on a glass of brandy and bake a light brown. This pudding is very nice made of stale pound of sponge cake instead of light bread.—*Mrs. M. C. C.*

Mrs. Spence's Pudding. (*Original.*)

One pint grated bread crumbs put into one quart fresh sweet milk. Beat the yolks of five eggs very light. Add one teacup of sugar to them. Stir in the milk and crumbs and add three-quarters of a pound clipped raisins and one-quarter of a pound sliced citron. Season with mace. Bake nicely.

Whip the whites of the five eggs to a stiff froth. Add one teacup pulverized sugar and season with extract of vanilla Put this over the pudding and set in the stove again to brown it slightly. Serve hot with a rich sauce made of sugar and butter seasoned with nutmeg and Madeira wine.

Teacup Pudding.

1 teacup grated bread.
1 teacup raisins.
1 teacup chopped apples.
1 teacup chopped suet.
3 eggs.
1 gill of cream.
Wine glass of brandy.
Spice and sugar to taste.—*Mrs. Dr. J.*

French Pudding.

Grate one pint stale bread. Pour over it one quart fresh milk, yolks of four eggs, rind of one lemon and part of juice, one teacup of sugar, piece of butter size of an egg. Mix all well, put in a pudding-dish and bake until it looks like custard. Then set it to cool, after which spread the top with jelly or preserves. Beat the whites of the four eggs to a stiff froth, adding the remaining juice of the lemon and three tablespoonfuls of sugar. Spread this on top the preserves, then put the pudding again in the oven and bake a light brown.—*Mrs. C.*

Fruit Pudding.

1 pint grated bread crumbs.
1 pound raisins.

¾ pound suet chopped fine.
½ pound sugar.
½ pint chopped apples.
Yolks of three eggs, well beaten.

Pour over the top the whites of the three eggs, frothed and sweetened Bake an hour.—*Mrs.* ——

Pudding without Milk or Eggs.

Put into a buttered baking-dish, alternate layers of grated bread, and finely chopped apples seasoned with brown sugar, bits of butter and allspice. Pour over it a pint of wine and water mixed. Let the top layer be bread crumbs, and bake one hour.—*Miss N.*

Marrow Pudding.

Grate a large loaf of bread and pour on the crumbs a pint of rich milk, boiling hot. When cold, add four eggs, a pound of beef marrow, sliced thin, a gill of brandy with sugar and nutmeg to your taste. Mix all well together and bake it. When done stick slices of citron on the top. You may make a boiled pudding of this, if you prefer.—*Mrs. E.*

Original Pudding.

Crumb up four rolls. Pour over them a quart of fresh milk at the breakfast table. A half hour before dinner, beat up separately the yolks and whites of six eggs. After beating, put them together and stir them up. Take a piece of butter the size of a walnut, cut it in bits and throw it on top.

Sauce. Throw in a bowl, a tablespoonful of flour and a large piece of butter. Cream it round and round. Add two teacups of sugar, one wine-glass of light wine, and nutmeg, and boil up.—*Miss R. S.*

Cracker Pudding.

Put into a deep dish six or eight large soda crackers. Add a large lump of butter and a teacup of sugar. Grate the rind of two lemons and squeeze the juice over the crackers. Then pour boiling water all over them, and allow them to stand till they have absorbed it and become soft. Beat the yolks and whites of three eggs separately. Stir them gently into the crackers. Butter a deep dish and pour in the mixture, baking it a nice brown. If not sweet enough, add sugar to the eggs before mixing them.—*Mrs. M. C. C.*

Rice Pudding.

Boil half a pound of rice in milk, till quite tender. Then mash the grains well with a wooden spoon. Add three-quarters of a pound of sugar, and the same of melted butter, half a nutmeg, six eggs, a gill of wine, and some grated lemon peel. Bake it in a paste. For a change, it may be boiled, and eaten with butter, sugar, and wine.—*Mrs. E.*

Rice Pudding.

Sweeten three pints of sweet milk, and flavor with lemon or vanilla. Put in this a small cupful of raw rice, thoroughly washed. Bake, and serve cold.—*Mrs. H. S.*

Rice Pudding.

3 cupfuls boiled rice.
6 eggs.
1½ cupful sugar.
1½ pint milk.
1 wine-glassful wine and brandy.
1 tablespoonful melted butter.
Flavor with nutmeg.—*Mrs. Col. S.*

Rice Pudding.

Boil a cup of rice till nearly done, then add a pint of milk. When perfectly done, mash, and, while hot, add half a pound of butter, one pound of sugar, six fresh eggs, beaten till light.

(Beat the sugar with   eggs.) Season with wine or brandy, and one grated nutmeg. Lemon is another good seasoning for it. Put in rich puff paste, and bake till a light brown.—*Mrs Dr. R. W. W.*

Rice Pudding.

Boil one cup of rice in one quart of milk. Add six eggs and a small tablespoonful of butter. Sweeten and flavor to the taste, and bake.—*Mrs. B.*

Irish Potato Pudding.

1 pound mashed Irish potatoes.
1 pound sugar.
2 cupfuls butter, well creamed.
5 eggs.
1 teacup cream.
1 wine-glassful brandy.

Stir the ingredients thoroughly together. Bake in pastry without tops.—*Mrs. Dr. J. F. G.*

Sweet Potato Pudding.

1 quart grated sweet potatoes.
10 eggs, well beaten.
3 cupfuls sugar.
1 cupful flour.
1 cupful butter.
1 quart milk.

Bake slowly in a pan. Serve with sauce.—*Mrs. G. A. B.*

Sweet Potato Pudding.

Grate three or four large sweet potatoes and put them immediately in three pints of sweet milk to prevent them from turning dark. Beat six eggs light, add four ounces melted butter, and mix well with potatoes and milk. Add eight tablespoonfuls of sugar, and season with lemon or vanilla. Bake without a crust.—*Mrs. W. C. R.*

Sweet Potato Pudding.

Boil one and a half pounds potatoes very tender. Add half a pound butter, and rub both together through a sieve. Then add a small cupful milk, six eggs, one and a half cupful sugar. Beat all together and add a little salt, the juice and rind of a lemon. Then beat again, and prepare pastry. Bake twenty minutes. It may be baked without pastry. Irish potato pudding may be made by the same recipe.—*Mrs. A. C.*

CREAM PUDDING.

Beat six eggs to a froth and stir into them three tablespoonfuls sugar and the grated rind of a lemon. Mix one pint milk, one pound flour, and two teaspoonfuls salt. Add eggs and sugar. Just before baking, add a pint of thick cream. Bake in cups or pudding dishes.—*Mrs. Col. W.*

TYLER PUDDING.

4 eggs.
3 cupfuls sugar.
1 cupful butter, washed and melted.
1 cupful cream, seasoned with lemon.

Bake in a paste.—*Mrs. C. N.*

MOLASSES PUDDING.

1 cupful molasses.
½ cupful butter and lard mixed.
1 cup not quite full of buttermilk.
3 eggs.
1 teaspoonful soda.

Flour enough to make it as thick as cake batter. If you wish to eat it cold, add another cup of sugar. Bake it quickly.—*Mrs. M. S. C.*

Molasses Pudding.

1 teacup sugar.
1 teacup butter.

2 teacups molasses.
2 teacups flour.
4 eggs.
1 tablespoonful ginger.

1 teaspoonful soda dissolved in a few spoonfuls of buttermilk Eat with sauce. Excellent.

Molasses Pudding.

9 eggs.
4 cupfuls molasses.
1 teacup butter.

Bake in a paste.—*Mrs. P. W.*

Cottage Pudding.

Beat to a cream one large cupful of sugar and two and a half tablespoonfuls of lard and butter mixed. Stir in one well beaten egg, one large cup of buttermilk with soda dissolved in it. Add nutmeg to the taste. Take one pint of flour and rub into it, dry, two tablespoonfuls cream of tartar. Then add the other ingredients. Bake three-quarters of an hour and serve with wine sauce.—*Mrs. A. F.*

Texas Pudding.

3 eggs (yolks and whites beaten separately).
3 cupfuls sugar.
1 cupful butter.
1 cupful sweet milk.

Two tablespoonfuls of flour. Bake in a crust. This will fill three pie-plates.—*Mrs. McN.*

Snowball Pudding.

Boil one quart of rich milk and then thicken it with a tablespoonful of flour or arrow-root. Beat up the yolks of four eggs with three tablespoonfuls of white sugar. Then pour the milk slowly into the eggs and sugar, stirring all the time. Pour this custard into a pudding dish and brown it slightly. Beat up the whites to a stiff froth, adding four tablespoonfuls of sugar, and flavoring with lemon. Drop it on the custard (when browned) in the form of balls, as large as an egg. Set it back in the stove to brown a little.—*Mrs. S. T.*

THICKENED MILK PUDDING.

Boil one pint of milk and one-half pint of water. Thicken with one pint of flour, and stir in three ounces butter, while warm. When cold, add nine eggs (well beaten), one pound sugar, one wine-glassful wine, and powdered cinnamon and mace to your taste.—*Mrs. R.*

DELICIOUS HASTY PUDDING.

Seven eggs beaten separately. Add to the yolks gradually ten tablespoonfuls of sifted flour, alternately with a quart of milk and half a teaspoonful of salt. Beat till perfectly smooth. Then add the whites, pour into a buttered dish, and bake twenty minutes. Eat with nun's butter or wine sauce.—*Mrs. P. McG.*

FEATHER PUDDING.

2 cupfuls flour.
1 cupful sugar.
1 cupful sweet milk.
1 egg.
1 tablespoonful butter.
1 teaspoonful cream of tartar.
½ teaspoonful soda.

Season with nutmeg and eat with sauce.—*Mrs. D. C. K.*

WASHINGTON PUDDING.

6 eggs (well beaten).
½ pound butter.
½ pound sugar.
½ pound marmalade.

Beat well together, season with nutmeg, and bake in a paste.
—*Mrs. Dr. S.*

ONE EGG PUDDING.

1 egg.
1 cupful sugar.
1 cupful milk.
2 cupfuls flour.
1 tablespoonful butter.
1 teaspoonful soda.
2 teaspoonfuls cream of tartar.

Eat with sauce.—*Mrs. A. C.*

DELICIOUS PUDDING.

Beat the yolks of six eggs very light. Stir in alternately three tablespoonfuls of flour and a pint of milk. Put a tablespoonful of melted butter and half a teaspoonful of salt in the batter. Then stir in the whites of the six eggs, beaten to a stiff froth. Butter the baking dish or cups, fill them a little more than half full, and bake quickly. Eat with wine sauce. Make this pudding half an hour before dinner, as it must be eaten as soon as done.—*Mrs. S. T.*

BALLOONS.

6 eggs.
7 tablespoonfuls of flour.
1 quart of milk.
1 teacup of sugar.
1 tablespoonful of butter.
1 tablespoonful of lard.

Cream the butter and lard with the flour. Beat the eggs and sugar together. Mix the milk in gradually, bake quickly, and eat with sauce.—*Mrs. Dr. E.*

VIRGINIA PUDDING.

Scald one quart of milk. Pour it on three tablespoonfuls of

sifted flour. Add the yolks of five eggs, the whites of two, and the grated rind of one lemon. Bake twenty minutes.

Sauce.—The whites of three eggs, beaten to a stiff froth, a full cup of sugar, then a wine-glass of wine and the juice of a lemon. Pour over the pudding just as you send it to the table.—*Miss E. S.*

Extra Fine Pudding.

Make a batter of two teacupfuls of flour and four of milk. Beat the yolks and whites of four eggs separately. Then mix all together and add one tablespoonful of melted butter. Bake in a buttered pan and serve with wine sauce.—*Mrs. McG.*

Superior Pudding.

4 eggs.
1 quart of milk.
1 cup of sugar.
2 tablespoonfuls of flour.

Beat the sugar, flour, and yolks of the eggs together, with one cup of the milk, scald the remainder of the milk and put the above in it. Flavor with lemon or vanilla. Beat the whites of the eggs to a stiff froth, add a little sugar, spread on top of the pudding, and brown slightly.—*Mrs. D. C. K.*

Baked Indian Pudding.

Take nearly one pint sifted meal and make into a mush. Pour over it one quart of boiled sweet milk. Add one gill of molasses, one gill of sugar, six eggs beaten separately, half a pint chopped suet. If you like, add a few currants, raisins, or a little citron. Bake nearly two hours. Eat with sauce.—*Mrs J. A. B.*

Excellent Batter Pudding.

1 quart flour.
7 eggs.
½ cupful melted butter.

1 teaspoonful salt.

1 teaspoonful soda, dissolved in lukewarm water.

2 teaspoonfuls cream of tartar, also dissolved.

Enough sweet milk to make a batter the consistency of sponge cake batter. Bake in a mould and eat with brandy sauce.—*Mrs. M. C. C.*

Puff Pudding.

10 eggs (beaten separately).

10 tablespoonfuls sifted flour.

1 quart milk.

A little salt.

Beat the eggs to a stiff froth. Then put the flour with the yolks, then add the milk and lastly the whites, well beaten. Eat with cold or hot sauce.—*Mrs. D. C. K.*

Penny Pudding.

Beat five eggs very light. Mix with five tablespoonfuls of flour, one large spoonful of butter and one pint of milk. Eat with sauce.—*Mrs. A. T.*

Economical Pudding.

1 cup chopped suet.

1 cupful golden syrup.

1 cupful milk.

2 cupfuls chopped raisins.

3 cupfuls flour.

1 teaspoonful soda (put in the milk).

2 teaspoonfuls cream of tartar put in the dry flour.

Boil three hours and a half.—*Miss E. T.*

Poor Man's Pudding.

6 eggs.

1 pint sour cream.

1 cupful melted butter.

1½ cupful sugar.

not enough butter), which must be spread on the dough four times and rolled in.

It must be made thin, put in tins, and baked in a moderate oven.

LEMON PIE.

Grate the rind and squeeze the juice of two lemons. Stir two tablespoonfuls corn-starch into two teacups hot water, and boil, stirring well. Add three-quarters of a pound of granulated sugar. When cool, add the yolks of four eggs well beaten, then the lemon-juice and grated rind, stirring the whole well together. Line the plates with rich pastry, and pour the mixture in. Bake until the crust is done. Beat the whites of the eggs very light, add six ounces powdered sugar, pour over the pies, set them again in the oven, and slightly brown. This will make two pies.—*Mrs. T. M. C.*

Lemon Pie.

One cupful sugar, one cupful sweet milk, one tablespoonful flour, one tablespoonful butter, three eggs, one lemon. Mix the grated rind and juice of the lemon with the yolks of the eggs and the sugar. Add the milk next, and then the butter and flour. Bake in a paste. After it is cold, spread on the whites of the eggs, frothed and sweetened.—*Mrs. McG.*

Lemon Pie.

Yolks of four eggs, white of one, beaten very light; grated rind and juice of one large lemon; five heaping tablespoonfuls sugar. Bake in an undercrust till the pastry is done. Froth the whites of three eggs with five tablespoonfuls sugar. Spread over the pies and bake again till brown.—*Mrs. Col. S.*

Lemon Pie.

One tablespoonful butter, creamed with two cups of sugar, yolks of six eggs, grated rind and juice of four lemons, four heaping tablespoonfuls flour. Mix well. Add a cupful butter-

Brandy Sauce.

Cream together one-quarter pound fresh butter, and one quarter pound pulverized white sugar. Mix with it one gill of lemon brandy, or half the quantity of brandy; the juice of one lemon, and half a nutmeg grated. Stir it slowly into half a cup of boiling water, and after letting it simmer a moment, pour into a warm sauce tureen.—*Miss E. P.*

French Sauce.

Cream half a pound butter, and stir in half a pound sugar. Then add the yolk of an egg, and a gill of wine. Put it on the fire; stir till it simmers. Grate nutmeg over it, after taking it off the fire.—*Mrs. F. D.*

A Nice Sauce for Puddings.

Half a pound of butter; eight tablespoonfuls brown sugar; one nutmeg (grated), the white of one egg.

The butter must be creamed and the sugar beaten into it, then the egg. The wine poured gently in and stirred till the sauce is cold, then grate the nutmeg. Make it in a common sauce tureen, on the hearth, stirring all the while. Do not let it boil.
—*Mrs. M. E. J. B.*

Rich Sauce for Puddings.

One pint cream; half pound sugar; one tablespoonful butter; one glass of wine. Season to the taste. Do not let it boil.—*Miss E. P.*

Sauce for Pudding.

Two large cupfuls brown sugar; one large cupful butter; one teacup wine; a little rose water. Boil the sugar and wine together. Then add the butter and grated nutmeg.—*Mrs. McG.*

Pudding Sauce.

One cupful cream, from morning's milk; two cupfuls sugar; one egg, well beaten; one tablespoonful butter; one teaspoonful corn-starch. Boil all together till a thick syrup. Take off the fire and add grated nutmeg and a glass of wine.—*Mrs. S. T.*

COLD SAUCE.

Whites of five eggs beaten to a stiff froth. Sweeten to the taste. Pour in some hot melted butter, stirring well. Season with lemon.—*Mrs. M. G. H.*

Cold Sauce.

Half a pound of butter and half a pound of sugar (powdered), beaten to a froth. The juice and grated rind of a lemon, or essence of any kind, as a flavor.—*Mrs. M. F. G.*

Cold Sauce (for about eight people).

One heaping tablespoonful of butter, creamed till very light, adding sugar till as thick as you can stir. Then add two tablespoonfuls of very rich milk, a glass of good wine, and a little grated nutmeg.—*Mrs. P. McG.*

PUDDING SAUCE.

One cupful of butter; two cupfuls sugar; three eggs; one wine-glass of wine. Stir well, and let it come to a boil.—*Mrs. F. D.*

Pudding Sauce.

Cream together half a pound of sugar and butter. Add the yolk of one egg, the juice of a lemon, and a glass of wine. Stir over a slow fire, but don't boil.—*Mrs. McG.*

LEMON SAUCE.

One pound sugar; three ounces butter; half a teacup of water. Juice and sliced rinds of two lemons. Pour this into a saucepan, and while it is coming to a boil, beat the yolks of two eggs and add them. When well boiled, take it from the fire and add the whites of the two eggs, beaten to a froth. To be eaten hot with sponge cake.—*Mrs. K.*

Sauce for Boiled Pastry.

Stew for fifteen minutes one pint of water, half a pound of sugar, and a piece of butter as large as an egg. Beat the yolks of three eggs. Remove the pan from the fire, and pour several spoonfuls of its contents into the beaten eggs, stirring briskly. Then pour all into the pan, place it over a slow fire and stir till it thickens. Season with lemon or vanilla.—*Mrs I. H.*

Molasses Sauce.

Moderately boil a pint of molasses from five to twenty minutes, according to its consistency. Add three eggs well beaten. Stir them and continue to boil a few minutes longer. Season with nutmeg and lemon.—*Mrs. Dr. J.*

PASTRY.

Pastry has fallen somewhat into disfavor, on account of its unwholesome properties, but as many persons still use it, we will give some directions for making it as wholesome and palatable as possible.

It is a great mistake to use what is called "cooking butter" and old lard for pastry. Only fresh butter and sweet lard should be employed for the purpose, and in summer these should be placed on ice before being used for pastry. Pastry, like cake, should be made in the cool of the morning, and it should be eaten fresh, as, unlike cake, it will not admit of being kept.

If a marble slab cannot be obtained, it is well to keep a thick wooden board exclusively for rolling out pastry. Handle as little as possible, and if anything should prevent you from putting it on to bake as soon as it is rolled out, put it on ice in the interim, as this will make it nicer and more flaky. Sometimes there is a delay about getting the oven or fire ready, in which case the cook generally leaves the pastry lying on the kitchen table; but its quality would be much improved if it were put on the ice instead, whilst waiting to be baked.

Excellent Recipe for Pastry.

Four teacups flour, one teacup firm butter, one teacup nice lard, one teacup ice water, one teaspoonful salt. Mix the lard and butter in the flour with a large, flat knife, then add the ice water. Do not touch it with the hands. Take it up in a rough-looking mass, roll it out quickly—not too thin. Cut it with a very sharp knife around the edges of the patty-pans. When intending to bake lemon puddings or cheese-cakes, let the pastry bake four or five minutes before adding butter, as this prevents the pastry from being heavy at the bottom. In summer it is best to put five teacups of flour, instead of four.—*Mrs. M. C. C.*

Pastry.

One pound fresh butter, one quart flour. Make up the dough with ice water. Divide the butter into parts. Roll out, and cover thickly with one part of the butter. Continue till all is rolled, sifting flour each time. Don't handle much, or it will be heavy.—*Mrs. W.*

Pastry.

Mix with water one quart flour and two teaspoonfuls salt. Work well and roll out thin. Spread over with lard, sift flour over the dough, and cut it in strips of two inches. Lay them in a pile one above another, cut them in squares, and again pile them up. Press down with the hands, and roll out thin as before. Repeat this several times, and the pastry will be improved each time. Do not use your hands after the roller is applied.

Puff Paste.

One pound flour, to be made up with cold water and beaten fifteen minutes. One pound butter (or half lard, if you have not enough butter), which must be spread on the dough four times and rolled in.

It must be made thin, put in tins, and baked in a moderate oven.

LEMON PIE.

Grate the rind and squeeze the juice of two lemons. Stir two tablespoonfuls corn-starch into two teacups hot water, and boil, stirring well. Add three-quarters of a pound of granulated sugar. When cool, add the yolks of four eggs well beaten, then the lemon-juice and grated rind, stirring the whole well together. Line the plates with rich pastry, and pour the mixture in. Bake until the crust is done. Beat the whites of the eggs very light, add six ounces powdered sugar, pour over the pies, set them again in the oven, and slightly brown. This will make two pies.—*Mrs. T. M. C.*

Lemon Pie.

One cupful sugar, one cupful sweet milk, one tablespoonful flour, one tablespoonful butter, three eggs, one lemon. Mix the grated rind and juice of the lemon with the yolks of the eggs and the sugar. Add the milk next, and then the butter and flour. Bake in a paste. After it is cold, spread on the whites of the eggs, frothed and sweetened.—*Mrs. McG.*

Lemon Pie.

Yolks of four eggs, white of one, beaten very light; grated rind and juice of one large lemon; five heaping tablespoonfuls sugar. Bake in an undercrust till the pastry is done. Froth the whites of three eggs with five tablespoonfuls sugar. Spread over the pies and bake again till brown.—*Mrs. Col. S.*

Lemon Pie.

One tablespoonful butter, creamed with two cups of sugar, yolks of six eggs, grated rind and juice of four lemons, four heaping tablespoonfuls flour. Mix well. Add a cupful buttermilk, and one teaspoonful soda. Froth and sweeten the whites of the eggs and put them on top the pies.—*Mrs. N.*

LEMON CREAM PIE.

One cupful sugar, one of water; one raw potato, grated; juice and grated rind of one lemon. Bake in pastry, top and bottom.

ORANGE PIE.

Pulp and juice of two oranges, a little of the grated peel, the yolks of three eggs, one cupful sugar, one cupful milk. Stir the yolks with the sugar, then a tablespoonful of butter, then the juice, lastly the milk. Bake in a dish. After the pie has cooled, spread on it the whites of the three eggs, stiffly frothed and sweetened. Then set it again on the fire, to brown slightly. —*Mrs. McG.*

Orange Pie.

One quart milk, eight eggs, one small teacup rolled cracker, half a cupful butter, two grated fresh oranges, or the juice and chopped peel of two, one wine-glassful wine. Cream the butter and sugar, add the wine, oranges, and eggs beaten to a foam, the whites separately, the milk and the cracker. Bake half an hour, in puff paste.—*Mrs. M. B. B.*

Orange Pie.

One pint of milk, three oranges, one cupful of sugar, three eggs, one and a half tablespoonful of corn-starch. Bake in puff paste.—*Mrs. H. H. S.*

PEACH MÉRINGUE PIE.

Pare and stew ripe peaches. When nearly done, sweeten, take from the fire. Stir in a heaping teaspoonful fresh butter to each pie. Pour in a deep pie-plate, lined with paste. Bake; when done, remove from the oven and cover with the whites of three eggs beaten to a stiff froth, and sweetened with three tablespoonfuls powdered sugar. Set back in the oven to brown slightly. Apple méringue pie may be made in the same way, only flavoring the fruit.—*Mrs. S. T.*

PEACH PIE.

Pare and stew a quart of peaches with a pint of sugar, stirring often; when boiled to look nearly as thick as marmalade, take from the fire and when nearly cool, add one tablespoonful fresh butter. Have ready three crusts, baked in shallow tin plates. Spread and pile up the fruit on each.—*Mrs. S. T.*

Peach Pie.

Pare and stew the peaches till nearly done. Sweeten and boil a little longer. Set aside and when nearly cool, pour into deep pie-plates, lined with paste. Put bits of butter over the top, dredge with flour, then cover with a top crust, and bake.—*Mrs. T.*

PRUNE PIE.

Wash the prunes through several waters. Put in a preserving kettle in the proportion of two pounds fruit to one pound sugar. Pour a quantity of boiling water over them and let them boil at least two hours. When they are thoroughly done and the syrup thickens, take from the fire and pour into tin plates, lined with paste. Add one teaspoonful of butter. Cover with a rich paste and bake.—*Mrs. S. T.*

DAMSON PIE.

Scald the damsons slightly, in just enough water to prevent burning. Set aside till cool enough to handle. Remove the stones, sweeten well, and put in a deep pie-plate, lined with paste. Dredge with a little flour, cover with a top crust, and bake.—*Mrs. T.*

STRAWBERRY SHORT-CAKE.

Bake a rich paste in pie-plates. Have six ready. In these spread stewed strawberries well sweetened; lay one upon another, six deep. In winter, use preserved or canned berries.—*Mrs. H.*

Cherry Pie.

Seed the cherries first, then scald them in their own juice. Sweeten liberally and pour into a deep pie plate lined with a rich paste. Dredge with flour, cover with a top crust and bake. Scarlet or short-stem cherries are best. It is necessary to scald most fruits, as otherwise the pastry will burn before the fruit is thoroughly done.—*Mrs. S. T.*

Cranberry Pie.

Prepare as for sauce, stewing two pounds fruit to one pound sugar. Pour into a pie plate lined with paste, cover with a top crust and bake.

Currant Pie.

Wash and thoroughly pick the fruit. Sweeten liberally and put in a yellow baking-dish, adding a little boiling water to melt the sugar; let it simmer a little; then set it aside to cool. Pour into a pie plate, covered with paste. Dredge with flour. Cover with paste and bake.

Apple Pie.

Put a crust in the bottom of a dish. Put on it a layer of ripe apples, pared, cored, and sliced thin, then a layer of powdered sugar. Do this alternately, till the dish is filled. Add a few teaspoonfuls rose water and some cloves. Put on a crust and bake it.—*Mrs. E.*

Apple Pie.

Pare and stew the apples till thoroughly done and quite dry. Rub through a colander and sweeten with powdered sugar. When cool add the whites of eggs—three eggs to a pint of apples—and a teacup of cream, whipped. Beat all the ingredients together with a patent egg-whip—one with a wheel if convenient. Spread upon crusts of rich paste, baked in shallow tin pie-plates. Grate nutmeg on each one and pile up three or four deep.—*Mrs. S T.*

Apple Pie.

Pare and slice the apples. Make a little thick syrup of white sugar, into which throw a few cloves, allspice, or mace, as you prefer. In this syrup, scald a few apples at a time, taking them out and putting more in till all are slightly cooked. Set aside to cool, then pour into deep pie plates lined with paste. Dredge with flour. Put bits of butter over all. Dredge again. Cover with paste and bake. A glass of brandy or wine will improve it.—*Mrs. S. T.*

BLACKBERRY PIE.

Pick the berries, but do not wash them. Stew slightly, sweeten, pour into a pie plate, lined with paste. Grate in a little nutmeg, dredge with flour, put on a top crust and bake.

WHORTLEBERRY PIE.

Pour just enough boiling water on the fruit to prevent it from sticking to the bottom of the preserving kettle. Boil a minute, sweeten and pour into a pie-plate lined with paste. Dredge with flour, cover with paste and bake.—*Mrs. S. T.*

GOOSEBERRY PIE.

Put one pound sugar to one of fruit, adding just enough water to prevent it from burning. Cook till it begins to jelly. Then spread over shapes of rich puff paste, already baked.—*Mrs. M. C. C.*

TOMATO PIE.

Slice green tomatoes and stew in a thick syrup of sugar and lemon juice. Grate in the yellow rind of a lemon. When transparent, spread evenly over the bottom of a pie-plate that has been lined with paste. Spread strips of pastry across or cut into ornamental leaves with a cake-cutter, place over the fruit and bake.—*Mrs. S. T.*

Sliced Potato Pie.

Steam or boil the potatoes. Slice and lay in a syrup of sugar seasoned with whole cloves or allspice. Scald and set aside till nearly cool. Then place the slices evenly on the bottom of a deep pie-plate lined with crust. Put in each pie a tablespoonful of butter in bits, a wine-glass of brandy or Madeira wine.—*Mrs. S. T.*

Sweet Potato Pie.

One pint potatoes, boiled and mashed with a teacup sweet milk, and run through a colander. Beat separately four eggs; cream one teacup butter with one of sugar. Beat in the yolks, then the potatoes, grate in half a nutmeg, pour in a large wine-glass of brandy or good whiskey, and last of all, stir in the frothed whites. Bake in deep pie plates, lined with paste, without a top crust. Sift powdered sugar over the pies.

Irish potato pie may be made in the same way; only adding the juice and grated rind of a lemon.—*Mrs. T.*

Rhubarb Pie.

Carefully skin the stalks, cut in pieces half an inch long. Scald in a little rich syrup, but not long enough to become soft. Set aside, and when nearly cool, pour into a pie plate, lined with paste. Put a little grated lemon rind and a piece of butter the size of a walnut, in each pie. Dredge with flour, put on a top crust and bake.—*Mrs. T.*

Mincemeat.

Two quarts boiled beef, two quarts suet, chopped fine (or a part butter, for suet). Six quarts apples, one quart molasses (best quality). Four pounds sugar, three pounds raisins, one pound citron. Nutmeg, cinnamon, cloves, allspice, and wine to your taste. Mix well, pack in jars, with melted butter on top, if to keep long. Put in a cool place.—*Mrs. J. W.*

Mincemeat.

Three pounds meat (after it is boiled). Four pounds suet, three and one-half pounds raisins, one and one-half pounds currants, one-half pound dried cherries, two nutmegs, and mace to your taste. Four pints white wine, one pint brandy, four pounds brown sugar.—*Mrs. M. E. J. B.*

Mincemeat.

Six cupfuls beef, twelve cupfuls apples, three cupfuls sugar, two cupfuls molasses, two cupfuls butter, two pounds raisins, one quart cider, three tablespoonfuls cinnamon, two tablespoonfuls allspice, two nutmegs.

Mincemeat.

Two pounds lean fresh beef, boiled and chopped. Two pounds beef suet chopped fine, four pounds pippin apples, two pounds raisins stoned and chopped, two pounds currants, one-half pound citron, two grated nutmegs, one ounce powdered cinnamon, one-half ounce each of cloves and mace, two large oranges, one teaspoonful salt, one quart brandy, one quart wine, one wineglass rose water.

CREAM PIE.

One quart morning's milk, 1 cupful sugar, yolks of six eggs, three tablespoonfuls sifted flour. Boil twenty minutes, after seasoning with nutmeg, wine, and vanilla or lemon. Have rich pastry already baked, in deep pie plates. Fill with the above mixture and bake. Make a méringue of the whites and some sugar, pour over the pie, and set it in the stove again to brown.—*Mrs. T.*

Cream Pie.

One half pound butter, four eggs, sugar and nutmeg to taste, two tablespoonfuls flour well mixed with milk. Pour over it one quart boiling milk, stir all together and bake in deep dishes.—*Mrs. A. B.*

Soda Cracker Pie.

Pour water on two large or four round soda crackers and let them remain till thoroughly wet. Then press out the water and crush them up together. Stir in the juice and grated peel of a lemon, with a cupful or more of powdered sugar. Put in pastry and bake.—*Miss H. L.*

Silver Pie.

Peel and grate one large white potato. Add the juice and grated rind of a lemon, the beaten white of one egg, one cupful of white sugar, and one of cold water.

Bake in a nice paste. After baking, spread on top the whites of three eggs, frothed, sweetened and flavored with lemon. Set again on the fire and brown. Lay on small pieces of jelly or jam, just before taking it to the table.—*Mrs. M. B. B.*

Custard Pie.

One quart milk, five eggs, five tablespoonfuls sugar; flavor with lemon.

Bake slowly, half an hour.—*Mrs. M. B. B.*

Washington Pie.

One cupful sugar, one-half cupful butter, one-half cupful sweet milk, one-half cupful flour, one egg, one teaspoonful cream of tartar, one-half teaspoonful soda; flavor with lemon. Put on dinner plates—spread with apple sauce between each layer.—*Mrs. Dr. J.*

Sugar Pie.

Three cupfuls light brown sugar, one-half cupful melted butter, one-half cupful cream, three eggs. Season with lemon; beat well together; bake in pastry, without tops.—*Mrs. J. F. G.*

Molasses Pie.

Three eggs, beaten separately, one pint molasses, one tablespoonful melted butter. Bake on a rich crust.—*Mrs. Dr. J.*

Molasses Pie.

One teacup molasses, one teacup sugar, four eggs, four tablespoonfuls butter. Mix sugar and eggs together, pour in butter, and add molasses.—*Mrs. Dr. S.*

Cheese Cakes.

Yolks of twelve eggs, one pound sugar, one-half pound butter, one cupful flour, one pint milk, juice of two lemons. The milk, flour, and butter, creamed, and lemons put in together, after the eggs are well beaten. Stir all well together till it curds.

Bake in paste.—*Mrs. A. C.*

Lemon Cheese Cakes.

Yolks of sixteen eggs, one pound sugar, three-quarters pound butter, four lemons, boiling rinds twice before using, two tablespoonfuls powdered cracker.

Bake in paste.—*Mrs. Dr. E.*

Lemon Cheese Cakes.

Mix and gently melt four ounces of sugar and four ounces of butter; add yolks of two eggs, white of one; grated rind of three lemons, juice of one and a half lemon, one small Savoy or sponge biscuit, some almonds blanched and pounded, three spoonfuls brandy. Mix well and bake in rich pastry.—*Mrs. V. P. M.*

Lemon Cheese Cakes.

Yolks of eight eggs or yolks of five and whites of three, one-half pound sugar, a lump of butter, juice of one lemon and grated rind of three. Bake in rich pastry—*Miss D. D.*

Corn-starch Cheese Cakes.

Juice and rind of three lemons, three cupfuls water, three cupfuls sugar, three eggs, three tablespoonfuls corn starch, two tablespoonfuls butter. Boil the water, mix the corn starch with a little cold water and pour on the boiling water. Let it boil up once and then pour it on the butter and sugar. After it cools add the lemons and eggs.—*Miss D. D.*

Almond Cheese Cakes.

Beat up together very light one-half pound powdered sugar, and the whites of four eggs.

Blanch and cut in small pieces four ounces of almonds, which must be beaten up with the eggs and sugar. Add a little oil of almonds or rose water, and bake with pastry, in tins.—*Mrs. I. H.*

Almond Cheese Cakes.

Soak one-half pound Jordan almonds in cold water all night. Next morning, blanch them in cold water, lay them on a clean cloth to dry, and then beat them fine in a marble mortar with a little orange-flower or rose water. Then beat and strain six yolks and two whites of eggs, add a half-pound white sugar, and a little powdered mace. Rub all well together in the mortar. Melt ten ounces fresh butter, and add a grated lemon peel. Mix all the ingredients and fill the pans, after putting a paste at the bottom. Small tin shapes are best for cheese cakes.

Cream Tarts.

Make them small, of rich paste. Fill them after baking, with whipped cream, and drop a small spot of jelly in each one. The prettiest and most delicate of tarts.—*Mrs. M. B. B.*

Lemon Tarts.

Chop or grate a lemon; add a cupful white sugar, a cupful water, one egg, one tablespoonful flour. Line small patties with paste, put a spoonful in each and bake.—*Mrs. M. B. B.*

Prune Tarts.

Scald the prunes, take out the stones, break them and put the kernels in a little cranberry juice with the prunes, and some sugar. Simmer them, and when cold put in tart shapes in pastry and bake.—*Mrs. V. P. M.*

FRENCH FRITTERS.

One quart of milk (half to be boiled, and the other half mixed with a quart of flour, and used to thicken the boiling milk with).

Let it get done. While cooking, beat ten eggs very light; add a spoonful at a time to the batter, beating all the time, till well mixed. Add salt to your taste. Have a small oven full of nice lard, boiling hot. Put not quite a spoonful of batter to each fritter. Take them out before they turn dark and put them in a colander to drain the lard off of them.—*Mrs. Dr. E.*

FRITTERS (*made with yeast*).

One quart flour, three tablespoonfuls yeast, five eggs, one pint milk. Beat into a tolerably stiff batter. Stir a cupful of boiled rice into the batter, a short time before baking. A good deal of lard (boiling hot) is required for frying the fritters. Drop the batter in with a spoon, which must be dipped, each time, in boiling water. In cool weather, make the fritters about nine in the morning, in the summer, about eleven.—*Mrs. A. C.*

BELL FRITTERS.

Put a pint of boiling water in a preserving kettle, and as it boils, put in a tablespoonful of fresh butter. Have ready a pint of the best flour, sifted and wet with cold water, as for starch. Dip up some of the boiling water and pour to this, being careful to have it smooth. Return this to the kettle, stirring rapidly to prevent lumps. Turn into a wooden tray, and while hot, beat in six well beaten eggs, a spoonful at a time. Beat till very light, and beat quickly that the eggs may not cook in lumps. Have ready a pint of boiling lard in a pan. Make the fritters the shape of an egg, drop in and fry a light brown.

To be eaten with a pint of molasses, a heaping tablespoonful of butter, a little ginger and cinnamon, boiled to a thick syrup and served hot.

A great deal of lard is required to fry fritters nicely; yet it is not extravagant, as it may be used again. Strain what remains and put it by for use.—*Mrs. S. T.*

Quire of Paper Pancakes.

Mix with half a pint of rich milk the yolks of four eggs, well beaten. Add three tablespoonfuls fine flour, four ounces sugar, five ounces fresh butter, melted and cooled, four tablespoonfuls Madeira wine, half a nutmeg. Grease the pans once with fresh butter, and this will answer for all. The above quantity will suffice for five or six persons.—*Mrs. R.*

Common Pancakes.

Eight eggs, four tablespoonfuls flour, one pint of milk, one teaspoonful salt.

JELLY, BLANC-MANGE, CHARLOTTE RUSSE, BAKED CUSTARD, CREAMS, ETC.

Jelly made of the feet of calves, hogs, etc., is more troublesome, but is also considered more nutritious than jelly made of gelatine. It is very desirable, for country housekeepers in particular, to make this sort of jelly, as the materials are generally in their reach. It is well, however, in all cases, to keep on hand Cox's or Nelson's gelatine, on account of the expedition with which jelly may be made from these preparations.

As jelly is considered more wholesome when not colored by any foreign substance, no directions will be given in the subsequent pages for coloring it. The palest amber jelly, clear and sparkling, flavored only by the grated rind and juice of a lemon and pale Madeira or sherry wine, is not only the most beautiful, but the most palatable jelly that can be made.

Though the recipes accompanying boxes of gelatine do not always recommend boiling, it is a great improvement to jelly, adding brilliancy, transparency, and a better flavor. Only the grated yellow rind and strained juice of the lemon should be used, and these, with the requisite quantity of pale Madeira or sherry, should be added after the other ingredients have been well boiled together. The white rind or one single lemon seed will render the jelly bitter. A delicious preserve (for which a receipt is given under the proper heading), may be made of lemons, after the yellow rind has been grated off and the juice pressed out for jelly.

The best and most simple arrangement for straining jelly is to invert a small table, fold an old table-cloth four double, tie each corner to a leg of the table; set a bowl under the bag thus formed, with another bowl at hand to slip in its place when the jelly first run through is returned to the bag, as will be necessary, the first never being transparently clear. Catch a little in a glass. If clear as crystal, it will be unnecessary to return it again to the bag. You may then put a thick cloth over the bag to keep in the heat, and if in winter, place before a fire. Shut up the room, and let it drip. The jelly will run through the bag more rapidly if the bag is first scalded.

Jelly should never be made in hot weather. Ices are much better and more seasonable.

Always serve jelly with a pitcher of whipped cream, but do not mix it beforehand with the cream, as it is best to leave it to the taste of each person.

For blanc-mange and gelatine, it is best to use gelatine and as few spices as possible, as spices turn gelatine dark. As such explicit directions are given in the subsequent pages for the making of these dishes, it is unnecessary to say anything further on the subject at present.

A nice custard is made in the following manner: Mix the

beaten yolks of six eggs with a teacup of sugar. Have a quart of milk boiling in a kettle. Dip up a teacup of milk at a time and pour on the eggs, till the kettle is emptied, stirring rapidly all the time. Wash out the kettle, pour the mixture back, and stir constantly till it thickens. Then pour it into a bowl and stir till cool, to make it smooth and prevent it from curdling. Put in the bottom of glass mugs slips of preserved orange, lemon, or citron. Fill nearly full with custard; put whipped cream and grated nutmeg on top.

Or, the yolks may be mixed with boiled milk and sugar in the same proportions, but instead of being returned to the kettle, may be poured into china or earthenware custard-cups, set in a pan of boiling water, placed in a stove or range, and baked. The boiled milk must be seasoned by boiling a vanilla bean in it, or a few peach leaves, or it may be flavored with caromel. Serve the custard with whipped cream on top.

Stock Jelly.

To one and a half gallons of stock, put the whipped whites of eight eggs. Put in six blades of mace and the rind of three lemons, 4½ pounds sugar. Let it boil ten minutes, then add three pints of Madeira wine, juice of eight lemons, a little vinegar or sharp cider. Let it boil only a few minutes. Strain through a dripper. If the stock is not very nice, it may require the whites of one dozen eggs to clear it.—*Mrs. T.*

Calves' Foot Jelly.

One quart nice jelly stock, one pint wine, half a pound white sugar, whites of four eggs beaten up, three spoonfuls lemon juice. Boil all well and pass through a jelly-bag, kept hot before the fire. Try some at first, till it drips clear, and then pour out the whole. Peel the lemons as thin as possible and strain the jelly on the peelings. Should you wish to turn out the jelly in moulds, put one ounce isinglass to three pints of jelly.—*Mrs. I. H.*

Isinglass Jelly.

Dissolve two ounces isinglass in two quarts of boiling water. When cold, add juice of three lemons and skin of one, whites of three eggs, well beaten, one and a half pounds of sugar, one pint cider, four pieces cinnamon (size of the little finger), eight blades of mace. Let it boil up well. Be careful not to stir after the ingredients are thoroughly mixed. Let it stand ten minutes after removing from the fire, and just before straining pour in a pint of wine.—*Mrs. W. R. R.*

Crystal Jelly.

Pare off the rind of one large lemon. Boil in one pint water with one ounce isinglass; add one pound sugar and one cup pale wine. As soon as the isinglass is dissolved, strain through a muslin and let it stand till cold. Grate the rind of another lemon and let it stand in the juice of the two lemons for a short time. Strain all in a bowl, and whisk it till it begins to stiffen. Pour in moulds.—*Mrs. E. P. G.*

Gelatine Jelly.

Soak one box of Cox's gelatine, three hours, in a pint of cold water. Then add one pint of cooking wine, the rind and juice of one lemon, two pounds white sugar, a little mace. Stir these ingredients till the sugar dissolves, then add two quarts of boiling water, gently stirring till mixed. Strain at once, through a flannel bag twice. This recipe makes the best jelly I ever saw.—*Mrs. M. M. D.*

Gelatine Jelly.

To one package of gelatine add one pint cold water, the rind of one lemon and juice of three. Let it stand an hour. Then add three pints of boiling water, one pint wine, two and a quarter pounds loaf sugar, a wineglass of brandy or the best rum. Strain through a napkin and let it stand to jelly.—*Mrs. Col. S.*

Gelatine Jelly (*without straining*).

Add a pint cold water to one box Cox's gelatine. Let it

stand fifteen minutes, then add three pints boiling water, one pint wine, the strained juice and peelings (cut thin) of three lemons, half a teacup of best vinegar, one and a half pounds loaf sugar, one wine-glass French brandy, mace or any other spice you like, and a little essence of lemon. Let it stand an hour, then take out the lemon peel and mace. Let it stand in a cool place to congeal.—*Mrs. Dr. J.*

JELLY WITHOUT EGGS OR BOILING.

Dissolve one package gelatine, an hour, in a pint of cold water. Then add three pints of boiling water, the strained juice of four lemons and the rind of two, one quart of wine, two pounds of sugar. Stir all well together until dissolved.— *Mrs. E. B.*

Jelly without Boiling.

To one of the shilling packages of Cox's gelatine, add one pint cold water. After letting it stand an hour, add one and a half pounds of loaf sugar, the juice of four lemons, one pint light wine, three pints boiling water, and cinnamon to the taste. In cold weather this is ready for use in four or five hours. Set the vessel with the jelly on ice, in summer.—*Miss D. D.*

CREAM JELLY.

Two measures of stock, one of cream; sweeten and flavor to the taste. Pour in moulds to congeal.

BLANC-MANGE.

Dissolve over a fire an ounce of isinglass in a gill of water. Pour the melted isinglass in a quart of cream (or mixed cream and milk), and half a pound of loaf sugar. Put in a porcelain kettle, and boil fast for half an hour. Strain it, and add a quarter of pound of almonds, blanched, and shaved fine. Season to the taste with vanilla and wine, but do not add the wine while hot. Pour into moulds.—*Mrs. C. C.*

Blanc-mange.

Pour two tablespoonfuls cold water on one ounce gelatine to soften it. Boil three pints rich cream. Stir the gelatine into it whilst on the fire, and sweeten to the taste. When it cools, season with three tablespoonfuls peach water. Four ounces almonds, blanched and pounded very fine and boiled with the blanc-mange, are a great improvement. When it begins to thicken, pour into moulds. Serve with plain cream.—*Mrs. J. H. T.*

Blanc-mange.

Sweeten a pint of cream and flavor it with lemon juice. Then whip it over ice, till a stiff froth. Add one-quarter of an ounce gelatine, dissolved in a little boiling water, and whip it well again to keep the gelatine from settling at the bottom. Pour in a mould, and set on ice till stiff enough to turn out Eat with cream, plain or seasoned. A delicious dish.—*Mrs. G. D. L.*

Blanc-mange. (*Very fine.*)

Dissolve one box gelatine in two quarts milk, let stand for two hours. Boil six almonds in the milk. Strain through a sifter while this is being boiled. Pound together in a mortar, two handfuls blanched almonds and half a cupful granulated sugar. Stir into the boiled milk. Add one tablespoonful vanilla, and sweeten to your taste.—*Mrs. W. S.*

CUSTARD BLANC-MANGE.

Make a custard with one quart milk, four eggs, one teacup sugar. Stir into it while boiling, half a box gelatine after it has soaked ten minutes. Season with vanilla, and pour in moulds. Eat with whipped cream.—*Mrs. E. P. G.*

ARROW-ROOT BLANC-MANGE.

Boil in a saucepan (tightly covered) one quart milk and a piece of vanilla bean. Stir into half a pint cream, a teacup arrow-root, and a little sauce, mixing them smoothly. Pour into this the quart boiling milk, stir it well, put it in the saucepan again and let it simmer ten minutes. Sweeten to your taste. Set it in moulds to cool. Eat with cream, flavored to your taste.—*Mrs. H.*

Chocolate Mange.

Dissolve one ounce Cox's gelatine in a pint cold water. Let it stand an hour. Then boil two quarts of milk, and add to it six ounces chocolate with the gelatine. Sweeten to your taste and pour into moulds. Eat with sauce made of cream, wine, and sugar.—*Mrs. W. H. L.*

Coffee Mange.

One cupful very strong coffee, one cupful sugar, one cupful rich cream. Dissolve half a box gelatine in two cupfuls milk, over the fire. Add the cream last, after the rest is cool. Pour in a mould to congeal.—*Mrs. McG.*

Charlotte Russe.

One pint milk made into a custard with the yolks of six eggs, sweetened with half a pound sugar, and flavored with vanilla. Strain into the custard, one ounce isinglass, dissolved in two cupfuls milk. When this mixture is cold and begins to stiffen, mix with it gradually, one pint rich cream, previously whipped to a froth. Then put strips of sponge cake around the mould and put the Charlotte Russe in. Turn it out when ready to serve.—*Mrs. W. C. R.*

Charlotte Russe.

Soak three-quarters of a package of gelatine in three teacups fresh milk. Make a custard of one and a half pint fresh milk, three-quarters of a pound of sugar, and the yolks of eight eggs. When it has boiled, add the gelatine, and flavor with vanilla

When it begins to congeal, stir in a quart rich cream, whipped to a froth.—*Mrs. M.*

Charlotte Russe.

Have a tin or earthernware mould six inches high, and the same in diameter (or oblong, if you like). Slice sponge cake or lady-fingers and line the mould with them. Then beat three pints rich cream to a froth, and put the froth on a sieve to drain the milk from it. Take one pint calf's-foot jelly (or one and a half ounces gelatine), half a pint rich milk, and the yolks of six eggs. Place over a slow fire, and beat till they nearly boil. Then take them off the fire and beat till cool. Put in the frothed cream, sweeten to your taste, flavor with vanilla, and stir all well together. Fill the mould and place it on ice to cool.—*Mrs. W. H. L.*

Strawberry Charlotte Russe.

Six eggs, one ounce isinglass, one quart milk. Sweeten to the taste and flavor with vanilla. Pour into moulds. Then put it on sponge cake, covered with strawberry jam, and pour around the dish whipped cream, sweetened and flavored with wine.—*Mrs. McG.*

CHARLOTTE RUSSE.

Sweeten one quart cream, flavor it with wine and whip it lightly. Dissolve half a box gelatine in a tablespoonful cold water and the same quantity of boiling water. Set over the steam of a kettle to dissolve. Then add half a pint of cream. When cold, stir it into the whipped cream. Beat the whites of four eggs very light, and stir into the cream. When it begins to stiffen, pour into a glass bowl, lined with thin strips of sponge cake. Whip, sweeten and flavor another pint of cream, and garnish the dish.—*Mrs. D.*

Charlotte Russe.

One ounce gelatine; one quart rich cream; eight eggs; one

quart new milk. Sugar and flavoring to taste. Whip the cream to a stiff froth. Make a custard of the milk, gelatine and yolks of the eggs. When cool, add the whites of the eggs well beaten and the whipped cream. Line the mould with sponge cake, and if in summer put it on ice.—*Miss M. C. L.*

Baked Custard.

Boil a quart or three pints of cream, or rich milk, with cinnamon, and three dozen beaten peach kernels, tied in a piece of muslin, or you may substitute some other flavoring, if you choose. After boiling, let it cool.

Then beat the yolks of fourteen eggs and whites of four, sweeten and strain in a pitcher. After it has settled, pour it in cups and set them in the oven, putting around them as much boiling water as will reach nearly to the top of the cups. Let it boil till you see a scum rising on top the custard. It will require at least ten minutes to bake.—*Mrs. R.*

Baked Custard.

Seven eggs; one quart milk; three tablespoonfuls sugar. Flavor to taste.—*Mrs. Dr. E.*

Baked Custard.

Scald eight teacups milk. (Be careful not to boil it.) After cooling, stir into it eight eggs and two teacups sugar. Bake in a dish or cups. Set in a stove pan and surround with water, but not enough to boil into the custard cups. An oven for baking puddings is the right temperature. Bake when the custard is set, which will be in twenty minutes.—*Mrs. J. J. A.*

Spanish Cream.

Boil, till dissolved, one ounce of gelatine in three pints of milk. Then add the yolks of six eggs, beaten light, and mixed with two teacups sugar. Put again on the fire and stir till it thickens. Then set it aside to cool, and meantime beat the six whites very stiff and stir them into the custard when almost cold. Pour into moulds. Flavor to your taste, before adding the whites.—*Mrs. W.*

Spanish Cream.

Dissolve half a box gelatine in half a pint milk. Boil one quart milk, and while boiling beat six eggs separately and very light. Mix the yolks with the boiling milk, and when it thickens add the gelatine. Sweeten and season to the taste. Pour all while hot on the whites of the eggs. Pour into moulds.—*Mrs. J. T. B.*

Italian Cream.

Soak a box of gelatine in one pint cold water. Then add one quart nice cream, season with fresh lemons, sweeten to your taste, beat well together, and set away in a cool place. When hard, eat with cream, flavored with wine.—*Mrs. A. B.*

Russian Cream.

Boil, till dissolved, one ounce gelatine in three pints milk. Then add the yolks of four eggs, well beaten, and five ounces sugar. Mix the whole and let it cook. Then strain and set aside to cool. Beat the four whites to a stiff froth, and when the cream is nearly congealed, beat them in. Flavor to your taste, and mould.—*Mrs. A. P.*

Bavarian Cream.

Sweeten one pint thick cream to your taste and flavor it with lemon or vanilla. Churn the cream to a froth, skim off the froth as it rises and put it in a glass dish. Dissolve one and a half tablespoonfuls gelatine in warm water, and when dissolved pour into the froth and stir fifteen minutes. Set in a cold place and it will be ready for use in a few hours.—*Mrs. D. R.*

Bavarian Cream.

Soak half a box gelatine in cold water till thoroughly dissolved. Then add three pints milk or cream, and put on the fire till scalding hot, stirring all the while. Then take it off and add three teacups sugar and the yolks of eight eggs (by spoonfuls) stirring all the time. Set on the fire again and let it remain till quite hot. Then take it off and add the eight beaten whites and eight teaspoonfuls vanilla. Put into moulds to cool.—*Mrs. N. A. L.*

TAPIOCA CREAM.

Three tablespoonfuls tapioca, one quart milk, three eggs, one cupful sugar. Flavor with lemon or vanilla.

Soak the tapioca, in a little water, overnight. After rinsing, put it in milk and let it cook soft. Add sugar and yolks of eggs. Whip the whites stiff and pour on the tapioca, as you remove it from the fire. It should be cooked in a tin pail, set in a kettle of boiling water, to prevent the milk from scorching. Eat cold.—*Mrs. G. W. P.*

TAPIOCA.

Boil the pearl tapioca (not the lump kind) as you do rice. When cool, sweeten to the taste and season with nutmeg. Pour rich cream over it and stir it to make it smooth. Put one pint cream to two tablespoonfuls before boiling.—*Mrs. J. H. T.*

LEMON FROTH.

Dissolve a box of gelatine in a pint of warm water, then add a pint of cold water. In winter three pints may be used instead of two.

Add the juice of six lemons and the rind; cut them as for jelly. Let it stand till it begins to harden. Then take out the rind and add the whites of twelve eggs beaten to a stiff froth. Beat them into the jelly, put in a glass bowl, and serve in saucers.—*Mrs. A. C.*

SYLLABUB.

Half a pound sugar, three pints lukewarm cream, one cupful wine. Dissolve the sugar in the wine, then pour it on the milk

from a height and slowly, so as to cause the milk to froth.—
Mrs. E.

SLIP.

One quart milk (warm as when milked), one tablespoonful wine of the rennet. After the milk is turned, eat it with a dressing of cream, sugar and wine.—*Mrs. Dr. E.*

BONNY-CLABBER.

Set away the milk in the bowl in which it is brought to the table. If the weather is warm, set it in the refrigerator after it has become clabber.

Help each person to a large ladleful, being careful not to break it. Eat with powdered sugar, nutmeg and cream.—*Mrs. S. T.*

FLOAT.

To a common-sized glass bowl of cream, sweetened with loaf sugar and flavored with wine, take the whites of six eggs, three large tablespoonfuls sugar, and three of fruit jelly. Do not beat the eggs to a froth, but put in the jelly and sugar and beat all together.—*Mrs. T.*

APPLE FLOAT.

Mash a quart cooked or coddled apples smooth through a sieve; sweeten with six tablespoonfuls sugar, and flavor with nutmeg. Then add the apples, a spoonful at a time, to the whites of four eggs, well beaten. Put a pint of cream, seasoned with sugar and nutmeg, at the bottom of your dish, and put the apples on top.—*Mrs. I. H.*

APPLE SNOW.

Pare and slice one dozen large apples; stew them perfectly done, and run through a colander. Then add whites of twelve eggs, beaten to a stiff froth, and one pound white sugar. Eat with sweet cream.

A Nice Dessert of Apples.

Pare and weigh two pounds green apples. Cut them in small pieces, and drop them in a rich syrup, made of a pound and a quarter of "A" sugar and a little water. As soon as the syrup begins to boil, add the juice and grated rind of one large lemon or two small ones.

Boil till the apples become a solid mass. Turn out in a wet mould to stand till cold. Serve on a dish surrounded with boiled custard, or eat with seasoned cream.—*Mrs. A. F.*

A Nice, Plain Dessert.

Peel and slice the apples, stew till done, then run through a colander and sweeten, season. Beat the whites of three eggs to a stiff froth, and just before serving whip them into a quart of the stewed apples. Eat with cream.—*Mrs. T.*

Apple Compote.

Pare, core, and quarter the apples, wash them, and put them in a pan with sugar and water enough to cover them. Add cinnamon, and lemon peel which has been previously soaked, scraped and cut in strings. Boil gently till done; lay in a deep dish. Boil the syrup to the proper consistency, and pour over the apples.—*Mrs. E.*

Nice Preparation of Apples.

Quarter and core some well-flavored apples, place in a shallow tin pan or plate, sprinkle thickly with white sugar and a few small pieces of cinnamon. Pour on enough cold water to half cover the apples, and scatter a few small pieces of butter over them. Cook slowly till thoroughly done, then set away to cool. —*Mrs. McG.*

Baked Apples.

Pare and core the apples, keeping them whole. Put in a baking-dish, and fill the holes with brown sugar. Pour into each apple a little lemon juice, and stick into each a piece of lemon peel. Put enough water to prevent their burning. Bake till tender, but not broken. Set away to cool. Eat with cream or custard. They will keep two days.—*Mrs. Dr. J.*

Iced Apples.

Pare and core one dozen fine, firm apples, leaving them whole. Place in a stewpan, with enough water to cover them, and stew till you can pierce them with a straw. Then remove from the fire, and set in a dish to cool. Then fill the centre with currant or some other jelly, and ice over as you would cake. Serve in a glass dish, and eat with rich cream or custard.—*Mrs. A. D.*

ICE CREAM AND FROZEN CUSTARD.

After having tried many new and patent freezers, some of the best housekeepers have come to the conclusion that the old-fashioned freezer is the best. It is well, however, to keep a patent freezer on hand, in case of your wanting ice cream on short notice; but for common use an old-fashioned one is the best, especially as servants are so apt to get a patent freezer out of order.

The great secret of freezing cream quickly in a common freezer is to have the cream and salt in readiness before breaking the ice into small pieces the size of a walnut. There must be a space of two inches between the freezer and the tub in which it is set. Put a little ice and salt under the bottom of the freezer, then pack alternate layers of ice and salt several inches higher than the cream is in the freezer. If there is no top to the tub, with an aperture to admit the freezer, pin a woollen cloth over it and turn the freezer rapidly. When the cream begins to harden on the sides of the freezer, cut it down with a knife, scrape from the sides, and beat with a large iron spoon. Then cover again, and turn rapidly till it is as hard as mush. When the ice begins to melt, drain off the salt and water, adding more salt and ice, which must be kept above the level of the cream in the freezer. When done, tie large newspapers over the tub and freezer. Put a woollen cloth or blanket over these, and set the cream in a dark, cool closet till wanted. In this way it may be kept for hours in summer, and for days in winter, and will grow harder instead of melting. As cream can be kept thus, it is well to make it early in the day and set it aside, leaving more leisure for other preparations that are better made immediately before dinner.

Ice cream making, like other branches of housekeeping, is much facilitated by having all the ingredients at hand before beginning on it. As such explicit directions for the process are given in the subsequent pages, it is unnecessary for me to add anything further on the subject. Unless you have pure cream to freeze, it is better to make plain boiled custard rather than to attempt an imitation of ice cream.

It is a good plan to make jelly and custard at the same time, so that the yolks of eggs not used in the jelly may be utilized in custard either boiled or baked. The same proportions are generally used for boiled and baked custard. Instead of flavoring with extract of vanilla, it is much better to boil a vanilla bean in the milk, or to boil some peach leaves tied up in a piece of muslin (six or eight leaves to a quart of milk), or to flavor it with burnt sugar. Never flavor custard with extract of lemon, when you can obtain fresh lemons for the purpose.

When you have no yolks left from making jelly, boil a quart of milk (flavored by the above directions). Have ready three eggs, whites and yolks beaten together to a stiff froth, and into these stir a teacup of powdered white sugar. Dip up the boiling milk, pour slowly on the eggs, stirring rapidly. When all the milk has been stirred in the eggs, wash out the kettle, put the milk and eggs back into it, and let the mixture boil till it begins to thicken, when it must be taken immediately from the fire, poured into a bowl, and stirred till cold and smooth.

Many persons, before freezing, stir in the frothed whites of three eggs. The same directions given for freezing cream apply to the freezing of custard.

Boiled custard should never be used as a substitute for cream in making fruit ice creams, nor should it ever be eaten with jelly.

Ice Cream.

Dissolve five teaspoonfuls Oswego starch or arrow-root in a teacup milk. Add to it the whites of three eggs well frothed, and the yolk of one, well beaten.

Sweeten with loaf sugar and boil half a gallon new milk. As soon as it begins to boil, pour it in small quantities over the mixture of eggs and starch, till about half the milk is taken out of the kettle. Then pour all back in the kettle and stir a few moments. After it cools, add one quart rich cream; season to the taste and freeze.—*Mrs. Dr. E.*

Ice Cream.

One quart milk, two eggs, one teaspoonful corn starch, one teaspoonful arrow-root. A small lump of butter.—*Mrs. E. B.*

Ice Cream.

Cream one tablespoonful butter from which the salt has been washed. Add three tablespoonfuls corn starch. Dissolve this in half a gallon new milk, heated, sweetened and seasoned. Beat the whites of four eggs, and stir in just before freezing.—*Mrs. McG.*

Lemon Ice Cream.

One gallon rich cream, six lemons, first rubbed till soft, and then grated. Tie the yellow peel, which has been grated off, in a piece of coarse muslin. Cut each lemon in half and squeeze the juice from it. Strain the juice, and soak the muslin bag of lemon peel in it, squeezing it frequently till it becomes highly flavored and colored by it. Then add two teacups of sugar.

In sweetening the cream, allow a teacup of sugar to each quart. Pour the juice into it slowly, carefully stirring. Froth and freeze, reserving a portion of cream to pour in as it sinks in freezing.—*Mrs. S. T.*

Orange Ice Cream.

Four oranges, one gallon cream. Rub four or five lumps of sugar on the orange peel, squeeze the juice out, put the lumps of sugar in it and pour into the cream. Sweeten heavily with pulverized sugar before freezing.—*Mrs. M.*

Strawberry Cream.

Four quarts thick sweet cream, four quarts strawberries. The berries must be mashed or bruised, caps and all, with a teacup of granulated sugar to each quart. After standing several hours, strain through a thin coarse cloth.

Put four teacups of white sugar to the cream, and then add the juice of the berries. Whip or froth the cream with a patent egg-whip or common egg-beater. Pour two-thirds of the cream into the freezer, reserving the rest to pour in after it begins to freeze. Raspberry cream may be made by the same recipe.—*Mrs. S. T.*

Peach Cream.

Take nice, soft peaches, perfectly ripe. Pare and chop fine, make them very sweet, and mash to a fine jam. To each quart of peaches, add one pint of cream and one pint of rich milk. Mix well and freeze. If you cannot get cream, melt an ounce of Cox's gelatine in a cup of water. Boil the milk, pour it on the gelatine, and when cold, mix with the peaches.—*L. D. L.*

Peach Cream.

To two quarts of rich, sweet cream, add two teacups of sugar. Whip to a stiff froth with a patent egg-whip, one with a wheel, if convenient; if not, use the common egg-whip. Then peel soft, ripe peaches till you have about two quarts. As you peel, sprinkle over them two teacups powdered white sugar. Mash quickly with a silver tablespoon, or run through a colander, if the fruit is not soft and ripe. Then stir into the whipped cream, and pour into the freezer, reserving about one-fourth to add when the cream begins to sink in freezing. When you add the remainder, first cut down the frozen cream from the sides of the freezer. Beat hard with a strong iron spoon, whenever the freezer is opened to cut down the cream, till it becomes too hard. This beating and cutting down is required only for the common freezer, the patent freezer needing nothing of the kind.

Tie over the freezer large newspapers, to exclude the air, and set aside till wanted.

Apricot cream may be made exactly by this receipt.—*Mrs. S. T.*

Pineapple Ice Cream.

Whip two quarts rich, sweet cream to a froth, with two teacups powdered white sugar. Use a patent egg-whip with a wheel, if convenient; if not, use the common egg-whip.

Grate two ripe pineapples, and add to them two teacups white sugar. When well mixed, stir into the cream.

Pour into the freezer, reserving one-fourth. When it begins to freeze, it will sink; then beat in the remainder with a strong iron spoon. Beat every time the freezer is opened to cut down the cream from the sides. Never cook fruit of any sort to make cream.—*Mrs. S. T.*

Vanilla Ice Cream.

Boil half a vanilla bean, cut in small pieces, in half a pint of rich new milk. When cool, strain and add to two quarts thick sweet cream. Sweeten with two heaping teacups powdered sugar, and whip to a stiff froth. Pour into a freezer, reserving one-fourth of the cream. As soon as it begins to freeze, stir from the sides with a large iron spoon, and beat hard. Add the remaining cream when it begins to sink. Beat every time the freezer is opened. When frozen, tie newspapers over the freezer and bucket, throw a blanket over them, and set in a close, dark place till the ice cream is wanted.—*Mrs. S. T.*

NORVELL HOUSE CARAMEL ICE CREAM.

One gallon rich, sweet cream, four teacups powdered sugar, five tablespoonfuls caramel. Mix well and freeze hard.

CARAMEL.

Put in a stewpan one teacup nice brown sugar and half a teacup water. Stew over a hot fire till it burns a little. If too thick, make it of the consistency of thin molasses, by adding a little boiling water. Bottle and cork, ready for use.—*Mrs. J. W. II.*

Caramel Ice Cream.

Three quarts cream, two pints brown sugar, put in a skillet and stir constantly over a brisk fire until it is dissolved. Be careful not to let it burn, however. While it is melting, heat one pint milk, and stir a little at a time with the dissolved sugar. Then strain it, and when cool, pour it into the cream, well beaten. Then freeze.—*Mrs. W. C. R.*

CHOCOLATE ICE CREAM.

Half a pound sweet chocolate, twelve eggs, one gallon milk, two tablespoonfuls arrow-root, sugar and vanilla to the taste. Dissolve the chocolate in one pint and a half boiled milk. Whip the eggs. Mix the arrow-root in a little cold milk, and add to the eggs. Then pour on one gallon boiled milk, and put on the fire to thicken. When cool, season and freeze.—*Mrs. D. R.*

Chocolate Ice Cream.

Three quarts milk, eight eggs, six ounces chocolate dissolved in a pint of boiling water, three heaping tablespoonfuls arrow-root well mixed in cold milk, one pound and a half of brown sugar, vanilla to the taste. Made like custard, and boiled very thick.—*Miss D. D.*

Chocolate Ice Cream.

One quart morning's milk, one-quarter of a pound chocolate, one teaspoonful vanilla, sugar to the taste. Boil as for table use. When ready to freeze, whip in one quart rich cream.

Cocoanut Ice Cream.

One pound grated cocoanut, one pound sugar, one pint cream. Stir the grated nut gradually into the cream. Boil gently, or merely heat it, so as to thoroughly get the flavor of the nut. Then pour the cream into a bowl and stir in the sugar. When cold, stir in three pints fresh cream, then freeze.

Cocoanut Ice Cream.

One cocoanut, pared and grated. Mix with a quart of cream, sweeten, and freeze.—*Mrs. E. I.*

Cocoanut Ice Cream.

One grated nut, three and a half quarts of milk, one pint of cream, two tablespoonfuls arrow-root mixed in a little cold milk. Sweeten to the taste, and freeze.—*Mrs. D. R.*

Gelatine Ice Cream.

Soak one-half package of Cox's gelatine in a pint of morning's milk. Boil three pints of milk, and while hot, pour on the gelatine, stirring till dissolved. When cold, add two quarts of cream, and sweeten and season to your taste. Then freeze. It is improved by whipping the cream before freezing.—*Miss E. T.*

White Ice Cream.

Three quarts milk, whites of four eggs beaten light, three tablespoonfuls arrow-root mixed in a little cold water and added to the eggs. Boil the milk and pour over the eggs, etc.

Then put on the fire and thicken a little. When nearly cold, add a quart of cream. Sweeten and season to the taste and freeze.—*Mrs. D. R.*

Ice Cream without Cream.

One gallon milk, yolks of two eggs well beaten, whites of twelve eggs well beaten. Sweeten and scald the milk, and pour it on the eggs, stirring all the time. Put it in the kettle again and let it come to a boil. Season to the taste and freeze at once.—*Mrs. E. W.*

Bisque Ice Cream.

One half-gallon of freshly turned clabber, one-half gallon rich sweet cream, one good vanilla bean boiled in one-half pint sweet milk, sugar to the taste. Churn this five minutes before freezing. One can of condensed milk may be used with less clabber. *Mrs. H L. S.*

Buttermilk Cream.

One gallon buttermilk, yolks of eight eggs, and whites of four, well beaten; three pints sweet milk. Boil the sweet milk and pour on the eggs; then thicken, stirring all the time. When cool stir in the buttermilk slowly, season and sweeten to the taste, then freeze.—*Mrs. D. R.*

Caramel Custard (*Frozen*).

Make a rich custard, allowing a cup of nice brown sugar to every quart. Stew the sugar till it burns a little. Then mix it with the custard while both are hot. Boil two sticks cinnamon in the custard.—*Mrs. J. J. B.*

Frozen Custard.

One quart fresh milk, eight eggs, yolks and whites beaten separately. Put the milk on the fire, sweetened to the taste, and let it come to boiling heat; then take it off and add the yolks. Then wash the kettle and put the custard on the fire again, and let it boil till quite thick. Take it off, and when cool enough, add the whites. Flavor with lemon or vanilla, and freeze. —*Mrs. C. N.*

Frozen Custard.

Twelve eggs, one gallon milk, four lemons, sugar to taste, freeze.—*Mrs. Dr. S.*

Bisque.

Make one-half gallon rich boiled custard, allowing six eggs to each quart. Add, before taking it from the fire, two pounds of macaroon almonds. When cold, freeze.—*Mrs. A. P.*

Plumbière.

Make a rich custard, and flavor it when cool with wine and extract of lemon. When half frozen, add blanched almonds, chopped citron, brandy peaches cut up, and any other brandied or crystallized fruit. Make the freezer half full of custard and fill with fruit.

Frozen Pudding.

Forty blanched almonds pounded rather fine, one ounce citron cut in small squares, two ounces currants, two ounces raisins stoned and divided. Soak all in two wine-glasses wine, all night. Make custard of a pint of cream or milk. If cream, use yolks of four eggs; if milk, yolks of eight eggs. Make a syrup of one pound white sugar and a pint of water. When nearly boiling, put in the fruit and wine and boil one minute. When cool, mix with the custard. Whip whites of the eggs to a stiff froth, and add to the custard and syrup after they are mixed. Add last a wine-glass of brandy.—*Miss E. W.*

Plum Pudding Glacé.

To one pint cream or new milk, stir in thoroughly two table-spoonfuls arrow-root. Boil three pints milk, and while boiling add the cold cream and arrow-root, also three eggs well beaten, and sugar to the taste. When cold season with vanilla bean, and stir in half a pound cut citron, half a pound currants, half a pound raisins cut and seeded. Freeze hard and serve in moulds.—*Mrs. T.*

Cream Sherbet.

Three quarts water, four lemons, whites of six eggs, one pound and two ounces sugar, one pint sweet cream. Mix one-half the sugar with the cream and eggs, which must be beaten to a stiff froth; mix the rest of the sugar with the water and lemons. Mix all together just before freezing.—*Mrs. A. P.*

Lemon Sherbet.

Take one dozen lemons, squeeze out the juice, then slice the rind and pour over it six quarts boiling water. Mix three pounds sugar with the lemon juice, and one quart milk, brought to a boil and thickened with three tablespoonfuls arrow-root or corn-starch. Be careful to remove all the seed and most of the rind, leaving only a few slices to make the dish pretty. After the lemonade begins to freeze, stir in the thickened milk, and the whites of six eggs beaten very light.

Lemon Sherbet.

One dozen good lemons, whites of twelve eggs beaten stiff, three pounds white sugar, one gallon water. Stir all well together and add one quart nice fresh cream. Stir often while freezing.—*Miss E. T.*

Lemon Sherbet.

Two quarts water, four large lemons, one pound and a half sugar, whites of six eggs. Rub some lumps of sugar on the rind of the lemons. Powder some of the sugar, beat it with the whites of the eggs, and mix with the lemonade when it begins to freeze.—*Mrs. M.*

A new Recipe for Lemon Sherbet.

Make one and a half gallon rather acid lemonade, grating

the peel of three or four of the lemons before straining the juice into the water. Let it stand fifteen minutes. Then make and add to it the following mixture: pour a pint cold water over one box gelatine and let it stand half an hour; then pour over it one pint boiling water, and let it stand till thoroughly dissolved. Beat the whites of eight eggs with two pounds pulverized sugar till as thick as icing; then churn a quart rich cream till it is reduced to a pint; then beat the froth of the cream into the egg and sugar. Pour in gradually the lemonade, beating all the time so as to mix thoroughly, and then freeze. Delicious.—*Mrs. F. C. W.*

ORANGE SHERBET.

One gallon water, twelve oranges, juice of three lemons, whites of six eggs. Rub some lumps of sugar on the orange peel. Mix as lemon sherbet, and freeze.—*Mrs. M.*

ORANGE ICE.

One dozen oranges, juice of two lemons, two quarts water; sugar to the taste. Rind of four oranges grated on sugar. Freeze as usual.—*Mrs. G. D. L.*

Orange Ice.

Juice of nine oranges, juice of one lemon, one and one-quarter pounds powdered sugar, two quarts water. To be frozen.—*Mrs. I. H.*

PINEAPPLE ICE.

To a two-pound can of pineapples add three quarts water, half a box gelatine (prepared as for jelly), juice of two oranges, whites of four eggs. Remove the black and hard pieces of pineapple, then pass it through the colander by beating with a potato-masher. Sweeten to your taste and freeze.—*Mrs. I. H.*

Pineapple Ice.

One large pineapple peeled and finely grated, juice of one

lemon, two quarts water. Sweeten to the taste, and freeze hard.—*Mrs. G. D. L.*

Pineapple Ice.

Dissolve one box gelatine in one gallon water. Beat two pounds pineapple through a colander with a wooden pestle. Add the juice of two lemons and the juice of two oranges; sweeten to your taste, but add more sugar than is required for ice cream.

Beat six eggs separately and stir in the mixture. When half-frozen, beat rapidly half a dozen times, at intervals.

This makes two gallons when frozen.—*Mrs. E. T.*

Citron Ice.

Slice citron, pour on it a rich, hot lemonade, and freeze — *Mrs. E. I.*

Raspberry Ice.

Three quarts juice, one quart water. Sweeten heavily, and after putting in the freezer add the whites of six eggs beaten very light. The same recipe will answer for currant or cherry ice.—*Mrs. M. C. C.*

Watermelon Ice (*beautiful and delicious*).

Select a ripe and very red melon. Scrape some of the pulp and use all the water. A few of the seeds interspersed will add greatly to the appearance. Sweeten to the taste and freeze as you would any other ice. If you wish it very light, add the whites of three eggs, thoroughly whipped, to one gallon of the icing just as it begins to congeal. Beat frequently and very hard with a large iron spoon.—*Mrs. J. J.*

Gelatine Ice.

Let one ounce sparkling gelatine stand an hour in a pint of cold water. Then add three pints boiling water, one and one-half pounds loaf sugar, one and one-half pint wine, juice of three lemons, rind of two lemons. Stir all these ingredients and freeze before allowing it to congeal. Delicious.

AMBROSIA.

Pare and slice as many oranges as you choose, in a glass bowl Sprinkle sugar and grated cocoanut over each layer.—*Mrs. W. C. R.*

Ambrosia.

Cut pineapple and orange in slices, sprinkle with sugar, and put in a deep dish alternately to form a pyramid. Put grated cocoanut between each layer. If you like, pour good Madeira or sherry wine over the dish.—*Mrs. T.*

PINEAPPLE.

Peel and slice thin, just before eating. Sprinkle pulverized sugar over it, but nothing else, as the flavor of this delicious fruit is impaired by adding other ingredients. Keep on ice till wanted.—*Mrs. S. T.*

WATERMELONS.

Keep on ice till wanted. If lacking in sweetness, sprinkle powdered sugar over them.—*Mrs. S. T.*

CANTALEUPES.

Cut out carefully the end with the stem, making a hole large enough to admit an apple. With a spoon, remove the seed. Fill with ice, replace the round piece taken out, and place on end. Eat with powdered sugar, salt, and pepper.—*Mrs. S. T.*

PEACHES AND CREAM.

While the first course is being served, peaches should be pared and split, and the stones removed. Lay in a glass bowl and sprinkle liberally with powdered sugar. No fruit should be sweetened till just before eating. Ornament the edges of the bowl with any handsome, glossy leaves convenient, and serve with cream.—*Mrs. S. T.*

STRAWBERRIES

Should never be washed unless sand or earth adheres to them. Cap carefully while the first course is being served, or, if more convenient, you may cap in the morning, but never sweeten till just before eating, as sweetening long beforehand extracts the juice and makes the fruit tough. Set it on ice, or in a refrigerator. No ice must be put on fruit. Serve with cream that has been set on ice. Decorate the edges of the bowl with strawberry leaves.

The same directions will apply to raspberries, blackberries, and dewberries. Whortleberries may be washed, picked, and drained, though not sweetened till dinner.—*Mrs. S. T.*

PRESERVES AND FRUIT JELLIES.

Always make preserves in a porcelain or brass kettle. If the latter, have it scoured first with sand, then with salt and vinegar. Then scald it and put in the sugar and water for the syrup.

In peeling fruit, throw it into cold water to keep it from turning dark, and let it remain there till you are ready to throw it in the boiling syrup. Bear in mind that exposure to the air turns peeled fruit dark.

Boil rather quickly. In preserving fruit whole, boil it a short time in the syrup, take it out, let it get cold, and then put it again in the kettle.

Cut sugar is best for preserves which you wish to be clear and light-colored, but nice brown sugar is best for dark-colored jams and marmalades, such as those made of blackberries, raspberries, whortleberries, etc.

The best peaches for preserving, brandying, or pickling, are white freestone peaches, not quite ripe enough to eat with cream. Pears and quinces also should be preserved before they are quite ripe enough for eating. They should be parboiled before eating. No fruit should be over-ripe when preserved. Damsons and blue plums should be slit lengthwise with a pen knife, and set in the sun before preserving, which will render it easy to extract the stones. Cherries also should be stoned before preserving. A piece of paper dipped in brandy and laid on top the preserves will help to keep them. I would suggest to housekeepers that they always put their preserves in glass jars with screw tops. By this means they can readily inspect it and see if it is keeping well, without the trouble of untying the jar and looking inside, as would be necessary in the case of stone jars.

Set the jar of preserves, if they become dry or candied, in a pot of cold water, which allow to come gradually to a boil. If the preserves ferment, boil them over with more sugar.

The great secret of making nice fruit jelly is to boil the syrup well before adding the sugar (which should always be loaf or cut), and you should allow a pound of sugar to a pint of the juice in acid fruit jellies, though less will answer for sweet fruit. By boiling the syrup well before adding the sugar, the flavor and color of the fruit are retained. Keep the jelly in small, common glasses.

SWEETMEAT PRESERVES.

Cut the rind in any shapes fancied (such as flowers, fruits, leaves, grapes, fish, etc.), put it in brine strong enough to float an egg, cover closely with grape leaves, and set away the jar. When ready to make the preserves, soak the rind in fresh water, changing it till all taste of salt is removed from the rind. Dissolve four tablespoonfuls pulverized alum in one gallon water. Lay the rind in this, covered closely with grape or cabbage leaves. Simmer till it becomes a pretty green, then soak out the alum by throwing the rind in soft water.

Pour boiling water on half a pound white ginger, and let it

stand long enough to soften sufficiently to slice easily in thin pieces (retaining the shapes of the races as much as possible). Then boil it an hour in half a gallon water, and add one ounce mace and two pounds best cut sugar. This makes a thin syrup, in which boil the rind gently for half an hour, adding water to keep the rind covered with syrup.

Set the kettle away for four days and then boil again as before, adding two pounds sugar and more water, if necessary. Repeat the boiling six or seven times, till the syrup is rich and thick and sufficient to cover the rind.

The quantity of seasoning given above is for three gallons rind. Allow two pounds sugar to each pound fruit. This sweetmeat keeps indefinitely and never ferments.—*Mrs. F. M. C.*

Watermelon or Muskmelon Marmalade.

Weigh twelve pounds rind, previously soaked in brine, and the salt extracted by fresh water, parboil, put on with twelve pounds sugar made into a thin syrup, and boil to pieces. Add the peelings of twelve oranges and twelve lemons, previously soaked in water, cut in strips and boiled extrmeley soft, the water being changed three times while boiling. Stir constantly from the bottom with a batter-cake turner. Cook very thick. Put in wide-mouthed glass jars —*Mrs. S. T.*

Ripe Muskmelon or Watermelon Preserves.

During the summer, peel and slice indifferent cantaleupes (such as you do not care to eat), especially such as are not quite ripe. Throw them into brine, together with your thickest watermelon rinds, peeling off the outside skin. When you have enough, weigh them, throw them in fresh water, which change daily till the salt is extracted. Boil in a preserving kettle till soft enough to pierce with a straw. Make a syrup, allowing one pound sugar for each pound fruit. When it boils, put the rind in it and simmer steadily till the rind is transparent and the syrup thick. When cool, add the juice and grated rind of twelve lemons. Let it stand in a bowl several days. Then strain the syrup (which will have become thin), boil it again, pour over the rind, and put the preserves in glass jars with screw tops.—*Mrs. S. T.*

RIPE MUSKMELON PRESERVES.

Peel and slice the melons, soak them twenty-four hours in salt water, twenty-four hours in alum water, and twenty-four hours in fresh water, changing the latter several times. Then make a strong ginger tea, in which boil them slowly till they taste of ginger.

Make a syrup, allowing a pound and a half sugar to each pound fruit, and adding mace and sliced ginger (the latter must be soaked in boiling water twelve hours before it is wanted). Cook the melon in the syrup till clear and tender. You may use sliced lemons as a seasoning instead of ginger.—*Mrs. R. L.*

PINEAPPLE PRESERVES.

Parboil the pineapples, then peel and cut in thick slices, carefully taking out the cores, which, if allowed to remain, will cause the preserves to ferment. Put a pound of sugar to a pound of fruit, and let it remain all night to make the syrup. Boil then till done, without adding a drop of water to the syrup. —*Mrs. F. C.*

ORANGE PRESERVES.

Peel a thin rind off the oranges and make a hole in each end, getting out all the seed. Pour boiling water over them and let them stand till next morning. If the water tastes bitter, search for seed. Pour boiling water over them every day, as long as the bitterness remains. Boil till soft enough to run a straw through them. Add a pound and a half sugar to each pound fruit. Make a thin syrup of half the sugar, and boil the oranges in it a short time. Let them stand in the syrup three days, then pour the syrup from the fruit, put the rest of the sugar to it, and boil it down thick. Then pour it over the fruit. A few lemons added is a great improvement.—*Mrs. J. H.*

ORANGE MARMALADE.

Peel the oranges, taking all the seed and tough skin out of them. Cut the peel in small pieces, put in cold water and boil till tender. Make a syrup, one pound sugar to one pint water. Put a pound of the oranges (mixed with the peel) to a pint of the syrup, and boil all for two hours.—*Mrs. C. C. McP.*

Orange Marmalade.

The day before making, peel one dozen oranges (no matter how sour and indifferent). Throw the peel in a bucket of water, take out the seed, cut up the pulp fine with a pair of old scissors. Then take the peel, cut it in thin strips and throw it into fresh water. Pare and slice pippins (or any other nice apple). Weigh six pounds of them, stew with a little water till perfectly done, and set away. Next day, run this pulp through a colander into a preserving kettle. Add six pounds sugar and boil slowly, constantly scraping from the bottom.

Take the orange peel (which should have been left in soak all night), boil till perfectly soft and free from bitterness, changing the water three times while boiling. In another preserving kettle, simmer this with the orange pulp and two pounds sugar. When both are nearly done, turn the oranges into the apples and cook them very thick. Cool in a bowl, and then put in a glass jar with a screw top.—*Mrs. S. T.*

SLICED LEMON PRESERVES.

Take large, firm lemons, not quite ripe, cut in slices one-quarter inch thick, and take out the seed. Soak in brine a week. Then soak several days in clear water, changing the water twice a day. When all the salt and the bitter taste are extracted, weigh the lemons and boil till tender enough to pierce with a straw. Make a thin syrup, allowing one pound of sugar to each pound of fruit. Put the lemons in and let them simmer slowly a good many hours. Pour into a large bowl and let it remain there several days. At the end of that time strain the syrup (which will have become thin), put the lemons in it again, and boil till they jelly. When cool put in a glass jar with a screw top. The same recipe may be used for oranges.—*Mrs. S. T.*

LEMON MARMALADE.

Every housekeeper should keep a large jar, or other nice vessel, filled with brine, in which she may throw lemon peels after being deprived of the grated rind and juice, used for creams, jellies, etc. These may remain any length of time, to suit one's convenience. Before preserving, soak in pure water till all the taste of salt is extracted. Boil till soft enough to pierce with a straw. Then put in a preserving kettle nine pounds cut sugar and one quart water. As soon as it boils, add six pounds lemon peel and three pounds nice sliced apples (pippins are best). Boil till very thick.—*Mrs. S. T.*

LEMON PRESERVES

May be made of lemon peel, prepared exactly by the above recipe. Put the peel in a preserving kettle and keep covered, while boiling in clear water, till you can run a straw through it. Then throw it into a rich syrup (one pound sugar to one of lemon peel), and boil a long time. Put in a bowl till the next day; then take the syrup (which will be somewhat thin) and boil again till very thick. Pour it over the lemon, and when cold it will be jellied.—*Mrs. S. T.*

PEACH PRESERVES.

Pare white freestone peaches, not quite ripe. Split in half, take out the stones, and throw the peaches in a bucket of water to prevent them from turning dark. Make a syrup of white sugar, using as many pounds of sugar as you have pounds of peaches. When it has boiled thick, put in as many peaches as will cover the bottom of the kettle. Let them boil till nearly done; then take them out, one by one, in a perforated spoon. Lay them in dishes and set in the sun. When all the peaches have been carried through this process, put back the first dish of peaches in the kettle, taking them out when a pretty amber color, and so on till all have been boiled twice. Meantime the peach-kernels should have been scalded and skinned. Put them in the boiling syrup, which must be kept on the fire till very thick. Put the peaches when cool in glass jars, and pour the syrup over them. In a few days examine, and if the syrup has become thin, boil again.—*Mrs. S. T.*

Peach Preserves.

Pare, and add to a pound of peaches one and one-quarter pounds best sugar. Cook very fast for a few moments, in a porcelain kettle. Turn out in a bowl, cover with muslin or cambric, set in the sun, stirring every day till they seem quite transparent. They retain their flavor much better this way than when cooked on the fire. Put in jars, cover with paper saturated with brandy, and tie up tightly to exclude the air.—*Mrs. P. W.*

Peach Marmalade.

Boil twelve pounds soft peaches in a little water. When reduced to a pulp, run through a colander and boil again till very thick, constantly scraping from the bottom. Add half a pound sugar to one pound fruit. Cool in a bowl, and then put in glass jars with screw tops. Pear marmalade may be made by the same recipe, and also apple marmalade, except that you flavor the last with lemon juice and rind.—*Mrs. S. T.*

Brandy Peaches.

For twelve pounds large freestone Heath peaches, not quite ripe and delicately pared, make a syrup of four pounds sugar. Scald a few peaches at a time in the syrup, till all have gone through this process. Place on dishes to cool. Then put in glass jars and add enough good whiskey or brandy to the syrup to cover the peaches. Any spirit will do, if strong enough. Add a few blanched peach-kernels. In a few days see if more liquor or sugar is required. If so, drain off the syrup, add what is needed, and pour again over the fruit. It is a mistake to put too much sugar. Always use freestone peaches.—*Mrs. S. T.*

Brandy Peaches.

Put the peaches (a few at a time) in boiling lye. Let them remain five minutes, to loosen the fur. Then take them out and wipe perfectly clean and white. Then drop them in cold water. Boil them gently in a rich syrup till a straw will pierce them. Then put in a jar, and mix equal parts of French brandy with the syrup. Carefully exclude the air.—*Mrs. G. N.*

Pear Preserves.

Scald the fruit, but do not let it remain till it comes to pieces. Boil till clear, in a syrup made of as many pounds of sugar as you have of fruit.—*Mrs. J. J. A.*

Preserved Apples for Winter Use.

Pare and slice pippins. Put to each pound apples half a pound sugar, and to every eight pounds thus sweetened one quart water, a few cloves, the thin rind and juice of a lemon. Stew till clear, and eat with cream.—*Mrs. B. J. B.*

Apple Mange.

Stew and mash well three pounds pippins, then add three pounds sugar. Just before they are done, add a few drops lemon juice. Put in moulds and it will keep two years. Turned out and sliced, it is a nice dish for tea. Quinces are as nice as apples, prepared this way.—*Mrs. B. J. B.*

Crab Apple Preserves.

Put the crab apples in a kettle, with some alum, keeping

them scalding hot for an hour. Take them out, skin and extract the seed with a small knife, leaving on the stems. Put them in cold water awhile, then take them out, wipe them and put them in a syrup made of as many pounds sugar as you have of fruit. Let them stew gently till they look clear, then take them out and let the syrup boil longer. Siberian crabs may be preserved in the same way, except that they are not peeled and cored.

QUINCE JAM.

Pour boiling water over them and let them remain till the skin rubs off easily. Then peel them and cut off the fair slices. To each pound put twelve ounces sugar, and let them stew together till the syrup is sufficiently thick.

Quince preserves may be made by the same recipe as that used for pears.

DAMSON PRESERVES.

With a sharp penknife, cut a long slit lengthwise in each damson. Spread in dishes and set in the sun till the seed comes out readily. Then boil till thoroughly done in a thick syrup made of as many pounds sugar as there are pounds of damsons.

Preserve green gage plums and other plums by the same recipe.—*Miss P.*

FOX GRAPE PRESERVES.

Seed the grapes, then pour scalding water on them and let them stand till cold; then draw off the water, put one pound sugar to one pound of grapes, and boil gently about twenty minutes.—*Mrs. A. D.*

CHERRY PRESERVES.

Wash, pick and stone the cherries, saving the juice. Allow one pound sugar to each pound fruit. Boil the juice and sugar to a thick syrup, then put in half the cherries and stew till nearly done. Take them out with a perforated spoon and lay on dishes. Put in the other half, let them stew as long as the first; then take out and lay in dishes. Meantime boil the syrup gently. When the cherries are cool, put them again in the syrup and boil a short time. Pour in a large bowl and cool, then put in glass jars and cover tightly.

Scarlet short stems and large wax cherries are best for preserving.—*Mrs. S. T.*

STRAWBERRY PRESERVES.

Cap the berries. Put one and a half pounds sugar to each pound fruit. Let them stand two or three hours, and then boil thirty minutes.

STRAWBERRY JAM.

Cap and wash the berries, and put them on to stew with a very small quantity of water. Stir constantly. When thoroughly done and mashed to a soft pulp, add one pound sugar to each pound fruit. The advantage of adding sugar last is that it preserves the color and flavor of the fruit. Stew till sufficiently thick, scraping constantly from the bottom with a batter-cake turner.—*Mrs. S. T.*

RASPBERRY JAM.

Wash and pick the berries, boil with a little water, mashing and scraping from the bottom as they simmer. When reduced to a thick pulp, add one-half pound sugar to each pound berries. Stew till very thick, scraping constantly from the bottom. Cool in a large bowl, then put in a glass jar with screw top. Blackberry, Dewberry, and Whortleberry Jam may be made by the same recipe.

FIG PRESERVES.

Pick the figs fully ripe the evening before. Cut off about half the stem, and let them soak all night in very weak salt and water. Drain off the salt water in the morning and cover them with fresh. Make a thick syrup, allowing three-quarters pound loaf sugar to each pound fruit. When it boils, drop the figs carefully in and let them cook till they look clear. When done take from the fire and season with extract of lemon or ginger.

The figs must not be peeled, as the salt water removes the roughness from the skin and keeps the fruit firm and hard.—*Miss A. S.*

TOMATO PRESERVES (*either ripe or green*).

The day before preserving, peel and weigh eight pounds pale yellow, pear-shaped or round tomatoes, not quite ripe; spread on dishes alternate layers of tomato and sugar, mixing with the latter the grated rind and juice of four lemons. In the morning, drain off the juice and sugar and boil to a thick syrup. Drop in half the tomatoes and boil till transparent. Take up with a perforated spoon and put on dishes to cool. Then carry the other half through exactly the same process. Then strain the juice, wash the kettle, and put in the juice again. When it boils hard, put in again the first boiled tomatoes. Take them out when they become amber color, and put in the rest. When they are all boiled to an amber color, and cooled on dishes, put them in half-gallon glass jars, and add the syrup after it has been boiled to a thick jelly.—*Mrs. S. T.*

GREEN TOMATO SWEETMEATS.

Slice the tomatoes and soak them a day and night in salt and water, then in fresh water for an hour or two, then scald in alum water with grape leaves. When taken out of alum water, put in cold water to cook. Scald in ginger-tea and again put in cold water, while you make the syrup. To each pound tomatoes put one and a quarter pounds sugar and a few races of white ginger. Cook the tomatoes till clear, the syrup till thick. When cool, season the syrup with essence of lemon and pour over the tomatoes.—*Mrs. C. M.*

RECIPE FOR PUTTING UP FRUIT.

For fruit not very acid, weigh one-quarter of a pound white sugar to one pound fruit perfectly ripe. After sprinkling the fruit with sugar, put it in a preserving kettle and let it just come to a boil. Then put it quickly in glass self-sealing cans, being careful to screw down the tops tightly.—*Mrs. Dr. E. T. R.*

CANDIED FRUIT.

Preserve the fruit, then dip it in sugar boiled to a candied thickness, and dry it. Grapes and some other fruits may be dipped in uncooked.

LEMON CONSERVES.

Wash and dry ten lemons. Pare the yellow rind off clear of the white, and beat it in a mortar with double its weight of sugar. Pack closely in a jar and cover with part of the sugar.—*Mrs. T.*

ORANGE CONSERVES.

Cut the peel in long, thin strips, and stew in water till all bitterness is extracted. Drain off this water and stew again in a thick syrup, allowing one pound sugar to each pound peel. Put away in a cool place for flavoring puddings, pies, etc.

PEACH CONSERVES.

Pare the peaches and cut them from the stone in thick slices. Make a syrup, allowing three-quarters pound sugar to each pound fruit. Boil the peaches and put them on dishes to dry. As they dry, roll them in granulated sugar, and pack in jars or boxes.—*Mrs. W. P.*

GOLDEN SYRUP.

Five pounds white sugar; one quart water. Let it boil two or three minutes, then add two pounds strained honey. It will keep for months.—*Mrs. D. C.*

BLACKBERRY JELLY.

Crush one quart blackberries with one pound best loaf sugar. Cook it over a gentle fire till thick, then add one gill best brandy. Stir it while over the fire, then put it in pots.—*Mrs. E.*

CURRANT JELLY WITHOUT COOKING.

Press the juice from the currants and strain it. To one pint juice put one pound white sugar. Mix together till the sugar is dissolved. Then put them in jars, seal them and expose them to a hot sun two or three days.—*Mrs. E.*

Currant Jelly.

Pick ripe currants from the stem, and put them in a stone jar. Then set the jar in an iron pot and let the fruit boil till the juice is extracted. Pour in a flannel bag and let it drip through—without squeezing, however, as this makes it cloudy.

To each pint of juice add one pound good white sugar. Boil about twenty minutes and keep it well skimmed. Put in the glasses while hot, and sun daily.—*Mrs. P. W.*

Cranberry Jelly.

Wash and pick the cranberries, put them in the preserving kettle with a very small quantity of water, cover closely and stew till done. Pour through a jelly bag or coarse towel, without squeezing, as this will prevent it from being clear. Measure and pour the liquid into the preserving kettle. Let it boil up and remove the scum, then add the sugar, cut or loaf, one pound to a pint. Boil about twenty minutes, or until it jellies. It preserves the color of fruit jellies to add the sugar as late as possible.—*Mrs. S. T.*

Apple Jelly.

Take half a peck of pippin apples, wash them clean, slice them from the core, put them in a preserving kettle with a quart of water. Boil till entirely soft, then strain through a flannel bag. To each pint of juice add one pound white sugar and the juice of three lemons. Boil till jellied. Do not stir while boiling.—*Mrs. P. W.*

Apple Jelly.

Pare and stew sour, juicy apples (Greenings are best), in enough water to cover them. Strain as for currant jelly.

Allow a pound of sugar for each pound of juice. Put them together and strain. Boil four or five minutes, skimming thoroughly.—*Mrs. M. B. B.*

Apple Jelly.

Take any number of juicy apples, put them in a porcelain kettle, and boil to rags. Then strain them through a cloth or sieve. Put a pound of loaf sugar to each pint of the juice, and boil till it jellies. Flavor with the seed beaten in a mortar, and put in while the apples are cooking.—*Mrs. G. W.*

Crab Apple Jelly.

Slice the apples, take out the cores and seed, as they make the jelly bitter. Put them in a kettle cover with water, and boil till quite soft, keeping it well skimmed. Pour the pulp in a jelly bag, and let it drip through. To each pint of juice, add one pound and a half of sugar. Pour in the glasses while hot. Delicious with meats.—*Mrs. P. W.*

Quince Jelly.

Make the same as apple jelly, only do not pare or core the fruit, as much of the jelly is contained in those parts. Or, you may take the sound parings and cores, stew them and strain the liquor twice, and you will have a jelly as nice as that made from the fruit. To each pound of juice allow one pound of sugar. Boil fifteen minutes.—*Mrs. M. B. B.*

Orange Jelly.

Grate the rinds of two Seville and two China oranges, and two lemons. Squeeze the juice of six oranges and three lemons. Add one and a quarter pounds of loaf sugar and one-quarter of a pint of water, and boil till it jellies. Have ready a quart of isinglass jelly, made quite stiff. Put it to the syrup and let it boil up once. Then strain it and put it in a mould.—*Mrs. V. P. M.*

Jelly Oranges.

Dissolve one package gelatine in one cup cold water, afterwards adding two cups boiling water to thoroughly dissolve it. Add then three cups white sugar, one-quarter teaspoonful cinnamon, grated rind of three oranges, juice of twelve fine oranges. Strain through a flannel bag into a pitcher, without shaking or squeezing. Extract the pulp from the orange, by making a hole in one end of it large enough to admit a mustard spoon. Soak the rind a few hours, and then pour the jelly into each orange through the whole at the end. Then set aside to congeal. Garnish with orange leaves. Cut each orange in two. A very ornamental dish.—*Mrs. McG.*

Green Grape Jelly.

Gather Catawba grapes before ripening. Pick them from the stem, wash them, and put them in a stone jar. Set the jar in a kettle of cold water over a hot fire. When the juice comes out of the grapes, take the kettle off and strain the grapes. To each pint of juice put one pound of the best loaf sugar. Boil twenty minutes in the kettle. Ripe grape jelly may be made in the same way.—*Mrs. E.*

Grape Jelly.

The chief art in making jelly is to boil it continuously, slowly and gently. It will not harden well if the boiling stops, even for a few moments. To preserve the true color and flavor of fruit in jellies or jams, boil well before adding the sugar; in this way the water contained in all fruit juices is evaporated. Heat the sugar before adding it. In making grape jelly, pick the grapes from their stems, wash them, put them over the fire in a vessel containing a little water, to keep them from burning. Stew a few moments; mash gently with a silver spoon, strain, and to every pint of juice, allow one pound of white sugar After the juice comes to the boiling point, boil twenty minutes, pour it over the heated sugar, and stir constantly till all is dissolved. Then fill the jelly glasses.—*J. I. M.*

Remedy for Mouldiness in Fruit Jellies.

Fruit jellies may be preserved from mouldiness by covering the surface one-quarter of an inch deep with finely pulverized loaf sugar. Thus protected, they will keep for years.—*Mrs. R. C. M. W.*

Tomato Jelly.

Take ripe tomatoes, peel them carefully, cutting out all the seams and rough places. To every pound put half a pound of sugar. Season with white ginger and mace. Boil to a stiff jelly, then add enough good cider vinegar to keep it.—*Mrs. Dr. P. C.*

Sugar Candy.

Two cupfuls sugar, one cupful water, one wineglassful vinegar, one tablespoonful butter. Cook ten or fifteen minutes.—*Mrs. Dr. J.*

Sugar Candy.

Three cupfuls sugar, half a cupful vinegar, half a cupful water, juice of one lemon. Boil without stirring, till brittle. Pour on a buttered dish and pull till white and light.—*Mrs. McG.*

Sugar Kisses.

Whisk the whites of four eggs to a stiff froth and stir in half a pound sifted white sugar. Flavor as you like. Lay it when stiff in heaps the size of a small egg, on white paper. Lay on a board half an inch thick and put in a hot oven. When a little yellowish, slip off two of the kisses with a knife and join the bottom parts together. Continue till all are thus prepared.—*Mrs. R.*

Nut Candy.

Make sugar candy by one of the foregoing receipts, but instead of pouring it into a dish, drop it at intervals over a buttered dish. On each bit of candy thus dropped, lay half the kernel of an English walnut, and when a little cool, pour half a spoonful of sugar candy on top. Candy of almonds, pecans, or palm nuts may be made by the same recipe.—*Mrs. S. T.*

CREAM CANDY.

Two pounds of sugar, half a cup water, two tablespoonfuls vinegar, one tablespoonful butter. Boil twenty minutes. Season with lemon or vanilla, just as you take it off. Put in a dish and stir till cold.—*Mrs. McN.*

MOLASSES CANDY.

Boil one quart molasses in a rather deep vessel. Boil steadily, stirring from sides and bottom. When a little, poured in a glass of cold water, becomes brittle, it is done. Pour in a buttered dish and pull as soon as cool enough to handle, or you may stir in, when it is nearly done, some picked kernels of the common black walnut. Boil a little longer, pour on a buttered dish, and cut in squares just before it gets cold.—*Mrs. S. T.*

CARAMELS.

One cake (half a pound) of Baker's chocolate broken up, four pounds brown sugar, half a pound fresh butter, one pint of milk. Pour the milk in a preserving kettle and pour the other ingredients into this. Let it boil at least half an hour, stirring frequently. When done, a crust of sugar will form on the spoon and on the side of the kettle. Pour in a large tablespoonful extract of vanilla, take from the fire and stir rapidly till it begins to thicken like mush. Then pour quickly into buttered dishes or pans, and when nearly cold cut into small squares.—*Mrs. S. T.*

Caramels.

Three pounds white sugar, half a pound of chocolate, one pint milk, six ounces of butter. Boil three-quarters of an hour and stir constantly.—*Mrs. R. C.*

Chocolate Caramels.

Two and one-half pounds of sugar, three-quarters pound of chocolate, one quarter pound of butter, half a pint of milk or cream.—*Mrs. W. C. R.*

Cream Chocolate.

One cupful of cream, with enough white sugar to thicken it. Boil till thick, and when cold, roll up in little balls and put them on a dish on which has been poured some melted chocolate. Then pour over them with a spoon some melted chocolate. When quite cool, cut apart and trim off the edges, if uneven. This cream should be seasoned with a few drops of vanilla and the dish should be buttered.—*Miss N.*

Cocoanut Caramels.

One-quarter pound Baker's chocolate (half cake), one-quarter pound butter, two pounds nice brown sugar, one teacup rich milk. Stew half an hour or till thick. Add a grated cocoanut. Stir till it begins to boil again. Take from the fire, stir in a tablespoonful vanilla, and pour into buttered dishes. When cool enough to handle, make into balls, the size of a walnut and place on buttered dishes.—*Mrs. S. T.*

Cocoanut Caramels.

Pour a teacup of boiling milk over one-quarter cake of pounded chocolate. Let it steep an hour, then add one and one-quarter pounds of white sugar, and the milk of a cocoanut. Boil till perfectly done. Then remove from the fire, adding the grated cocoanut. Season with vanilla, pour in buttered dishes, and cut in blocks.—*Mrs. W. C.*

Cocoanut Balls.

Wet two pounds of sugar with the milk of a cocoanut. Boil

and stir till it begins to granulate. Then stir in the cocoanut grated fine. Boil a short time longer, then pour into buttered dishes, and as soon as it can be handled make into balls.—*Mrs. J. M.*

COCOANUT DROPS.

The white part of a grated cocoanut, whites of four eggs well beaten, one-half pound sifted white sugar. Flavor with rose water or lemon. Mix all as thick as can be stirred; lay in heaps half an inch apart, on paper or on a baking-pan, in a hot oven. Take them out when they begin to look yellowish.—*Mrs. R.*

ALMOND MACAROONS.

One-half pound almonds, blanched and pounded, with a teaspoonful essence of lemon, till a smooth paste. Add an equal quantity of sifted white sugar and the whites of two eggs. Work well together with a spoon. Dip your hand into water and work them into balls the size of a nutmeg. Lay them on white paper an inch apart, then dip your hand in water and smooth them. Put them in a slow oven for three-quarters of an hour. Cocoanut may be used instead of almonds.—*Mrs. M G. H.*

WINE.

Be sure to get perfectly ripe fruit for making wine, but do not gather it immediately after rain, as it is watery then and less sweet than usual.

Be very careful to stop the wine securely as soon as fermentation ceases, as otherwise it will lose its strength and flavor. Watch carefully to see when fermentation ceases.

Strawberry wine makes a delicious flavoring for syllabub, cake, jelly, etc., and so does gooseberry wine. Dewberries make a prettier and better wine than blackberries, and have all the medicinal virtues of the latter.

The clearest wine is made without straining, by the following process: Take a tub or barrel (a flour-barrel for instance), and make a little pen of sticks of wood at the bottom. On top of this pen lay an armful of clean straw. Bore a hole in the side of the tub or barrel as near the bottom as possible, and set it on a stool or box so as to admit of setting a vessel underneath it. After mashing the berries intended for wine, put them on top the straw, and let the juice drain through it and run through the hole at the side of the tub or barrel into the vessel set beneath to catch it. Be careful to have this vessel large enough to avoid its being overrun. Any open stone vessel not used before for pickle will answer, or a bucket or other wooden vessel may be used. Let the berries remain on the straw and drain from evening till the next morning. Some persons make a slight variation on the process above described, by pouring hot water over the berries after putting them on the straw. After the draining is over, an inferior sort of wine may be made by squeezing the berries.

The following process will make wine perfectly clear: To a half-gallon of wine put two wine-glasses of sweet milk. Stir it into the wine and pour it all in a transparent half-gallon bottle. Stop it and set it by for twenty-four hours, at the end of which time the wine will be beautifully clear, the sediment settling with the milk at the bottom. Pour off the wine carefully into another bottle, not allowing any of the sediment or milk to get into the fresh bottle. The same directions apply to vinegar.

BLACKBERRY WINE.

Fill large stone jars with ripe black or dewberries. Cover them with water, mash them, and let them stand several hours, or, if freshly gathered, let them stand all night. Then strain through a thick cloth and add three pounds white sugar to each gallon of juice. Let the wine stand a few days in the jars, stirring and skimming each day. Put it in a demijohn, but do not cork it up for some time.—*Mrs. M. D.*

Blackberry Wine.

Measure the berries and bruise them; to every gallon adding one quart of boiling water. Let it stand twenty-four hours, stirring occasionally; then strain off the liquor into a cask, adding two pounds sugar to every gallon. Cork tight and let it stand till the following October, when it will be ready for use without further boiling or straining.

Blackberry Wine.

One bushel very ripe berries makes ten gallons wine. Mash the berries as fine as possible and pour over them a water-bucket of clear spring water. Cover it and let it stand twenty-four hours to ferment. Next day strain through a cloth, and to every three quarts juice add two quarts clear cold water and five pounds common brown sugar. Pour in a demijohn or runlet, reserving some to fill the vessel as fermentation goes on. After six or eight days, put to every ten gallons one-half box gelatine. After two weeks, cover the bung-hole with a piece of muslin. Two or three weeks later, cork tightly and then leave undisturbed for six months. After that time, bottle and seal. Superior currant wine may be made by this recipe.—*Mrs. F.*

Blackberry Wine.

Fill a large stone jar with the ripe fruit and cover it with water. Tie a cloth over the jar and let them stand three or four days to ferment; then mash and press them through a cloth. To every gallon of juice add three pounds of brown sugar. Return the mixture to the jar and cover closely. Skim it every morning for more than a week, until it clears from the second fermentation. When clear, pour it carefully from the sediment into a demijohn. Cork tightly, set in a cool place.

When two months old it will be fit for use.—*Mrs. Gen. R. E. Lee.*

[Copied from a recipe in Mrs. Lee's own handwriting.]

Grape Wine.

Take any convenient quantity of perfectly ripe grapes. Mash them so as to break all the skins, and put them in a tub or other clean vessel, and let them remain twenty-four hours; with a cider-press or other convenient apparatus, express all the juice, and to each gallon of juice thus obtained add from two to two and a half pounds of white sugar (if the grapes are sweet, two pounds will be enough), put the juice and sugar in a keg or barrel, and cover the bung-hole with a piece of muslin, so the gas can escape and dust and insects cannot get in; let it remain perfectly quiet until cold weather, then bung up tightly. This wine will need no clarifying; if allowed to rest perfectly still it can be drawn off perfectly clear.—*Mr. W. A. S.*

Grape Wine.

Pick the grapes from the bunch, mash thoroughly, and let them stand twenty-four hours. Then strain and add three pounds of sugar to every gallon of juice. Leave in a cask six months, and then bottle, putting three raisins in each bottle.—*Mrs. R. L.*

Grape Wine.

Press the grapes, and when the juice settles, add two pounds of white sugar to four quarts of juice. Let it stand twenty-four hours, drain, put in a cask; do not stop tightly till the fermentation is over.—*Mrs. R. A.*

Catawba Grape Wine.

Mash ripe grapes to a pulp, and let them stand twenty-four hours. Then squeeze through a cloth, and add two pounds of sugar to each gallon of pure juice. Put in a cask, leave the bung out, and put coarse muslin over the hole to admit the air.

Let it stand six weeks, or till fermentation ceases. Then close the mouth of the cask and let the wine stand several months, after which it may be drawn off.—*Mrs. R. D.*

Catawba Grape Wine.

To every gallon of grape juice add one quart of cold, clear water, and three pounds of "A" sugar. Pour into a runlet and let it remain uncorked fourteen days, and then cork loosely. Add half a box gelatine to every ten gallons, fourteen days after making it. At the end of a month tighten the cork, then let it remain undisturbed for six months, after which it may be carefully racked, bottled, and sealed.—*Mrs. Dr. E.*

Fox Grape Wine.

To every bushel of fox grapes add twenty-two quarts of water. Mash the fruit and let it stand twenty-four hours. Strain through a linen or fine sieve that will prevent the seed from getting through. To every gallon of juice add two pounds of brown sugar. Fill the cask not quite full. Let it stand open fourteen days, and then close the bung.—*Mrs. Gen. R. E Lee.*

[The above was copied from an autograph recipe of Mrs. Lee's, kindly furnished by her daughter.]

Wild Black Grape Wine.

Pick the grapes from the stem and cover with water. Mash and strain immediately. Add three pounds white sugar to one gallon juice. Garden grape wine is made in the same way. If you prefer a red wine, let the water stand on the grapes all night. The light wine is the best, however.

This wine has to be kept much longer than blackberry wine before it is fit for use.—*Mrs. M. D.*

Native Grape Wine.

Pick all the perfect grapes from the bunches, wash them and pack them down in a wooden or stone vessel. Pour over them boiling water—about one quart to every bushel of grapes. Tie a cloth over them and let them stand a week or ten days. Then strain it and add three pounds sugar to every gallon juice, mixing it well. Put in demijohns and tie a cloth over the top. Let it stand six months, and then cork it tightly. The wine will be fit for use in nine months.—*Mrs. Dr. S.*

GOOSEBERRY WINE.

To every gallon of gooseberries add three pints of boiling water. Let it stand two days, then mash and squeeze out the juice, to every gallon of which add three pounds of sugar. Put it in a cask and draw off about the usual time of drawing off other wines.—*Mrs. R. T. H. A.*

CURRANT WINE.

Put three pounds of brown sugar to every squeezed gallon of currants. Add a gallon of water, or two, if juice is scarce. It is better to put it in an old wine-cask and let it stand a year before you draw it off.—*Mrs. Gen. R. E. Lee.*

[Copied from a recipe in her own handwriting.]

Currant Wine.

Mash the currants well and strain through a linen towel. Add a gallon of water to every gallon of juice. Allow three pounds sugar to every gallon of the mixture. Put in a cask and cork loosely till fermentation is over. Bottle in September.—*Mrs. Dr. S.*

Currant Wine.

To one gallon well picked and washed currants, add one gallon water. Let it stand twenty-four hours, then strain through a flax linen cloth. Add to a gallon of juice and water three pounds brown sugar. Let it stand fourteen days in a clean, open cask.—*Mrs. Dr. E.*

Cherry Wine.

Measure the berries and bruise them, adding to every gallon one quart boiling water. Let it stand twenty-four hours, stirring occasionally. Then strain off the liquor, put in a jar, adding two pounds sugar to every gallon. Stop tightly, and let it stand till the next October, when it will be fit for use without straining or boiling.

Strawberry Wine.

Mash the berries and add to each gallon of fruit a half-gallon boiling water. Let it stand twenty-four hours, then strain and add three pounds brown sugar to each gallon juice. Let it stand thirty-six hours, skimming the impurities that rise to the top. Put in a cask, reserving some to add as it escapes from the cask. Fill each morning. Cork and seal tightly after the fermentation is over.—*Mrs. E.*

Orange Wine.

One gallon juice of sour oranges, four gallons water, twenty pounds sugar. Boil it and clarify with the whites of two eggs; skim the liquid till the scum has disappeared. Pour into a vessel of suitable size, taking the precaution to first strain it through flannel. Add three-quarters of a bottle of raw juice and let it ferment. Bottle in six months. Put less sugar if you prefer a wine less sweet.—*Mrs. N.*

Cider Wine.

One gallon sweet cider, three pounds sugar. Put in a cask and let it ferment. Keep the vessel full so that it will run over. Let it stand fifteen days. Put the corks in a little tighter every day. Let it stand three months, then bottle and seal up.—*Mrs. E. B.*

Tomato Wine.

Pick small, ripe tomatoes off the stems, put them in a clean bucket or tub, mash well, and strain through a linen rag (a bushel will make five gallons of juice). Add from two and a half to three pounds brown sugar to each gallon. Put in a cask and let it ferment like raspberry wine. If two gallons water be added to a bushel of tomatoes, the wine will be as good.—*Mrs. A. D.*

Eggnog.

To each egg one tablespoonful of sugar, one wine-glassful of milk, one wine-glassful of liquor. The sugar and yolks to be well beaten together, and the whites (well beaten) added by degrees. To twelve eggs, put eight glassfuls of brandy and four of wine. Put the liquor in the yolks and sugar, stirring slowly all the time; then add the whites, and lastly the milk.—*Mrs. F.*

Eggnog.

Three dozen eggs, three pounds of sugar, half a gallon of brandy, half a pint of French brandy, half a gallon of milk. Beat the yolks and whites separately. Stir the sugar thoroughly into the yolks, add the brandy slowly so as to cook the eggs, then add the milk, and lastly the whites, with grated nutmeg, reserving enough for top-dressing.—*Mrs. P. W.*

Eggnog.

Take any number of eggs you wish, beat the whites and yolks separately and as light as possible. Stir into the yolks, while beating, a tablespoonful of sugar to each egg. Then pour on the yolks and sugar a small wine-glassful of wine, flavored with a little vanilla, to each egg. On that pour a wine-glassful of rich milk or cream to each egg. Beat the whites as if for cake, then beat in enough sugar to make them smooth and stiff. Stir this into the eggnog for twenty minutes, and grate nutmeg on the top.—*Mrs. R. C.*

Apple Toddy.

Half a gallon of apple brandy, half a pint of French brandy, half a pint of peach brandy, half a pint of Madeira wine, six apples, baked without peeling, one pound of sugar, with enough hot water to dissolve it; spice, if you like. This toddy, bottled after straining, will keep for years, and improve with age.—*Mrs. C. C. McP.*

Apple Toddy.

One gallon of apple brandy or whiskey, one and a half gallon of hot water, well sweetened, one dozen large apples, well roasted, two grated nutmegs, one gill of allspice, one gill of cloves, a pinch of mace. Season with half a pint of good rum. Let it stand three or four days before using.—*Col. S.*

Rum Punch.

Make a rich, sweet lemonade, add rum and brandy to taste, only dashing with brandy. It must be sweet and strong.—*Mrs. D. R.*

Regent Punch.

One pint of strong black tea (in which put the rind of four lemons cut very thin). Two pounds of sugar, juice of six lemons, juice of six oranges, one pint of French brandy, one pint of rum, two quarts of champagne. Serve in a bowl, with plenty of ice.—*Mrs. C. C. McP.*

Tea Punch.

Three cups of strong green tea (in which put the rind of six lemons, pared very thin), one and one-half pound of sugar, juice of six lemons. Stir together a few minutes, then strain, and lastly add one quart of good rum. Fill the glasses with crushed ice when used. It will keep any length of time bottled. Fine for hot weather.—*Mrs. A. B.*

Roman Punch.

Grate the rind of four lemons and two oranges upon two pounds of sugar. Squeeze the juice of these, and let it stand several hours. Strain them through a sieve. Add one quart of champagne and the whites of three eggs, beaten very light. Freeze, and serve in hock glasses.—*Mrs. C. C. McP.*

Roman Punch.

To make a gallon. One and a half pint of lemon juice, rinds of two lemons grated on sugar, one pint of rum, half a pint of brandy, two quarts of water, three pounds of loaf sugar. A pint-bottle of champagne is a great improvement. Mix all together, and freeze.—*Mrs. B. C. C.*

BLACKBERRY CORDIAL.

Two quarts blackberry juice, one pound loaf sugar, four grated nutmegs, one-quarter ounce ground cloves, one-quarter ounce ground allspice, one-quarter ounce ground cinnamon. Simmer all together, for thirty minutes, in a stewpan closely covered, to prevent evaporation. Strain through a cloth when cold and add a pint of the best French brandy. Soothing and efficacious in the summer complaints of children. Dose, one teaspoonful poured on a little pounded ice, once or several times a day, as the case may require.

Whortleberry cordial may be made by the same recipe. Good old whiskey may be used for either, in the absence of brandy.—*Mrs. Gen. S.*

Blackberry Cordial.

Half a bushel of berries, well mashed, one-quarter pound of allspice (pulverized), two ounces cloves (pulverized). Mix and boil slowly till done. Then strain through homespun or flannel, and add one pound white sugar to each pint of juice. Boil again, and, when cool, add half a gallon best brandy. Good for diarrhœa or dysentery. Dose, one teaspoonful or more according to age.—*Mrs. S. B.*

DEWBERRY CORDIAL.

To one quart juice put one pound loaf sugar and boil these

together fifteen minutes. When cool, add one gill brandy, one tablespoonful mace, cloves, and allspice powdered. Bottle and cork tightly.—*Mrs. A. D.*

Dewberry Cordial.

Two quarts strained juice, one pound loaf sugar, four grated nutmegs, one-half ounce pulverized cinnamon, one-quarter ounce pulverized cloves, one-quarter ounce pulverized allspice. Simmer all together for thirty minutes, in a saucepan tightly covered to prevent evaporation. Then strain through a cloth, and, when cold, add one pint best French brandy. Bottle and cork tightly. —*Mrs. D. R.*

Strawberry Cordial.

One gallon apple brandy, four quarts strawberries. After standing twenty-four hours, press them through a cotton bag, and add four quarts more of berries. After twenty-four hours more, repeat this process. To every quart of the cordial add one pound of sugar, or sweeten it with a syrup made as follows: two pounds sugar, one pint water, white of one egg whipped a little—all boiled together. When cold, add one pint syrup to one quart cordial.—*Mrs. C. F. C.*

Cherry Cordial.

Extract the juice from ripe Morella cherries as you would from berries. Strain through a cloth, sweeten to your taste, and when perfectly clear, boil it. Put a gill of brandy in each bottle, cork and seal tightly. Will keep all the summer in a cool place. Delicious with iced water.

Cherry Cordial or Cherry Brandy.

Take three pounds Morella cherries. Stone half and prick the rest. Throw into a jar, adding the kernels of half slightly bruised. Add one pound white sugar. Cover with brandy, and let it stand a month.—*Mrs. E.*

Mint Cordial.

Pick the mint early in the morning while the dew is on it. Do not bruise it. Pour some water over it, and then drain it off. Put two handfuls in a pitcher with a quart of French brandy. Cover and let it stand till next day. Take out the mint carefully, and put in as much more, which take out next day. Add fresh mint a third time, taking it out after twenty-four hours. Then add three quarts water and one pound loaf sugar to the brandy. Mix well, and, when clear, bottle.—*Mrs. Dr. J.*

Strawberry Acid.

Put twelve pounds fruit in a pan. Cover it with two quarts water, having previously acidulated the water with five ounces tartaric acid. Let it remain forty-eight hours. Then strain, taking care not to bruise the fruit. To each pint of juice add one pound and a half powdered sugar. Stir till dissolved, and leave a few days. Then bottle and cork lightly. If a slight fermentation takes place, leave the corks out for a few days. The whole process to be cold. When put away, the bottles must be kept erect.—*Mrs. Col. R.*

Royal Strawberry Acid.

Dissolve two ounces citric acid in one quart spring water, which pour over three pounds ripe strawberries. After standing twenty-four hours, drain the liquor off, and pour it over three pounds more of strawberries. Let it stand twenty-four hours more, and again drain the liquor off. Add to the liquor its own weight of sugar. Boil three or four minutes, put in cool bottles, cork lightly for three days, then cork tightly and seal.—*Mrs. G.*

Strawberry Vinegar.

Four pounds strawberries, three quarts vinegar. Put fresh, ripe berries in a jar, adding to each pound a pint and a half of fine, pale white-wine vinegar. Tie a thick paper over them and let them remain three or four days. Then drain off the vinegar, and pour it over four pounds fresh fruit. After three days drain it again, and add it a third time to fresh fruit. After draining the last time, add one pound refined sugar to each pint of vinegar. When nearly dissolved, stir the syrup over a fire till it has dissolved (five minutes). Skim it, pour it in a pitcher, cover it till next day. Then bottle it, and cork it loosely for the first few days. Use a few spoonfuls to a glass of water.—*Mrs. E. P. G.*

Raspberry Vinegar.

Put a quart red raspberries in a bowl. Pour over them a quart strong apple vinegar. After standing twenty-four hours, strain through a bag, and add the liquid to a quart of fresh berries. After twenty-four hours more, strain again, and add the liquid to a third quart of berries. After straining the last time, sweeten liberally with pounded loaf sugar, refine and bottle. Blackberry vinegar may be made by the same recipe.—*Mrs. C. N.*

Raspberry Vinegar.

Put two quarts ripe, fresh gathered berries in a stone or china vessel, and pour over them a quart of vinegar. After standing twenty-four hours, strain through a sieve. Pour the liquid over two quarts fresh berries, which strain after twenty-four hours. Allow one pound loaf sugar to each pint of juice. Break up the sugar and let it melt in the liquid. Put the whole in a stone jar, cover closely, and set in a kettle of boiling water, which must be kept boiling briskly an hour. Take off the scum, and, when cold, bottle.—*Miss N. L.*

Raspberry Acid.

Dissolve five ounces tartaric acid in two quarts water, and pour it over twelve pounds berries. Let it stand twenty-four hours, and then strain without bruising the fruit. To each pint clear juice add one pound and a half dissolved sugar, and leave a few days. If a slight fermentation takes place, delay corking a few days. Then cork and seal.—*Mrs. G.*

LEMON VINEGAR.

Fill a bottle nearly full of strong cider vinegar. Put in it the rind of two or three lemons, peeled very thin. In a week or two it will be ready for use, and will not only make a nice beverage (very much like lemonade), but will answer for seasoning.—*Mrs. M. C. C.*

LEMON OR ORANGE SYRUP.

Put one pound and a half white sugar to each pint of juice. Add some peel, and boil ten minutes, then strain and cork. It makes a fine beverage, and is useful for flavoring pies and puddings. The juice of any acid fruit may be made into a syrup by the above recipe.

ORGEAT.

Make a syrup of one pound sugar to one pint water. Put it aside till cold. To five pounds sugar put one gill rose-water and two tablespoonfuls essence of bitter almonds.—*Mrs. I. H.*

SUMMER BEER.

Twelve quarts water, one quart molasses, one quart strong hop-tea, one-half pint yeast. Mix well and allow to settle. Strain through a coarse cloth, and bottle. It will be good in twenty-four hours.—*Mrs. E. W.*

CREAM BEER.

Two ounces tartaric acid, two pounds white sugar, three pints water, juice of one lemon. Boil all together. When nearly cold, add whites of three eggs, well beaten, with one-half cupful flour, and one-half ounce essence wintergreen. Bottle and keep in a cool place. Take two tablespoonfuls of this mixture for a tumbler of water, in which put one-quarter teaspoonful soda. —*Mrs. E.*

Lemon Beer.

Cut two large lemons in slices and put them in a jar. Add one pound white sugar and one gallon boiling water. Let it stand till cool; then add one-quarter cupful yeast. Let it stand till it ferments. Bottle in the evening in stone jugs and cork tightly.—*Mrs. G. W. P.*

Ginger Beer.

One and a half ounce best ground Jamaica ginger, one and a half ounce cream of tartar, one pound brown sugar, two sliced lemons, four quarts boiling water, one-half pint yeast. Let it ferment twenty-four hours. In two weeks it will be ready for use.—*Mrs. G. W. P.*

Small Beer.

Fifteen gallons water, one gallon bran, one and a half gallon molasses, one quart corn or oats, one-quarter pound hops. Let it boil up once; take it off and sweeten with the aforementioned molasses. Put it in a tub to cool. When a little more than milk warm, add one and a half pint yeast. Cover it with a blanket till next morning, and then bottle.—*Mrs. M. P.*

Mulled Cider.

To one quart cider take three eggs. Beat them light and add sugar according to the acidity of the cider. When light, pour the boiling cider on, stirring briskly. Put back on the fire and stir till it fairly boils. Then pour off.—*Mr. R. H. M.*

Crab Cider.

To a thirty-gallon cask put one bushel clean picked grapes. Fill up with sweet cider, just from the press—crab preferred. Draw off in March, and it is fit for use. Add brandy, as much as you think best.—*Mrs. A. D.*

THE SICK-ROOM—DIET AND REMEDIES FOR THE SICK.

First of all, let me say that after a reliable physician has been called in, his directions should be strictly followed, and his instructions should be the law in the sick-room. Have everything in readiness for his admission immediately after his arrival, as his time is valuable and it occasions him both annoyance and loss of time to be kept waiting outside of the sick-room, after reaching the house of the patient.

Pure air is of vital importance in the sick-room. Many persons exclude fresh air for fear of dampness, but even damp air is better than impure. Even in cold weather, there should be a free circulation of air. If there are no ventilators, let the air circulate from the tops of the windows, rather than admit it by opening the door, which is apt to produce a draft. Meantime keep up a good fire; if practicable, let it be a wood fire, but if this be not attainable, have an open grate, with a coal fire. The sight of a bright blaze is calculated to cheer the patient, while the sight of a dark, close stove is depressing. By no means allow a sick person to be in a room warmed by a flue or register.

The old idea of darkening the sick-room is exploded. It should be darkened only when the patient wishes to sleep. If the eyes are weak, admit the sunshine from a quarter where it will not fall upon them. The modern science of physics has come to recognize sunshine as one of the most powerful of remedial agencies, and cases are not rare in which invalids have been restored to health by using sun-baths, and otherwise freely enjoying the sunshine.

It is best to have no odors in the sick-room unless it be bay rum, German cologne, or something else especially fancied by the sick person. Where there is any unpleasant exhalation, it is far better to let it escape by properly ventilating the room, than to try to overcome it by the aid of perfumery. In fevers, where there are offensive exhalations from the body, sponging with tepid water will help to remove the odor, and will also prove soothing to the patient. In winter, expose but a small portion of the body at a time, in sponging. Then rub gently with the hand or a coarse towel, and there will be no danger of the patient's taking cold, even in winter.

Be careful to keep warm, soft flannels on the sick person in winter. In summer, do not keep a pile of bedclothes on the patient, even though chilly. It is better to keep up the circulation by other means, such as rubbing or stimulants. Scrupulous neatness should be observed about the bed-linen (as well as the other appointments of the sick-room). Never use bed-quilts or comforts; they are not only heavy, but retain the exhalations from the body. Use soft, fleecy blankets instead.

The nurse should watch her opportunity of having the bedclothes taken into the fresh air and shaken, and the bed made up, when the patient has been lifted up and set in an easy-chair near the fire. The arrangements about the bed should be quickly made, so that the patient may be able to lie down again as soon as fatigued. Let such sweeping and dusting as are necessary be also done with dispatch, using a dust-pan to receive the dust from the carpet. Avoid clouds of dust from the carpet, and of ashes from the fireplace.

The nurse has a very important part to play, as physicians say that nursing is of equal importance as medical attendance. The nurse should be careful not to wear a dress that rustles, nor shoes that creak, and if the patient has any fancy, or any aversion connected with colors, she should regard it in her dress. Indeed, the patient should be indulged in every fancy that is not hurtful.

The nurse should be prompt in every arrangement. Where blisters or poultices are to be used, she should not wait till the last moment to prepare them, but should do so before uncovering the patient to apply them, or even broaching the subject

If anything painful or distasteful has to be undergone by the patient, it should not be discussed beforehand with or before the patient; but when all is in readiness, with cheerful and soothing words, let it be done.

The patient should never be kept waiting for food, medicine, bath, or any other requisite. Every arrangement should be made beforehand to supply his or her needs in good time. Crushed ice and other needful things should be kept always at hand, so the patient may have them at any moment without delay. Especially on the approach of night, try to provide everything needed during the night, such as ice, mustard, hot water, kindling wood, a large piece of soapstone for the feet, as this is more cleanly and retains heat better than other things used for the purpose. Other things, such as the nature of the sickness may call for, should be thought of and provided before nightfall.

As the sick are very fastidious, all food for them must be prepared in the most delicate manner. Do not bring the same article of food several times consecutively, but vary it from time to time. Do not let a sick person have any article of food forbidden by a physician, as there are many reasons known to them only, why dishes fancied by the sick should be injurious.

Avoid whispering, as this excites nervousness and apprehension on the part of the sick. Do not ask in a mournful tone of voice how the patient is. Indeed, it is best to ask the sick as few questions as possible. It is far better to watch their symptoms for yourself than to question them. Examine for yourself if their feet are warm, and endeavor to discover their condition and their wants, as far as possible, without questions.

In a case of illness, many well-meaning persons crowd to see the patient; do not admit them into the sick-room, as it is both exciting and fatiguing to an ill person to see company, and, when in a critical condition, the balance might be disastrously turned by the injudicious admission of visitors. Both mind and body must be kept quiet to give the patient a chance for recovery. When well enough to listen to conversation, the patient should hear none but what is cheerful and entertaining, never any of an argumentative or otherwise unpleasant nature.

Do not allow the patient to read, as it is too great a tax on the sight and brain before convalescence. Suitable books, in large print, are a great resource to the patient when arrived at this stage, but should be read only in moderation.

Driving out is a delightful recreation for convalescents, and they should be indulged in it as soon as the physician pronounces it safe. In winter, they should be carried driving about noon, so as to enjoy the sunshine at its warmest. In summer, the cool of the morning or evening is the best time to drive them out; but if the latter time be chosen, be careful to return immediately after sundown. Make arrangements for the patient on returning to find the room thoroughly cleaned, aired, and adorned with fresh flowers (always so cheering in a sick-room), and let the bed be nicely made up and turned down. It is well to have some little refreshment awaiting after the drive—a little cream or milk toddy, a cup of tea or coffee, or, if the weather be hot, some cooling draught perhaps would be more acceptable. It is well to keep the convalescent cheered, by projecting each day some new and pleasant little plan for the morrow.

ARROWROOT.

Break an egg. Separate the yolk and white. Whip each to a stiff froth. Add a tablespoonful of arrowroot and a little water to the yolk. Rub till smooth and free from lumps. Pour slowly into half a pint of boiling water, stirring all the time. Let it simmer till jelly-like. Sweeten to the taste and add a tablespoonful of French brandy. Stir in the frothed white and take hot in winter. In summer, set first on ice, then stir in the beaten white. Milk may be used instead of water.—*Mrs. S. T.*

Arrowroot.

Mix one tablespoonful arrowroot with enough cold water to make a paste, free from lumps. Pour this slowly into half a pint boiling milk and let it simmer till it becomes thick and jelly-like. Sweeten to the taste and add a little nutmeg or cinnamon.—*Mrs. R. C. M. W.*

Seamoss Farina.

One tablespoonful in one quart hot water makes jelly; one tablespoonful in one quart milk makes blanc-mange. Stir fifteen minutes, and, while simmering, flavor with vanilla or lemon. Suitable for sick persons.—*M. L. G.*

Racahaut.

One pound rice flour, one pound chocolate, grated fine, two tablespoonfuls arrowroot. From a half-pound to a pound of sugar. Mix well together and put in a close jar. To one quart milk, rub in four dessertspoonfuls of the above mixture. Give it a boil up and season with vanilla.—*Mrs. J. H. T.*

Cracked Wheat.

Soak the wheat in cold water all night. Pour off this water in the morning. Pour boiling water then over the wheat and boil it about half an hour, adding salt and butter. Eat with cream.—*Mrs. A. M.*

Breakfast for an Invalid.

Bread twelve hours old, an egg and black tea.—*Mrs. A.*

Food for a Sick Infant.

Gelatine two inches square, milk half a pint, water half a pint, cream one-half to one gill, arrowroot a teaspoonful. Sweeten to the taste.—*Mrs. J. D.*

Wine Whey.

Put half pint milk over the fire, and, as soon as it begins to boil, pour slowly into it a wine-glass of sherry wine, mixed with a teaspoonful white sugar. Grate into it a little nutmeg, and as soon as it comes to a boil again, take it off the fire. When cool, strain for use.—*Mrs. R. C. M. W.*

MILK PUNCH.

Pour two tablespoonfuls good brandy into six tablespoonfuls milk. Add two teaspoonfuls ground loaf sugar and a little grated nutmeg. An adult may take a tablespoonful of this every two or three hours, but children must take less.—*Mrs. R. C. M. W.*

BEEF ESSENCE.

Cut one pound beef in small bits, sprinkle with a very little salt, tie up in a close stone jar, and set in boiling water. Boil it hard an hour or more, then strain it. Chicken may be prepared the same way. Nice for the sick.—*Mrs. Col. W.*

BEEF-TEA.

Take half a pound fresh beef for every pint of beef-tea required. Carefully remove all fat, sinew, veins, and bone from the beef. Cut it in pieces under an inch square and let it soak twelve hours in one-third of the water required to be made into tea. Then take it out and let it simmer three hours in the remaining two-thirds of the water, the quantity lost by evaporation being replaced from time to time. The boiling liquor is then to be poured on the cold liquor in which the meat was soaked. The solid meat is to be dried, pounded in a mortar, and minced so as to cut up all strings in it, and mixed with the liquid. When the beef-tea is made daily, it is convenient to use one day's boiled meat for the next day's tea, as thus it has time to dry and is more easily pounded. Avoid having it sticky and too much jellied, when cold.

ESSENCE OF CHICKEN.

In a case of extreme sickness, when it is important that what little nourishment the patient can take should be highly condensed, the following is an excellent mode for concentrating, in a small compass, all the nutritive properties of a chicken.

After picking the chicken, sprinkle a little salt over it and cut it in pieces, as if for frying. Put the pieces in a small glass jar (or wide-mouthed bottle), stop it tightly, and put it in a pot of cold water, gradually heating the latter till it boils. Let the jar of chicken remain in the water till the juices are well extracted, then pour them off for the patient.—*Mrs. M. C. C.*

Chicken Jelly.

Take a large chicken, cut the flesh from its bones, break the bones, soak an hour in weak salt and water to extract the blood. Put on in a stewpan with three pints of cold water. Simmer till reduced to less than half its original quantity. Sprinkle a little salt on it, and strain in a bowl. Keep on ice.—*Mrs. S. T.*

A Nourishing Way to Prepare Chicken, Squirrel, or Beef for the Sick.

Put in a clean, glazed jar or inner saucepan. Set this in another vessel of boiling water. Cover closely, and keep boiling for hours. Season the juice thus extracted with a little salt, stir in a teaspoonful of fresh milk, and give to the patient.—*Mrs. T.*

Panada.

Lay six nice crackers in a bowl. Sprinkle over them powdered sugar and a pinch of salt, adding a very small piece of fresh butter. Pour boiling water over the crackers, and let them remain near the fire half an hour. Then add a teaspoonful of good French brandy, or a tablespoonful of Madeira wine, and a little grated nutmeg.—*Mrs. T.*

Dry Toast.

Slice thin, some nice, white bread, perfectly sweet. Toast a light brown, and butter with fresh butter.—*Mrs. S. T.*

Scalded Toast.

Prepare and toast the bread as above directed. Then lay in a covered dish and pour boiling water over it. Turn to one side, and drain out the water. Then put fresh butter on each slice, with a small pinch of salt. Serve in a covered dish.—*Mrs. S. T.*

Milk Toast.

Slice the bread thin, toast a light brown, butter each side, and sprinkle with a little salt. Put in a covered dish, and pour over it boiling milk.—*Mrs. S. T.*

Carolina Small Hominy.

Wash and pick. Drain, and soak an hour in cold water. Drain again, and put in a saucepan, with one pint boiling water to one pint hominy. Boil till dry like rice. Eat with cream, butter and salt, or with sugar, butter and nutmeg.—*Mrs. S. T.*

Dishes Suitable for the Sick

May be found in various parts of this work, such as rice pudding, baked custard, and various preparations of tapioca, sago, and arrowroot. Grapes are valuable in fever, and also good for chronic sore-throat.—*Mrs. S. T.*

Thieves' Vinegar.

A handful of sage and the same of mint, tansy, rue, rosemary, lavender, and thyme; one ounce of camphor. Put in a gallon demijohn, and fill with good vinegar. Set in the sun two weeks with a piece of leather over the mouth, then stop tightly.—*Mrs. D. R.*

Aromatic Vinegar.

Acetic acid (concentrated), eight ounces; oil of lavender (Eng.), two drachms; oil of rosemary, one drachm; oil of cloves, one drachm; gum camphor, one ounce. Dissolve the camphor (bruised) in the acid, then add perfumes. After standing a few days, with occasional shaking, strain, and it is ready for use.—*Dr. E. A. C.*

Soda Mint.

Bicarb. soda (Eng.), one drachm; pure water, three ounces spearmint water, four ounces; glycerine, one ounce; ar. spts. ammonia, thirty-two drops. Mix and filter. Dose, from twenty drops to a tablespoonful, according to age.—*Dr. E. A. C.*

Lime-Water.

This is easily prepared, and a bottle should always be kept ready for use. It is an antidote to many poisons and a valuable remedy in a sick-room. Put some pieces of unslacked lime in a bottle, fill up with cold water, keep it corked and in a cool, dark place. It does not matter about the quantity of lime, as the water will not dissolve more than a certain quantity. It is ready for use in a few minutes, and the clear lime-water can be poured off as needed. When all the water is used, fill up again, which may be done several times before it is necessary to use fresh lime.—*Mrs. T.*

Tarrant's Effervescent Seltzer Aperient

Is an invaluable remedy for sick headache, nausea, constipation, and many of the attendant evils of dyspepsia. Directions accompany each bottle. Colic and other violent pains of the stomach are sometimes instantly relieved by adding to the dose of Seltzer Aperient a teaspoonful of Brown's Jamaica Ginger.

Brown's Jamaica Ginger

Is not only an invaluable remedy, but a refreshing and delightful drink may be made from it in summer, when iced lemonade would be unsafe and iced juleps, etc., would be too heating for one suffering from over-fatigue. Fill a goblet with crushed ice, add two tea-poonfuls of powdered sugar and one of Jamaica ginger. Fill up with water, stir and drink.—*Mrs. S. T.*

Mustard.

It is not safe to pass a day without mustard in the house, so valuable are its medicinal properties. When a large plaster is wanted, put into a plate or bowl two tablespoonfuls ground mustard. Wet it with cold water and stir with a spoon or knife till a smooth paste. Lay on an inverted tea-board a piece of newspaper twice the size of the plaster wanted. On one-half spread evenly and thinly the mustard. Fold over the other half and fold over the edges as if to hem a piece of cloth, to prevent the mustard from getting on the skin or clothing. In winter, warm slightly before applying. Keep it on an adult fifteen minutes; on a child, half that time. In this way, painful blisters will always be avoided. If the pain is in the chest or stomach, place the same plaster on the back just opposite, and let it remain on twenty minutes the second time. Colman's mustard is considered the best by many persons.

Mustard Leaves or Plasters.

It is well in travelling to carry a package of these plasters, in case of sudden sickness. It is important also to keep them at home, as sometimes they are needed suddenly in the night, and even one moment gained is important in great emergencies. Those manufactured by Seabury & Johnson, N. Y., are considered excellent and superior to the foreign article.

Compound Syrup of Horehound and tar

Is excellent for coughs, colds, bronchitis, and diseases of the chest. Manufactured by Faulkner & Craighill, Lynchburg, Va.

For Sore-Throat.

Carbolic acid crystals, pure, half a drachm; tincture kino, one drachm; chlorate potash, two drachms; simple syrup, half an ounce. Water sufficient to make an eight-ounce mixture. Gargle the throat every few hours.—*Dr. T. L. W.*

For Sore-Throat.

Rub the throat well with camphorated oil, and gargle frequently with a strong solution chlorate of potash.—*Mrs. S. T*

For Sore-Throat.

Carbolic acid, fifteen grains; chlorate potash, thirty grains; rose-water, one and a half ounces; glycerine, one-half ounce. Use as a gargle, three or four times daily.—*Mr. E. C.*

A CURE FOR EPILEPSY (*one I have known to succeed in many cases*).

Procure the fresh root of a white peony. Scrape and cut in pieces an inch square. Eat one three times a day, never taking any food after four P.M. Use a month, stop two weeks and begin again. The best way to keep the root is to string it on a cord. The red peony will do, if you cannot get the white. *Mrs. R. C.*

CURE FOR CRAMP.

Wet a cloth in spirits turpentine and lay it over the place where the pain is felt. If the pain moves, move the cloth. Take five drops spirits turpentine at a time on white sugar till relieved.—*Mrs. R.*

FOR CRAMP-COLIC, OR PAIN RESULTING FROM DISORDERED BOWELS.

One teaspoonful paregoric, one teaspoonful Jamaica ginger, one teaspoonful spirits camphor, one-half teaspoonful carbonate soda, two tablespoonfuls water, two tablespoonfuls whiskey. This is for one dose. If it does not relieve in an hour, repeat. —*Dr. J. T. W.*

FOR CHILBLAINS.

Take common furniture glue from the pot, spread it on a linen rag or piece of brown paper, and apply hot to the chilblain, letting it remain till the glue wears off.

FOR FRESH CUTS.

Varnish them with common furniture varnish. This remedy has been known to prove very efficacious.—*Mr. W.*

THE OCEAN SALT

Is now much used by those who cannot go to the seaside

Seventy-five cents for half a bushel. Dissolve a large handful in a pitcher of water. Use a sponge to rub the flesh.—*Mrs. A.*

Breast Salve.

Linseed oil (raw), four ounces; mutton tallow, four ounces; yellow wax, two ounces; Burgundy pitch, one ounce; Venice turpentine, one ounce; oil lavender, one-half ounce; rosin, one-half ounce.

Melt together and strain through flannel. Spread lightly on a soft linen rag, apply to the breast, and the relief is almost instantaneous.—*Dr. E. A. C.*

An Excellent Wash for Inflamed Eyes.

Sulph. zinc, two grains; wine of opium, ten drops; distilled water, one ounce. Mix. Drop two or three drops in the outer corner of the eye several times a day.—*Dr. E. A. C.*

Eye-Water for Weak Eyes.

One teaspoonful laudanum, two teaspoonfuls Madeira wine, twelve teaspoonfuls rose-water.—*Mrs. E. I.*

For Earache.

Equal parts of laudanum and tincture of arnica. Mix, saturate a piece of wool in the mixture, and insert in the ear.—*Dr. E. A. C.*

Toothache Drops. (*Sure cure.*)

Morphia, six grains; half an ounce each of tincture aconite root, chloroform, laudanum, creosote, oil cloves, cajuput. Add as much gum camphor as the chloroform will dissolve. Saturate with the above mixture a piece of wool and put it in the hollow tooth, being certain that the cavity is cleaned out.—*Dr. E. A. C.*

Preventive of Scarlet Fever.

Extract belladonna (pure), three grains; cinnamon-water, one drachm; distilled water, seven drachms. Mix, label poison, and give the child for a dose as many drops as the years of his age. --*Dr. E. A. C.*

For Preventing Scarlet Fever.

Extract belladonna, six grains; cinnamon-water, one drachm; white sugar, two drachms; alcohol, two drachms; pure water, thirteen drachms. Mix thoroughly and label belladonna, *poison.* Dose, one drop for each year of the child's age, repeated twice a day.—*Dr. E. A. C.*

To Relieve "Prickly Heat."

Sulphate of copper, grains ten; pure water, f. ℥ i. Mix sol. Apply with camel-hair brush daily or oftener.—*Dr. E. A. C.*

For Snake Bites.

Apply ammonia or hartshorn immediately to the bite, and swallow ten drops, dissolved in a wine-glass of water. Said to be a certain remedy.—*Mrs. T.*

Remedy for Chicken Cholera.

Dip a small feather or brush into tincture of iodine, hold the chicken's mouth open, and mop the inside of the throat thoroughly with the iodine. This treatment has proved successful whenever tried.—*Mrs. N. G.*

Mashed Finger.

Bind up with old linen and keep constantly wet with cold water. If there is much pain, add laudanum or tincture of arnica. If discoloration and swelling remain, after the pain subsides, use stimulating liniment to encourage a flow of pure blood and the washing away of the injured blood.

Burns and Scalds.

If the burn or scald is serious, send immediately for a physician. In the meantime, cover with wet linen cloths, pouring on more water without removing them, till the pain is alleviated, when pure hog's lard may be applied, which is one of the best and most easily procured dressings. If the scald or burn is trifling, this is all that is needed. Lather of soap from the shaving-cup applied by the brush often produces relief. White of egg applied in the same way is a simple and useful dressing. Never tamper with a bad burn. This requires the skilful treatment of a physician. If the shock is great, and there is no reaction, administer frequently aromatic spirits of ammonia or a little brandy and water till the patient rallies.

LINIMENT FOR RECENT BURNS AND SCALDS.

Take equal parts of lime-water, linseed oil, and laudanum. Mix and apply on a soft linen rag. Some add about one-quarter quantity commercial sol. carbolic acid.—*Dr. E. A. C.*

COMPOUND CHALK MIXTURE FOR INFANTS AND YOUNG CHILDREN.

Prepared chalk, powdered white sugar, gum arabic, two drachms each. Tincture kino, paregoric, each six drachms. Lime-water, one ounce; peppermint water, sufficient for four ounces.

Mix thoroughly and shake well before administering. Dose, from half to a teaspoonful, according to age and urgency of the case.—*Dr. E. A. C.*

A SIMPLE REMEDY FOR DYSENTERY.

Black or green tea steeped in boiling water and sweetened with loaf sugar.—*Mrs. R. C. M. W.*

FOR DIARRHŒA.

Take equal parts of laudanum, tincture capsicum, tincture camphor, and aromatic syrup rhubarb. Mix. Dose, from half to a teaspoonful, in water, when needed.—*Dr. E. A. C.*

CHILL PILLS.

Sulph. quinine, two drachms; arsenious acid, one grain; strychnia, one grain; Prussian blue, twenty grains; powdered capsicum, one drachm. Mix, and make sixty pills. Take one pill three times a day.—*Dr. E. A. C.*

Cure for Cold in the Head.

Muriate of morphia, two grains; powdered gum arabic, two drachms; sub. nit. bismuth, six drachms.

Mix and snuff frequently.—*Dr. E. A. C.*

Prompt Remedy for Cold in the Head.

Sulph. quinine, twenty-four grains; cayenne pepper, five grains. Make twelve pills, and take one every three hours.—*Mr. E. C.*

Cure for Dyspepsia.

Best Turkish rhubarb, one ounce; gentian root, bruised, one-half ounce; columbo, one-half ounce; orange peel, one-half ounce; fennel seed, one-half ounce; best French brandy, one quart. This will bear filling up several times.

For Whooping-Cough.

Drop a fresh, unbroken egg in lemon juice. When dissolved, sweeten and give a spoonful occasionally when the cough comes on.—*Mrs. E. I.*

An Excellent Remedy for Coughs.

Boil three fresh lemons till quite soft. Then slice them on a pound of brown sugar. Stew them together fifteen or twenty minutes, or till they form a rich syrup. When cool, add one tablespoonful oil of sweet almonds.

Take one spoonful or more when the cough is troublesome.—*N. A. L.*

Remedy for Coughs.

Boil one ounce licorice root in one-half pint of water, till it is reduced one-half. Then add one ounce gum arabic and one ounce loaf sugar. Take a teaspoonful every few hours.—*N. A. L.*

Remedy for Coughs.

Boil three lemons for fifteen minutes. Slice them thin while hot over one pound of loaf sugar. Put on the fire in a porcelain-lined saucepan and stew till the syrup is quite thick. After taking it from the fire, add one tablespoonful of oil of sweet almonds. Stir till thoroughly mixed and cool. If more than a small quantity is desired, double the above proportions. —*Mrs. J. D. L.*

Remedy for Asthma, Sore-Throat, or a Cough.

Cut up two or three bulbs of Indian turnip, put the pieces in a quart bottle, which fill up with good whiskey. Dose, a tablespoonful, three or four times a day. It is especially desirable to take it just after rising and just before going to bed. Wonderful cures of asthma have been effected by this remedy, and many persons living near the writer have tested its efficacy. The bottle will bear refilling with whiskey several times. Great care must be taken in procuring the genuine Indian turnip for this preparation, as there is a poisonous plant much resembling it.—*Mrs. M. L.*

Remedy for Poison Oak.

Make a strong decoction of the leaves or bark of the common willow. Bathe the parts affected frequently with this decoction, and it will be found a very efficacious remedy.—*Gen. M.*

Remedy for Poison Oak.

Forty grains caustic potash to five ounces of water. Apply to the eruption with a small mop, made by tying a soft linen rag to a stick. Often a speedy cure.—*Mrs. S. T.*

Cure for Jaundice.

Fill a quart bottle a third full of chipped inner cherry bark. Add a large teaspoonful soda, and fill the bottle with whiskey or brandy. Take as large a dose three times a day as the system will tolerate. If it affects the head unpleasantly, lessen the quantity of bark. It will be fit for use in a few hours.—*Dr. B.*

Cure for Bone Felon.

One ounce assafœtida in one pint vinegar, as hot as the hand can bear. Keep it hot by placing the vessel over the top of a teakettle. Use it frequently through the day, an hour at a time. A painful but effective remedy.—*Mrs. J. D. P.*

For Treating Corns.

Apply night and morning with a brush one or two drops of protoxide of iron for two weeks.—*Mrs. W.*

Cure for Corns between the Toes.

Wet them several times a day with hartshorn, and in a short time they will disappear.—*Mrs. W. B.*

Carrot Salve for Blisters.

Scrape two carrots and stew in two tablespoonfuls hog's lard. Add two plantain leaves. When the carrots are well done, strain.—*Mrs. E. I.*

Liniment for Rheumatism.

Half an ounce gum camphor, half an ounce saltpetre, half an ounce spirits ammonia, half a pint alcohol. Old-fashioned liniment, good for man or beast.—*Mrs. T.*

A Good Liniment.

One egg beaten light, half a pint spirits turpentine, half a pint good apple vinegar. Shake well before using. Good for sprains, cuts, or bruises.—*Mrs. H.*

A Good Treatment for Croup.

When the child is taken with a hoarse, tight cough, give it immediately from ten drops to half a teaspoon of hive or croup syrup, or if you have not these, use ipecac syrup, though this is less rapid in its effects. Put a mustard plaster on the windpipe, and let it redden the skin, but not blister. Put the feet in mustard-water as hot as they can bear it. Then wipe them dry and keep them covered warm. A child from three to six years old will require from ten drops to half a teaspoon of the syrup every half-hour till relieved. From six to twelve, give from a half teaspoon to a full teaspoon, according to the age of the patient. Croup requires very prompt treatment. If home treatment does not relieve, send immediately for a physician.—*Mrs. P. W.*

To Take Quinine without Tasting it.

Put a little of the mucilage from slippery elm in a teaspoon. Drop the quinine on it, and put some mucilage on top. This will make the quinine slip down the throat without leaving any taste.—*Mrs. J. A. S.*

Dressing for Blisters.

The first dressing should be of collard leaves, prepared thus. With a sharp knife carefully pare smooth all the stalk and veining. Then scald and squeeze each one to a pleasant moisture, keeping them blood-warm until applied. Second dressing—pure lard or mutton suet spread evenly and thinly on a soft linen rag.—*Mrs. S. T.*

An Excellent and Simple Salve for Boils.

Melt together, in equal parts, the white rosin that exudes from the common pine tree and mutton suet. This makes a good plaster for the boil, both before and after it breaks.—*Mrs. S. T.*

For Boils.

Slippery elm flour wet with cold water, and put in a soft muslin bag, and applied to the boil till the inflammation subsides, is an admirable remedy. Then apply carbolic salve spread on a linen rag, which is a good dressing for the boil, both before and after it breaks.—*Mrs. S. T.*

To Extinguish the Flames when the Clothing has taken Fire.

First, throw the person on the ground to prevent the upward

flames from being inhaled. Then quickly roll the person in a carpet hearth-rug or blanket; if neither is at hand, use any woollen garment, such as a coat, overcoat, or cloak. Keep the blaze as much as possible from the face, wrapping the woollen garment first around the neck and shoulders. Jumping into bed and covering up with the bedclothes is also a good plan.

For Weak Back.

Two tablespoonfuls finely powdered rosin, four tablespoonfuls white sugar, whites of two eggs, one quart best whiskey. Dose, a tablespoonful three times a day, either before or after meals. Excellent also for colds or weak lungs; will stop an irritating cough. Taken half a teaspoonful at a time.—*Mrs. G.*

Poisons and Antidotes.

Acids—Sulphuric, Nitric, Muriatic, Phosphoric, Oxalic, Citric, Tartaric, Acetic.—Give freely of magnesia or soap-water (half an ounce white soap to two quarts tepid water). Also very weak solutions of carbonate of soda or potassa may be used. Give demulcent drinks and milk-baths, cataplasms, antiphlogistics. Avoid lime-water.

Alkalies—Caustic, Potassa, Soda, Lime, Strontia, Baryta, and their Carbonates.—Give diluted vinegar in abundance, four ounces vinegar to one quart water. Citric or tartaric lemonade, whites of eggs with tepid water, milk, sweet-oil. Baths, lotions, fomentations.

Arsenic.—Prompt emetic. Give freely of hydrated peroxide of iron; dose, half an ounce, frequently repeated. If this is not at hand, give magnesia in large quantities of tepid water. Demulcent drinks, baths, and counter-irritants over the stomach to relieve spasms.

Carbolic Acid.—Saccharated lime in water; also demulcent drinks.

Chloral.—Keep the patient warm in bed, with hot blankets and hot water bottles, the bottles also to be applied over the heart. A warm bath may be of advantage. If respiration threatens to fail, maintain it artificially, and apply galvanic battery (induced current), one pole over pit of stomach and the other over lower cervical vertebræ.

Chloroform.—Draw out the tongue, if retracted. Give plenty of air. Raise the body and lower the head, till the body is almost inverted. Maintain artificial respiration. Use the galvanic battery as above directed.

Copper, Salts of.—Cause vomiting, and then give freely of whites of eggs and water, demulcent drinks, soothing clysters, lotions, fomentations. Avoid vinegar.

Corrosive Sublimate.—First, cause vomiting, then give whites of eggs in water, four whites to one quart water. Milk, demulcent drinks, and gargles.

Gases.—The antidote for chlorine is to inhale ammonia. Asphyxia by other gases, treated by cold applications to the head, plenty of air, artificial respiration.

Glass, in powder.—Farina or light food in abundance. Then an emetic, then milk and demulcent drinks.

Iodine.—Starch-water containing albumen in large quantities, or starch-water alone.

Lead, Salts of.—White of eggs, epsom salts, or sulphuric acid lemonade. (One drachm diluted acid to a quart sweetened water.)

Nitrate of Silver (lunar caustic).—Give salt water freely.

Opium and Salts of Morphine.—Cause free vomiting by sulphate of zinc, sulphate of copper, and tartar emetic, and use the stomach-pump. Then administer one-sixteenth grain atropine, hypodermically, and repeat with caution till the pupils dilate. Also give strong coffee or tea. Keep the patient awake. If depression and drowsiness are extreme, bleeding may do the patient good.

Phosphorus.—Emetic, then water with whites of eggs, magnesia in suspension, milk. Avoid oils.

Prussic Acid.—Affusions of water over the cervical vertebræ Cause the gas from chlorine water to be inhaled. Give from twenty to forty drops of Labbaraque's solution largely diluted, also coffee.

Strychnine.—Cause vomiting. Give ether or chloroform by inhalation, and chloral internally. Insufflate the lungs.

Tartar Emetic.—If there is vomiting, favor it by giving whites of eggs with water in large quantities, then give infusion of gall or oak bark. If vomiting is not free, use the stomach-pump.

Venomous Bites, Serpents.—Apply a moderately tight ligature above the bite. Wash the wound freely with warm water to encourage bleeding, then cauterize thoroughly. Afterwards apply lint dipped in equal parts of olive-oil and spirits hartshorn. Internally give freely of alcoholic stimulants, with liquid ammonia, largely diluted.

Rabid Dogs.—Apply ligature as above described, wash the wound thoroughly with warm water, and cauterize immediately with nitric acid or lunar caustic, leaving no part of the wound untouched.

HOUSE-CLEANING.

Do not clean but one room at a time, as it is a bad plan to have the whole house in confusion at once. It is best to commence with the attic.

Before beginning on your spring cleaning, remove the curtains, all the movable furniture, and the carpets. With a broom and dust-pan remove all dust from the floor. Then with a wall-brush thoroughly sweep and dust the ceiling and side-walls, window and door frames, pictures and chandeliers. Then go over the floor again, removing the dust that has fallen from the ceiling and walls. Then proceed to wash all the paint in the room. If it be white paint, use whiting or such other preparations as are recommended for the purpose in the subsequent pages. If it be varnished, or in imitation of oak or walnut, wipe with a cloth dipped in milk-warm water. If the wood work in the room be of unvarnished walnut or oak, wipe it off first, and then oil it, rubbing in the oil well.

Then with a soft flannel rag and a cake of sapolio clean every piece of marble in the room. Next wipe the mirrors carefully with a flannel rag, wrung out of warm water and dipped in a little whiting, or you may rub a little silver soap on the rag. The gilding must be merely dusted, as the least dampness or a drop of water will injure it.

The windows (sash and all) must then be washed in soap and water, with a common brush such as is used for washing paint. A little soda dissolved in the water will improve the appearance of the windows. It is unnecessary to use such a quantity of soap and water as to splash everything around. After being washed, the windows should be polished with newspapers. Except in a general house-cleaning, windows may be cleaned by the directions given above for mirrors.

The metal about the door-knobs, tongs, etc., may be cleaned by electro-silicon, and the grates may be varnished with the black varnish kept for the purpose by dealers in grates, stoves, etc. Every chair and article of furniture should be carefully cleaned before being brought back into the room, and linen covers should be put on the chairs. If you are going to put down matting, do so before bringing back the first article of furniture. Some housekeepers, however, allow their matting to remain during the winter under their carpets. Spots on matting may be removed by being scoured with a cloth, dipped first in hot water and then in salt. This, however, will cause wet spots to appear on it in damp weather. After the spots are removed, scrub the matting with dry corn-meal and a coarse cloth. Sweep it over several times, till all the meal is removed.

For persons who do not use matting in summer, a recipe is given later for beautifully coloring the floor with boiled linseed oil and burnt sienna. Where different woods are used alternately in the floor, this oil answers better than revarnishing the floor every spring.

As soon as the carpets are taken up, have them nicely shaken, swept, and brushed on both sides. Every spot should be carefully washed and wiped dry. The carpets should then be rolled up smoothly, with tobacco sprinkled between the folds, sewed up in coarse linen cloths, and put away till autumn. A cedar closet is an excellent place to keep carpets as well as other woollens. If you have no cedar closet, however, a cedar chest will serve to protect your woollen clothes against moths, and it is better to preserve them in this way than to sprinkle them with tobacco, which imparts an unpleasant scent to them.

WHITEWASH FOR OUTDOOR USE.

Take good quick-lime in lumps. Slack it with hot water, and while slacking add to what will make a pailful one pound tallow or other grease, free from dirt. It may be rancid, smoked, or otherwise unfit for kitchen use.

When the violent slacking is over, stir thoroughly. All the water should be added before the slacking ceases, and the mixing together should be thorough. Do not dilute with cold water. If well made, it will be very smooth and but little affected by rain.—*Mrs. E.*

INDOOR WHITEWASHING.

We have recently seen recommended in a journal a fine and brilliant whitewash preparation of chalk, called "Paris White," and said to be admirable for whitewashing walls. It sells in paint stores at three cents per pound, retail. For every sixteen pounds Paris White, get half a pound white transparent glue. Cover the glue with cold water at night, and in the morning heat it, without scorching, till dissolved. Stir in the Paris White with hot water to give it a milky consistency. Then add and mix well the glue. Apply with a common lime whitewash brush. A single coating will do, except on very dingy walls. Almost as brilliant as "Zinc White."—*Mrs. S. T.*

To Oil Floors.

To one gallon boiled linseed oil add half a pound burnt sienna. The druggist who sells these articles will mix them. If economy is necessary, instead of employing a painter to put it on, dip a large woollen rag into the mixture, and with this wipe over the floor.—*Mrs. S. T.*

To Dye Floors a Pretty Color.

Make a strong decoction of the inside bark of red oak. Set it a dark color with copperas.

Have the floors well swept and cleaned of spots. Then with a cloth rub the dye in well, taking care to wipe up and down the floor, so as to prevent streaking.

Let it dry, then wipe over with weak lye, and as soon as this dries off, rub with a waxed brush.—*Mrs. Dr. P. C.*

To Clean Paint.

Wring out a clean flannel, take up as much powdered whiting as will adhere to it, then rub the paint. Wash off with clean water and rub dry with a soft cloth, and it will look new. Not for paint in imitation of oak.—*Mrs. R.*

To Wash Oil-Cloth.

Wash oil-cloths with salt water; say, one pint salt dissolved in a pailful water. When dry wipe over with a little milk and water.—*Mrs. H. D.*

To Wash Oil-Cloth.

Sweep it well. Wash with cold water, using a brush. Then wash with milk and wipe dry. Never use hot water.—*Mrs. R.*

To Wash Carpets.

Shake, beat, and sweep well. Tack firmly on the floor. Mix three quarts soft, cold water with one quart beef's gall. Wash with a flannel, rub off with a clean flannel, immediately after putting it on each strip of carpet.—*Mrs. R.*

Carpets should be washed in spots, with a brush or flannel, one tablespoonful ox-gall in one or two quarts water.—*Mrs. A.*

To Remove Ink from Carpets.

Take up the ink with a spoon. Pour cold water on the stained spot, take up the water with a spoon, and repeat this process frequently. Then rub on a little oxalic acid and wash off immediately with cold water. Then wet with hartshorn.—*Mrs. R.*

To Clean Marble Slabs, etc.

Sal soda, four ounces; powdered pumice-stone, two ounces; prepared chalk, two ounces. Mix well, add sufficient water, rub well on the marble, and then wash with soap and water.—*Dr. E. A. C.*

Sapolio, rubbed on a flannel rag which has just been dipped in hot water and squeezed, is also good for cleaning marble.—*Mrs. S. T.*

To Remove Grease from Wall Paper.

Dip a flannel in spirits of wine and go carefully over the soiled places once or twice.—*Mrs. R.*

To Clean Furniture.

One-half pint linseed oil, one half pint vinegar, one-half pint turpentine. Apply with a flannel rag, and then rub with a dry flannel.—*Mrs. H. S.*

To Clean Varnished Furniture, Mahogany Especially.

Wash the piece of furniture with warm water and soap, and then rub dry; afterwards take a flannel rag, and rub with the following mixture: equal proportions of vinegar, sweet-oil, and spirits of turpentine, in a bottle which must be shaken before using.—*Mrs. McG.*

An Excellent Furniture Polish.

Alcohol, three ounces; linseed oil, boiled, two ounces

oxalic acid, one drachm; gum shellac, two drachms; gum benzoin, two drachms; rosin, two drachms. Dissolve the gums in the alcohol, and then add oil and oxalic acid. Apply with a woollen cloth.—*Dr. E. A. C.*

Furniture Polish.

One pint of alcohol, one pint of spirits of turpentine, one and one-half pint of raw linseed oil, one ounce balsam fir, one ounce ether. Cut the balsam with the alcohol, which will take about twelve hours. [That is to say, dilute the balsam with the alcohol.] Mix the oil with the turpentine in a separate vessel and add the alcohol, and last the ether.— *G. C. W.*

To Clean Silver.

There is nothing better for this purpose than Colgate's Silver Soap, and Robinson's Indexical Silver Soap, made in Boston. After the silver has been cleaned, according to the directions accompanying each package of the aforementioned kinds of soap, wash it in a pan of hot water in which a tablespoonful of ammonia has been poured.—*Mrs. S. T.*

To Clean Silver.

Make a paste of whiting and spirits of wine. Put it on with a soft cloth, then rub it off also with a soft cloth, and polish with chamois skin.—*Mrs. R.*

To Remove Egg Stains from Silver Spoons.

Rub with salt, and it will entirely remove the discoloration produced by eating a boiled egg with a silver spoon. Rubbing with salt will also remove the grayish streaks that collect on white tea-china by careless usage.—*Mrs. M. C. C.*

To Clean Brasses, etc.

Electro-silicon, manufactured by J. Seth Hopkins & Co., Baltimore, is the best article that can be procured for this purpose. The price is twenty-five cents per box, with full directions for use. It may be procured of any druggist. If not convenient to get it, use powdered brick-dust.—*Mrs. S. T.*

FOR THE KITCHEN.

Sapolio, manufactured by Enoch Morgan & Sons, should be in every kitchen. It is invaluable for cleaning tins, iron-ware, knobs, and is so neat a preparation that it does not blacken the hands.

THE DOVER EGG-BEATER

Is indispensable to housekeepers. It froths eggs in less than a fourth of the time a spoon or an ordinary egg-beater requires to froth them.—*Mrs. S. T.*

TO REMOVE RUST FROM KNIVES OR ANY STEEL.

Rub very hard with a piece of wash leather, dipped in powdered charcoal, moistened with spirits of wine. Rub off quickly, wash in hot water, and renew as may be necessary.—*Mrs. K.*

TO CLEAN KNIVES, TINS, ETC.

Crystal Kitchen Soap, manufactured by Eastman & Brooke, Philadelphia, is excellent for this purpose, being so neat a compound that the knives and coffee-pot, as well as the tins used in the preparation of breakfast, may be quickly cleaned at the table while the tea-china is being washed.

When not convenient to obtain the Crystal Kitchen Soap, knives may be cleaned with ashes either of coal or wood.—*Mrs. S. T.*

TO WHITEN THE IVORY ON THE HANDLES OF KNIVES.

The ivory handles of knives sometimes become yellow from being allowed to remain in dish-water. Rub them with sandpaper till white. If the blades have become rusty from careless usage, rub them also with sandpaper and they will look as nice as new.—*Mrs. S. T.*

Mixture for Shading Glass.

Spanish whiting, one pound; white glue, one-quarter pound; litharge, one ounce; alum, one ounce. Boil the glue and alum in a sufficient quantity of water. Let it cool, then add the whiting and litharge. Stir well and use at once. It may be washed or scraped off, if desired.—*Dr. E. A. C.*

Cement for Rubber and Glass.

Pulverized gum shellac in ten times its weight of strong spirits hartshorn.—*Dr. E. A. C.*

To Destroy Bedbugs.

Dissolve one ounce corrosive sublimate in one pint strong spirits. Put it on the bedsteads with a feather, and it will destroy the bugs and their eggs also.—*Mrs. Dr. P. C.*

Bedbug Poison.

Alcohol, two and a half pints; camphor, one ounce; spirits turpentine, one ounce; corrosive sublimate, half an ounce. Mix and dissolve. If the scent is not objectionable, two ounces commercial carbolic acid will greatly improve the above.—*Dr. E. A. C.*

To Destroy Bugs, Ants, etc.

Dissolve two pounds alum in three quarts boiling water. Apply boiling hot with a brush. Add alum to whitewash for store-rooms, pantries, and closets. It is well to pound alum fine and sprinkle it about beds infested with bugs.—*Mrs. S. T.*

Remedy for Red Ants.

Kerosene oil is a sure remedy for red ants. Place small blocks under a sugar barrel, so as not to let the oil touch the barrel.—*Mrs. J. W.*

Cayenne pepper will keep the store-room and pantry free from ants and cockroaches.—*Mrs. S. D.*

Remedy for Mosquitoes or other Blood-sucking Insects.

Uncork a bottle of oil of pennyroyal, and it will drive them away, nor will they return so long as the scent of it is in the room.—*Mrs. S. D.*

For the stings of insects, wasps, hornets, bees, etc. Apply to the place soda, hartshorn, or arnica.

Rats.

Mix a little powdered potash with meal and throw it into the rat-holes and it will not fail to drive the rats away. If a mouse enters into any part of your dwelling, saturate a rag with cayenne in solution and stuff it into his hole.—*Mrs. S. D.*

Concentrated Lye Soap.

All fat and grease from the kitchen should be carefully saved, and should be made into soap before accumulating and becoming offensive.

Boil for six hours ten gallons of lye made of green wood ashes. Then add eight or ten pounds of grease, and continue to boil it. If thick or ropy, add more lye till the grease is absorbed. This is ascertained by dropping a spoonful in a glass of water, and if grease remains it will show on the water.

If hard soap is desired, put one quart of salt in half-gallon of hot water. Stir till dissolved and pour into the boiling soap. Boil twenty minutes, stirring continually. Remove from the fire, and when cold cut in cakes and dry. A box of concentrated lye may be used instead of salt, as it will obviate the necessity of using more dripped lye to consume the grease.—*Mrs. P. W.*

A Washing Mixture.

Mix and boil twenty minutes one gallon soft soap; half a gallon of weak boiled lye; four ounces sal soda; half a gill of spirits turpentine. Soak the clothes overnight in milk-warm water. In the morning, rinse and wring them. To every gallon cold water add one pint of the above mixture. Stir it well in the water. Open the clothes and boil fifteen or twenty minutes; rinse out of those suds. If the articles are not thoroughly cleansed, rub a little of the mixture on the soiled places, and the result will be satisfactory.—*Mrs. Dr. E.*

RECIPES FOR RESTORING OLD CLOTHES, SETTING COLORS, REMOVING STAINS, ETC.

For Cleaning Clothes.

Castile soap, one ounce; aqua ammonia (34), a quarter-pound; sulphur ether, one ounce; glycerine, one ounce; spirits wine, one ounce. Shave the soap into thin pieces, dissolve it in two quarts rain (or any other soft water). Then add the other ingredients. Rub the soiled spots with a sponge or piece of flannel and expose to the air.—*Mrs. B.*

Soap to Remove Grease from Cloth.

Detersive soap, three pounds; alcohol, two pints; oxalic acid, half an ounce; essential oil to flavor. First bring the alcohol to a boil, then gradually add the soap (pared in thin shavings) and stir constantly. Then add the acid and oil, pour into moulds while hot, and let it cool. You may, of course, make it in smaller quantities, observing the same relative proportions.—*Dr. E. A. C.*

To Remove Spots from Cloth.

Aqua ammonia, two ounces; alcohol, two ounces; spirits camphor, one ounce; transparent soap, one ounce; rain-water, one quart.—*Mr. E. C., Jr.*

To Wash Black Cashmere.

Wash in hot suds, with a little borax in the water. Rinse in bluing water, and iron very damp.

To Restore the Pile of Velvet.

Heat a large flat-iron, place it in a pan, and lay on it a wet cloth. The steam will rise rapidly. Hold the right side of the velvet over it. If this does not restore the pile, wet it on the wrong side. Have a smooth flat-iron very hot. Set it on the edge of the table, upright. If it is a narrow piece of velvet, it may be easily ironed by passing the wet side against the iron. If a large piece, have some one to hold the botton of the iron upwards while the wet side of the velvet is passed over it.—*Mrs. S. T.*

To Restore old Black Silk.

Pour one pint boiling water on two tablespoonfuls gum arabic. When a little cooled, add one teaspoonful spirits turpentine and the same of spirits ammonia. With a large sponge wipe the silk on both sides with this mixture. Then lay the silk on an ironing-table, place over it a thin piece of colored rice cambric, and iron it very hard with a hot iron. This makes old silk look like new.—*Mrs. S. T.*

To Freshen old Black Silk.

Boil one ounce crushed soap bark in one quart water till reduced to one pint. Strain it; sponge the material with the liquid, and while wet iron on the wrong side. Good for black woollens also.—*Mrs. M. E. L. W.*

To Renew Black Crape Veils.

Wring two large towels out of water. Then put the veil (folded across the middle, lengthways) on the lower towel; spread the other on top and roll the veil, when between, in a small tight roll. Let it stand an hour, or till it is damp through. Take it out and air it a little before it dries. Fold it then in smooth squares, put it in a large book, such as an atlas, put heavy weights on it, and let it; stand an hour or two.—*Mrs. M. C. C.*

To Set Colors.

Wash in strong salt or alum water and rinse in water in which Irish potatoes have been sliced and boiled, to stiffen.

A strong tea of hay or fodder preserves the color of brown linen. One spoonful gall to a gallon of water will set the colors of almost any goods. A teaspoonful sugar of lead in a gallon cold water (some say a tablespoonful in a quart soft water) will set colors. Let the material soak in it an hour.

A teacup of lye in a pail of water will improve black calicoes.

To Restore Colors that have been Taken Out.

Rub the spots with hartshorn and place in the sun till dry.

To Keep Blue Calicoes Bright and Fresh.

The first time they are washed, put them in water with a cupful spirits of turpentine to each pail of water. This will set the color, and they will always look well.

Mildew.

Moisten the mildewed spot with clear water, then rub over it a thick coating of castile soap. Scrape chalk with the soap, mixing and rubbing with the end of the finger. Then wash it off. Sometimes one coating suffices, but generally several are required.

Labaraque Solution

Will remove mildew, ink, or almost any fruit stain from cloth. The solution should be washed off soon after applying, as it may injure the cloth—*Dr. E. A. C.*

To Prevent Fruit Stains from being Permanent.

Wet the stained spot with whiskey before sending it to wash, and there will be no sign of it when the article comes in.

For Removing Fruit or Ink Stains.

Two drachms chloride of lime, two drachms acetic acid, one and a half ounce water. Mix well—*Dr. E. A. C.*

Iron Rust.

Salts of lemon applied to the place and exposed to the sun will remove all iron rust in linen, etc.

MISCELLANEOUS RECIPES.

Ammonia.

No housekeeper should be without a bottle of spirits of ammonia, for, besides its medical value, it is highly useful for household purposes. It is nearly as useful as soap, and its cheapness brings it in the reach of all. Put a teaspoonful ammonia in a quart of warm soapsuds, dip in a flannel cloth, wipe off the dust and fly-specks, and see how much scrubbing it will save you.

For washing windows and mirrors, it is very desirable. A few drops on a piece of paper will take off every spot or finger-mark on the glass.

It cleanses and brightens silver wonderfully. Dip your forks, spoons, etc., in a pint of suds, mixed with a teaspoonful spirits ammonia. Then rub with a brush and polish with chamois skin.

It will take grease spots from every fabric. Put on the ammonia nearly clear. Lay blotting paper on the place, and press a hot flat-iron on it a few moments. A few drops of it will clean and whiten laces, also muslins.

It is highly useful and refreshing at the toilet-table. A few drops in the bath will remove all offensive perspiration and glossiness (if the skin is oily). Nothing is better for cleansing the hair from dust and dandruff. A teaspoonful in a pint of water will cleanse the dirtiest brushes. Shake the brushes through the water, and when they look white, rinse them in water and put them in the sunshine or a warm place to dry.

For medicinal purposes ammonia is almost unrivalled

Inhaling it will often cure headache and catarrhal cold. Ten drops aromatic spirits of ammonia in a wine-glass of water is excellent for heartburn or dyspepsia. The ordinary spirits of ammonia may be used also for the purpose, but it is not so palatable.

Ammonia is also good for vegetation If you desire roses, fuschias, geraniums, etc., to become more flourishing, add five or six drops ammonia to every pint of lukewarm water you give them. Do not repeat this more than once in five or six days, lest you should stimulate them too highly.

Be sure to keep a large bottle of ammonia in the house, and use a glass stopper for it, as it is very evanescent and is injurious to corks.

[The above remarks on the usefulness of ammonia were furnished and endorsed by Mrs. A. D., of Virginia.]

Borax.

It is very desirable to keep borax in the house. Its effect is to soften the hardest water, and it is excellent for cleansing the hair. Some washerwomen use borax for a washing powder, instead of soda, in the proportion of a handful of borax powder to ten gallons boiling water, and they save in soap nearly half, whilst the borax, being a neutral salt, does not injure the texture of the linen.—*Mrs. S. T.*

Red Ink.

Bicarb. potash, half an ounce; cochineal, half an ounce; bitart. potash, half an ounce; powdered alum, half an ounce; pure rain-water, four ounces. Mix, and add ten drops creosote.—*Dr. E. A. C.*

Black Ink.

Extract logwood (pulv.), two ounces; hot rain-water, one gallon. Simmer over water-bath one hour, till logwood is dissolved. Put into a bottle the following: bichromate potash., one hundred grains; prus. of potass., forty grains; warm rainwater, four ounces. Shake till dissolved, put into the logwood solution, stir well together, strain through flannel, and, when cold, add corrosive sublimate, ten grains; warm rainwater, one ounce. Dissolve thoroughly, put with the above, and add pure carbolic acid crys., one drachm. This makes the best black ink in the world, at a cost of about ten cents a gallon.—*Dr. E. A. C.*

COMMON BOTTLE WAX.

Rosin, eighteen ounces; shellac, one ounce; beeswax, two ounces. Melt together and color to suit the fancy.—*Dr. E. A. C.*

GRAFTING WAX.

Rosin, two pounds; beeswax, one pound; tallow, one pound. Melt together, pour into a tub of cold water, and work with the hands till pliable.—*Dr. E. A. C.*

LIQUID GLUE.

Acetic acid, one ounce; water, half an ounce; glue, two ounces; gum tragacanth, one ounce. Mix and dissolve.—*Dr. E. A. C.*

SHOE BLACKING (*equal to Mason's*).

Ivory black, twelve ounces; molasses, four ounces; sperm-oil, one ounce; oil of vitriol, by weight, two drachms; vinegar, one pint. Mix the black, molasses, and oil, and add the vinegar gradually, stirring all the time. Then add the oil of vitriol very carefully, stirring constantly, till effervescence ceases.—*Dr. E. A. C.*

LIQUID BLACKING.

Ivory black, in fine powder, one pound; molasses, twelve ounces; sweet-oil, two ounces; beer and vinegar, two pints of each. Mix thoroughly together.—*Dr. E. A. C.*

WHAT MOST OF THE BAKING POWDERS ARE COMPOSED OF.
(*One of the Best.*)

Cream tartar, twelve and one-quarter ounces; bicarb. soda

(Eng)., six and one-half ounces; tartaric acid, one and one-third ounces; carbonate of ammonia, four-fifths of an ounce; good wheat flour, four ounces. Mix thoroughly, and pass through a fine sieve.—*Dr. E. A. C.*

To Dry Herbs.

Gather on a dry day, just before they flower. Put them in an oven, and when dry take them out, pick off the leaves, put in bottles, cover tightly, and keep in a dry place.—*Mrs. R.*

To Keep Weevil out of Wheat.

Put the wheat in barrels, smooth it, and sprinkle a layer of salt over the top. Keep the barrels well covered by tying cloths over them. A sure preventive.—*Mrs. Dr. P. C.*

Fertilizer for Strawberries.

Nitrate of potash, one pound; glauber salts, one pound; sal soda, one pound; nitrate of ammonia, one-quarter pound. Dissolve the above in forty gallons of water, one-third to be applied when the leaves begin to appear, one-third ten days later, and the rest when the vines begin to bloom. This quantity is for forty feet square.—*Mrs. R.*

Red Lip Salve.

Oil of sweet almonds, two ounces; pure olive-oil, six ounces; spermaceti, one and one-half ounce; white wax, one ounce. Color with carmine, and perfume with oil of roses.—*Dr. E. A. C.*

Lotion for Chaps.

Borax, two drachms; strong rose-water, twelve ounces; glycerine, three ounces; mucilage of quince seed, ten drachms. Mix.—*Dr. E. A. C.*

Cold Cream.

Rose-water, half an ounce; oil of sweet almonds, half an ounce; pure olive-oil, two ounces; spermaceti, half an ounce;

white wax, one drachm. Melt sperm and wax with the oil by means of water-bath. Then add the rose-water, and stir till cool. When nearly cool, add oil of roses or any other perfume desired.—*Dr. E. A. C.*

CAMPHOR ICE.

White wax, two ounces; spermaceti, two ounces and two drachms; camphor, six drachms. Melt, and add olive-oil, five ounces and five drachms; glycerine, three drachms. Make into eighteen cakes.—*Dr. E. A. C.*

CAMPHOR SALVE FOR CHAPPED LIPS, HANDS, ETC.

Spermaceti, two drachms; white wax, two drachms; pulverized camphor, two drachms; washed lard, half an ounce; pure olive-oil, half an ounce. Melt in water-bath, and stir with it, while cooling, two drachms glycerine.

Note.—This is excellent, will relieve almost instantly, and will cure in a few applications.—*Dr. E. A. C.*

TOOTH POWDER.

Prepared chalk, two pounds; powdered orris-root, two pounds; powdered white castile soap, quarter of a pound; powdered white sugar, quarter of a pound; powdered pumice-stone, half an ounce; powdered carmine, half an ounce; oil of lemon, half an ounce; oil of lavender, half an ounce. Powder the carmine as fine as possible; then add to it the pumice-stone, then the sugar, then the soap, orris, and chalk in succession. Then add the flavoring drop by drop, mixing it thoroughly with all the ingredients. Sift through the finest apothecaries' sieve. —*Dr. E. A. C.*

For the Teeth.

Van Buskirk's Sozodont, manufactured by Hall & Ruckel, N. Y., is all that it claims to be. I have known it tried ten years consecutively with the happiest results.—*Mrs. S. T.*

Charcoal Tooth Powder.

Powdered charcoal, six ounces; gum myrrh, one ounce; pale Peruvian bark, one ounce. Mix thoroughly.—*Dr. E. A. C.*

Hair-Oil.

Pure olive-oil, six ounces; perfumed with oil of jessamine. —*Dr. E. A. C.*

Hair-Oil.

Castor-oil, ten ounces; pure alcohol, six ounces. Perfume with oil of bergamot or any other perfume preferred.—*Dr. E. A. C.*

Hair Tonic.

Glycerine, one and a half ounces; tincture cantharides (95 per cent.), half an ounce; sulph. quinine, twenty grains; alcohol, four ounces. Mix together; perfume with oil of roses.— *Dr. E. A. C.*

Another Hair Tonic,

Claimed to restore falling out hair, when baldness is not hereditary. Tincture of cantharides (officinal), one ounce; glycerine, one and a half ounce; rose-water, three and a half ounces.— *Dr. E. A. C.*

Hair Dye, No. 1.

Pyrogallic acid, one drachm; distilled water, three ounces. Dissolve.—*Dr. E. A. C.*

No. 2.

Nitrate of silver (crystals), one drachm; aqua ammonia, strong, two drachms; distilled water, six drachms. Mix.—*Dr. E. A. C.*

Hair Restorative.

Sugar of lead (chemically pure), one drachm; milk of sulphur, two drachms; rose-water, four ounces; glycerine, one ounce. Mix.—*Dr. E. A. C.*

Shampoo Liquor.

Bay rum, three quarts; tincture cantharides (officinal), one and a half ounces; carb. ammonia, half an ounce; salts of tartar, one ounce. Mix. Thoroughly cleanse the hair with clean water after using.—*Dr. E. A. C.*

Rose Bandoline.

Gum tragacanth, six ounces; rose-water, one gallon; otto of roses, half an ounce. Steep the gum in the water a day or two. Agitate frequently while forming into a gelatinous mass. After standing forty-eight hours, strain through a clean, coarse linen cloth. Again let it stand a few days, and then strain a second time. When the consistency is uniform, add the otto of roses, and color with carmine.—*Dr. E. A. C.*

Almond Bandoline

Is made as the above, except that no coloring is used, and it is scented with quarter of an ounce of oil of bitter almonds instead of rose.—*Dr. E. A. C.*

To Clean the Hair and Hair-Brushes and Combs.

Dissolve one ounce borax and half an ounce camphor in a quart boiling water. For cleaning combs and brushes use two teaspoonfuls supercarbonate soda dissolved in half a pint boiling water, or else use one teaspoonful hartshorn dissolved in a little water.—*Mrs. R.*

To Remove Dandruff.

Wash the hair thoroughly in rain-water with a good deal of borax dissolved in it.—*Mrs. C. C.*

To Remove Blood Stains.

Make a thin paste of starch and water. Spread over the stain. When dry, brush the starch off and the stain is gone. Two or three applications will remove the worst stains.—*Mrs. D.*

INDEX.

BREAD.

	PAGE
Batter bread	56
" " 2d recipe	57
" " 3d "	57
Brown bread	40
Biscuit, beaten	43
" " 2d recipe	42
" " cream	42
" " French	41
" " excellent light	43
" " light	43
" " soda	42
" " thick	43
" " thin or crackers	43
Box bread	40
Bunns	39
Cakes, Virginia ash	61
" batter	55
" " 2d recipe	55
" " made of stale bread	55
" " cheap recipe	56
" old Virginia batter cakes	55
" " " 2d	56
Cakes, Boston cream	53
" breakfast	50
" buckwheat	51
" " 2d recipe	52
" " 3d "	52
" " 4th "	52
" buttermilk	54
" corn	58
" cream	52
" " 2d	53
" " 3d	53
" farina	54
" flannel	51
" " 2d method	51
" " 3d "	51
" Indian griddle	56
" Madison	50
" orange	50
" rice	54
" sour milk	54
" velvet	50
Corn-bread, plain	61
" " light	59

	PAGE
Crackers, Huntsville	44
" soda	43
" water	44
Cracklin-bread	60
Egg-bread	60
" " old-fashioned	59
" " soft	59
Family bread	29
Graham bread	40
Grit or hominy bread	58
" " " 2d recipe	58
Henrietta bread	45
Indian "	60
Lapland "	45
" " plain recipe	45
New bread	45
Leaven	27
Light bread	31
Jenny Lind bread	46
Loaf, cottage	39
Loaf bread	29
" " old Virginia	29
" " 3d method	30
Lunch bread	46
Lunn, quick Sallie	36
" Sallie 2d	34
" " 3d	35
" " 4th	35
" " 5th	35
Old maids	39
Muffins	36
" 2d	37
" 3d	38
" bread	38
" corn	57
" cream	38
" white egg	38
" Parker House	37
" salt sulphur	36
" soda	38
" superior	37
" sweet spring	36
Mush bread	59
Pockets	34
Pone, St. Nicholas	58
Potato bread	89

Puffs, breakfast	46
" nun's	44
Rice bread	60
Rolls, hot or cold loaf bread	31
" French	31
" " 2d	33
" " or twist	32
" pocket-book	33
" velvet	32
Rusks	40
" egg	41
" German	41
Salt risen bread	47
" " " 2d	47
Turnovers	33
Twist	34
Wafers	44
Waffles	47
" 2d	48
" 3d	48
" corn meal	57
" mush	49
" rice	49
" " 2d	49
" superior rice	49
" soda	48
" another recipe	48
Yeast	25
" alum	27
" another recipe	26
" Irish potato	26
" that never fails	26

COFFEE, TEA AND CHOCOLATE.

Café au lait	63
Coffee, to make	62
" " 2d	62
" boiled	61
" dripped or filtered	63
" " " 2d	63
" to toast	61
Broma	65
Chocolate	65
Cocoa	65
Black tea	64
" " 2d	64
Green "	63
" " 2d	64
" " a good cup of	64
Iced "	64

MILK AND BUTTER.

Butter, to secure nice for the table in winter	67
Butter, putting up	67
Clabber	67
Cottage cheese	68

SOUP.

Asparagus soup	83
" " 2d	83
Beef "	74
" " 2d	74
Beef's head, to prepare as stock for soup	74
Calf's head soup	75
" " " 2d	75
" " " 3d	76
" " " 4th	76
" " " 5th	77
" " " brown	77
Clam soup	72
" " 2d	73
Chicken soup	78
" " 2d	79
Crab "	73
" " 2d	74
Giblet "	79
Gumbo "	80
" " 2d	80
Okra "	79
Oxtail "	78
Oyster "	69
" " 2d	70
" " 3d	70
" " economical	69
" " purée of	70
Pea "	83
" " green	84
" " " 2d	84
Potato "	84
" " 2d	84
Terrapin soup, mock	72
Turtle "	71
" " 2d	71
" " 3d	72
" " mock	72
Tomato "	82
" " 2d	82
" " clear	83
Veal " roast, and chicken bone soup	79
Vegetable soup	81
" " fine	80

OYSTERS AND OTHER SHELL FISH.

Clam or oyster fritters	90

INDEX.

	PAGE		PAGE
Crabs, to cook	94	Mackerel, boiled	105
" devilled	94	" to broil	105
" " 2d	94	" salt, to cook	106
" hard, to devil	95	Perch, to fry	104
Crab stew	94	Rock fish, baked	101
" soft	95	Rock, to boil	101
Lobster curry	95	" boiled, 2d	101
Terrapin	96	" pickled	102
" or turtle in batter	96	" to stew	101
" " steaks	96	Shad, baked	102
" " stew	96	" to barbecue	103
Turtles, to cook	96	" " broil	102
" stewed	96	" " fry	102
Oysters, broiled	90	" potted	103
" to cook	86	" to roast	102
" "	89	Salmon, to bake, to boil and steak	106
" devilled	88	" to pickle	107
" "	88	Sheep's head, to bake	100
" fritters	89	" or rock, to boil	100
" "	89	" to bake, 2d	100
" to fry	89	" " " 3d	101
" fried	89	" boiled	100
" " 2d	90	Sturgeon, baked	104
" to fry	90	" cutlet	103
" " 2d	90	" scolloped	103
" to keep alive and fatten	94	Trout, to fry	104
" pâtés	92		
" pie	92	**GAME.**	
" " 2d	92		
" pickled	91	Duck, wild	111
" " 2d	91	" " to cook for breakfast	111
" " 3d	92	Fowl " " roast in a stove	110
" raw	93	Goose "	111
" to roast	91	" " 2d	111
" sausage	93	Partridges, to broil	112
" steamed	90	" and pheasants, to cook	112
" shortcake	93	" to roast	112
" scalloped	86	Pigeon, to broil	112
" " 2d	87	" pie	113
" " 3d	87	" to stew	113
" " 4th	88	Rabbit, barbecue	109
		" roast	109
FISH.		" stewed	109
		" " 2d	109
A la crême	98	Reed birds, to dress	113
Cat fish	99	Sora, ortolans and other small birds, to cook	113
" " or hog fish	99	Sora, ortolans and other small birds, to cook	114
Cod fish balls	104	Sora, ortolans, robins and other small birds, to cook	114
" " boiled	104		
" " salt, to dress	105		
" " Nantucket	105		
Chowder	99	Squirrel, to barbecue	108
Chowder, 2d	100	Turkey, wild	110
Drum or sturgeon	104	" " simple way of preparing	110
German fish stew	107		
Halibut	98	Venison, haunch	108
" 2d	98	" " of	107

	PAGE
Venison, stewed	108
" " 2d	108

MEATS.

	PAGE
Backbone or chine, to cook	120
" pie	120
Bacon, to cure	125
" curing	125
" fried	130
" and greens	129
" shoulder of	129
Chine, to dress	121
" roast	121
Ham, baked	127
" " 2d	128
" or tongue, bake	127
" broiled	129
" of pork, to cook	121
" for curing	125
" Virginia mode of curing	124
" to boil	126
" " " 2d	127
" weighing 10 lbs	126
" fried	129
" an improvement to	126
" relish	131
" spiced	129
" stuffed and baked	128
" to stuff, fresh cured	128
" toast	131
" " 2d	131
Jowl and turnip salad	130
Lard, to cure	124
Leg of pork stuffed	121
Pickled pork, equal to fresh	130
Pork royal	122
" steak	119
Sausage meat	122
" " excellent recipe	122
" seasoning for	122
Salt pork, how to cook	131
Spare ribs	119
" " pork	119
" " 3d	119
" " 4th	119
" " grisken and short ribs, to cook	120
Souse cheese	123
" to make from hogs' feet	123
Sweetbread of hog	123
Tongue or ham, potted	131
Barbecue shoat	132
Forequarter of shoat to roast	132
Head of shoat	134
" " " to stew	135
" " pig to hash	135
Head and jowl of pig to stew	134
Jowl of shoat	133
Roast pig	133
" shoat	132

BEEF AND VEAL.

	PAGE
A-la mode	140
" " 2d	140
" " 3d	141
Boiled beef and turnips	141
Brine for beef	154
Brains, croquettes	151
" to dress	150
" " fry	150
" " " 2d	150
" " stew	150
Collaps, beef	146
Collar	142
Cow heel	153
" " fried	153
Corned beef	154
" " 2d	156
" " 3d	156
" " and tongues	155
" " or pork	155
" round, to cook	158
" beef, how to cook	159
" " tongue, to cook	158
Cure " for drying	159
" " ham	160
Daube Froide	153
Dry beef and tongue	160
French dish	153
Frizzled beef	144
Fricasseed beef	145
Gravy brown	152
" for roast beef	152
Heel of beef to fry	153
Hunter's beef or spiced round	156
" " " " " 2d	157
Heart of "	147
Kidneys, broiled	148
" fried	148
" " 2d	148
" grilled	148
" stewed	147
" " 2d	147
Liver	149
" fried	149
" to fry	149
" to fry with onions	149
" dried for relish	149
Ox-heart, to roast	147
Roast beef	138
" " 2d	139
Rib roast of beef	139

INDEX.

	PAGE
Round of beef, to spice	157
Rump " " to stew	145
Steak, broiled	142
" " 2d	143
" how to cook	143
" fried	144
" to fry	144
" fried with onions	143
Stew, Lebanon	146
Sausage, beef	152
" bologna	152
Smoked beef	159
Spiced "	157
Tongue à la terrapin	146
" toast	147
" to stew	146
" to pickle	155
Tripe	151
" 2d	151
" to fry	152
" " prepare	151
Calves' brains	167
Cake, of veal	164
Chops, veal	161
Cutlets, veal	162
" " 2d	162
" " 3d	162
Cold veal, dressed with white sauce	163
Daub veal	167
Feet, calf's, dressed as terrapins	165
Head, calf's	167
" " to bake	167
Liver, bewitched	166
" broiled	165
" to fry	166
" " 2d	166
" simple way of cooking	166
Loaf, veal	163
" " 2d	164
Loin of veal, stewed	160
Minced "	163
Roast "	161
Steak "	161
Sweetbreads	165
" " 2d	165
" " 3d	165

MUTTON AND LAMB.

Broiled	170
Chops, mutton	172
" " 2d	172
" " 3d	173
" " broiled	173
Corned "	171
Leg of mutton, boiled	170

	PAGE
Leg of mutton, boiled, 2d	170
" " roast	169
Roast mutton	169
Saddle of mutton, to cook	171
" " "	171
" " iced	171
" " to roast	170
Shoulder " corned	172
Slices, grilled	174
Stew	173
" 2d	173
Tongues, sheep	174
Lamb's head	175
" " to fricassee	175
Roast lamb	174
Shoulder of lamb, to grill	174
Decorations and garnishes for cold meat and salads	175

POULTRY.

Chickens	183
" to boil	184
" " broil	187
" " dress with tomatoes	186
" " fricassee	187
" fried	186
" " 2d	186
" pie	187
" " 2d	188
" pudding	188
" " 2d	188
" " with potatoes	188
" to roast	184
" smothered	185
" to steam	184
" " stew	185
" " "	185
Ducks, young, to prepare	190
" to stew	190
Goose, devilled	189
" to roast	189
Turkey, boiled	180
" " 2d	180
" boned	181
" devilled	181
" hash	181
Turkey, meat jelly for	183
" roast	178
" " 2d	178
" " 3d	179
" " with truffles	179
" to steam	180

SALADS.

Celery salad	196
Chicken "	194

	PAGE
Chicken salad, 2d	195
" " 3d	195
" " 4th	196
" for 35 people	195
Fish salad	192
Irish potato salad	198
Lettuce salad	198
" dressed	200
" "	200
Lobster salad	192
Oyster "	191
Potato "	197
" " 2d	198
Salmon salad, and lobster	191
Slaw	199
" cold	199
" " 2d	199
Terrapin salad	192
Tomato "	197
Turnip "	197
Turkey "	193
" " 2d	193
" " 3d	194
Veal and potato salad	197

	PAGE
Egg sauce	205
Mushroom sauce	206
Oyster "	205
Sauce for boiled poultry	205
White sauce	204

SALAD DRESSING.

Cabbage dressing	208
Celery dressing	211
" " 2d	211
Chicken salad dressing	208
Cold slaw "	210
Lettuce "	208
" " 2d	210
Sana Mayonnaise	209
Salad dressing	207
" " 2d	207
" " 3d	207
" " 4th	208
" " 5th	210

SAUCES.

Anchovy sauce	202
Apple "	204
Cod's head " for	201
Fish "	200
" " 2d	201
" " 3d	202
" " or sauce for salad.	200
Dutch " for fish	201
Horseradish sauce	202
Maitre d'Hôte sauce	202
Mint sauce	204
Mushroom sauce	203
" "	203
Nasturtium "	204
Onion "	204
Pepper vinegar	203
Tomato sauce	203

SAUCES ESPECIALLY SUITABLE FOR FOWLS.

Asparagus sauce	205
Celery "	205
Cranberry "	206
Drawn butter	205
" " 2d	206
" " 3d	206

BRUNSWICK STEWS, GUMBO, SIDE DISHES.

Apples, fried	231
" spiced	232
Bacon fraize	227
Beef cakes	226
Beefsteak and potatoes	226
Breakfast dish	221
" " 2d	222
Broth, Scotch	216
Cassa rolls	221
Calf's head pudding	223
Cold chicken, devilled	225
" " with vinegar	225
Croquettes	217
" 2d	217
" 3d	218
" 4th	218
Chicken croquettes	217
Croquettes balls	218
" potato	218
" sausage	219
" " 2d	219
" meat	217
Crumb pie	224
Dried apples, peaches, quinces and pears, to stew	231
Fish and potatoes	226
Forcemeat balls	219
Fondee	230
Giblet pie	220

INDEX.

	PAGE		PAGE
Gumbo	213	Egg with toast	236
" 2d	213	Ham and eggs	236
" 3d	213	" egg pudding	237
" filet à la Creole	214	Omelette	234
Haggis	225	" 2d	234
Hash	220	" 3d	234
" baked	222	" 4th	234
Hominy, to boil	228	" cheese	235
" " 2d	229	" German	235
" croquettes	228	" ham	235
" fried	229	" mock	235
Hotch potch	216	" soufflé	235
Liver pudding	223	Pie, egg	237
Loaf, meat	216	Poached eggs	236
Macaroni	237	Rumble "	236
" 2d	227	Scrambled eggs	233
" 3d	227	" "	233
" Italian method	227	Stuffed	237
Mince, with bread crumbs	219		
" " potatoes	220		
Mushrooms, broiled	230	**VEGETABLES.**	
" to stew	230		
" " fry or broil	229	Artichokes, burr	249
" and sweetbread patés	229	Asparagus, to cook	238
Mutton, hashed	215	" " 2d	239
" " 2d	215	Beans, lima, to boil	245
" " 3d	215	" " " 2d	245
Nice pie	223	" " " 3d	254
Pig's head pudding	223	Beets, to boil	239
Potato pie	223	Cabbage, with bacon, to boil	251
" 2d	223	" boiled without bacon	251
Pot pouri	220	" fried	252
Prunes, stewed	232	" pudding	251
Ragout souse	221	" " 2d	251
Rice and egg patés	231	Cauliflower	252
Sandwiches	222	Celery	240
" 2d	222	Corn fritters	242
Squab pie	225	" " 2d	243
Side dish	216	" " for breakfast	243
Stew, black	216	" green, to boil	241
Stew, Brunswick	211	" pudding	242
Stew " 2d	212	" " 2d	242
" " 3d	212	" put in brine	254
" " 4th	212	Cucumbers, to dress raw	246
Terrapin, mock	221	Cucumbers, to fry	246
Tongue and prunes	231	Cymlins, with bacon	240
Veal patés	214	" to fry	241
Welsh rarebit	231	" fritters	241
		" pudding	241
		" or squash to stew	240
EGGS.		Egg-plant, to bake	249
		" " to fry	249
À-la-crême	237	" " pudding	249
Boiled eggs	233	" " to stew	248
" " soft	333	Okra	246
Baked for dinner	237	Onions, to bake	239
Egg cups, breakfast dish	233	" cook	239
" for breakfast	233	" dress raw	240

		PAGE
Onions, to fry		239
Parsnips, to cook		250
" " fry		249
" " stew		249
Peas, cornfield or black-eye		254
" dried, to boil		254
" green, "		238
Pees, kon-feel		253
Potato chips, Irish		247
" cakes		247
Potatoes creamed		247
" Irish, to boil		246
Potato hash		247
" pudding		247
" snow		247
Potatoes, sliced, to fry		247
" sweet, to boil		248
" " to cook inferior		248
" " to fry		248
Radishes		240
Ropa Viga		244
Salsify, to cook		250
" " fry		250
" " stew		250
" " "		250
Slaw, warm		251
" " 2d		252
" " 3d		252
Snaps, to boil		240
Spinach		252
Succotash		246
Tomatoes, baked		243
" " 2d		243
" fried		244
" omelet		244
" raw, to dress		245
" " " 2d		245
" stewed		244
" " 2d		244
Tomato toast		245
Turnips		253
" salad		253
" to stew		253
Yams, to dress		248

PICKLE AND CATSUPS.

Apple pickle		294
Blackberry pickle		295
Cabbage " for present use		262
" " cut		262
" " chopped		263
Cantaloupe pickle, 3	287,	288
Composition "		291
Cherry "		295
Chow-chow " 5	282–	284
" " (Leesburg)		285

		PAGE
Cucumber pickle 4	266–	268
" " boiled		268
" " ripe		269
" " sweet, 2		269
Damson " 2	290,	291
French " 2		292
Green " 3	264–	266
German "		290
Honolulu melon pickle		287
Hyden salad, 5	273–	275
Ingredients for one gallon green pickle		258
Kentucky pickle		292
Lemon " 2		294
Mangoes, oil, 3		276
" to green		270
" stuffing for 60		270
" peach, 4	278,	279
" pepper		279
Martinas pickle	281,	282
Muskmelon pickle		288
Onion " 2	293,	294
Peach " 4	286,	287
" " spiced		286
" " sweet		286
Pear, peach or quince pickle		287
Plum pickle		289
Preparing pickles		258
Ragout pickle		291
Spanish "		293
Sweet "	287,	290
Tomato " (green) 3	269,	270
" " (sweet) 3		272
" " (ripe)		272
" sauce (green) 3	270,	271
" marmalade or sauce for meats		273
Vinegar for pickle, 3		256
" " yellow pickle		257
Walnut pickle, 4	280,	281
Watermelon pickle, 4		289
" " sweet		288
Yellow " 7	258–	261
Bay sauce, 2		299
Caper sauce		302
Celery vinegar		301
Cucumber catsup, 4		297
Horseradish sauce		301
Mushroom catsup, 4	299,	300
" sauce		300
Mustard, to mix		303
" aromatic		303
Pepper catsup		302
" sauce		301
" vinegar		302
Tomato catsup, 2	295,	296
Tartan sauce		302
" " (Morcan's)		303

	PAGE
Walnut catsup, 3	298
" leaves, catsup from	298

CAKE.

	PAGE
Almond cake, 2	328
Angel's "	311
" bread	323
Black cake	314, 315
Brides' cake, 4	309, 310
Capital "	342
Citron " 4	327, 328
Cocoanut cake, 6	323, 324
Chocolate " 5	325, 326
" jelly cake	327
Corn-starch "	313
Clay "	323
Cream " 2	340, 341
Currant "	329
Cup " 3	342
Custard "	344
Cake	343
" with sauce	344
" that never fails	344
Delicate cake, 2	312
Delicious " 2	343
Fruit " 7	316–319
Fig "	329
Gold "	311
Mrs. Galt's cake	345
Jelly for " 2	334, 335
Jelly " 2	335
Jelly cake (lemon) 2	335, 336
" " (rolled) 2	336
" " filling for	337
Kettle cake	345
Lady " 2	311, 312
Lee " (R. E.) 2	321
Leighton cake	306
Lemon " 2	320, 321
Mountain cake	307
" ash-cake	308
Merry Christmas cake	312
Marble cake	337, 339
" or Bismarck cake	339
Norfolk "	345
Naples biscuit	347
Orange cake, 3	319, 320
Parson's "	346
Pound " 7	329, 331
Pineapple "	319
Risen "	346
Rose or clouded cake	339
Ruggles' "	346
Silver "	310
Snow "	308
" mountain "	307

	PAGE
Spice mountain cake	340
Sponge " 2	332
Sponge cake (confederate)	332
" " (cream)	333
" " (butter) 2	331, 332
" " (extra)	333
" " that never fails	333
" " roll, 2	334
Tipsy cakes	347
Velvet "	347
White " 2	305
" " (superior)	305
" mountain cake, 4	306, 307
" " ash-cake	308
" fruit cake, 4	313, 314
Whortleberry	347
Icing for cakes	349
Icing, 5	348, 349
" boiled, 2	348, 349
" cold	348
" hot	348, 349
Ginger bread	350, 351
Ginger bread, cup cake	351
" " lightened	351
" " risen	351
" " soft	350
Ginger loaf	350
Molasses cake, 2	351, 352
" or black cake	352
" pound cake	352
Small cakes	353
Albany cakes	353
Bonnefeadas	361
Coffee cakes	357
Cookies	358
Cinnamon cakes, 2	357
Coffee "	357
Cream "	354
Crullers	359
Delicate tea cakes, 2	360
Delicious small cakes	361
Dimples	362
Drop cakes	358
Ginger cakes, 2	362, 363
" " (drop)	364
" " (cheap)	363
" bunns	363
" snaps, 2	363, 364
Gloucester cakes	359
Holmcroft	358
Jumbles, 3	356
" (Jackson)	356
" (lemon)	361
Macaroons	356
Marguerites, 3	354, 355
Molasses cakes	364
Nothings	358
Scotch cakes	353

524   INDEX.

	PAGE
Strawberry cakes	357
Sugar "	358
Shrewsbury "	355
Sweet crackers	353
Spice nuts	364
Tea cakes, 2	359, 360
Tartaric cakes	360
Wafers, 2	362

PUDDINGS.

	PAGE
Apple pudding, 5	376
Apple charlotte	377
Apple custard	378
Apple custard pudding	377
Apple méringue, 2	377
Apple dumplings	373
Apple roll (baked)	377
Almond pudding	381
Amherst "	370
Arrowroot "	389
Batter "	398
Balloons	398
Bread pudding	390
Boiled bread pudding, 2	372
Boiled pudding of acid fruit	371
" sweetmeat pudding	372
" molasses "	373
" pudding, 2	370, 372
" dumplings, paste for	373
Cake pudding	387
Caramel pudding	383
Citron " 2	378
Cocoanut " 5	381, 382
Chocolate " 2	382, 383
Cherry "	371
Cheesecake pudding	388
Cracker "	392
Cream "	395
Currant "	375
Custard "	390
Cottage "	396
Delicious pudding	398
" hasty pudding	397
Eve's pudding	374
Economical pudding	400
Extra fine "	399
Fruit "	374, 391
French "	391
Feather "	397
Irish potato "	394
Indian "	399
Jelly roll	387
Lemon pudding, 4	380
Lemon méringue, 2	381
Molasses pudding, 3	395, 396

	PAGE
Marrow pudding	392
Original " 2	369, 392
Orange " 4	378, 379
One egg "	398
Peach dumplings	375
Penny pudding	400
Plain "	401
Plum " 4	365–368
" " Christmas	368
" " economical, 2	369
" " English	367
" " rich	367
" " simpler kind of	369
Poor man's pudding	400
Puff "	400
Preserve "	387
Pudding without milk or eggs	382
Queen of puddings, 5	383–385
Raspberry pudding	375
Rice " 3	393, 394
Sago "	389, 390
Sippet "	390
Snow " 3	386, 387
Snowball "	396
Sweet potato "	394, 395
" " roll	372
Suet pudding, 2	373
" dumplings	374
Steam pudding	370
Superior "	399
Sweetmeat pudding, 2	388
Mrs. Spence's "	391
Tapioca "	385
" with apples	386
Teacup pudding	391
Texas "	396
Thickened milk pudding	347
Transparent "	388, 389
Troy "	371
Tyler "	395
Virginia "	398
Washington "	397

PUDDING SAUCES.

	PAGE
Brandy sauce	402
Cold " 3	403
French "	402
Lemon "	403
Molasses "	404
Nice "	403
Rich "	403
Sauce for pudding, 3	402, 403
" for boiled pastry	404
Wine sauce, 3	406

INDEX.

PASTRY.

	PAGE
Apple pie, 1, 2, 3	409, 410
Blackberry pie	410
Cherry "	409
Cream " 1, 2	412
Currant "	409
Custard "	413
Cream tarts	415
Cheese cakes, almond, 1, 2	415
" cornstarch	414
" lemon	414
Damson pie	408
Gooseberry pie	410
Lemon " 1, 2, 3, 4	406
Lemon cream pie	406
Lemon tarts	415
Mince meat, 1, 2, 3, 4	411, 412
Molasses pie, 1, 2	413, 414
Orange pie, 1, 2, 3	407
Pastry, 1, 2, 3	405
Puff paste	405
Peach pie	408
Peach méringue pie	407
Potato pie (sliced)	411
" " (sweet)	411
Prune "	408
Prune tarts	415
Rhubarb pie	411
Soda cracker pie	413
Silver "	413
Sugar "	413
Strawberry shortcake	408
Washington pie	413
Whortleberry "	410
Fritters (Bell)	416
" (French)	416
" (made with yeast)	416
Pancakes (common)	417
" (quire of paper)	417

JELLIES, BLANC-MANGE, CHARLOTTE RUSSE, BAKED CUSTARDS, CREAMS, ETC.

Jelly (calves' feet)	419
" cream	421
" crystal	420
" gelatine, 2	420
" " without straining	420
" " without eggs or boiling	421
Jelly without boiling	421
" (stock)	419
Blanc-mange, 4	421, 422
" (arrowroot)	422
" (coffee)	423
Blanc-mange, (chocolate)	423
" (custard)	422
Charlotte russe, 6	423, 424
" " (strawberry)	424
Baked custard, 3	425
Apples (baked)	429
Apple compote	429
" float	428
Apples (nice dessert of)	429
" (nice plain dessert of)	429
" (iced)	430
" (nice preparation of)	429
Apple snow	428
Bonny clabber	428
Cream (Bavarian) 2	426
" Italian	426
" Russian	426
" Spanish, 2	425, 426
" Tapioca, 2	427
Float	428
Lemon froth	427
Slip	428
Syllabub	427

ICE-CREAM.

Bisque ice-cream	437
Buttermilk ice-cream	437
Caramel ice-cream	435
" " (Norvell House)	435
Cocoanut " 3	436
Chocolate "	435, 436
Gelatine "	436
Ice-cream, 3	432
" (without cream)	437
Lemon ice-cream	432
Orange "	433
Peach "	433
Pineapple "	434
Strawberry ice-cream	433
Vanilla "	434
White "	436

Frozen Custards.

Bisque	438
Caramel custard	437
Frozen custard, 2	437, 438
" pudding	438
Plumbière	438
Plum pudding glacé	438

Sherbet

Cream sherbet	439
Lemon " 4	439
Orange "	439

Water Ices.

	PAGE
Citron ice	441
Gelatine ice	441
Orange " 2	440
Pineapple ice, 3	440, 441
Raspberry "	441
Watermelon ice	441

Fruit Desserts.

Ambrosia, 2	442
Canteleupes	442
Peaches and cream	442
Pineapple	442
Strawberries	443
Watermelons	442

PRESERVES AND FRUIT JELLIES.

Apples (preserved for winter use)	450
Apple mange	450
" preserves (crab)	450
Cherry "	451
Candied fruit	454
Damson preserves	451
Fig "	452
Fox grape "	451
Fruit (putting up)	453
Lemon preserves	448
" (sliced)	447
" marmalade	448
" conserves	454
Muskmelon preserves (ripe)	446
Orange "	446
" marmalade, 2	447
" conserves	454
Peach preserves, 2	448, 449
" marmalade	449
" (brandy) 2	449, 450
" conserves	454
Pear preserves	450
Pineapple preserves	446
Quince jam	451
Raspberry jam	452
Sweetmeat preserves	444
Strawberry "	452
" jam	452
Syrup (golden)	454
Tomato preserves	453
" sweetmeats	453
Watermelon marmalade	445
" or muskmelon preserves	445
Apple jelly, 3	455, 456
" (crab)	456
Blackberry jelly	454
Currant "	455
" " (without cooking)	454
Cranberry jelly	455
Grape "	457
Green grape jelly	457
Orange "	456
Jelly oranges	457
Quince jelly	456
Tomato	458

CONFECTIONERY.

Almond macaroons	460
Caramels, 2	459
" (chocolate)	460
Cocoanut balls	460
" caramels, 2	460
" drops	460
Cream candy	459
Cream chocolate	460
Nut candy	458
Molasses candy	459
Sugar " 2	458
" kisses	458

WINE.

Blackberry wine, 4	462, 463
Cider "	467
Cherry "	467
Currant " 3	466
Gooseberry "	466
Grape Wine, 3	464
" " (Catawba)	464, 465
" " (wild black)	465
" " (native)	465
Fox grape wine	465
Orange "	467
Strawberry "	467
Tomato "	467
Apple toddy, 2	468, 469
Beer (cream)	474
" (ginger)	475
" (lemon)	475
" (small)	475
" (summer)	474
Blackberry cordial, 2	470
Cherry "	471
Crab cider	475
Cider (mulled)	475
Dewberry cordial, 2	470, 471
Eggnog	468
Lemon vinegar	474
" or orange syrup	474
Mint cordial	472
Orgeat	474
Raspberry acid	473
" vinegar, 2	473
Regent punch	469
Roman punch	469, 470
Rum "	468

INDEX.

	PAGE
Strawberry acid, 2	472
" cordial	471
" vinegar	472
Tea punch	469

THE SICK-ROOM DIET AND REMEDIES FOR THE SICK.

	PAGE
Aromatic vinegar	483
Arrowroot, 2	479, 480
Asthma, sore-throat and cough, remedy for	491
Beef essence	481
" tea	481
Boils	493
" salve for	493
Bone felon	492
Blisters, dressing for	493
Breakfast for an invalid	480
Breast salve	487
Burns and scalds	488
Carolina small hominy	483
Carrot salve for blisters	492
Cold in the head, cure for, 2	490
Colic, cure for	486
" cramp, cure for	486
Corns, remedy for	492
Coughs, remedies for	490
Chalk mixture for infants and young children	489
Chicken essence	481
" jelly	482
" cholera	488
Chilblains	486
Chill pills	489
Cuts	486
Cracked wheat	480
Croup, good treatment for	492
Diarrhœa, remedy for	489
Dysentery " "	489
Earache " "	487
Inflamed eyes, remedy for	487
Epilepsy " "	486
Food for sick infants	480
Flames, to extinguish clothing in	492
Jaundice, remedy for	491
Jamaica ginger (Brown's)	484
Lime-water	484
Liniment (a good)	492
" for rheumatism	492
" for recent burns	489
Mashed finger	488
Milk punch	481
Mustard	484
" leaves	485
Nourishing way to prepare chicken, squirrel, or beef for the sick	482

	PAGE
Ocean salt	486
Panada	482
Prickly heat, remedy for	488
Poison oak " " 2	491
Poisons, antidotes to	494-496
Acids	494
Alkalies	494
Arsenic	494
Carbolic acid	494
Chloral	494
Chloroform	495
Copper	495
Corrosive sublimate	495
Gases	495
Glass, in powder	495
Iodine	495
Lead	495
Nitrate of silver	495
Opium	495
Phosphorus	495
Prussic acid	495
Strychnine	496
Tartar emetic	496
Venomous bites of rabid dogs and serpents	496
Quinine, to take without tasting	493
Racahaut	480
Seamoss farina	480
Seltzer aperient	484
Soda mint	484
Sore throat, remedy for, 3....485,	486
Sick-room	476, 496
Scarlet fever, preventive to, 2, 487,	488
Snake bites	488
Toast, dry	482
" milk	483
" scalded	483
Toothache drops	487
Thieves' vinegar	483
Weak back, remedy for	494
Wine whey	480
Whooping-cough, remedy for	490

HOUSE-CLEANING.

	PAGE
Ants and bugs, to destroy	503
Bedbugs " "	503
" poison	503
Brasses, to clean	501
Carpets, to wash	499
" to remove ink from	500
Cement for rubber and glass	503
Egg-beater	502
Egg stains, to remove from silver spoons	501
Floors to oil	499
" to dye	499

INDEX.

	PAGE
Furniture to clean	500
" unvarnished, to clean	500
" polish, 2	500, 501
House-cleaning (directions for)	496–498
Knives and tins, to clean	502
" to remove rust from	502
" to whiten handles of	502
Mosquitoes	504
Marble slabs, to clean	500
Oil-cloth, to wash, 2	499
Paint, to clean	499
Rats	504
Red ants, remedy for	503
Sapolio for kitchen use	502
Silver, to clean, 2	501
Shading glass, mixture for	503
Soap, concentrated lye	504
Wall paper, to remove grease from	500
Washing mixture	504
Whitewash, outdoor	498
" indoor	498

RECIPES FOR RESTORING OLD CLOTHES, SETTING COLORS, REMOVING STAINS, ETC.

	PAGE
Black cashmere, to wash	505
Black crape veils, to renew	506
Black silk, to renew old	506
" " to freshen old	506
Blue calicoes, to keep bright and fresh	507
Colors, to set	507
Colors, to restore	507
Cloth, to remove spots from	505
Cloth, soap for removing grease from	505
Clothes to clean	505
Fruit stains, to remove	507
" or ink stains, to remove	507
Iron rust, to remove	508
Mildew, " "	507
" Labaraque solution for	507
Velvet, to restore the pile of	506

MISCELLANEOUS RECIPES.

	PAGE
Almond bandoline	514
Ammonia	508
Borax	509
Bottle wax	510
Blood stains, to remove	514
Camphor ice	512
" salve	512
Cold cream	511
Chaps, lotion for	511
Dandruff, to remove	514
Fertilizer for strawberries	511
Grafting wax	510
Hair-oil, 3	513
" dye, 2	513
" tonic	513
" restorative	513
" to clean	514
" brushes, to clean	514
Herbs, to dry	511
Ink (black)	509
" (red)	509
Liquid glue	510
" blacking	510
Lip salve (red)	511
Rose bandoline	514
Shoe blacking	510
Shampoo liquor	513
Sozodont	512
Tooth powder	512
" " charcoal	513

THE END.